500

LOW-CARB
RECIPES

FAIR WINDS
PRESS
GLOUCESTER, MASSACHUSETTS

500
LOW-CARB
RECIPES

Dana Carpender

First published in the U.S.A. by
Fair Winds Press
33 Commercial Street
Gloucester, Massachusetts 01930-5089

10 9 8 7 6 5 4 3 2 1

Cover design by DW Design
Cover photography by Bobbie Bush, www.bobbiebush.com
Design by Leslie Haimes

Printed in Canada

To my husband, Eric Schmitz,
who has unfailingly helped me,
supported me, and believed in me.
I couldn't have done it without you.
I love you with all my heart.

And to the readers of my Internet newsletter,
Lowcarbezine! You have taught me how
much enthusiasm, humor, intelligence,
caring, and love can come through
a fiber-optic cable. You have also taught me my job.
This book is for you, and for low-carbers everywhere.

CONTENTS

Welcome to Low-Carbohydrate Variety!

What's the hardest thing about your low-carb diet? And what's the most common reason that people abandon their low-carb way of eating and all the health benefits and weight loss that come with it?

Boredom. People just plain get bored. After a few weeks of scrambled eggs and bacon for breakfast, a hamburger with no bun for lunch, and a steak—no baked potato—for dinner, day after day, people get fed up and quit. They just can't face a life of food monotony. Sound familiar?

If you've been getting bored with your low-carb diet, this is the book for you. You'll find dozens of exciting ways to vary a hamburger, a steak, pork chops, chicken, and even fish. You'll find a wide variety of side dishes and salads. You'll find snacks and party foods that you can eat without feeling like you're depriving yourself. You'll even find recipes for bread—really, truly bread—not to mention muffins, waffles, pancakes, and granola. In short, this book has recipes for all sorts of things you never *dreamed* you could have on a low-carb diet.

Did I come up with these recipes for you? Heck, no! I came up with these recipes for *me*.

Who am I? I'm a person who, through circumstances that surely could have happened to anyone, has spent the past several years writing about low-carbohydrate dieting. In fact, I spent so much time answering questions for the curious that I finally wrote a book, *How I Gave Up My Low Fat Diet and Lost Forty Pounds!* To supplement the book, I started an "e-zine"—an Internet newsletter—for low-carb dieters, called *Lowcarbezine!* So for the past few years, through the wonders of the Internet, I've been writing and developing recipes for a growing audience of low-carb dieters around the world.

I've always loved to cook, and I've always been good at it. My friends long ago dubbed me "The God of Food." So when low-fat, high-carb mania hit in the 1980s, I learned how to make a killer low-fat fettuccine Alfredo, curried chicken and mixed grain pilau, black beans and rice, blue corn pancakes, low-fat cheesecake, you name it.

And I got fat. Really fat. And sick. And tired. Thank heavens, in 1995 I got smart and tried going low carb, instead. Within two days my energy levels skyrocketed and my clothes were looser. It was overwhelmingly clear that this was the way my body wanted to be fed and that this was the way of eating that would make me well. I had set my foot upon a path from which there was no turning back; I was low carb for life.

The only thing that nearly derailed me was a terrible sense of Kitchen Disorientation. I had to discard the vast majority of my recipes when I dropped the grains, beans, potatoes, and sugar from my diet. For the very first time in my life, I'd walk into my kitchen and have no idea what to cook—and I had always known what to cook and how to put together a menu. It really was pretty scary, and it certainly was depressing. But I set out to become as good a low-carb cook as I had been a low-fat cook.

Seven years later, my mission has been accomplished, and then some! What you hold in your hands is the end result of years and years of trial and error, of learning what works and what doesn't, of experimenting to find out which substitutes are yummy and which are just plain lame.

This is not, for the most part, a gourmet cookbook, which means that the recipes you find here are recipes you'll actually use. You'll find a lot of fairly simple recipes and a few more complex ones for special occasions. There's lots of family fare here—pork chops and meat loaf, burgers and chicken. You'll find lots of meals you can cook on the stove top in a simple skillet and plenty of salads you can make ahead and stash in the refrigerator, ready to be pulled out and served when you dash in the door at a quarter-to-dinnertime. You'll find many one-dish meals that are protein and vegetables combined, from main dish salads to thick, hearty soups to casseroles. You'll also find ethnic flavors from around the world right alongside comfort foods you won't believe are low carb!

Why Is There Such a Wide Range of Carb Counts in the Recipes in This Book?

If carbs are your problem, then they're going to be your problem tomorrow, and next week, and next year, and when you're old and gray. If you hope to keep your weight off, you cannot think in terms of going on a low-carb diet, losing your weight, and then going off your diet—you'll gain back every ounce, just as sure as you're born. You'll also go back to blood-sugar swings, energy crashes, and nagging, insatiable hunger, not to mention all the health risks of hyperinsulinemia. In short, you are in this for life.

So if you are to have any hope of doing this forever—and at this writing, I've been doing this for going on seven years—you're going to need to enjoy what you eat. You're going to need variety, flavor, color, and interest. You're going to need festive dishes, easy dishes, and comfort foods—a whole world of things to eat. You're going to need a cuisine.

Because of this, I have included everything from very low-carb dishes, suitable for folks in the early, very low-carb "induction" stage of their diet, to "splurge" dishes, which would probably make most of us gain weight if we ate them every day but which still have far fewer carbs than their "normal" counterparts.

There's another reason for the range of carb counts: Carbohydrate intolerance comes in degrees, and different people can tolerate different daily carbohydrate intakes. Some of you, no doubt, need to stay in that 20-grams-a-day-or-less range, whereas many others—lucky souls—can have as much as 90 to 100 grams a day and stay slim. This cookbook is meant to serve you all.

Only you can know, through trial and error, how many grams of carbs you can eat in a day and still lose weight. It is up to you to pick and choose among the recipes in this book while keeping an eye on the carbohydrate counts provided. That way, you can put together menus that will please your palate and your family while staying below that critical carb level.

However, I do have this to say: Always, always, always the heart and soul of your low-carbohydrate diet should be meat, fish, poultry, eggs, healthy fats, and low-carb vegetables. This book will teach you a boggling number of ways to combine these things, and you should try them all. Don't just find one or two recipes that you like and make them over and over. Try at least one new recipe every week; that way, within a few months you'll have a whole new repertoire of familiar low-carb favorites!

You will, as I just mentioned, find recipes in this book for what are best considered low-carb treats. Do not take the presence of a recipe in this book to mean that it is something that you can eat every day, in unlimited quantities, and still lose weight. I can tell you from experience that even low-carb treats, if eaten frequently, will put weight on you. Recipes for breads, cookies, muffins, cakes, and the like are here to give you a satisfying, varied diet that you can live with for life, but they should not become the new staples of your diet. *Do not try to make your low-carbohydrate diet resemble your former Standard American Diet.* That's the diet that got you in trouble in the first place, remember?

One other thought: It is entirely possible to have a bad reaction to a food that has nothing to do with its carbohydrate count. Gluten, a protein from wheat that is essential for baking low-carb bread, causes bad reactions in a fair number of people. Soy products are problematic for many folks, as are nuts. Whey protein, used extensively in these recipes, contains lactose, which some people cannot tolerate. And surely you've heard of people who react badly to artificial sweeteners of one kind or another. I've also heard from diabetics who get bad blood-sugar spikes from eating even small quantities of onions or tomatoes.

Yet all of these foods are just fine for many, many low-carb dieters, and there is no way I can know which foods may cause a problem for which people. All I can tell you is to pay attention to your body. If you add a new food to your diet and you gain weight (and you're pretty certain it's not tied to something else, like your menstrual cycle or a new medication), or you find yourself unreasonably hungry, tired, or "off" despite having stayed within your body's carbohydrate tolerance, you may want to consider avoiding that food. One man's meat is another man's poison, and all that.

What's a "Usable Carb Count"?

You may or may not be aware of the concept of the usable carb count, sometimes called the "effective carb count"; some low-carb books utilize this principle, whereas others do not. If you're not familiar with the concept, here it is in a nutshell:

Fiber is a carbohydrate and is, at least in American nutritional breakdowns, included in the total carbohydrate count. However, fiber is a form of carbohydrate made of molecules so big that you can neither digest nor absorb them. Therefore fiber, despite being a carbohydrate, will not push up your blood sugar and will not cause an insulin release. Even better, by slowing the absorption of the starches and sugars that occur with it, fiber actually lessens their bad influence. This is very likely the reason that high-fiber diets appear to be so much better for you than "American Normal."

For these reasons many (if not most) low-carb dieters now subtract the grams of fiber in a food from the total grams of carbohydrate to determine the number of grams of carbohydrates that are actually a problem. These are the "usable" carbs, or the "effective carb count." These non-fiber grams of carbohydrates are what we count and limit. Not only does this approach allow us a much wider variety of foods, and especially lots more vegetables, but it actually encourages us to add fiber to things such as baked goods. I am very much a fan of this approach, and therefore I give the usable carbohydrate count for these recipes. However, you will also find the breakdown of the total carb count and the fiber count.

Using This Book

I can't tell you how to plan your menus. I don't know if you live alone or have a family, if you have hours to cook or are pressed for time every evening, or what foods are your favorites. I can, however, give you a few pointers on what you'll find here that may make your meal planning easier.

There are a lot of one-dish meals in this book—main dish salads, skillet suppers that include meat and vegetables both, and hearty soups that are a full meal in a bowl. I include these because they're some of my favorite foods, and to my mind, they're about the simplest way to eat. I also think they lend a far greater variety to low-carb cuisine than is possible if you're trying to divide up your carbohydrate allowance for a given meal among three or four different dishes. If you have a carb-eating family, you can appease them by serving something on the side, such as whole wheat pitas split in half and toasted, along with garlic butter, brown rice, a baked potato, or some noodles. (Of course I don't recommend that you serve them something like canned biscuits, Tater Tots, or Minute Rice, but that shouldn't surprise you.)

When you're serving these one-dish meals, remember that most of your carbohydrate allowance for the meal is included in that main dish. Unless you can tolerate more carbohydrates than I can, you probably don't want to serve a dish with lots of vegetables in it with even more vegetables on the side. Remember, it's the total usable carb count you have to keep an eye on. Complement simple meat dishes—such as roasted chicken, broiled steak, or pan-broiled pork chops—with the more carbohydrate-rich vegetable side dishes.

There's one other thing I hope this book teaches you to do, and that's break out of your old ways of looking at food. There's no law insisting that you eat eggs only for breakfast, have tuna salad for lunch every day, and serve some sort of meat and two side dishes for dinner. Short on both time and money? Serve eggs for dinner a couple of nights a week; they're fast, cheap, and unbelievably nutritious. Having family video night or game night? Skip dinner and make two or three healthy snack foods to nibble on. Can't face another fried egg at breakfast? Throw a pork chop or a hamburger on the electric tabletop grill while you're in the shower, and you've got a fast and easy breakfast. Sick of salads for lunch? Take a protein-rich dip in a snap-top container and some cut up vegetables to work with you.

Helpful General Hints

🧁 **If you're not losing weight, go back to counting every carb.** Remember that snacks and beverages count, even if they're made from recipes in this book. A 6-gram muffin may be a lot better for you and your waistline than a convenience store muffin, but it's still 6 grams, and it counts! Likewise, don't lie to yourself about portion sizes. If you make your cookies really big, so that you only get two dozen instead of four dozen from a recipe, the carb count per cookie doubles, and don't you forget it.

🧁 **Beware of hidden carbohydrates.** It's important to know that the government lets food manufacturers put "0 grams of carbohydrates" on the label if a food has less than 0.5 gram per serving, and "less than 1 gram of carbohydrate" if a food has between 0.5 gram and 0.9 gram. Even some diet sodas contain trace amounts of carbohydrates! These amounts aren't much, but they do add up if you eat enough of them. So if you're having trouble losing, count foods that say "0 grams" as 0.5 gram and foods that say "less than 1 gram" as 1 gram.

🧁 **Remember that some foods you may be thinking of as carb-free actually contain at least traces of carbohydrates.** Eggs contain about 0.5 gram apiece, shrimp have 1 gram per 4-ounce portion, natural cheeses have about 1 gram per ounce, and heavy cream has about 0.5 gram per tablespoon. And coffee has more than 1 gram in a 10-ounce mug before you add cream and sweetener. (Tea, on the other hand, is carb-free.) If you're having trouble losing weight, get a food counter book and use it, even for foods you're sure you already know the carb counts of.

How Are the Carbohydrate Counts in These Recipes Calculated?

Most of these carbohydrate counts have been calculated using MasterCook software. This very useful program allows you to enter the ingredients of a recipe and the number of servings it makes, and it then spits out the nutritional breakdown for each serving. MasterCook does not include every low-carb specialty product, so these were looked up in food count books or on the product labels and added in by hand. Some figures were also derived from Corinne T. Netzer's *The Complete Book of Food Counts* and *The NutriBase Complete Book of Food Counts*. I have also used the USDA's Nutrient Database, a hugely useful online reference.

The carb counts for these recipes are as accurate as we can make them. However, they are not, and cannot be, 100 percent accurate. MasterCook gets its nutritional information from the USDA Nutrient Database, and my experience is that the USDA's figures for carbohydrate content tend to run a bit higher than the food count books. This means that the carbohydrate counts in this book are, if anything, a tad high, which beats being too low!

Furthermore, every stalk of celery, every onion, every head of broccoli is going to have a slightly different level of carbohydrates in it, because it grew in a specific patch of soil, in specific weather, and with a particular kind of fertilizer. You may use a different brand of vanilla-flavored whey protein powder than I do. You may be a little more or a little less generous with how many bits of chopped green pepper you fit into a measuring cup.

Don't sweat it. These counts are, as the old joke goes, close enough for government work. You can count on them as a guide to the carbohydrate content in your diet. And do you really want to get obsessed with getting every tenth of a gram written down?

In this spirit, you'll find that many of these recipes call for "1 large rib of celery," "half a green pepper," or "a clove of garlic." This is how most of us cook, after all. These things do not come in standardized sizes, so they're analyzed for the average. Again: Don't sweat it! If you're really worried, use what seems to you a smallish stalk of celery, or green pepper, or clove of garlic, and you can count on your cumulative carb count being a hair lower than what is listed in the recipe.

Low-Carb Specialty Foods

When I went low carb in 1995, it was a radical concept. Low-fat, high-carb diets were practically scriptural, and although there were loads and loads of low-fat specialty foods in every grocery store, from Healthy Choice dinners to Snackwells cookies, there were virtually no low-carb specialty foods to be found. As a result, eating a low-carbohydrate diet back then virtually *forced* me to eat real, unprocessed foods. Meat, poultry, fish, vegetables, low-sugar fruits, nuts and seeds, cheese, and butter were pretty much the whole of the diet.

What a difference seven years make! As more and more people have discovered low-carbohydrate eating, boatloads of low-carb specialty products have hit the market. Some are good, some are bad, some are middlin', pretty much like products in every other category.

I see this proliferation of low-carb specialty products as a double-edged sword. On the one hand, anything that helps carbohydrate-intolerant people remain happily on their diets is a good thing. On the other hand, most of these specialty products are highly processed foods, and they do not equal genuine foodstuffs in nutritional value. I fear that too many people are eating these things as staples of their diet, displacing the real foods that should be the bedrock of any healthy low-carb diet.

Another drawback is that low-carb specialty foods tend to be extremely expensive. Don't mistake what I'm saying—these products are not, in general, a rip-off. Low-carb products are more expensive to make, partly because they call for more expensive ingredients and partly because they are made in smaller quantities by smaller companies than are regular processed foods. These are, after all, specialty foods, and you're going to pay specialty prices for them. But I'd hate for you to start basing your diet on specialty products, decide that a low-carb diet is too expensive, and go back to eating junk. Use these products wisely to add a little variety, to provide an occasional treat, or to fight off cravings, but not as a major part of your diet.

Here's a taste of the variety of low-carb specialty products now available on the market:

- **Breads and bagels.** These are often quite good, but keep an eye on the portion size listed on the label. I've seen low-carb bagels with a label claiming only 4 grams per serving, but discovered that a serving was only 1/3 of a bagel!

- **Tortillas.** Useful not only for eating with fajitas and burritos and for making quesadillas, but also in place of Chinese mu shu pancakes. Be aware that low-carb tortillas, although tasty, are not identical to either flour or corn tortillas in either flavor or texture.

- **Jams, jellies, and condiments.** These do contain the carbohydrates from whatever fruit or vegetable was used to make them, but not added sugars. Generally very good in quality, especially Jok'n Al brand, imported from New Zealand.

- **Pastas.** I have yet to find a brand of low-carb pasta that has really impressed me, but some of them are okay. I find that the texture of the pastas is off, so they cook up either too soft or too chewy. Still, the stuff sells like low-carb hotcakes, so somebody must really like it. If you are having a hard time passing up pasta, these products are worth a try.

- **Cold cereals.** I've tried two low-carb cold cereals. One, called Keto Crisp, is quite similar to Rice Krispies in texture and flavor. This is now available in a chocolate flavor, as well. The other is called Nuttlettes, and it's very much like Grape Nuts. They're both good if you're fond of the cereals they imitate. Both of these "cereals" are made from soy, which some people think is a life-saving wonder food but others—including me—aren't sure is safe in large quantities. It's a moot point for me, since I just don't miss Rice Krispies or Grape Nuts enough to bother with these cereals. (Although Keto Crisp makes a mean cookie bar!) However, if you do miss cold cereal, these products are quite good, as well as low in carbohydrates and high in protein.

- **Protein chips.** These are okay, but not so wonderful that I've bothered to buy them often. Of the "regular" chips, these most closely resemble tortilla chips, but the texture is noticeably different. If you're mad for a bag of chips, these are worth a try. But for me, I'd rather have pumpkin seeds.

- **Protein meal replacement shakes.** Mostly quite good, and certainly useful for folks who can't face cooked food first thing in the morning. They're available in a wide range of flavors.

- **Protein bars**. These seem to be everywhere these days. They range from pretty darned good to absolutely wretched, sometimes within the same brand. You'll have to try a few brands and flavors to see which ones you like. Be aware that there is a lot of controversy about low-carb protein bars. Virtually all of them contain glycerine, to make them moist and chewy. The controversy is over whether or not glycerine acts like a carbohydrate in some ways in the body. Many people find that these bars knock them out of ketosis, whereas others don't have a problem. So I'll say it again: Pay attention to your body!

- **Hot cereal**. There is one low-carb hot cereal on the market at this writing: Flax-O-Meal. I haven't tried it, but by all reports it is very good.

- **Cookies and brownies**. These are getting better every day, and many are quite good already. I've had low-carb brownies that were superb, and some very nice oatmeal cookies, as well. See "About Polyols," on page 18.

- **Muffins**. Although some of these are quite good, others are not so brilliant, and often the same brand varies widely depending on which flavor you choose. You'll just have to try them and see which you like.

- **Other sweet low-carb baked goods**. I've tried commercially made low-carb cheesecake and cake rolls. The cheesecake was pretty good, but I can make better for far less money. I didn't like the cake rolls at all because I found them overwhelmingly sweet. But I know that they sell quite well, so somebody must like them.

- **Chocolate bars and other chocolate candy**. These, my friend, are generally superb. The best of the low-carb chocolate candies, including Carbolite, Pure De-Lite, Ross, Darrell Lea, and Low Carb Chef, are indistinguishable from their sugar-laden counterparts. You can get low-carb chocolate in both milk and dark. There are peanut butter cups, crispy bars, turtles, you name it. I haven't had a really bad sugar-free chocolate yet. See "About Polyols," on page 18.

- **Other sugar-free candy**. You can, if you look, find sugar-free taffies, hard candies, marshmallows, jelly beans, and other sweet treats. Again, the quality of these tends to be excellent. See "About Polyols," on page 18.

About Polyols

Polyols, also known as sugar alcohols, are widely used in sugar-free candies and cookies. There are a variety of polyols, and their names all end with "ol"—lactitol, maltitol, mannitol, sorbitol, xylitol, and the like. Polyols are, indeed, carbohydrates, but they are carbohydrates that are made up of molecules that are too big for humans to digest or absorb easily. As a result, polyols don't create much, if any, rise in blood sugar, nor do they create much of an insulin release.

Polyols are used in commercial sugar-free sweets because, unlike Splenda and other artificial sweeteners, they will give all of the textures that can be achieved with sugar. Polyols can be used to make crunchy toffee, chewy jelly beans, slick hard candies, chewy brownies, and creamy chocolate, just as sugar can. Yet they are far, far easier on your carbohydrate metabolism, and on your teeth, as well.

However, there are one or two problems with polyols. First of all, there is some feeling that different people have different abilities to digest and absorb these very long chain carbohydrates, which means that for some people, polyols may cause more of a derangement of blood sugar than they do for others. Once again, my only advice is to pay attention to your body.

The other problem with polyols is one that is inherent in all indigestible, unabsorbable carbohydrates: They can cause gas and diarrhea. Unabsorbed carbs ferment in your gut, creating intestinal gas as a result. It's the exact same thing that happens when people eat beans. I find that even half of a low-carb chocolate bar is enough to cause me social embarrassment several hours later. And I know of a case where eating a dozen and a half sugar-free taffies before bed caused the hapless consumer 45 minutes of serious gut-cramping intestinal distress at 4 a.m.

Don't think, by the way, that you can get around these effects of polyol consumption by taking Beano. This will work, but it will work by making the carbohydrates digestible and absorbable. This means that any low-carb advantage is gone. I know folks who have gained weight this way.

What we have here, then, is a sweetener that enforces moderation. Personally, I think this is a wonderful thing.

How much you can eat in the way of polyol-sweetened products without getting into digestive trouble will vary with each food's polyol content. For instance, sugar-free taffy is almost solid polyols, just as its sugary counterpart is virtually all sugar. Sugar-free chocolate, on the other hand, has much of its bulk made up of the chocolate. The bottom line is, I wouldn't eat sugar-free candies at all if you have an important meeting or a hot date a few hours later, or if you'll be getting on an airplane. (Altitude can make gas swell very uncomfortably in your gut.) If you can afford some gaseousness, for lack of a better word, I'd stick to no more than one chocolate bar or three or four taffies or caramels in a day.

One more good thing to know about polyols: It's not just candies that are labeled "low carbohydrate" that are made with these sweeteners. Many well-known candy companies, such as Fannie May and Fannie Farmer, make sugar-free chocolates, and virtually all of them use polyols. The only difference is that they count the carbohydrate grams in the polyols in their nutrition counts, even though the polyols are not, for the most part, absorbed. If you see a candy labeled "sugar free" that you're interested in, don't ask for the carb count, ask what it's sweetened with. If it's sweetened with something ending in "ol," chances are that it's okay for you. But once again, do pay attention to your body's reaction.

Where to Find Low-Carbohydrate Specialty Products

The availability of low-carbohydrate specialty products varies a great deal. Health food stores are good places to start your search, but even though some will carry these products, others still are caught up in low-fat, whole grain mania, and therefore shun them. Some carry things like fiber crackers and protein powder, but refuse to carry anything artificially sweetened because they pride themselves on carrying "natural" products only. Still, you'll want to find a good health food store to use as a source of many ingredients called for in this book, especially those for low-carb baking, so you may as well go poke around any health food stores in your area and see what you can find.

Little specialty groceries often carry low-carbohydrate products as a way to attract new and repeat business. In my town, Sahara Mart, a store that has long specialized in Middle Eastern foods, has become the best source for low-carb specialty products, as well. If a store carries a broad line of products specifically for low-carb dieters, they'll generally advertise it with signs in the windows, so keep your eyes open.

If you can't find a local source for such things as sugar-free chocolate, low-carb pasta, or whatever else you want, your best bet is to go online. Hit your favorite search engine, and search for "low-carbohydrate products," "sugar-free candy," or whatever it is you're looking for. There are a whole lot of low-carb "e-tailers" out there; find the ones with the products and prices you want. If you don't care to use your credit card online, most of them have toll-free order numbers you can call, and others have the ability to take checks online, as well as credit cards. A few companies I've done business with happily are Carb Smart, Low Carb Grocery, and Synergy Diet, but there are tons of them out there if you take the time to look.

On the Importance of Reading Labels

Do yourself a favor and get in the habit of reading the label on every food product, and I do mean every food product, that has one. I have learned from long, hard, repetitive experience that food manufacturers can, will, and do put sugar, corn syrup, corn starch, and other nutritionally empty, carb-laden garbage into every conceivable food product. I have found sugar in everything from salsa to canned clams, for heaven's sake! (Who it was who thought that the clams needed sugaring, I'd love to know.) You will shave untold thousands of grams of carbs off your intake in the course of a year by simply looking for the product that has no added junk.

There are also a good many classes of food products out there to which sugar is virtually always added; the cured meats come to mind. There is almost always sugar in sausage, ham, bacon, hot dogs, liverwurst, and the like. You will look in vain for sugarless varieties of these products, which is one good reason why you should primarily eat fresh meats, instead. However, you will find that there is quite a range of carb counts among cured meats, because some manufacturers add more sugar than others do. I have seen ham that has 1 gram of carbohydrates per serving, and I have seen ham that has 6 grams of carbohydrates per serving—that's a 600 percent difference! Likewise, I've seen hot dogs that have 1 gram of carbohydrates apiece, and I've seen hot dogs that have 5 grams of carbohydrates apiece.

If you're in a position where you can't read the labels (for instance, at the deli counter at the grocery store), ask questions. The nice deli folks will be glad to read the labels on the ham and salami for you, and they can tell you what goes into the various items they make themselves. You'll want to ask at the meat counter, too, if you're buying something they've mixed up themselves, such as Italian sausage or marinated meats. I've found that if I simply state that I have a medical condition that requires me to be very careful about my diet—and I don't come at the busiest hour of the week—folks are generally very nice about this sort of thing.

In short, you need to become a food sleuth. After all, you're paying your hard-earned money for this stuff, and it is quite literally going to become a part of you. Pay at least as much attention as you would if you were buying a car or a computer.

CHAPTER ONE

Ingredients You Need To Know About

This is by no means an exhaustive rundown of every single ingredient used in this book; these are just the ones I thought you might have questions about. I've grouped them by use, and within those groupings they're alphabetized, so if you have a question about something used in a recipe, flip back here and read up on whatever you're curious about.

Eggs

There are a few recipes in this book that call for raw eggs, an ingredient currently frowned upon by nutritional "officialdom" because of the risk of salmonella. However, I have it on pretty good authority that only 1 out of every 16,000 uncracked, properly refrigerated eggs is actually contaminated. As one woman with degrees in public health and food science put it, "The risk is less than the risk of breaking your leg on any given trip down the stairs." So I use raw eggs now and again without worrying about it, and we've never had a problem around here.

However, this does not mean that there is no risk. You'll have to decide for yourself whether this is something you should worry about. I generally use very fresh eggs from local small farmers, which may well be safer than eggs that have gone longer distances, and thus have a higher risk of cracking or experiencing refrigeration problems.

One useful thing to know about eggs: Although you'll want very fresh eggs for frying and poaching, eggs that are at least several days old are better for hard boiling. They're less likely to stick to their shells in that maddening way we've all encountered. So if you like hard-boiled eggs (and they're certainly one of the most convenient low-carb foods), buy a couple of extra cartons of eggs and let them sit in the refrigerator for at least three or four days before you hard boil them.

Fats and Oils

Bland Oils

Sometimes you want a bland oil in a recipe, something that adds little or no flavor of its own. In that case, I recommend peanut, sunflower, or canola oil. These are the oils I mean when I simply specify "oil" in a recipe. Avoid highly polyunsaturated oils such as safflower; they deteriorate quickly both from heat and from contact with oxygen, and they've been associated with an increased risk of cancer.

Butter

When a recipe says butter, use butter, will you? Margarine is nasty, unhealthy stuff, full of hydrogenated oils, trans fats, and artificial everything. It's terrible for you. So use the real thing. If real butter strains your budget, watch for sales and stock up; butter freezes beautifully. Shop around, too. In my town I've found stores that regularly sell butter for anywhere from $2.25 a pound to $4.59 a pound. That's a big difference, and one worth going out of my way for.

Coconut Oil

Coconut oil makes an excellent substitute for hydrogenated vegetable shortening (Crisco and the like), which you should shun. You may find coconut oil at health food stores, or possibly in Oriental food stores. One large local grocery store carries it in the "ethnic foods" section, with Indian foods. My health food store keeps coconut oil with the cosmetics. They're still convinced that saturated fats are terrible for you, so they don't put it with the foods, but some folks use it for making hair dressings and soaps. Coconut oil is solid at room temperature, except in the summer, but it melts at body temperature. Surprisingly, it has no coconut flavor or aroma; you can use it for sautéing or in baking without adding any "off" flavor to your recipes.

Olive Oil

It surely will come as no surprise to you that olive oil is a healthy fat, but you may not know that there are various kinds. Extra-virgin olive oil is the first pressing. It is deep green, with a full, fruity flavor, and it makes all the difference in salad dressings. However, it's expensive and also too strongly flavored for some uses. I keep a bottle of extra-virgin olive oil on hand, but use it exclusively for salads.

For sautéing and other general uses, I use a grade of olive oil known as "pomace." Pomace is far cheaper than extra-virgin olive oil, and it has a milder flavor. I buy pomace in gallon cans at the same Middle Eastern grocery store where I buy my low-carb specialty products. These gallon cans are worth looking for because they're the cheapest way to buy the stuff. If you can't find gallon cans of pomace, feel free to buy whatever cheaper, milder-flavored type of olive oil is available at your grocery store.

Be aware that if you refrigerate olive oil it will become solid. This is no big deal, as it will be fine once it warms up again. If you need it quickly, you can run the bottle under warm water. Or, if the container has no metal and will fit in your microwave, microwave it for a minute or so on low power.

Flour Substitutes

As you are no doubt aware, flour is out, for the most part, in low-carb cooking. Flour serves a few different purposes in cooking, from making up the bulk of most baked goods and creating stretchiness in bread dough to thickening sauces and "binding" casseroles. In low-carb cooking, we use different ingredients for these various purposes. Here's a rundown of flour substitutes you'll want to have on hand for low-carb cooking and baking:

Brans

Because fiber is a carbohydrate that we neither digest nor absorb, brans of one kind or another are very useful for bulking up (no pun intended!) low-carb baked goods. I use different kinds in different recipes. You'll want to have at least wheat bran and oat bran on hand; both of these are widely available. If you can also find rice bran, it's worth picking up, especially if you have high cholesterol. Of all the kinds of bran tested, rice bran was most powerful for lowering high blood cholesterol.

Ground Almonds and Hazelnuts

Finely ground almonds and hazelnuts are wonderful for replacing some or all of the flour in many recipes, especially cakes and cookies. If you can purchase almond meal and hazelnut meal locally, these should work fine in the recipes in this book. If you can't (I don't have a local source for these), simply grind nuts in your food processor, using the S blade. The nuts are not the texture of flour when ground, but more the consistency of coarsely ground cornmeal. Whenever a recipe in this book calls for ground almonds or hazelnuts, this is what I used.

It's good to know that these nuts actually expand a little during grinding. This surprised me because I thought they'd compress a bit. Figure that between $^2/3$ and $^3/4$ of a cup of either of these nuts will become 1 cup when ground.

Guar and Xanthan Gums

These sound just dreadful, don't they? But they're in lots of your favorite processed foods, so how bad can they be? If you're wondering what the heck they are, anyway, here's the answer: They're forms of water-soluble fiber, extracted and purified. Guar and xanthan are both flavorless white powders; their value to us is as low-carb thickeners. Technically speaking, these are carbs, but they're all fiber, nothing but, so don't worry about using them.

You'll find guar or xanthan used in small quantities in a lot of these recipes. Don't go dramatically increasing the quantity of guar or xanthan to get a thicker product, because in large quantities they make things gummy, and the texture is not terribly pleasant. But in these tiny quantities they add oomph to sauces and soups without using flour. You can always leave the guar or xanthan out if you can't find it; you'll just get a somewhat thinner result.

You'll notice that I always tell you to put the guar or xanthan through the blender with whatever liquid it is that you're using. This is because it is very difficult to simply whisk guar into a sauce and not get little gummy lumps in your finished sauce or soup, and the blender is the best way to thoroughly combine your ingredients.

If you don't own or don't want to use a blender, there is one possible alternative: Put your guar or xanthan in a salt shaker, and sprinkle it, bit by bit, over your sauce, stirring madly all the while with a whisk. The problem here, of course, is there's no way to know exactly how much you're using, so you'll just have to stop when your dish reaches the degree of thickness you like. Still, this can be a useful trick.

Your health food store may well be able to order guar or xanthan for you (I slightly prefer xanthan, myself) if they don't have it on hand. You can also find suppliers online. Keep either one in a jar with a tight lid, and it will never go bad. I bought a pound of guar about 15 years ago, and it's still going strong!

Low-Carbohydrate Bake Mix

There are several brands of low-carbohydrate bake mix on the market. These are generally a combination of some form of powdery protein and fiber, such as soy, whey, and sometimes oat, plus baking powder, and sometimes salt. These mixes are the low-carb world's equivalent of Bisquick, although low-carb bake mixes differ from Bisquick in that they do not have shortening added. You will need to add butter, oil, or some other form of fat when using them to make pancakes, waffles, biscuits, and such. I mostly use low-carb bake mix in lesser quantities, for "flouring" chicken before baking or frying, or replacing flour as a "binder" in a casserole. If you can't find low-carbohydrate bake mix locally, there are many Web sites that sell it.

Oat Flour

One or two recipes in this book call for oat flour. Because of its high fiber content, oat flour has a lower usable carb count than most other flours. Even so, it must be used in very small quantities. Oat flour is available at health food stores. In a pinch, you can grind up oatmeal in your blender or food processor.

Psyllium Husks

This is another fiber product. It's the same form of fiber that is used in Metamucil and similar products. Because psyllium has little flavor of its own, it makes a useful high-fiber "filler" in some low-carb bread recipes. Look for plain psyllium husks at your health food store. Mine carries them in bulk, quite cheaply, but if yours doesn't, look for them among the laxatives and "colon health" products. (A brand called "Colon Cleanse" is widely available.)

Rice Protein Powder

For savory recipes such as entrees, you need a protein powder that isn't sweet, and preferably one that has no flavor at all. There are a number of these on the market, and some are blander than others. I tried several kinds, and I've found that rice protein powder is the one I like best. I buy Nutribiotics brand, which has 1 gram of carbohydrates per tablespoon, but any unflavored rice protein powder with a similar carb count should work fine. For that matter, I see no reason not to experiment with other unflavored protein powders, if you like.

Rolled Oats

Also known as old-fashioned oatmeal, rolled oats are oat grains that have been squashed flat. These are available in every grocery store in the Western Hemisphere. Do not substitute instant or quick-cooking oatmeal.

Soy Powder, Soy Flour, and Soy Protein Isolate

Some of my recipes call for soy *powder*. None call for soy *flour*, although a few recipes from other folks do. If you use soy flour in a recipe that calls for soy powder, you won't get the results I got. You also won't get the right results with *soy protein powder*, also known as *soy protein isolate*. What is the difference? Soy protein isolate is a protein that has been extracted from soybeans and concentrated into a protein powder. Soy flour is made from raw soybeans that have simply been ground up into flour, and it has a strong bean flavor. Soy powder, also known as *soy milk powder*, is made from whole soybeans, like soy flour, but the beans are cooked before they're ground up. For some reason I don't pretend to understand, this gets rid of the strong flavor and makes soy powder taste quite mild. If your local health food store doesn't stock soy powder or soy milk powder, they can no doubt order it for you.

You should be aware that despite the tremendous marketing buildup soy has enjoyed for the past several years, there are some problems emerging. Soy is well known to interfere with thyroid function, which is the last thing you need if you're trying to lose weight. It also can interfere with mineral absorption. It is also less certain, but still possible, that regular consumption of soy causes brain deterioration and genital defects in boy babies born to mothers with soy-heavy diets. For these reasons, although I do not shun soy entirely, I use other options when possible.

Vital Wheat Gluten

Gluten is a grain protein. It's the gluten in flour that makes bread dough stretchy so that it will trap the gas released by the yeast, letting your bread rise. We are not, of course, going to use regular, all-purpose flour, with its high carbohydrate content. Fortunately, it is possible to buy concentrated wheat gluten. This high-protein, low-starch flour is absolutely essential to making low-carbohydrate yeast breads.

Buying vital wheat gluten can be a problem, however, because the nomenclature is not standardized. Some packagers call this "vital wheat gluten" or "pure gluten flour," whereas others simply call it "wheat gluten." Still others call it "high-gluten flour." This is a real poser, since the same name is frequently used for regular flour that has had extra gluten added to it; that product is something you definitely do not want.

To make sure you're getting the right product, you'll simply have to read the label. The product you want, regardless of what the packager calls it, will have between 75 and 80 percent protein, or about 24 grams in 1/4 cup. It will also have a very low carbohydrate count, somewhere in the neighborhood of 6 grams of carbohydrates in that same 1/4 cup. If your health food store has a bulk bin labeled "high-gluten flour" or "gluten flour" but there's no nutrition label attached, ask to see the bulk food manager and request the information off of the sack the flour came in. If the label on the bin says "vital wheat gluten" or "pure gluten flour," you can probably trust it.

At this writing, the most widely distributed brand of vital wheat gluten in the United States is Bob's Red Mill. More and more grocery stores are beginning to carry this line of products. If your grocery store doesn't yet, you might request that they start.

Wheat Germ

The germ is the part of the wheat kernel that would have become the plant if the grain had sprouted. It is the most nutritious, highest protein part of the wheat kernel, and is much lower in carbohydrates than the starchy part that becomes white flour. A few recipes in this book call for raw wheat germ, which is available at health food stores. Raw wheat germ should be refrigerated, as it goes rancid pretty easily. If your health food store doesn't keep the raw wheat germ in the cooler, I'd look for another health food store.

If you can't get raw wheat germ, toasted wheat germ, such as Kretchmer's, is a usable second-best. It's widely available in grocery stores.

Whey Protein Powder

Whey is the liquid part of milk. If you've ever seen yogurt that has separated, the clearish liquid on top is the whey. Whey protein is of extremely good quality, and the protein powder made from it is tops in both flavor and nutritional value. For any sweet recipe, the vanilla-flavored whey protein powder is best, and it's readily available in health food stores. (Yes, this is the kind generally sold for making shakes with.) Keep in mind that protein powders vary in their carbohydrate counts, so look for the one with the fewest carbohydrates. Also beware of sugar-sweetened protein powders, which can be higher in carbs. The one I use is sweetened with stevia and has a little less than 1 gram of carbohydrates per tablespoon.

Natural whey protein powder is just like vanilla-flavored whey protein powder, except that it has not been flavored or sweetened. Its flavor is bland, so it is used in recipes where a sweet flavor is not desirable. Natural whey protein powder is called for in some of the recipes that other folks have donated to this book; I generally use rice protein powder when a bland protein powder is called for.

Liquids

Beer

One or two recipes in this book call for beer. The lowest carbohydrate beers I've been able to find are Miller Lite and Milwaukee's Best Light, both at 3.5 grams per can. They are what I recommend you use when you cook, and they are also what I recommend you drink, if you're a beer fan.

Broths

Canned or boxed chicken and beef broths are very handy items to keep around, and it's certainly quicker to make dinner with these than it would be if you had to make your own from scratch. However, the quality of most of the canned broth you'll find at your local grocery store is appallingly bad. The chicken broth has all sorts of chemicals in it and often sugar, as well. The "beef" broth is worse, frequently containing no beef whatsoever. I refuse to use these products, and you should, too.

However, there are a few canned and boxed broths worth buying. Many grocery stores now carry a brand called Kitchen Basics, which contains no chemicals at all. It's packaged in 1-quart boxes, much like soy milk, and it's available in both chicken and beef. Health food stores also have good quality canned and boxed broths. Both Shelton and Health Valley brands are widely distributed in the United States.

Decent packaged broth won't cost you a whole lot more than the stuff that is made of salt and chemicals. If you watch for sales, you can often get it as cheaply as the bad stuff; stock up on it then. (When my health food store runs a sale of good broth for 89 cents a can, I buy piles of the stuff!)

One last note: You will also find canned vegetable broth, particularly at health food stores. This is tasty, but it runs much higher in carbohydrates than the chicken and beef broths. I'd avoid it.

Vinegar

Various recipes in this book call for wine vinegar, cider vinegar, sherry vinegar, rice vinegar, tarragon vinegar, white vinegar, balsamic vinegar, and even raspberry vinegar, for which you'll find a recipe. If you've always thought that vinegar was just vinegar, think again! Each of these vinegars has a distinct flavor all its own, and if you substitute one for the other, you'll change the whole character of the recipe. Add just one splash of cider vinegar to your Asian Chicken Salad (see page 368), and you've traded your Chinese accent for an American twang. Vinegar is such a great way to give bright flavors to foods while adding very few carbs that I keep all of these varieties on hand. This is easy to do, because vinegar keeps for a very long time.

As with everything else, read the labels on your vinegar. I've seen cider vinegar that has 0 grams of carbohydrates per ounce and I've seen cider vinegar that has 4 grams of carbohydrates per ounce—a huge difference. Beware, also, of apple cider–flavored vinegar, which is white vinegar with artificial flavors added. I bought this once by mistake. (You'd think someone who constantly reminds others to read labels would be beyond such errors, wouldn't you?)

Wine

There are several recipes in this cookbook calling for either dry red or dry white wine. I find the inexpensive box wines, which come in a mylar bag inside a cardboard box, very convenient to keep on hand for cooking. The simple reason for this is that they don't go bad because the contents are never exposed to air. These are not fabulous vintage wines, but they're fine for our modest purposes, and they certainly are handy. I generally have both Burgundy and Chablis wine-in-a-box on hand. Be wary of any wine with "added flavors." Too often, one of those flavors will be sugar. Buy wine with a recognizable name, such as Burgundy, Rhine, Chablis, Cabernet, and the like, rather than stuff like "Chillable Red," and you'll get better results.

Nuts, Seeds, and Nut Butters

Nuts and Seeds

Low in carbohydrates and high in healthy fats, protein, and minerals, nuts and seeds are great foods for us. Not only are they delicious for snacking or for adding crunch to salads and stir-fries, but when ground, they can replace some of the flour in low-carb baked goods. In particular, you'll find quite a few recipes in this book calling for ground almonds, ground hazelnuts, and ground sunflower seeds. Since these ingredients can be pricey, you'll want to shop around. In particular, health food stores often carry nuts and seeds in bulk at better prices than you'll find at the grocery store. I have also found that specialty ethnic groceries often have good prices on nuts. I get my best deal on almonds at my wonderful Middle Eastern grocery, Sahara Mart.

By the way, along with pumpkin and sunflower seeds, you can buy sesame seeds in bulk at health food stores for a fraction of what they'll cost you in a little shaker jar at the grocery store. Buy them "unhulled" and you'll get both more fiber and more calcium. You can also get unsweetened coconut flakes at health food stores.

Flaxseed comes from the same plant that gives us the fabric linen, and it is turning out to be one of the most nutritious seeds there is. Along with good-quality protein, flaxseeds have tons of soluble, cholesterol-reducing fiber and are a rich source of eicosapentaenoic acid (EPA), the same fats that make fish so heart-healthy.

Most of the recipes in this book that use flaxseed call for it to be ground up into a coarse meal. You can buy pre-ground flaxseed meal (Bob's Red Mill sells it, among others), but I much prefer to grind my own. The simple reason for this is that the fats in flaxseeds are very stable so long as the seeds are whole, but they go rancid pretty quickly after the seed coat is broken.

Grinding flaxseed is very easy if you have a food processor. Simply put the seeds in your food processor with the S blade in place, turn on the machine, and forget about it for about 5 minutes. (Yes, it takes that long!) You can then add your flaxseed meal to whatever it is you're cooking.

If you don't have a food processor, you'll just have to buy flaxseed meal pre-ground. If you do, keep it in an airtight container, refrigerate or freeze it, and use it up as quickly as you can.

Nut Butters

The only peanut butter called for in this cookbook is "natural" peanut butter, the kind made from ground, roasted peanuts; peanut oil; salt; and nothing else. Most big grocery stores now carry natural peanut butter; it's the stuff with the layer of oil on top. The oil in standard peanut butter has been hydrogenated to keep it from separating out (that's what gives big name-brand peanut butters that extremely smooth, plastic consistency) and it's hard to think of anything worse for you than hydrogenated vegetable oil—except for sugar, of course, which is also added to standard peanut butter. Stick to the natural stuff.

Health food stores carry not only natural peanut butter but also almond butter, sunflower butter, and sesame butter, generally called "tahini." All of these are useful for low-carbers. Keep all natural nut butters in the refrigerator unless you're going to eat them up within a week or two.

Seasonings

Bouillon or Broth Concentrates

Bouillon or broth concentrate comes in cubes, crystals, or liquids. It is generally full of salt and chemicals, and it doesn't taste notably like the animal it supposedly came from. It definitely does not make a suitable substitute for good-quality broth if you're making a pot of soup. However, these products can be useful for adding a little kick of flavor here and there, more as seasonings than as soups, and for this, I keep them on hand. I generally use chicken bouillon crystals because I find them easier to use than cubes. I also keep liquid beef broth concentrate on hand. I chose this because, unlike the cubes or crystals it actually has a bit of beef in it. I use Wyler's, but see no reason why any comparable product wouldn't work fine. If you can get the British product Bovril, it might even be better!

Fresh Ginger

Many recipes in this book call for fresh ginger, sometimes called ginger-root. Fresh ginger is an essential ingredient in Asian cooking, and dried, powdered ginger is not a substitute. Fortunately, fresh ginger freezes beautifully; just drop your whole gingerroot (called a "hand" of ginger) into a zipper-lock freezer bag, and toss it in the freezer. When the time comes to use it, pull it out, peel enough of the end for your immediate purposes, and grate it. (It will grate just fine while still frozen.) Throw the remaining root back in the bag, and toss it back on the freezer.

Ground fresh gingerroot in oil is available in jars at some very comprehensive grocery stores. I like freshly grated ginger better, but this jarred gingerroot will also work in these recipes.

Garlic

Garlic is a borderline vegetable. It's fairly high in carbohydrates, but it's very, very good for you. Surely you've heard all about garlic's nutritional prowess by now. Garlic also, of course, is an essential flavoring ingredient in many recipes. However, remember that there is an estimated 1 gram of carbohydrates per clove, so go easy. A "clove," by the way, is one of those little individual bits you get in a whole garlic bulb. If you read "clove" and use a whole bulb (also called a "head") of garlic, you'll get lots more carbs—and a *lot* stronger garlic flavor—than you expected.

I only use fresh garlic, except for in the occasional recipe that calls for a sprinkle-on seasoning blend. Nothing else tastes like the real thing. To my taste buds, even the jarred, chopped garlic in oil doesn't taste like fresh garlic. And we won't even talk about garlic powder. You may use jarred garlic if you like; 1/2 teaspoon should equal about 1 clove of fresh garlic. If you choose to use powdered garlic, well, I can't stop you, but I'm afraid I can't promise the recipes will taste the same, either. Figure that 1/4 teaspoon of garlic powder is roughly equivalent to 1 clove of fresh garlic.

By the way, the easiest way to crush a clove or two of garlic is to put the flat side of a big knife on top of it and smash it with your fist. Pick out the papery skin, which will now be easy, chop your garlic a bit more, and toss it into your dish. Keep in mind that the distinctive garlic aroma and flavor only develops after the cell walls are broken (that's why a pile of fresh garlic bulbs in the grocery store doesn't reek), so the more finely you crush or mince your garlic, the more flavor it will release.

Vege-Sal

If you've read my newsletter, *Lowcarbezine!*, you know that I'm a big fan of Vege-Sal. What is Vege-Sal? It's a salt that's been seasoned, but don't think "seasoned salt." Vege-Sal is much milder than traditional seasoned salt. It's simply salt that's been blended with some dried, powdered vegetables. The flavor is quite subtle, but I think it improves all sorts of things. I've given you the choice between using regular salt or Vege-Sal in a wide variety of recipes. Don't worry, they'll come out fine with plain old salt, but I do think Vege-Sal adds a little something extra. Vege-Sal is also excellent sprinkled over chops and steaks in place of regular salt. Vege-Sal is made by Modern Products and is widely available in health food stores.

Sweeteners

Blackstrap Molasses

What the heck is molasses doing in a low-carb cookbook? It's practically all carbohydrates, after all. Well, yes, but I've found that combining Splenda (see page 36) with a very small amount of molasses gives a good brown-sugar flavor to all sorts of recipes. Always use the darkest molasses you can find; the darker it is, the stronger the flavor and the lower the carb count. That's why I specify blackstrap—the darkest, strongest molasses there is. It's nice to know that blackstrap is also where all the minerals they take out of sugar end up, so it may be full of carbs, but at least it's not a nutritional wasteland. Still, I only use small amounts.

Most health food stores carry blackstrap molasses, but if you can't find it, always buy the darkest molasses available, keeping in mind that most grocery store brands come in both light and dark varieties.

Why not use some of the artificial brown sugar–flavored sweeteners out there? Because I've tried them, and I haven't tasted even one I would be willing to buy again. Ick.

Splenda

Splenda is the latest artificial sweetener to hit the market, and it blows all of the competition clear out of the water! Feed nondieting friends and family Splenda-sweetened desserts, and they will never know that you didn't use sugar. It tastes that good.

Splenda has some other advantages. The table sweetener has been bulked so that it measures just like sugar, spoon-for-spoon and cup-for-cup. This makes adapting recipes much easier. Also, Splenda stands up to heat, unlike aspartame, which means you can use it for baked goods and other things that are heated for a while.

However, Splenda is not completely carb-free. Because of the maltodextrin used to bulk it, Splenda has about 0.5 gram of carbohydrates per teaspoon, or about $1/8$ of the carbohydrates of sugar. So count half a gram per teaspoon, 1 $1/2$ grams per tablespoon, and 24 grams per cup. At this writing, McNeil, the company that makes Splenda, has no plans to release liquid Splenda in the United States, but I am hoping that they will change their minds. The liquid, available in some foreign countries, is carb-free. So while it will take a little more finesse to figure out quantities, it will also allow me to slash the carb counts of all sorts of recipes still further! Stay tuned.

Stevia/FOS Blend

Stevia is short for *Stevia rebaudiana*, a South American shrub with very sweet leaves. Stevia extract, a white powder from stevia leaves, is growing in popularity with people who don't care to eat sugar but who are nervous about artificial sweeteners.

However, stevia extract has a couple of faults: First, it's so extremely sweet that it's hard to know just how much to use in any given recipe. Second, it often has a bitter taste as well as a sweet one. This is why some smart food packagers have started blending stevia with fructooligosaccharide, also known as FOS. FOS is a sugar, but it's a sugar with a molecule so large that humans can neither digest nor absorb it, so it doesn't raise blood sugar or cause an insulin release. FOS has a nice, mild sweetness to it; indeed, it's only half as sweet as table sugar. This makes it the perfect partner for the too-sweet stevia.

This stevia/FOS blend is called for in just a few recipes in this book. It is available in many health food stores, both in packets and in shaker jars. The brand I use is called SteviaPlus, and it's from a company called Sweet Leaf, but any stevia/FOS blend should do for the recipes that call for it.

My favorite use for this stevia/FOS blend, by the way, is to sweeten my yogurt. I think it tastes quite good, and FOS actually helps the good bacteria take hold in your gut, improving your health.

Vegetables

Carrots

Because carrots have a higher glycemic index than many vegetables, a lot of low-carbers have started avoiding them with great zeal. But while carrots do have a fairly high blood sugar impact, you'd have to eat pounds of them to get the quantity that is used to test with. So don't freak when you see a carrot used here and there in these recipes, okay? I've kept the quantities small, just enough to add flavor, color, and a few vitamins, but certainly not enough to torpedo your diet.

Frozen Vegetables

You'll notice that many of these recipes call for frozen vegetables, particularly broccoli, green beans, and cauliflower. I use these because I find them very convenient, and I think that the quality is quite good. If you like, you may certainly substitute fresh vegetables in any recipe. You will need to adjust the cooking time, and if the recipe calls for the vegetable to be used thawed, but not cooked, you'll need to "blanch" your vegetables by boiling them for just three to five minutes.

It's important to know that frozen vegetables are not immortal, no matter how good your freezer is. Don't buy more than you can use up in four to six weeks, even if they're on sale. You'll end up throwing them away.

Onions

Onions are borderline vegetables. They're certainly higher in carbohydrates than, say, lettuce or cucumbers. However, they're loaded with valuable phytochemicals, so they're very healthful, and of course they add an unmatched flavor to all sorts of foods. Therefore I use onions a lot, but I try to use the smallest quantity that will give the desired flavor. Indeed, one of the most common things I do to cut carb counts on "borrowed" recipes is to cut back on the amount of onion used. If you have serious diabetes, you'll want to watch your quantities of onions pretty carefully, and maybe even cut back further on the amounts I've given.

If you're not an accomplished cook, you need to know that different types of onions are good for different things. There are mild onions, which are best used raw, and there are stronger onions, which are what you want if you're going to be cooking them. My favorite mild onions are sweet red onions; these are widely available, and you'll see I've used them quite a lot in the recipes here. However, if you prefer, you can substitute Vidalia or Bermuda onions anywhere I've specified sweet red onions. Scallions, also known as green onions, also are mild and are best eaten raw, or quickly cooked in stir-fries. To me, scallions have their own flavor, and I generally don't substitute for them, but your kitchen won't blow up or anything if you use another sort of sweet onion in their place.

When a recipe simply says "onion," what I'm talking about is good old yellow globe onions, the ones you can buy 3 to 5 pounds at a time in net sacks. You'll be doing yourself a favor if you pick a sack with smallish onions in it so that when a recipe calls for just a 1/4 or 1/2 cup of chopped onion, you won't be left with half an onion. For the record, when I say "small onion," I mean one about 1 1/2 inches in diameter, or about 1/4 to 1/3 cup when chopped. A medium onion would be about 2 inches in diameter, and would yield between 1/2 and 3/4 cup when chopped. A large onion would be 2 1/2 to 3 inches across, and would yield about a cup when chopped. Personally, I'm not so obsessive about exact carb counts that I bother to measure every scrap of onion I put in a dish; I think in terms of small, medium, and large onions, instead. If you prefer to be more exact, that's up to you.

Tomatoes and Tomato Products

Tomatoes are another borderline vegetable, but like onions they are so nutritious, so flavorful, and so versatile that I'm reluctant to leave them out of low-carb cuisine entirely. After all, lycopene, the pigment that makes tomatoes red, has been shown to be a potent cancer-fighter, and who wants to miss out on something like that?

You'll notice that I call for canned tomatoes in a fair number of recipes, even in some where fresh tomatoes might do. This is because fresh tomatoes aren't very good for much of the year, whereas canned tomatoes are all canned at the height of ripeness. I'd rather have a good canned tomato in my sauce or soup than a mediocre fresh one. Since canned tomatoes are generally used with all the liquid that's in the can, the nutritional content doesn't suffer the way it does with most canned vegetables.

I also use plain canned tomato sauce, canned pizza sauce, canned pasta sauce, and jarred salsa. When choosing these products, you need to be aware that tomatoes, for some reason, inspire food packers to flights of sugar-fancy. They add sugar, corn syrup, and other carb-laden sweeteners to all sorts of tomato products, so it is very important that you read the labels on all tomato-based products to find the ones with no added sugar. And keep on reading them, even after you know what's in them. The good, cheap brand of salsa I used for quite a while showed up one day with "New, Improved!" on the label. Can you guess how they improved it? Right—they added sugar. So I found a new brand.

Yeast

All of the bread recipes in this book were developed using plain old active dry yeast, not "bread machine yeast" and certainly not "rapid rise" yeast. Indeed, one of my testers had some spectacular failures using rapid rise yeast in her bread machine with one of my recipes, but the recipe worked brilliantly for another tester who used regular yeast.

The best place to buy yeast is at a good health food store, where yeast is generally available in bulk for a tiny fraction of what it would cost you in little packets at the grocery store. Yeast should be stored in a cooler at the health food store and the refrigerator at home.

One last note: Don't buy more yeast than you're likely to use up in, oh, four to six weeks. It will eventually die on you, and you'll end up with dough that won't rise. When you're using expensive ingredients, like we do, this is almost more than a body can bear.

Yogurt and Buttermilk

Yogurt and buttermilk both fall into the category of "cultured milks"—milk that has deliberately had a particular bacteria added to it and then been kept warm until the bacteria grows. These bacteria give yogurt and buttermilk their characteristic thick textures and tangy flavors.

If you look at the label of either of these cultured milk products, you'll see that the nutrition label claims 12 grams of carbohydrates per cup (and, by the way, 8 grams of protein). This is the same carbohydrate count as the milk these products are made from. For this reason, many low-carbers avoid yogurt and buttermilk.

However, in *GO-Diet*, Dr. Goldberg and Dr. O'Mara explain that in actuality, most of the lactose (milk sugar) in the milk is converted into lactic acid by the bacteria. This is what gives these foods their sour taste. The labels say "12 grams carbohydrate" largely, they say, because carbohydrate count is determined by "difference." What this means is that the calorie count is determined first. Then the protein and fat fractions are measured, and the number of calories they contribute is calculated. Any calories left over are assumed to come from carbohydrate.

However, Goldberg and O'Mara say, this is inaccurate in the cases of yogurt and buttermilk, and they say we should count just 4 grams of carbohydrates per cup for these cultured milks. Accordingly, I have added them back to my diet, and I have had no trouble with them, meaning no weight gain and no triggering of "blood sugar hunger." I really enjoy yogurt as a snack! Based on this, the carb counts in this book are calculated using that 4-grams-of-carbohydrates-per-cup figure.

Keep in mind that these numbers only apply to plain yogurt. The sweetened kind is always higher in carbohydrate. If you like fruit-flavored yogurt, flavor it yourself. You'll find a recipe for making your own plain yogurt, easy as pie, in the Eggs and Dairy chapter, but any store-bought plain yogurt is fine.

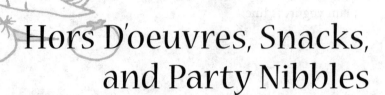

CHAPTER TWO

Hors D'oeuvres, Snacks, and Party Nibbles

Unlike most snack and party foods, the recipes in this chapter are actually nutritious and filling. This means two things: One, that if you serve one or two of these items before dinner, you may want to cut back a bit on quantities at the meal itself, and two, that you can actually use many of these recipes as light meals in and of themselves. This is a particularly nice idea for family movie night—just put out a big tray of cut up vegetables and dip, some wings, and a bowl of nut mix, and call it supper.

◌ Heroin Wings

Once you try these, you'll understand the name—they're utterly, totally addictive! These are a bit messy and time-consuming to make, but they're worth every minute. They'll impress the heck out of your friends, too, and you'll wish you'd made more of them. They also taste great the next day.

> 4 pounds chicken wings
> 1 cup grated Parmesan cheese
> 2 tablespoons dried parsley
> 1 tablespoon dried oregano
> 2 teaspoons paprika
> 1 teaspoon salt
> 1/2 teaspoon pepper
> 1/2 cup butter

1. Preheat the oven to 350°F.
2. Cut the wings into drumsticks, saving the pointy tips.

   🍓 Not sure what to do with those wingtips? Freeze them for soup
   —they make great broth.

3. Combine the Parmesan cheese and the parsley, oregano, paprika, salt, and pepper in a bowl.
4. Line a shallow baking pan with foil. (Do not omit this step, or you'll still be scrubbing the pan a week later.)
5. Melt the butter in a shallow bowl or pan.
6. Dip each drumstick in butter, roll in the cheese and seasoning mixture, and arrange in the foil-lined pan.
7. Bake for 1 hour,—and then kick yourself for not having made a double recipe!

Yield: About 50 pieces, each with only a trace of carbohydrates, a trace of fiber, and 4 grams of protein.

ဌ Chinese Peanut Wings

If you love Chinese barbecued spareribs, try making these.

1/4 cup soy sauce

3 tablespoons Splenda

3 tablespoons natural peanut butter

2 tablespoons dry sherry

1 tablespoon oil

1 tablespoon apple cider vinegar

2 teaspoons Chinese Five Spice powder

1/4 teaspoon red pepper flakes (or more, if you want them hotter)

1 clove garlic, crushed

12 chicken wings or 24 drumettes

1. Preheat the oven to 325°.

2. Put the soy sauce, Splenda, peanut butter, sherry, oil, vinegar, spice powder, pepper flakes, and garlic in a blender or food processor, and blend well.

3. If you have whole chicken wings and want to cut them into drumsticks, do it now. (This is a matter of preference and is not essential.)

4. Arrange the wings in a large baking pan, and pour the blended sauce over them, then turn them over to coat on all sides.

5. Let them sit for at least half an hour (an hour is even better).

6. Bake the wings for an hour, turning every 20 minutes during baking.

7. When the wings are done, put them on a serving platter and scrape the sauce from the pan back into the blender or food processor. Blend again for just a moment to make it smooth, and serve with the wings.

Yield: 24 pieces, each with 1 gram of carbohydrates, a trace of fiber, and 5 grams of protein.

⌒ Hot Wings

If you want to simplify this recipe, use store-bought Buffalo Wing sauce instead of the mixture of dry spices. Most wing sauces don't have any sugar in them and are quite low in carbs.

> 1 teaspoon cayenne pepper
>
> 2 teaspoons dried oregano
>
> 1 teaspoon curry powder
>
> 2 teaspoons paprika
>
> 2 teaspoons dried thyme
>
> 2 pounds chicken wings, cut into drumettes

1. Preheat the oven to 375°F.

2. Combine the pepper, oregano, curry, paprika, and thyme well in a bowl.

3. Arrange the wings in a shallow baking pan, and sprinkle the mixture evenly over them, turning to coat both sides.

4. Roast for 45 to 50 minutes, or until crisp. Serve with the traditional accompaniments of ranch or blue cheese dressing and celery sticks, if desired.

   Yield: About 24 pieces, each with a trace of carbohydrates, a trace of fiber, and 4 grams of protein.

↻ Paprika Wings

20 chicken wing drumsticks

3 tablespoons olive oil

2 cloves garlic, crushed

Salt

Pepper

Paprika

1. Preheat the oven to 350°F.

2. Arrange the wings in a baking pan so that they are not touching.

3. Combine the oil and garlic, and spoon the mixture over the wings. Make sure you get a little of the crushed garlic on each piece.

4. Sprinkle the wings with salt and pepper to taste, and then with enough paprika to make them reddish all over.

5. Roast for 15 to 20 minutes, then turn them over and sprinkle the other side with salt, pepper, and paprika.

6. Roast for another 45 minutes to 1 hour, turning every 15 to 20 minutes.

Yield: 20 pieces, each with a trace of carbohydrates, a trace of fiber, and 4 grams of protein.

Stuffed Eggs

Don't save these recipes for parties: If you're a low-carb eater, a refrigerator full of stuffed eggs is a beautiful thing. Here are six varieties. Feel free to double or triple any of these recipes—you know they'll disappear.

↻ Classic Deviled Eggs

These are everybody's potluck supper favorite.

>6 hard-boiled eggs
>
>5 tablespoons mayonnaise
>
>2 teaspoons spicy brown or Dijon mustard
>
>1/4 teaspoon salt or Vege-Sal
>
>Paprika

1. Slice the eggs in half, and carefully remove the yolks into a mixing bowl.
2. Mash the yolks with a fork. Stir in the mayonnaise, mustard, and salt, and mix until creamy.
3. Spoon the mixture back into the hollows in the egg whites. Sprinkle with a little paprika for color.

Yield: 12 halves, each with a trace of carbohydrates, a trace of fiber, and 3 grams of protein.

↻ Onion Eggs

>6 hard-boiled eggs
>
>5 tablespoons mayonnaise
>
>1 teaspoon spicy brown or Dijon mustard
>
>2 1/2 teaspoons very finely minced sweet red onion
>
>5 drops Tabasco
>
>1/4 teaspoon salt or Vege-Sal

1. Slice the eggs in half, and carefully remove the yolks into a mixing bowl.
2. Mash the yolks with a fork. Stir in the mayonnaise, mustard, onion, Tabasco, and salt, and mix until creamy.
3. Spoon the mixture back into the hollows in the egg whites.

Yield: 12 halves, each with a trace of carbohydrates, a trace of fiber, and 3 grams of protein.

⤳ Fish Eggs

That's eggs with fish, not eggs from fish. If you thought stuffed eggs couldn't go to an upscale party, these will change your mind.

6 hard-boiled eggs

2 tablespoons mayonnaise

2 tablespoons sour cream

1/4 cup moist smoked salmon, mashed fine

1 tablespoon jarred, grated horseradish

2 teaspoons finely minced sweet red onion

1/8 teaspoon salt

1. Slice the eggs in half, and carefully remove the yolks into a mixing bowl.

2. Mash the yolks with a fork. Stir in the mayonnaise, sour cream, salmon, horseradish, onion, and salt, and mix until creamy.

3. Spoon the mixture back into the hollows in the egg whites.

   Yield: 12 halves, each with a trace of carbohydrates, a trace of fiber, and 3 grams of protein.

⤳ Kali's Eggs

Curried and buttery and good!

6 hard-boiled eggs

1 tablespoon butter

1 teaspoon curry powder

1 clove garlic, crushed

1 scallion, including the crisp part of the green shoot, finely minced

1/3 cup mayonnaise

1/4 teaspoon Tabasco

1/2 teaspoon salt

1. Slice the eggs in half, and carefully remove the yolks into a mixing bowl.

2. In a small, heavy skillet over low heat, melt the butter. Add the curry powder and garlic, and stir for 2 minutes.

3. Scrape the butter mixture into the yolks. Stir in the scallion, mayonnaise, Tabasco, and salt, and mix until creamy.

4. Spoon the mixture back into the hollows in the egg whites.

Yield: 12 halves, each with 1 gram of carbohydrates, a trace of fiber, and 3 grams of protein.

Hammond Eggs

Deviled ham gives these eggs a country sort of kick.

> 6 hard-boiled eggs
>
> 1 can (2 1/4 ounces) of deviled ham
>
> 4 teaspoons spicy brown mustard
>
> 3 tablespoons mayonnaise
>
> 1/4 teaspoon salt
>
> Paprika

1. Slice the eggs in half, and carefully remove the yolks into a mixing bowl.
2. Mash the yolks with a fork. Stir in the ham, mustard, mayonnaise, and salt, and mix until creamy.
3. Spoon the mixture back into the hollows in the egg whites. Sprinkle with a little paprika for color.

Yield: Makes 12 halves, each with 1 gram of carbohydrates, a trace of fiber, and 4 grams of protein.

Cajun Eggs

> 6 hard-boiled eggs
>
> 1/3 cup mayonnaise
>
> 2 teaspoons horseradish mustard
>
> 1 teaspoon Cajun Seasoning (see page 405)

1. Slice the eggs in half, and carefully remove the yolks into a mixing bowl.
2. Mash the yolks with a fork. Stir in the mayonnaise and mustard, and mix until creamy.
3. Add the Cajun seasoning, and blend well.
4. Spoon the mixture back into the hollows in the egg whites.

Yield: 12 halves, each with 1 gram of carbohydrates, a trace of fiber, and 3 grams of protein.

↻ Artichoke Parmesan Dip

Serve this party favorite with pepper strips, cucumber rounds, celery sticks, or low-carb fiber crackers.

> 1 can (13 ½ ounces) artichoke hearts
>
> 1 cup mayonnaise
>
> 1 cup grated Parmesan cheese
>
> 1 clove garlic, crushed, or 1 teaspoon of jarred, chopped garlic
>
> Paprika

1. Preheat the oven to 325°F.
2. Drain and chop the artichoke hearts.
3. Mix the artichoke hearts with the mayonnaise, cheese, and garlic, combining well.
4. Put the mixture in a small, oven-proof casserole, sprinkle a little paprika on top, and bake for 45 minutes.

Yield: 4 servings, each with 3 grams of carbohydrates and 1 gram of fiber, for a total of 2 grams of usable carbs and 10 grams of protein.

↻ Spinach Artichoke Dip

This is a great, equally yummy version of the previous recipe, but keep in mind that it does make twice as much dip.

> 1 can (13 ½ ounces) artichoke hearts
>
> 1 package frozen chopped spinach (10 ounces), thawed
>
> 2 cups mayonnaise
>
> 2 cups grated Parmesan cheese
>
> 2 cloves garlic, crushed, or 2 teaspoons jarred, chopped garlic
>
> Paprika

1. Drain and chop the artichoke hearts.
2. Combine the spinach, mayonnaise, cheese, and garlic in a large casserole (a 6-cup dish is about right). Sprinkle with paprika.
3. Bake at 325°F for 50 to 60 minutes.

Yield: 8 servings, each with 4 grams of carbohydrates and 2 grams of fiber, for a total of 2 grams of usable carbs and 10 grams of protein.

↷ Guacamole

This is a very simple guacamole recipe, without sour cream or mayonnaise, that lets the taste of the avocados shine through.

  4 ripe black avocados
  2 tablespoons minced sweet red onion
  3 tablespoons lime juice
  3 cloves garlic, crushed
  1/4 teaspoon Tabasco
  Salt or Vege-Sal to taste

1. Halve the avocados, and scoop the flesh into a mixing bowl. Mash coarsely with a fork.

2. Mix in the onion, lime juice, garlic, Tabasco, and salt, stirring to blend well and mashing to the desired consistency.

Yield: 6 generous servings, each with 11 grams of carbohydrates and 3 grams of fiber, for a total of 8 grams of usable carbs and 3 grams of protein.

🍓 This recipe contains lots of healthy fats and almost three times the potassium found in a banana.

ꙮ Dill Dip

This easy dip tastes wonderful with all sorts of raw vegetables; try serving it with celery, peppers, cucumber, broccoli, or whatever else you have on hand.

1 pint sour cream
1/4 small onion
1 heaping tablespoon dry dill weed
1/2 teaspoon salt or Vege-Sal

1. Put the sour cream, onion, dill weed, and salt in a food processor, and process until the onion disappears. (If you don't have a food processor, mince the onion very fine and just stir everything together.)

2. You can serve this right away, but it tastes even better if you let it chill for a few hours.

Yield: 1 pint, containing 25 grams of carbohydrates and 1 gram of fiber, for a total of 24 grams of usable carbs and 16 grams of protein in the batch. (This is easily enough for 10 to 12 people, so no one's going to get more than a few grams of carbs.)

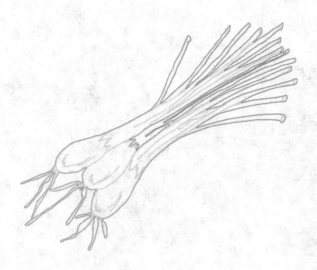

↷ Clam Dip

With some celery sticks and pepper strips for scooping, this would make a good lunch. Of course you can serve it at parties, too, with celery, green pepper, cucumber rounds, or fiber crackers for you and crackers or chips for the non low-carbers.

> 2 packages (8 ounces each) cream cheese, softened
>
> 1/2 cup mayonnaise
>
> 2 to 3 teaspoons Worcestershire sauce
>
> 1 tablespoon Dijon mustard
>
> 8 to 10 scallions, including the crisp part of the green shoot, minced
>
> 2 cans (6 1/2 ounces each) minced clams, drained
>
> Salt or Vege-Sal
>
> Pepper

Combine all the ingredients well, and chill. A food processor or blender works well for this, or if you prefer to leave chunks of clam, you could use an electric mixer.

Yield: 12 servings, each with just under 4 grams of carbohydrates, a trace of fiber, and 10 grams of protein.

Ꭷ Northwest Dip

Lowcarbezine! reader Pat Moriarty says, "This is my all-time favorite!"

> 1 package (8 ounces) cream cheese, softened
>
> 1/4 cup heavy cream
>
> 1 green onion, thinly sliced
>
> 2 teaspoons freshly squeezed lemon juice
>
> 1 dash red pepper sauce
>
> 4 ounces smoked salmon, gently shredded
>
> 1 ripe avocado, mashed

1. In a large mixing bowl, combine the cream cheese and heavy cream together until smooth and creamy.
2. Stir in the onion, lemon juice, and red pepper sauce. Gently fold in the smoked salmon and mashed avocado, being careful not to over-mix.
3. Serve with cucumber, celery, your choice of low-carb crackers, or pork rinds.

Yield: 6 servings, each with 4 grams of carbohydrates and 1 gram of fiber, for a total of 3 grams of usable carbs and 7 grams of protein.

Ꭷ Kathy's Pork Rind Dip

When she gets tired of eating plain pork rinds, *Lowcarbezine!* reader Kathy Rice makes this dip to go with them.

> 3 ounces cream cheese, softened
>
> 2 tablespoons salsa

Blend and enjoy—that's all there is to it.

Yield: 2 servings, each with 2 grams of carbohydrates and 0.5 gram of fiber, for a total of 1.5 grams of usable carbs and 3.5 grams of protein.

◌ Avocado Cheese Dip

This dip has been known to make my mom a very popular person at parties. Dip with pork rinds, vegetables, or purchased protein chips. It can also be served over steak, and it makes perhaps the most elegant omelets on the face of the earth.

> 2 packages (8 ounces each) cream cheese, softened
> 1 1/2 cups shredded white Cheddar or Monterey jack cheese
> 1 ripe black avocado, peeled and seeded
> 1 small onion
> 1 clove garlic, crushed
> 1 can (3 to 4 ounces) green chilies, drained, or jalapeños, if you like it hot

1. Combine all the ingredients in a food processor, and process until very smooth.
2. Scrape into a pretty serving bowl, and place the avocado seed in the middle.

> 🍓 For some reason, placing the seed in the middle keeps the dip from turning brown quite so quickly while it sits out. But if you're making this a few hours ahead of time, cover it with plastic wrap, making sure the wrap is actually touching the surface of the dip. Don't make this more than a few hours before you plan to serve it.

Yield: About 5 cups (plenty for a good-size party), with the batch containing 45 grams of carbohydrates and 9 grams of fiber, for a total of 36 grams of usable carbs and a whopping 83 grams of protein.

◌ Smoked Gouda Veggie Dip

Great with celery, peppers, or any favorite raw veggie. Combine your ingredients with a mixer, not a food processor, so you have actual little bits of Gouda in the dip.

    1 package (8 ounces) cream cheese, softened

    2/3 cup mayonnaise

    1 cup shredded smoked Gouda

    6 scallions, including the crisp part of the green shoot, sliced

    2 tablespoons grated Parmesan cheese

    1/2 teaspoon pepper

1. Beat the cream cheese and mayonnaise together until creamy, scraping the sides of the bowl often.

2. Add the Gouda, scallions, Parmesan, and pepper, and beat until well blended.

3. Chill, and serve with raw vegetables.

   Yield: At least 8 servings, each with 2 grams of carbohydrates, a trace of fiber, and 7 grams of protein.

⌒ Kim's Crab Dip

We have my sister to thank for coming up with this delicious, low-carb treat.

> 1 package (8 ounces) cream cheese, softened
>
> 1/2 cup sour cream
>
> 1 can (6 ounces) crabmeat, drained
>
> 1 teaspoon horseradish
>
> 2 tablespoons fresh chives, or dried if fresh are unavailable
>
> 1/4 teaspoon dry mustard
>
> 1/8 teaspoon salt
>
> 1/8 teaspoon pepper

1. Beat the cheese and sour cream together at a high speed until very smooth.
2. Set the beater to a low speed, and mix in the crab, horseradish, chives, mustard, salt, and pepper.
3. Chill. Serve with raw vegetables.

Yield: 12 servings, each containing 1 gram of carbohydrates, a trace of fiber, and 5 grams of protein.

↻ Bacon Cheese Spread

Another recipe from Jen Eloff's *Splendid Low-Carbing*. Jen, of sweety.com, says, "Your friends will beg you for this recipe!"

> 1 package (8 ounces) light cream cheese, softened
>
> 1/2 cup mayonnaise
>
> 1 1/2 cups shredded Cheddar cheese
>
> 2 tablespoons chopped fresh chives or scallions
>
> 1 teaspoon dried parsley
>
> 1/4 teaspoon garlic powder
>
> 8 slices bacon, cooked until crisp

1. Preheat the oven to 350°F.

2. In a food processor with the S blade in place or in a blender, process the cream cheese and mayonnaise until smooth.

3. In a medium bowl, combine the cream cheese mixture, Cheddar, chives, parsley, and garlic powder until well combined. Spread the mixture evenly on the bottom of a 9-inch glass pie plate.

4. Use a pair of kitchen scissors to cut the cooked bacon into small pieces. Garnish the top of the cheese spread with the bacon pieces, and bake for 15 minutes. Serve with low-carb crackers.

Yield: 12 servings, each with 2 grams of carbohydrates, a trace of fiber, and 7 grams of protein.

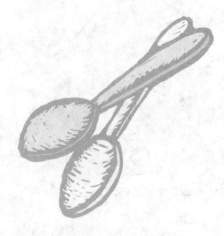

☾ Dukkah

My friend Lou Anne brought this Turkish "dry dip" along on a campout, and I've been nagging her for the recipe ever since. Although Dukkah is traditionally eaten with bread, it also adds an exotic, fascinating flavor to simple raw vegetables.

> 1/3 cup almonds or hazelnuts
>
> 1/4 cup white sesame seeds
>
> 1/4 cup coriander seeds
>
> 1/4 cup cumin seeds
>
> Salt and pepper to taste

1. Toast the nuts, sesame seeds, coriander seeds, and cumin seeds over high heat for 1 minute, stirring constantly.

2. Use a food processor, coffee grinder, or mortar and pestle to crush the toasted mixture, then season it with salt and pepper. (Don't over-grind; you want a consistency similar to coarse-ground cornmeal.)

3. Put your Dukkah in a bowl next to a bowl of olive oil, and set out cut-up raw vegetables. Dip the vegetables first into the oil, then into the Dukkah, and eat.

Yield: Just over a cup or about 10 servings, each with 4 grams of carbohydrates and 1 gram of fiber, for a total of 3 grams of usable carbs and. 2 grams of protein. (Analysis does not include vegetables.)

☽ Tuna Paté

If you throw in some veggies for dipping, this versatile dish makes a great snack, first course at a dinner party, or even a fine brown bag lunch.

 2 tablespoons butter

 2 cloves garlic, crushed

 1/2 medium onion, chopped

 1 can (4 ounces) mushrooms, drained

 1/2 teaspoon orange extract

 1 tablespoon Splenda

 1 package (8 ounces) cream cheese, softened

 1 can (6 ounces) tuna, drained

 2 tablespoons fresh parsley

 Grated rind of half an orange

 1/4 teaspoon salt

 1/4 teaspoon pepper

1. In a small, heavy skillet over medium heat, melt the butter and sauté the garlic, onion, and mushrooms until the onion is limp. Add the orange extract and Splenda, and stir well. Cool.

2. Place the cream cheese, tuna, parsley, orange rind, salt, and pepper in a food processor with the S blade in place. Pulse to blend. Add the sautéed mixture, and pulse until smooth and well blended.

3. Spoon into a serving bowl and chill. Serve with celery sticks, pepper strips, cucumber rounds, and crackers (for the carb-eaters).

   Yield: At least 6 servings, each with 3 grams of carbohydrates and1 gram of fiber, for a total of 2 grams of usable carbs and 11 grams of protein.

◯ Marinated Mushrooms

The quality of the vinaigrette dressing makes all the difference here, so use the best you can make or buy.

> 8 ounces small, fresh mushrooms
> 1 1/2 cups vinaigrette dressing (homemade or store-bought)

1. Thoroughly wipe the mushrooms clean with a soft cloth.
2. Place them in a saucepan, cover them with the dressing, and simmer over a medium low burner for 15 minutes.
3. Chill and drain the mushrooms, saving the dressing to store any leftover mushrooms in. (You can even simmer another batch of mushrooms in it when the first batch is gone.) Arrange the mushrooms on lettuce with toothpicks for spearing.

Yield: Depending on the size of your mushrooms, this will make about 12 to 15 servings, each with about 1 gram of carbohydrates and not enough fiber or protein to talk about.

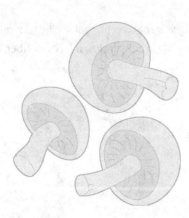

ᏑCheese Cookies

This recipe requires a food processor, so if you only have a tiny one, cut the recipe in half. Despite the name, these are not sweet; they're more like cheese crackers.

> 1/2 pound processed American loaf cheese, like Velveeta (store brand works fine)
>
> 1/2 pound sharp Cheddar cheese
>
> 1/4 pound butter
>
> 1 cup soy powder
>
> About 6 dozen pecan or walnut halves (optional)

1. Preheat the oven to 400°F.

2. Cut the loaf cheese, Cheddar, and butter into chunks.

3. Put the cheese chunks, butter, and soy powder in the food processor, and pulse until the dough is well combined.

4. Coat a cookie sheet with nonstick cooking spray. Drop spoonfuls of dough onto the cookie sheet, and press half a pecan or walnut in the top of each one (if using).

5. Bake for 8 to 10 minutes, or until the cookies are just getting brown around the edges.

Yield: This will depend on how big you make your cookies. I make mine small and get 6 dozen, each with 1 gram of carbohydrates, a trace of fiber, and 2 grams of protein.

ᢙ Snaps

Similar to the Cheese Cookies on previous page, but these bite back!

> 1 pound processed jalepeño Jack cheese
> 1/4 pound butter
> 1 cup soy powder

1. Preheat the oven to 400°F.
2. Cut the cheese and butter into chunks.
3. Put the cheese, butter, and soy powder in the food processor, and pulse until the dough is well combined.
4. Coat a cookie sheet with nonstick cooking spray. Drop spoonfuls of dough onto the cookie sheet.
5. Bake for 8 to 10 minutes, or until the cookies are just getting brown around the edges.

Yield: This will depend on how big you make your cookies. I make mine small, and get 6 dozen, each with 1 gram of carbohydrates, a trace of fiber, and 2 grams of protein.

ᢙ Roasted Nuts

Of course you can buy these in a can at the grocery store, but they're much better—and cheaper—when you roast them fresh at home.

> 2 cups shelled nuts of your choice (almonds, pecans, walnuts, or a combination)
> 4 tablespoons butter, melted
> Salt

1. Preheat the oven to 300°F.
2. Spread the nuts in a shallow roasting pan. Stir in the butter, coating all the nuts.
3. Roast for 20 to 25 minutes. Remove from the oven and salt to taste.

Yield: 8 servings. Each serving made with almonds will have 7 grams of carbohydrates and 4 grams of fiber, for a total of 3 grams of usable carbs and 7 grams of protein. Each serving made with pecans will have 5 grams of carbohydrates and 2 grams of fiber, for a total of 3 grams of usable carbs and 2 grams of protein. Each serving made with walnuts will have 5 grams of carbohydrates and 1 gram of fiber, for a total of 4 grams of usable carbs and 4 grams of protein.

ᛐ Soy and Ginger Pecans

I gave away tins of these for Christmas one year and got rave reviews.

> 2 cups shelled pecans
>
> 4 tablespoons butter, melted
>
> 3 tablespoons soy sauce
>
> 1 teaspoon ground ginger

1. Preheat the oven to 300°F.
2. Spread the pecans in a shallow roasting pan. Stir in the butter, coating all the nuts.
3. Roast for 15 minutes, then remove from the oven and stir in the soy sauce. Sprinkle the ginger evenly over the nuts, and stir that in as well.
4. Roast for another 10 minutes.

Yield: 8 servings, each with 6 grams of carbohydrates and 2 grams of fiber, for a total of 4 grams of usable carbs and 3 grams of protein.

ᛐ Worcestershire Nuts

I like to use this combination of nuts, but feel free to use just one or the other, or to experiment with your own proportions.

> 1 cup shelled walnuts
>
> 1 cup shelled pecans
>
> 4 tablespoons butter, melted
>
> 3 tablespoons Worcestershire sauce

1. Preheat the oven to 300°F.
2. Spread the nuts in a shallow baking pan, and stir in the butter, coating all the nuts.
3. Roast for 15 minutes, then remove from the oven and stir in the Worcestershire sauce.
4. Roast for another 10 minutes.

Yield: 8 servings, each with 6 grams of carbohydrates and 2 grams of fiber, for a total of 4 grams of usable carbs and 3 grams of protein.

↺ Curried Pecans

When I first came up with this combination of seasonings, I intended to use it on chicken, but I've discovered that it's also delicious on pecans.

  2 cups shelled pecans
  4 tablespoons butter, melted
  1 tablespoon Chicken Seasoning (see page 404)

1. Preheat the oven to 300°F.
2. Spread the nuts in a shallow baking pan, and stir in the butter, coating all the nuts.
3. Roast for 20 to 25 minutes.
4. Remove from the oven, sprinkle Chicken Seasoning over the nuts, and stir to coat.

Yield: 8 servings, each with 5 grams of carbohydrates and 2 grams of fiber, for a total of 3 grams of usable carbs and 2 grams of protein.

↻ Dana's Snack Mix

You can buy shelled sunflower seeds and pumpkin seeds in bulk at most health food stores, and you should be able to get raw cashew pieces there, too. For variety, try adding 2 1/2 cups of low-carb garlic croutons along with the seeds and nuts.

> 6 tablespoons butter
>
> 3 tablespoons Worcestershire sauce
>
> 1 1/2 teaspoons garlic powder
>
> 2 1/2 teaspoons seasoned salt
>
> 1 teaspoon onion powder
>
> 2 1/2 cups raw, shelled sunflower seeds
>
> 2 1/2 cups raw, shelled pumpkin seeds
>
> 1 cup almonds
>
> 1 cup pecans
>
> 1 cup walnuts
>
> 1 cup raw cashew pieces

1. Preheat the oven to 250°F.

2. In a small pan, melt the butter and stir in the Worcestershire sauce, garlic powder, seasoned salt, and onion powder.

3. In a large bowl, combine the seeds and nuts. Pour the melted butter mixture over them, and mix very well.

4. Put the mixture in large roasting pan, and bake for 2 hours, stirring occasionally.

5. Allow the mixture to cool, and store in an airtight container.

Yield: 18 servings, each with 14 grams of carbohydrates and 5 grams of fiber, for a total of 9 grams of usable carbs and 13 grams of protein.

◌ Ranch Mix

2 cups raw, shelled pumpkin seeds

2 cups raw, shelled sunflower seeds

2 cups dry-roasted peanuts

1 cup raw almonds

1 cup raw cashew pieces

2 tablespoons canola oil

1 packet dry ranch salad dressing mix

1 teaspoon lemon pepper

1 teaspoon dried dill

1/2 teaspoon garlic powder

1. Preheat the oven to 350°F.

2. In large mixing bowl, combine the pumpkin seeds, sunflower seeds, peanuts, almonds, and cashews. Add the canola oil, and stir to coat. Add the dressing mix, lemon pepper, dill, and garlic powder, and stir until well distributed.

3. Put the seasoned nuts in shallow roasting pan, and roast for 45 to 60 minutes, stirring occasionally, until the almonds are crisp through.

Yield: 16 servings, each with 15 grams of carbohydrates and 5 grams of fiber, for a total of 10 grams of usable carbs and 16 grams of protein.

☝ Asian Punks

Pumpkin seeds are terrific for you—they're a great source of both magnesium and zinc. And they taste great, too.

2 cups raw, shelled pumpkin seeds

2 tablespoons soy sauce

1/2 teaspoon powdered ginger

2 teaspoons Splenda

1. Preheat the oven to 350°F.
2. In a mixing bowl, combine the pumpkin seeds, soy sauce, ginger, and Splenda, mixing well.
3. Spread the pumpkin seeds in a shallow roasting pan, and roast for about 45 minutes,
   or until the seeds are dry, stirring two or three times during roasting.

Yield: 4 servings, each with 13 grams of carbohydrates and 3 grams of fiber, for a total of 10 grams of usable carbs and 17 grams of protein. (These are also a terrific source of minerals.)

↻ Indian Punks

You can actually buy curry-flavored pumpkin seeds, but these are better tasting and better for you.

> 4 tablespoons butter
> 2 1/2 tablespoons curry powder
> 2 cloves garlic, crushed
> 2 cups raw, shelled pumpkin seeds
> Salt

1. Preheat the oven to 300°F.
2. Melt the butter in a small skillet over medium heat. Add the curry and garlic, and stir for 2 to 3 minutes.
3. In a mixing bowl, add the seasoned butter to the pumpkin seeds, and stir until well coated.
4. Spread the pumpkin seeds in a shallow roasting pan and roast for 30 minutes. Sprinkle lightly with salt.

Yield: 4 servings, each with 15 grams of carbohydrates and 4 grams of fiber, for a total of 11 grams of usable carbs and 18 grams of protein.

🍓 In addition to all the minerals found in the pumpkin seeds, you get the turmeric in the curry powder, which is believed to help prevent cancer.

☾ Punks on the Range

Spicy-chili-crunchy. If you miss barbecue-flavored potato chips, try snacking on these.

     2 cups raw, shelled pumpkin seeds
     1 tablespoon canola oil
     1 tablespoon chili powder
     1 teaspoon salt

1. Preheat the oven to 350°F.
2. In a mixing bowl, combine the pumpkin seeds and canola oil, and stir until well coated. Add the chili powder and salt, and stir again.
3. Spread the seeds in a shallow roasting pan, and roast for about 30 minutes.

Yield: 4 servings, each with 13 grams of carbohydrates and 3 grams of fiber, for a total of 10 grams of usable carbs and 17 grams of protein.

↻ Barbecued Peanuts

    1 tablespoon Liquid Smoke flavoring

    1 teaspoon Worcestershire sauce

    Dash of Tabasco

    1/2 cup water

    1 1/2 cups dry-roasted peanuts

    3 tablespoons butter

    Garlic salt

1. Preheat the oven to 250°F.

2. In a saucepan, combine the Liquid Smoke, Worcestershire sauce, Tabasco, and water. Bring to a simmer.

3. Turn off the heat, and stir in the peanuts. Let the peanuts sit in the liquid for 30 minutes, stirring occasionally.

4. Drain off the liquid, and spread the peanuts in a shallow roasting pan. Bake for at least 1 hour, or until good and dry. (Stir occasionally to help speed up the process.)

5. When the peanuts are thoroughly dry, melt the butter and stir it into the peanuts to coat. Sprinkle lightly with garlic salt.

Yield: 3 servings, each with 16 grams of carbohydrates and 6 grams of fiber, for a total of 10 grams of usable carbs and 17 grams of protein.

ᗡ Antipasto

This easy dish makes a nice light summer supper. Use some or all of the ingredients listed here, adjusting quantities as necessary.

> Wedges of cantaloupe
>
> Salami
>
> Boiled ham
>
> Pepperoncini (mildly hot salad peppers,
>   available in jars near the pickles and olives)
>
> Halved or quartered hard-boiled eggs
>
> Marinated mushrooms
>
> Black and green olives (get the good ones)
>
> Strips of canned pimento
>
> Solid-pack white tuna, drizzled with olive oil
>
> Sardines
>
> Marinated artichoke hearts (available in cans)

Simply arrange some or all of these things decoratively on a platter, put out a stack of small plates and some forks, and dinner is served.

Yield: Varies with your taste and needs, but here are the basic nutritional breakdowns for the items on your antipasto platter:

Cantaloupe, 1/8 of a small melon: 4.5 grams of carbohydrates and 0.5 grams of fiber, for a total of 4 grams of usable carbs and 0.5 grams of protein

Salami, 1 average slice: 0.5 grams of carbohydrates, a trace of fiber, and 3 grams of protein

Boiled ham, 1 average slice: a trace of carbohydrates, no fiber, and 3.5 grams of protein

Pepperoncini, 1 average piece: 0.5 grams of carbohydrates, a trace of fiber, and no protein

Hard-boiled eggs, 1/2: 0.3 grams of carbohydrates, no fiber, and 3 grams of protein

Marinated mushrooms, 1 average piece: 1 gram of carbohydrates, a trace of fiber, and no protein

Black olives, 1 large: 0.5 grams of carbohydrates, a trace of fiber, and no protein

Green olives, 1 large: a trace of carbohydrates, a trace of fiber, and no protein

Pimento, 1 slice: a trace of carbohydrates, a trace of fiber, and no protein

Tuna, 3 ounces: no carbohydrates, no fiber, and 22 grams of protein

Sardines, 2 average: no carbohydrates, no fiber, and 5 grams of protein (not to mention 91 milligrams of calcium)

Artichoke hearts, 2 quarters: 2 grams of carbohydrates, 1 gram of fiber, and no protein

◯ Maggie's Mushrooms

Lowcarbezine! reader Maggie Cosey sends this recipe.

> 1 1/2 pounds large mushrooms
> 20 stuffed green olives
> 2 packages (8 ounces each) cream cheese, softened
> 1/8 to 1/4 cup Worcestershire sauce

1. Preheat the oven to 350°F.

2. Wash the mushrooms and remove their stems.

3. Chop the olives by hand or in a food processor.

4. In a mixing bowl, combine the olives, cream cheese, and Worcestershire sauce. (Be careful with the Worcestershire; there's a fine line between not enough and too much, it's better to err on the side of not enough.)

5. Spoon the mixture into the mushroom caps, and place them in a broiler pan.

6. Bake for 15 to 20 minutes, or until the cream cheese is slightly browned.

Yield: About 45 mushrooms, each with 1 gram of carbohydrates, a trace of fiber, and 1 gram of protein.

◯ Simple Low-Carb Stuffed Mushrooms

Lowcarbezine! reader Kayann Kretschmar says, "My Christmas Eve guests raved about them!"

>1 pound medium mushrooms
>
>1 pound bulk breakfast sausage, hot or sage
>
>1 package (8 ounces) cream cheese

1. Preheat the oven to 350°F.
2. Clean the mushrooms. Remove their stems and use a paring knife to make the hole for stuffing larger.

   🍄 **Waste not, want not**: If you freeze those stems and mushroom insides, you can use them for sautéed mushrooms the next time you have steak.

3. Brown and drain the sausage, and stir in the cream cheese. Spoon the mixture into the mushroom caps.
4. Bake for 20 minutes.

   Yield: About 30 mushrooms, each with 1 gram of carbohydrates, a trace of fiber, and 3 grams of protein.

◯ Kay's Crab-Stuffed Mushrooms

These are for my cyberpal Kay, who repeatedly begged me to come up with a low-carb recipe for crab puffs. I tried and tried, but all my attempts were relatively pathetic. So I made crab-stuffed mushrooms instead, and they were a big hit.

> 1 pound fresh mushrooms
>
> 1 can (6 1/2 ounces) flaked crab
>
> 2 ounces cream cheese
>
> 1/4 cup mayonnaise
>
> 1/4 cup grated Parmesan cheese
>
> 10 to 12 scallions, including the crisp part of the green shoot, finely sliced
>
> Dash of Tabasco
>
> 1/4 teaspoon pepper

1. Preheat the oven to 325°F.
2. Wipe the mushrooms clean with a damp cloth, and remove their stems.
3. In a good-size bowl, combine the crab, cream cheese, mayonnaise, parmesan, scallions, Tabasco, and pepper well.
4. Spoon the mixture into the mushroom caps, and arrange them in a large, flat roasting pan.
5. Bake for 45 minutes to 1 hour, or until the mushrooms are done through. Serve hot (although folks will still scarf 'em down after they cool off).

Yield: 25 to 30 mushrooms, each with 1 gram of carbohydrates, a trace of fiber, and 3 grams of protein.

> ☕ **Warning:** You may be tempted to make these with "fake crab" to save money. Don't. That stuff has a ton of carbohydrates added. Spend the extra couple of bucks and use real crab.

⌒ Vicki's Crab-Stuffed Mushrooms

Another tempter from Vicki Cash's *2002 Low Carb Success Calendar!*

> 10 ounces medium portobello mushrooms
>
> 2 Wasa Fiber Rye crackers
>
> 1 can (6 ounces) crabmeat
>
> 1 egg
>
> 2 tablespoons lemon juice
>
> 1 tablespoon dried dill weed
>
> 1 teaspoon dehydrated onion flakes
>
> 1/2 cup grated Parmesan cheese

1. Preheat the oven to 400ºF.

2. Wipe the mushrooms clean with a damp cloth, and remove their stems. Set aside 1/2 cup of stems. Place the caps on an ungreased baking sheet.

3. Use a food processor with the S blade attached to grind the crackers into coarse crumbs. Add the 1/2 cup of mushroom stems, processing until coarsely chopped. Add the crabmeat, egg, lemon juice, dill, onion, and cheese. Mix thoroughly.

4. Spoon the mixture into the mushroom caps and bake for 12 to 15 minutes, or until the top of the stuffing is slightly browned. Serve hot.

Yield: 6 appetizer-size servings, each with 4.5 grams of carbohydrates and 1 gram of fiber, for a total of 3.5 grams of usable carbs and 10 grams of protein.

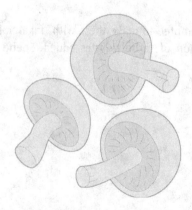

◌ Two-Cheese Tuna-Stuffed Mushrooms

Of all the stuffed mushrooms I've cooked or sampled, these are my absolute favorites.

> 1/2 pound fresh mushrooms
>
> 1 can tuna
>
> 1/2 cup shredded smoked Gouda
>
> 2 tablespoons grated Parmesan cheese
>
> 3 tablespoons mayonnaise
>
> 1 scallion, finely minced

1. Preheat the oven to 350°F.
2. Wipe the mushrooms clean with a damp cloth, and remove their stems.
3. Combine the tuna, Gouda, Parmesan, mayonnaise, and minced scallion, and mix well.
4. Spoon the mixture into the mushroom caps, and arrange them in a shallow roasting pan. Add just enough water to cover the bottom of the pan. Bake for 15 minutes and serve hot.

Yield: About 15 servings, each with 1 gram of carbohydrates, a trace of fiber, and 4 grams of protein.

↻ Turkey-Parmesan Stuffed Mushrooms

1 pound ground turkey

3/4 cup grated Parmesan cheese

1/2 cup mayonnaise

1 teaspoon dried oregano

1 teaspoon dried basil

2 cloves garlic, crushed

1 teaspoon salt or Vege-Sal

1/4 teaspoon pepper

1 1/2 pounds mushrooms

1. Preheat the oven to 350°F.

2. Combine the turkey, Parmesan, mayonnaise, oregano, basil, garlic, salt, and pepper, mixing very well.

3. Wipe the mushrooms clean with a damp cloth, and remove their stems.

4. Spoon the mixture into the mushroom caps, and place them in a shallow roasting pan. Add just enough water to cover the bottom of the pan. Bake for 20 minutes, and serve hot.

Yield: About 45 mushrooms, each with 1 gram of carbohydrates, a trace of fiber, and 3 grams of protein.

↻ Rumaki

These take a little extra effort, but I think it's worth it because my husband and I both love them.

> $1/2$ cup soy sauce
>
> $1/4$ cup dry sherry
>
> 1 clove garlic, crushed
>
> 1 slice fresh gingerroot, about $1/4$ inch thick, finely minced
>
> 12 strips bacon
>
> 12 chicken livers
>
> 24 canned whole water chestnuts

1. Mix together the soy sauce, sherry, garlic, and ginger to make the marinade.

2. Cut the bacon strips and chicken livers in half. (You'll find that the livers sort of have two halves naturally.)

3. Wrap each chicken liver half around a water chestnut, then wrap a half-strip of bacon around each chicken liver. Spear the whole thing with a large toothpick or bamboo skewer, making sure you pierce the water chestnut on the way through.

4. Submerge your speared bundles in the marinade, and let them marinate for at least an hour. (You can let them marinate overnight, if you want to prepare this dish well in advance of your company arriving.)

5. When you're ready to eat, take the bundles out of the marinade and broil or grill them for 5 to 7 minutes on each side, until the bacon is crisp.

Yield: Makes 24. When I analyzed this recipe, it came up with 10 grams of carbohydrates per piece, but the software was assuming that you consume all of the marinade, which of course you do not. These should actually have about 3 grams of carbohydrates apiece and 1 gram of fiber, for a total of about 2 grams of usable carbs and 5 grams of protein—plus all of the nutrients liver is famous for.

🍓 If you like, you may leave the water chestnuts out of these, and the carb count will drop to a mere trace.

☾ Country-Style Paté

This is really good. Plus, as paté goes, it's easy to make.

> 6 slices bacon
>
> 2 tablespoons butter
>
> 1 cup sliced mushrooms
>
> 1/2 cup chopped onion
>
> 1 cup chicken livers
>
> 1/2 teaspoon Worcestershire sauce
>
> 2 tablespoons mayonnaise
>
> Scant 1/2 teaspoon salt or Vege-Sal
>
> 1/4 teaspoon pepper

1. In a heavy skillet over medium heat, fry the bacon until it just starts to get crisp. Remove the bacon, and drain and reserve the grease.

2. Turn the burner down to low, and melt the butter and a little bacon grease in the skillet. Sauté the mushrooms and onion in the skillet until they're quite limp (about 15 minutes).

3. While they're sautéing, fill a medium saucepan with water, and bring it to a boil. Put the chicken livers in the water (make sure you keep stirring those sautéing vegetables), and bring the water back to a boil. Cover the pan, turn off burner, and let it sit for 15 minutes.

4. Drain the chicken livers. Put them in a food processor with the S blade in place and pulse two or three times to grind the chicken livers. Crumble and add the bacon and the mushroom and onion mixture. Pulse to combine. Add the Worcestershire, mayonnaise, salt, and pepper, and pulse again, until well combined. Serve with celery sticks, pepper strips, or low-carb crackers.

Yield: 12 servings, each with 2 grams of carbohydrates, a trace of fiber, and 5 grams of protein.

ᕫ Christmas Liver Paté

Lowcarbezine! reader Elizabeth Czilok sends this recipe, and says, "It's cute, Christmassy, yummy, and low-carb." Save it for Christmas if you like, but my recipe tester insists it's good any time, and on nearly anything.

> 8 ounces liverwurst (use the best you can find)
>
> 1 package (8 ounces) cream cheese, softened
>
> $1/3$ cup finely chopped onion
>
> 2 to 3 tablespoons sour cream
>
> $1/2$ teaspoon Worcestershire sauce
>
> $1/4$ teaspoon hot pepper sauce (optional)
>
> Stuffed olives to garnish

1. Mix the liverwurst, half the cream cheese, the onion, sour cream, Worcestershire sauce, and hot pepper sauce, combining well.

2. Form a mound of paté in the center of a serving dish. Place the dish and paté in the freezer for about 15 minutes.

3. Frost with the remaining softened cream cheese.

4. Slice a few green olives stuffed with pimentos so the green is a circle on the outside with the red pimento on the inside. Arrange them on the outside of the mound as a garnish, and serve with low-carb crackers and veggies.

Yield: Just over a pound of paté, or 16 servings, each with 1 gram of carbohydrates, almost no fiber, and 3 grams of protein. Four stuffed olives contain about 3 grams of carbohydrates, very little fiber, and no protein.

◌ Celery Stuffed with Bleu Cheese and Cream Cheese.

Lowcarbezine! reader Jeannette Regas sends this easy low-carb crowd-pleaser.

> 5 or 6 large ribs of celery
> 1/4 cup crumbled bleu cheese, at room temperature
> 1 package (8 ounces) cream cheese, at room temperature
> Heavy cream (optional)
> Salt and pepper

1. Clean the ribs of celery, and cut them into 3- to 4-inch pieces.
2. Mix the crumbled bleu cheese with the cream cheese, adding a little cream to make it smooth, if necessary. Add a little salt and pepper to taste.
3. Stuff into celery, and serve.

   Yield: 15 to 18 pieces, each with 1 gram of carbohydrates, a trace of fiber, and 2 grams of protein.

◌ Fried Cheese

This is the sort of decadence I would never have considered in my low-fat days. If you miss cheese-flavored snacks, you've got to try this.

> 2 or 3 tablespoons olive or canola oil
> 1/2 to 3/4 cup shredded Cheddar, Monterey Jack, or jalepeño Jack cheese

1. Spray a small, heavy bottomed, nonstick skillet with nonstick cooking spray, and place over medium-high heat.
2. Add the oil, and then the cheese. The cheese will melt and bubble and spread to fill the bottom of the skillet.
3. Let the cheese fry until it's crisp and brown around the edges. Use a spatula to lift up an edge, and check whether the cheese is brown all over the bottom; if it isn't, let it go another minute or so.
4. When the fried cheese is good and brown, carefully flip it and fry the other side until it, too, is brown.
5. Remove the cheese from the skillet, drain, and lie it flat to cool. Break into pieces and eat.

   Yield: 2 servings, each with 1 gram of carbohydrates, no fiber, and 11 grams of protein.

> 🍴 **Cheesy Bowls and Taco Shells**. For a tasty, cheesy, tortillalike bowl, follow the directions for Fried Cheese, until you get to Step 5. Then remove and drain the cheese, but drape it over the bottom of a bowl to cool. When it cools and hardens, you'll have a cheesy, edible bowl to eat a taco salad out of.
>
> You can also make a taco shell by folding the cheese disc in half and propping it partway open. Be careful when handling it, though; hot cheese can burn you pretty seriously.

Saganaki

If you've never tried the Greek cheese Kasseri, you're in for a treat. This dish is fantastically delicious, and has a dramatic, fiery presentation to boot.

> 1/4 pound Kasseri, in a slab 1/2 inch thick
> 1 egg, beaten
> 2 to 3 tablespoons rice protein powder, soy powder, or low-carb bake mix
> Olive oil
> 1 shot brandy
> 1/4 lemon

1. Dip the slab of cheese in the beaten egg, then in the protein powder, coating it all over.

2. Heat 1/4 inch of olive oil in a heavy skillet over medium heat. When the oil is hot, add the cheese.

3. Fry until golden and crisp on both sides, turning only once. Remove from the pan and put on a fire-proof plate.

4. Pour the brandy evenly over the hot cheese, strike a match, and light the brandy on fire. It is traditional to shout "Opa!" at this moment.

5. Squeeze the lemon over the flaming cheese, putting out the fire. Divide in half, and scarf it down!

Yield: 2 servings, each with 3 grams of carbohydrates, a trace of fiber, and 17 grams of protein.

↻ Southwestern Saganaki

A yummy twist on the traditional Saganaki and a perfect starter for a
fiery Mexican dinner for two.

> 1/4 pound pepper Jack cheese, in a slab 1/2 inch thick
>
> 1 egg, beaten
>
> 2 to 3 tablespoons rice protein powder, soy powder, or low-carb bake mix
>
> Olive oil
>
> 1 shot tequila
>
> 1/4 lime

1. Dip the slab of cheese in the beaten egg, then in the protein powder, coating it all over.

2. Heat 1/4 inch of olive oil in a heavy skillet over medium heat. When the oil is hot, add the cheese.

3. Fry until golden and crisp on both sides, turning only once. Remove from the pan and put on a fire-proof plate.

4. Pour the tequila evenly over the hot cheese, strike a match, and light the brandy on fire.

5. Squeeze the lime over the flaming cheese, putting out the fire.

Yield: 2 servings, each with 3 grams of carbohydrates, a trace of fiber, and 17 grams of protein.

꧂ Pickled Shrimp

This recipe will feed a crowd, so make it when you have plenty of people to share with.

 6 cups water

 1/4 cup dry sherry

 1/2 teaspoon peppercorns

 1 bay leaf

 6 teaspoons salt

 3 pounds raw shrimp, shelled and deveined

 1 cup oil

 2/3 cup lemon juice

 1/2 cup white vinegar

 3 tablespoons mixed pickling spice

 2 teaspoons Splenda

 2 sprigs fresh dill, coarsely chopped

1. In a large saucepan over high heat, bring the water, sherry, peppercorns, bay leaf, and 2 teaspoons of salt to a boil.

2. Add the shrimp, and bring back to a boil. Cook 1 minute longer, and drain.

3. In a large bowl, combine the oil, lemon juice, vinegar, pickling spice, Splenda, dill, and the remaining 4 teaspoons of salt. Add the shrimp, and toss with this pickling mixture.

4. Cover the bowl, and chill it and the platter you will serve the shrimp on in the refrigerator overnight.

5. To serve, drain off and discard the marinade, and arrange the shrimp on the platter. Garnish with additional dill, if desired.

   ꧂ If it's going to be a long party, it's a good idea to set the platter or bowl on a bed of crushed ice in another container, to keep the shrimp cold.

Yield: This is enough for a party of a few dozen people, but the carb count will differ according to how big your shrimp are, of course! Figure 24 servings, each with less than 1 gram of carbohydrates, a trace of fiber, and 12 grams of protein.

Crab and Bacon Bundles

This quick, hot hors d'oeuvre will impress your guests.

1 can (6 ounces) crab, drained

1 scallion, finely minced

1/2 pound bacon

Duck Sauce (see page 417)

1. Flake the crab, removing any bits of shell or cartilage. Stir in the minced scallion, and set aside.
2. Cut all your bacon strips in half crosswise, to make two shorter strips. Place a rounded 1/2 teaspoon or so of the crab mixture on the end of a bacon strip, and roll the strip up around it, stretching the bacon slightly as you go. Pierce the bundle with a toothpick, to hold. Repeat until all the crab and bacon strips are used up.
3. Broil about 8 inches from heat, turning once or twice, until the bacon is crisp—no more than 10 minutes. Serve with Duck Sauce for dipping.

Yield: About 2 dozen servings, each with only a trace of carbohydrates, a trace of fiber, and 4 grams of protein. (Analysis does not include Duck Sauce.)

↻ Low-Carb Margarita Mix

Okay, this is neither a snack nor a nibble, but it sure is good for parties! And although it's not super low in carbs, it's considerably less sugary than the commercial stuff.

1 1/2 cups lime juice, fresh or bottled

1/2 cup lemon juice, fresh or bottled

1 1/2 cups Splenda

2 cups water

1/2 teaspoon orange extract

Combine all the ingredients in a blender for 1 minute, and pour into a clean bottle. Refrigerate until ready to use.

🍓 To make a margarita, combine 2 ounces of tequila with 6 ounces of margarita mix, and either put it through the blender with lots of ice, or simply serve it on the rocks.

Yield: About 1 quart. This whole recipe has about 54 grams of carbs, so figure about 10 grams in each 6-ounce serving of the mix.

CHAPTER THREE

Eggs and Dairy

Before I get to the recipes, I'd like to urge you to stop thinking of eggs solely as a breakfast food. Eggs are wildly nutritious, infinitely versatile, they cook in a flash, and they're cheap, to boot. If you want a fast meal at any time of day, think eggs.

Omelets 101

There's this big mystique about omelets, maybe because they're a part of classic French cookery. People think that omelets are magically difficult and that only a true gourmet chef can get them right. But I say: Bah. Omelets are easy. Believe it or not, I've been known to turn out omelets for 20 on a propane camp stove. (This is when my friends started referring to my pop-up trailer as "Dana's House of Omelets.")

You can learn to do this quickly. Really—you can.

Before you begin, you'll need a good pan. What's a "good pan"? I prefer a 7-inch (medium-size) skillet with a heavy bottom, sloping sides, and a nonstick surface. However, what I currently have is a 7-inch skillet with a heavy bottom, sloping sides, and a formerly nonstick surface. I can still make omelets in it,— I just have to use a good shot of nonstick cooking spray. The heavy bottom and sloping sides, however, are essential.

Here's the really important thing to know about making omelets: The word "omelet" comes from a word meaning "to laminate," or to build up layers. And that's exactly what you do; you let a layer of beaten egg cook, then you lift up the edges and tip the pan so the raw egg runs under the cooked part. You do this all around the edges, of course, so you build it up evenly. The point is, you don't just let the beaten egg lie there in the skillet and wait for it to cook through. If you try to, the bottom will be hopelessly overdone before the top is set.

Dana's Easy Omelet Method

1. First, have your filling ready. If you're using vegetables, you'll want to sauté them first. If you're using cheese, have it grated or sliced and ready to go. If you're making an omelet to use up leftovers—a great idea, by the way— warm them through in the microwave and have them standing by.

2. Spray your omelet pan well with cooking spray if it doesn't have a good non-stick surface, and set it over medium-high heat.

3. While the skillet is heating, grab your eggs (two is the perfect number for this size pan, but one or three will work, too) and a bowl, crack the eggs, and beat them with a fork. Don't add water or milk or anything; just mix them up.

4. Test your pan to see if it's hot enough: A drop of water thrown in the pan should sizzle right away. Add a tablespoon of oil or butter, slosh it around to cover the bottom, then pour in the eggs, all at once. They should sizzle, too, and immediately start to set.

5. When the bottom layer of egg is set around the edges—and this should happen quite quickly—lift the edge using a spatula and tip the pan to let the raw egg flow underneath. Do this all around the edges, until there's not enough raw egg to run.

6. Turn your burner to the lowest heat if you have a gas stove. (If you have an electric stove, you'll have to have a "warm" burner standing by; electric elements don't cool off fast enough for this job.) Put your filling on one-half of the omelet, cover the pan with a lid, and let it sit over very low heat for a minute or two—no more. Peek and see if the raw, shiny egg is gone from the top surface (although you can serve it that way if you like; that's how the French prefer their omelets), and the cheese, if you've used it, is melted. If not, re-cover the pan and let it go another minute or two.

7. When your omelet is done, slip a spatula under the half without the filling, fold it over, and then lift the whole thing onto a plate. Or you can get fancy and tip the pan, letting the filling side of the omelet slide onto the plate and folding the top over as you go, but that takes some practice.

This makes a single-serving omelet. I think it's a lot easier to make several individual omelets than one big one, and omelets are so fast to make that it's not that big a deal. Anyway, that way you can customize your omelets to each individual's taste. If you're making more than two or three omelets, just set your oven to its very lowest heat setting and keep them warm in there.

Now here are some ideas for what to put in your omelets.

⌒ Cheese Omelet

This is pretty obvious, but you can't ignore a classic!

> 1 tablespoon butter
>
> 2 eggs, beaten
>
> 2 to 3 ounces sliced or shredded cheese (Cheddar, Monterey Jack, Colby, American, Swiss, Gruyère, Muenster, or whatever you prefer)

Make your omelet according to Dana's Easy Omelet Method (page 89), placing the cheese over half of your omelet when you get to step 6. Cover, turn the burner to low, and cook until the cheese is melted (2 to 3 minutes). Follow the directions to finish making the omelet.

Yield: 1 serving, with 2 grams of carbohydrates, no fiber, and 32 grams of protein.

⌒ Macro Cheese Omelet

My husband's favorite! With all that cheese, this is mighty filling.

> 1 tablespoon butter
>
> 2 eggs, beaten.
>
> 1 to 2 ounces Cheddar, sliced or shredded
>
> 1 to 2 ounces Monterey Jack, sliced or shredded
>
> 1 slice processed Swiss

Make your omelet according to Dana's Easy Omelet Method (page 89), placing the cheese over half of your omelet when you get to step 6. Cover, turn the burner to low, and cook until the cheese is melted (3 to 4 minutes). Follow the directions to finish making the omelet.

Yield: 1 serving, with 3 grams of carbohydrates, no fiber, and 46 grams of protein.

♫ Veggie Cheese Omelet

> Olive oil or butter
>
> 2 eggs, beaten
>
> 1/4 green pepper, sliced in small strips, sautéed
>
> 1/4 medium onion, sliced and sautéed
>
> 2 or 3 mushrooms, sliced and sautéed
>
> 2 ounces sliced or shredded Cheddar, Monterey Jack, Swiss, or Gruyère cheese

Make your omelet according to Dana's Easy Omelet Method (page 89), placing the filling over half of your omelet when you get to step 6. Cover, turn the burner to low, and cook until the cheese is melted (3 to 4 minutes). Follow the directions to finish making the omelet.

Yield: 1 serving, with 9 grams of carbohydrates and 2 grams of fiber, for a total of 7 grams of usable carbs and 27 grams of protein.

♫ Mexican Omelet

This will open your eyes in the morning! It's one of my favorites—I enjoy breathing fire.

> 1 tablespoon butter
>
> 2 eggs, beaten
>
> 2 ounces jalapeño Jack cheese, shredded or sliced
>
> 2 tablespoons salsa
>
> Hot sauce (optional)

Make your omelet according to Dana's Easy Omelet Method (page 89), placing the filling over half of your omelet when you get to step 6. Cover, turn the burner to low, and cook until the cheese is melted (3 to 4 minutes). Follow the directions to finish making the omelet. Top with salsa and hot sauce (if using).

Yield: 1 serving, with 5 grams of carbohydrates and 1 gram of fiber, for a total of 4 grams of usable carbs and 25 grams of protein.

☽ Taco Omelet

This is a great way to use up leftover taco filling.

> 1 tablespoon butter
>
> 2 eggs, beaten
>
> 1/4 cup beef, turkey, or chicken taco filling, warmed.
>
> 2 tablespoons shredded Cheddar cheese
>
> 2 tablespoons salsa
>
> 1 tablespoon sour cream

Make your omelet according to Dana's Easy Omelet Method (page 89), placing the taco filling over half of your omelet when you get to step 6. Cover, turn the burner to low, and cook until the cheese is melted (3 to 4 minutes). Follow the directions to finish making the omelet. Sprinkle with the cheese, and top with salsa and sour cream.

Yield: 1 serving, with 3 grams of carbohydrates and 1 gram of fiber, for a total of 2 grams of usable carbs and 24 grams of protein. (Analysis does not include garnishes.)

🍓 You can, if you like, jazz up this omelet with a little diced onion, olives, or whatever else you like on a taco.

☽ Denver Omelet

> 1 tablespoon butter
>
> 2 eggs
>
> 1 ounce Cheddar cheese, shredded or sliced
>
> 1/4 cup diced cooked ham
>
> 1/4 green pepper, cut in small strips, sautéed
>
> 1/4 small onion, sliced and sautéed

Make your omelet according to Dana's Easy Omelet Method (page 89), placing the cheese and the sautéed ham and vegetables over half of your omelet when you get to step 6. Cover, turn the burner to low, and cook until the cheese is melted (3 to 4 minutes). Follow the directions to finish making the omelet.

Yield: 1 serving, with 7 grams of carbohydrates and 1 gram of fiber, for a total of 6 grams of usable carbs (and you can cut that by using seriously low carb ham) and 25 grams of protein.

Artichoke Parmesan Omelet

This is a terrific combination.

> 1 tablespoon butter
>
> 2 eggs, beaten
>
> 1 to 2 tablespoons mayonnaise
>
> 1 canned artichoke heart, sliced
>
> 2 tablespoons grated Parmesan cheese

Make your omelet according to Dana's Easy Omelet Method (page 89), spreading mayonnaise over one-half of your omelet and topping it with the artichoke heart and Parmesan when you get to step 6. Cover, turn the burner to low, and cook until the cheese is melted (3 to 4 minutes). Follow the directions to finish making the omelet.

Yield: 1 serving, with 11 grams of carbohydrates and 5 grams of fiber, for a total of 6 grams of usable carbs and 18 grams of protein.

"My Day to Crab" Omelet

My grandmother never got to go crabbing when the family was at the shore, because she was too busy keeping house. Finally she declared, "It's my day to crab!" If it's your day to crab, this omelet will cheer you up.

> 1/4 cup canned crabmeat, flaked and picked over for shells and cartilage
>
> 2 scallions, sliced, including the crisp part of the green
>
> 1 tablespoon butter
>
> 2 eggs, beaten
>
> 1 to 2 tablespoons mayonnaise

Mix the crab meat with the scallions, and have the mixture standing by. Make your omelet according to Dana's Easy Omelet Method (page 89), spreading mayonnaise over half the omelet and topping it with the crab and scallion mixture when you get to step 6. Cover, turn the burner to low, and cook until the cheese is melted (3 to 4 minutes). Follow the directions to finish making the omelet.

Yield: 1 serving, with 3 grams of carbohydrates and 1 gram of fiber, for a total of 2 grams of usable carbs and 19 grams of protein.

◯ Leftover Lamblet

I adore roast lamb, and the leftovers are way too good to waste! This is very hearty, and would make a great quick supper.

> 1/4 pound leftover roast lamb, cut into small chunks
>
> 1/2 small onion
>
> 2 tablespoons grated Parmesan cheese
>
> 3 tablespoons mayonnaise
>
> 1/2 teaspoon prepared horseradish
>
> 1 tablespoon butter
>
> 2 eggs, beaten

1. In a food processor with the S blade in place, grind the lamb and the onion together. When you have a pretty uniform consistency, add the Parmesan, mayonnaise, and horseradish, and pulse until everything is combined. Place in a microwave-safe bowl, and microwave on 50 percent power for just 1 minute or so, to warm through.

2. Make your omelet according to Dana's Easy Omelet Method (page 89), placing the lamb mixture evenly over half of your omelet when you get to step 6. Cover, turn the burner to low, and cook until the eggs are set (60 to 90 seconds). Follow the directions to finish making the omelet.

Yield: 1 serving, with 6 grams of carbohydrates and 1 gram of fiber, for a total of 5 grams of usable carbs and 38 grams of protein.

◯ California Omelet

I've had breakfast down near the waterfront in San Diego. This is what it tastes like.

> 1 tablespoon olive oil
>
> 2 eggs, beaten
>
> 2 ounces Monterey Jack cheese, shredded
>
> 3 or 4 slices ripe avocado
>
> 1/4 cup alfalfa sprouts

Make your omelet according to Dana's Easy Omelet Method (page 89), placing the Monterey Jack over half of your omelet when you get to step 6. Cover, turn the burner to low, and cook until the cheese is melted (2 to 3 minutes). Arrange the avocado and sprouts over the cheese, and follow the directions to finish making the omelet.

Yield: 1 serving, with 4 grams of carbohydrates and 1 gram of fiber, for a total of 3 grams of usable carbs and 26 grams of protein (and as much potassium as a banana!).

℧ New York Sunday Brunch Omelet

My husband was absolutely blown away by this. It's unbelievably filling, by the way.

>   1 tablespoon butter
>   2 eggs, beaten
>   2 ounces cream cheese, thinly sliced
>   1/4 cup flaked smoked salmon
>   2 scallions, sliced

Make your omelet according to Dana's Easy Omelet Method (page 89), placing the cream cheese over half of your omelet when you get to step 6. (Don't try to spread the cream cheese—it won't work!) Top with the salmon, cover, turn the burner to low, and cook until hot all the way through (2 to 3 minutes). Scatter the scallions over salmon, and follow the directions to finish making the omelet.

Yield: 1 serving, with 5 grams of carbohydrates and 1 gram of fiber, for a total of 4 grams of usable carbs and 22 grams of protein.

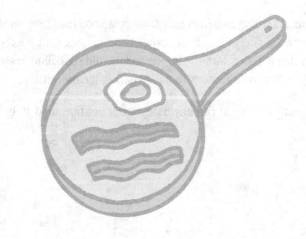

◌ Omelet Cordon Bleu

Canned asparagus is fine for this, but you may cook some up if you prefer, or use leftover asparagus, should you have any.

> 1 tablespoon butter
>
> 2 eggs
>
> 1/4 cup shredded Gruyère cheese
>
> 1 ounce boiled or baked deli ham (or sliced leftover ham)
>
> 3 asparagus spears, cooked

Make your omelet according to Dana's Easy Omelet Method (page 89), placing the Gruyère, ham, and asparagus over half of your omelet when you get to step 6. Cover, turn the burner to low, and cook until the cheese is melted (2 to 3 minutes). Follow the directions to finish making the omelet.

Yield: 1 serving, with 3 grams of carbohydrates and 1 gram of fiber, for a total of 2 grams of usable carbs and 25 grams of protein.

◌ Braunschweiger Omelet

Hey, don't look like that! Some of us love liverwurst!

> 1 tablespoon butter
>
> 2 eggs, beaten
>
> 2 ounces braunschweiger (liverwurst), mashed a bit with a fork
>
> 2 or 3 slices ripe tomato

Make your omelet according to Dana's Easy Omelet Method (page 89), spooning the mashed braunschweiger over half of your omelet and topping with the tomato slices when you get to step 6. Cover, turn the burner to low, and cook until heated through (2 to 3 minutes). Follow the directions to finish making the omelet.

Yield: 1 serving, with 4 grams of carbohydrates, a trace of fiber, and 19 grams of protein.

↷ Pizza Omelet

Remember that the pizza sauce is where the carbs are in this omelet, so govern yourself accordingly.

> 1 tablespoon olive oil
>
> 2 eggs, beaten
>
> 2 ounces mozzarella cheese
>
> 2 tablespoons jarred no-sugar-added pizza sauce, warmed
>
> 1 teaspoon grated Parmesan cheese

Make your omelet according to Dana's Easy Omelet Method (page 89), placing the mozzarella over half of your omelet when you get to step 6. Cover, turn the burner to low, and cook until the cheese is melted (2 to 3 minutes). Follow the directions to finish making the omelet, and top with the pizza sauce and Parmesan.

Yield: 1 serving, with 6 grams of carbohydrates (and you can lower that if you use the lowest-carb pizza sauce), no fiber, and 24 grams of protein.

↷ Tuna Melt Omelet

It's worth making extra tuna salad just to make this omelet. This is a great lunch.

> 1 tablespoon butter
>
> 2 eggs, beaten
>
> 1 ounce Swiss cheese or processed Swiss-style singles
>
> 1/2 cup leftover tuna salad, at room temperature

Make your omelet according to Dana's Easy Omelet Method (page 89), placing the Swiss cheese over half of your omelet when you get to step 6. Spread the tuna salad over the cheese, cover, turn the burner to low, and cook until hot all the way through (3 to 4 minutes). Follow the directions to finish making the omelet.

Yield: 1 serving. The carb count of this omelet will depend on your recipe for tuna salad. The eggs and cheese will add only 2 grams of carbohydrates, no fiber, and 19 grams of protein.

↻ Fajita Omelet

Again, a great way to use up leftovers!

> 1 tablespoon olive oil
>
> 2 eggs
>
> Leftover steak or chicken fajitas, warmed
>
> 1 tablespoon sour cream

Make your omelet according to Dana's Easy Omelet Method (page 89), placing the fajitas over half of your omelet when you get to step 6. Cover, turn the burner to low, and cook for 2 to 3 minutes. Follow the directions to finish making the omelet, and top with the sour cream.

Yield: 1 serving. The carb count for this omelet will depend on your recipe for fajitas. The eggs and sour cream will add only 2 grams of carbs, no fiber, and 11 grams of protein.

↻ Chili Omelet

Beef chili or turkey chili, it doesn't matter—they both make a great omelet.

> 1 tablespoon olive oil
>
> 2 eggs, beaten
>
> 1/2 cup all-meat chili, warmed
>
> 2 tablespoons shredded Cheddar cheese
>
> 1 tablespoon sour cream

Make your omelet according to Dana's Easy Omelet Method (page 89), placing the chili over half of your omelet when you get to step 6. Top with the Cheddar, cover, turn the burner to low, and cook until the cheese is melted (2 to 3 minutes). Follow the directions to finish making the omelet, and top with the sour cream.

Yield: 1 serving, with about 6 grams of carbohydrates (depending on your chili recipe), no fiber, and 33 grams of protein.

↻ Guacomelet

Should you happen to have leftover guacamole—an unlikely circumstance, I'll admit—this is a fine thing to do with it.

    1 tablespoon oil

    2 eggs, beaten

    2 ounces Monterey Jack cheese, sliced or shredded

    1/4 cup guacamole

Make your omelet according to Dana's Easy Omelet Method (page 89), placing the cheese over half of your omelet when you get to step 6. Spread the guacamole over the cheese, cover, turn the burner to low, and cook until the cheese is melted (3 to 4 minutes). Follow the directions to finish making the omelet.

Yield: 1 serving, with 6 grams of carbohydrates and 1 gram of fiber, for a total of 5 grams of usable carbs and 26 grams of protein (and a whopping 487 milligrams of potassium!).

↻ Avocado Cheese Dip Omelet

This is perhaps the most decadently delicious omelet I know how to make, and it's certainly a good enough reason to hide some of the Avocado Cheese Dip at your next party.

    1 tablespoon olive oil

    2 eggs, beaten

    1/3 cup Avocado Cheese Dip (see page 55)

Make your omelet according to Dana's Easy Omelet Method (page 89), placing the Avocado Cheese Dip over half of your omelet when you get to step 6. Cover, turn the burner to low, and cook until hot all the way through (3 to 4 minutes). Follow the directions to finish making the omelet.

Yield: 6 grams of carbohydrates and 1 gram of fiber, for a total of 5 grams of usable carbs and 19 grams of protein.

Frittatas

The frittata is the Italian version of the omelet, and it involves no folding! If you're still intimidated by omelets, try a frittata.

↷ Confetti Frittata

1/4 pound bulk pork sausage

1/4 cup diced green pepper

1/4 cup diced sweet red pepper

1/4 cup diced sweet red onion

1/4 cup grated Parmesan cheese

1 teaspoon Mrs. Dash, original flavor

8 eggs, beaten

1. In a large, oven-proof skillet, start browning and crumbling the sausage over medium heat. As some fat starts to cook out of it, add the green peppers, red peppers, and onion to the skillet. Cook the sausage and veggies until there's no pink left in the sausage. Spread the sausage and veggie mixture into an even layer in the bottom of the skillet.

2. Beat the Parmesan cheese and Mrs. Dash into the eggs, and pour the mixture over the sausage and veggies in the skillet.

3. Turn the burner to low, and cover the skillet. (If your skillet doesn't have a cover, use foil.) Let the frittata cook until the eggs are mostly set. This will take 25 to 30 minutes, but the size of your skillet will affect the speed of cooking, so check periodically.

4. When all but the very top of the frittata is set, slide it under the broiler for about 5 minutes, or until the top is golden. Cut into wedges, and serve.

Yield: 4 servings, each with 4 grams of carbohydrates and 1 gram of fiber, for a total of 3 grams of usable carbohydrates and 17 grams of protein.

↻ Fajita Frittata

This makes a good supper for a family that is taco- and burrito-oriented.

> 3 tablespoons oil
>
> 1/2 green pepper, cut into small strips
>
> 1 small onion, sliced
>
> 1 boneless, skinless chicken breast, cut into thin strips
>
> 1/2 teaspoon chili powder
>
> 1/2 teaspoon cumin
>
> 1 teaspoon lime juice
>
> 1/2 teaspoon salt
>
> 8 eggs, beaten
>
> 6 ounces shredded Monterey Jack or jalapeño Jack cheese
>
> Salsa
>
> Sour cream

1. Heat the oil in a large, heavy, oven-proof skillet, and sauté the green pepper, onion, and chicken until the chicken has turned white and is done through. Stir in the chili powder, cumin, lime juice, and salt.

2. Spread the fajita mixture in an even layer in the bottom of the skillet, and pour the beaten eggs over it.

3. Turn the burner to low, and cover the skillet. (If your skillet doesn't have a cover, use foil.) Let the frittata cook until the eggs are mostly set, but still soft on top (7 to 10 minutes).

4. Scatter the cheese evenly over the top and slide the skillet under the broiler, about 4 inches from the heat, for 2 to 3 minutes or until the eggs are set and the cheese is just turning golden.

5. Cut in wedges, top each serving with a tablespoon of salsa and a couple of teaspoons of sour cream, and serve.

Yield: 4 servings, each with 5 grams of carbohydrates and 1 gram of fiber, for a total of 4 grams of usable carbs and 36 grams of protein.

᠗ Artichoke Frittata

2 tablespoons butter

1 can (13 $^1/_2$ ounces) quartered artichoke hearts, drained

1 small onion, sliced

1 clove garlic

8 eggs, beaten

$^1/_3$ cup grated Parmesan cheese

6 ounces shredded Gruyère cheese

1. In a large, heavy skillet sprayed with nonstick cooking spray, melt the butter and begin sautéing the artichoke hearts, onion, and garlic over medium-low heat.

2. While sautéing, stir the eggs and Parmesan together.

3. When the onions are limp, spread the vegetables evenly over the bottom of the skillet, and pour the egg mixture over them.

4. Turn the burner to low, and cover the skillet. (If your skillet doesn't have a cover, use foil.) Let the frittata cook until the eggs are mostly set (7 to 10 minutes).

5. Top with the shredded Gruyère and slide the skillet under the broiler, about 4 inches from the heat. Broil for 2 to 3 minutes, or until the eggs are set on top and the cheese is lightly golden. Cut into wedges and serve.

Yield: 4 servings, each with 11 grams of carbohydrates and 4 grams of fiber, for a total of 7 grams of usable carbs and 29 grams of protein.

Artichoke Mushroom Frittata

Similar to the Artichoke Frittata on the opposite page, but adding mushrooms and leaving out the Parmesan cheese gives a whole new flavor.

> 3 tablespoons butter
>
> 1 cup canned, quartered artichoke hearts, drained
>
> 4 ounces fresh mushrooms, sliced
>
> 1/2 small onion, sliced
>
> 8 eggs, beaten
>
> 6 ounces shredded Gruyère cheese

1. In a heavy skillet, melt the butter and sauté the artichoke hearts, mushrooms, and onion over medium-low heat until the mushrooms are limp.

2. Spread the vegetables evenly over the bottom of the skillet, and pour the eggs over them.

3. Turn the burner to low, and cover the skillet. (If your skillet doesn't have a cover, use foil.) Let the frittata cook until mostly set (7 to 10 minutes).

4. Top with the Gruyère and slide the skillet under the broiler, about 4 inches from the heat. Broil for 2 to 3 minutes, or until the eggs are set on top and the cheese is lightly golden. Cut into wedges and serve.

Yield: 4 servings, each with 7 grams of carbohydrates and 3 grams of fiber, for a total of 4 grams of usable carbs and 26 grams of protein.

☽ Chorizo Frittata

Very South of the Border. If you like chorizo (Mexican sausage), you might cook some up, drain it well, and keep it in a container in the freezer so you can whip up one of these omelets on short notice.

> 1 tablespoon oil
>
> 1/2 green pepper, diced
>
> 1 small onion, sliced
>
> 2/3 cup cooked, crumbled, drained chorizo
>
> 2/3 cup salsa
>
> 8 eggs, beaten
>
> 6 ounces shredded Cheddar or Monterey Jack

1. In a large, heavy skillet over medium heat, heat the oil and sauté the green pepper and onion for a few minutes, until tender-crisp. Add the chorizo and the salsa, stir well, and heat through.

2. Spread the mixture into an even layer on the bottom of the skillet, and pour in the eggs.

3. Turn the burner to low, and cover the skillet. (If your skillet doesn't have a cover, use foil.) Let the frittata cook until the eggs are mostly set (7 to 10 minutes).

4. Top with the shredded cheese and slide the skillet under the broiler, about 4 inches from the heat. Broil for 2 to 3 minutes, or until the eggs are set and the cheese is melted. Cut into wedges and serve.

Yield: 4 servings, each with 8 grams of carbohydrates and 1 gram of fiber, for a total of 7 grams of usable carbs and 32 grams of protein.

Scrambles

When both omelets and frittatas are too much trouble, just make a scramble. The ways of varying scrambled eggs are endless, so you could have them several times a week and never get bored. These have been analyzed assuming a three-egg serving, but if you want a lighter meal, leave out one egg and subtract 0.5 gram of carbohydrates and 6 grams of protein from my analysis.

⟲ Country Scramble

This fast-and-filling family-pleaser is a great way to use up leftover ham.

> 1 tablespoon butter
> 1/4 cup diced cooked ham
> 1/4 cup diced green pepper
> 2 tablespoons diced onion
> 3 eggs, beaten
> Salt and pepper

1. Melt the butter in a skillet over medium heat. Add the ham, green pepper, and onion, and sauté for a few minutes, until the onion is softened.

2. Pour in the eggs, and scramble until the eggs are set. Add salt and pepper to taste, and serve.

   Yield: 2 servings, each with 7 grams of carbohydrates and 1 gram of fiber, for a total of 6 grams of usable carbs and 23 grams of protein.

   🍓 Don't look at the number of servings and assume you can't feed a hungry family with a scramble—these recipes are a snap to double, as long as you have a skillet large enough to scramble in.

◌ Curry Scramble

Okay, I admit it: I'd probably eat dog food if you curried it. But with a green salad, this makes a great light supper whether you're a devoted curry lover or not.

> 1 tablespoon butter
>
> 1/4 teaspoon curry powder
>
> 1/2 clove garlic, crushed
>
> 3 eggs
>
> 1 tablespoon heavy cream
>
> 3 slices bacon, cooked until crisp

1. Melt the butter in a heavy skillet, and sauté the curry powder and garlic over medium-low heat for a minute or two.

2. Beat the eggs and cream together, pour into the skillet, and scramble until the eggs are set. Crumble bacon over the top.

   Yield: 1 serving, with 3 grams of carbohydrates, a trace of fiber, and 23 grams of protein.

◌ Piperade

Say "peep-er-ahd." This Basque peasant dish has so many vegetables in it that it's a whole meal in itself.

> 2 tablespoons bacon grease
>
> 1/4 cup diced onion
>
> 1/2 cup diced green pepper
>
> 1/3 cup diced tomato (very ripe fresh or canned)
>
> 3 eggs, beaten
>
> Salt and pepper

1. Heat the bacon grease in a heavy skillet over lowest heat. Add the onion and sauté for 5 to 7 minutes, or until the onion is soft.

2. Add the pepper and the tomato. Stir, cover, and cook at lowest heat for 15 minutes, stirring once or twice. (You want the vegetables to be quite soft.)

3. Pour in the eggs, and scramble slowly until the eggs are just set. Add salt and pepper to taste, and serve.

Yield: 1 serving, with 13 grams of carbohydrates and 3 grams of fiber, for a total of 10 grams of usable carbs and 18 grams of protein.

Hearty Piperade. Make just as you would regular Piperade, but add ¹/₄ cup diced ham for each serving. (This is a great time to use up any leftovers you've been saving.) Sauté the ham with the vegetables, then add the eggs and scramble as usual.

Yield: 1 serving, with 14 grams of carbohydrates and 3 grams of fiber, for a total of 11 grams of usable carbs and 24 grams of protein.

Italian Scramble

This is a good quick supper. Serve it with a green salad and some garlic bread for the kids.

> 2 tablespoons olive oil
>
> 1/4 cup diced green pepper
>
> 1/4 cup chopped onion
>
> 1 clove garlic, crushed
>
> 3 eggs
>
> 1 tablespoon grated Parmesan cheese

1. Heat the olive oil in a heavy skillet over medium heat, and sauté the pepper, onion, and garlic for 5 to 7 minutes, or until the onion is translucent.

2. Beat the eggs with the Parmesan, and pour into the skillet. Scramble until the eggs are set, and serve.

Yield: 1 serving, with 8 grams of carbohydrates and 1 gram of fiber, for a total of 7 grams of usable carbs and 17 grams of protein.

Mushroom Scramble

> 1 to 2 teaspoons butter
>
> 1 tablespoon minced onion
>
> 1/4 cup sliced mushrooms
>
> 3 eggs, beaten

1. Melt the butter in a heavy skillet over medium heat, and sauté the onion and mushrooms for 4 to 5 minutes, or until the mushrooms are tender.

2. Add the eggs, scramble until set, and serve.

Yield: 1 serving, with 3 grams of carbohydrates, a trace of fiber, and 17 grams of protein.

☽ Greek Scramble

> 2 tablespoons olive oil
>
> 1 tablespoon minced onion
>
> 6 good, strong, black Greek olives, chopped
>
> 3 eggs, beaten
>
> 1/4 cup crumbled feta cheese

1. Heat the oil in heavy skillet over medium heat. Sauté the onion for a minute or two, then add the olives and sauté for a minute more.

2. Pour in the eggs and add the feta. Scramble until set, and serve.

Yield: 1 serving, with 6 grams of carbohydrates, a trace of fiber, and 22 grams of protein.

☽ Chicken Liver Scramble

> 1 tablespoon butter
>
> 1/4 small onion, sliced
>
> 1 chicken liver, cut into bite-size pieces
>
> 3 eggs, beaten
>
> Salt and pepper

1. Melt the butter in a heavy skillet over low heat. Sauté the onion for 2 to 3 minutes, then add the cut-up chicken liver.

2. Sauté, stirring frequently, until the chicken livers are no longer red but are still pinkish. Keep the heat very low, and don't overcook!

3. When the chicken liver pieces are cooked through, pour in the eggs and scramble until they're set. Add salt and pepper to taste, and serve.

Yield: 1 serving, with 5 grams carbohydrates, a trace of fiber, and 23 grams of protein.

⌒ Hot Dog Scramble

Okay, it's not haute cuisine, but I'll bet your kids will eat it without complaining.

  1 tablespoon butter

  1 hot dog, sliced into rounds

  1/2 small onion, chopped

  3 eggs, beaten

  1/4 cup shredded Cheddar cheese

1. Melt the butter in a heavy skillet over medium heat. Add the hot dog slices and onion, and sauté until the onion is limp and the hot dog slices are starting to brown.

2. Add the eggs, and scramble until half-set. Add the cheese, and continue to scramble until the eggs are set and the cheese is melted. Serve.

Yield: 1 serving, with 8 grams of carbohydrates and 1 gram of fiber, for a total of 7 grams of usable carbs and 31 grams of protein.

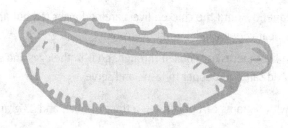

Fried Eggs

Tired of all that scrambling? These next few recipes are, in one form or another, good old fried eggs.

☽ Fried Eggs Not Over Really Easy

If you're like me, you like your eggs over-easy, so that the whites are entirely set, but the yolks are still soft – but you find it maddeningly difficult to flip a fried egg without breaking the yolk. Here's the solution!

> 3 eggs
> 1/2 tablespoon butter or oil
> 1 teaspoon water

1. Spray your skillet with nonstick cooking spray, and place it over medium-high heat. When the skillet is hot, add the butter and coat the bottom of the pan with it. Crack your eggs into the skillet—careful not to break the yolks!—and immediately cover them.

2. Wait about 2 minutes, and check your eggs. They should be well set on the bottom, but still a bit slimy on top. Add a teaspoon of water for each serving (you can approximate this; the quantity isn't vital), turn the burner to low, and cover the pan again.

3. Check after a minute; the steam will have cooked the tops of the eggs. If there's still a bit of uncooked white, give it another 30 seconds to 1 minute. Lift out and serve.

Yield: 1 serving, with about 1.5 grams of carbohydrates, no fiber, and 16 grams of protein.

> 🍓 For the easiest eggs, use a skillet that fits the number of eggs you're frying. A 7-inch skillet is just right for a single serving, but if you're doing two servings, use a big skillet.

☉ Huevos Rancheros

> 1 tablespoon butter or oil
>
> 2 eggs
>
> 3 tablespoons salsa (hot or mild, as you prefer)
>
> 2 ounces Monterey Jack cheese, shredded

1. Spray a heavy skillet with nonstick cooking spray, and set it over medium heat. Add the butter or oil, and crack the eggs into the skillet. Turn down the burner, and cover. Let the eggs fry for 4 to 5 minutes.

2. While the eggs are frying, warm the salsa in a saucepan or in the microwave.

3. When your fried eggs are set on the bottom but still a little underdone on top, scatter the cheese evenly over the fried eggs, add a teaspoon or two of water to the skillet, and cover it again. In a minute or two, the tops of the eggs should be set (but the yolks still soft) and the cheese melted.

4. Transfer the eggs to a plate with a spatula, top with warmed salsa, and serve.

Yield: 1 serving, with 4 grams of carbohydrates and 1 gram of fiber, for a total of 3 grams of usable carbohydrates and 25 grams of protein.

↻ Rodeo Eggs

This was originally a sandwich recipe, but it works just as well without the bread.

> 4 slices bacon, chopped into 1-inch pieces
>
> 4 thin slices onion
>
> 4 eggs
>
> 4 thin slices Cheddar cheese

1. Begin frying the bacon in a heavy skillet over medium heat. When some fat has cooked out of it, push it aside and put the onion slices in, too. Fry the onion on each side, turning carefully to keep the slices together, until it starts to look translucent. Remove the onion from the skillet, and set aside.

2. Continue frying the bacon until it's crisp. Pour off most of the grease, and distribute the bacon bits evenly over the bottom of the skillet. Break in the eggs and fry for a minute or two, until the bottoms are set but the tops are still soft. (If you like your yolks hard, break them with a fork; if you like them soft, leave them unbroken.)

3. Place a slice of onion over each yolk, then cover the onion with a slice of cheese. Add a teaspoon of water to the skillet, cover, and cook for 2 to 3 minutes, or until the cheese is thoroughly melted.

4. Cut into four separate eggs with the edge of a spatula, and serve.

Yield: This serves 2 if they're good and hungry or 4 if they're only a bit peckish, or if they're kids. In 2 servings, each will have 4 grams of carbohydrates, a trace of fiber, and 27 grams of protein.

◌ Gruyère Eggs

    1 tablespoon butter

    2 eggs

    1/4 cup shredded Gruyère cheese

    1 scallion, sliced

1. Spray a heavy skillet with nonstick cooking spray and melt the butter in it over medium-high heat. Crack the eggs into the skillet, and fry them until the bottoms are done, but the tops are still a little soft.

2. Scatter the Gruyère over the eggs. Add a couple of teaspoons of water to the skillet, cover, and let cook another couple of minutes, until the cheese is melted and the whites are set.

3. Move the eggs to a serving plate, scatter the sliced scallion on top, and serve.

Yield: 1 serving, with 2 grams of carbohydrates, a trace of fiber, and 19 grams of protein.

◌ Oeufs avec le Beurre Noire

This just might be the easiest French cooking you'll ever do, and it lends new interest to good old fried eggs.

    1 tablespoon butter

    3 eggs

    1/2 teaspoon lemon juice

1. Spray a skillet with nonstick cooking spray, put it over medium heat, and melt half of the butter in it. Crack the eggs into the skillet and fry as desired. Remove the eggs to a plate, and keep them warm.

2. Add the rest of the butter to the skillet, and let it cook until the foam on the butter shows a few flecks of brown. Stir in the lemon juice, pour the mixture over the eggs, and serve.

Yield: 1 serving, with 2 grams of carbohydrates, virtually no fiber, and 17 grams of protein.

Chili Egg Puff

Serve this versatile dish for brunch or supper. And don't be afraid of those chilies: The mild ones aren't hot, they're just very flavorful.(And if you like hot foods, feel free to use hotter chilies.)

>5 eggs
>
>3 tablespoons soy powder or rice protein powder
>
>1/2 teaspoon salt or Vege-Sal
>
>1/2 teaspoon baking powder
>
>1 cup small-curd cottage cheese
>
>8 ounces Monterey Jack cheese, grated
>
>3 tablespoons melted butter
>
>1 can (4 ounces) diced green chilies, drained

1. Preheat the oven to 350°F. Spray a 6-cup casserole with nonstick cooking spray, or butter it generously.

2. Break the eggs into a bowl and beat them with a whisk. Whisk in the soy powder, salt, and baking powder, mixing very well.

3. Beat in the cottage cheese, Monterey Jack, melted butter, and chilies. Pour the whole thing into the prepared casserole, put it in the oven, and bake for about 35 minutes. (It's okay if it's a little runny in the very center when you spoon into it; that part acts as a sauce for the rest.)

Yield: 4 servings, each with 7 grams of carbohydrates and 1 gram of fiber, for a total of 6 grams of usable carbohydrates and 30 grams of protein.

Don't know how big your casserole is? Fill it with water using a measuring cup. You want one that just holds 6 cups of water, although just a tad bigger or smaller won't matter.

↺ Ham and Cheese Puff

This dish reheats particularly well, making it the perfect leftover meal.

> 1/4 pound ham
>
> 1/4 pound Cheddar cheese
>
> 1 green pepper
>
> 1 can (4 ounces) mushrooms, well drained
>
> 5 eggs
>
> 3 tablespoons soy powder or unflavored protein powder
>
> 1/2 teaspoon baking powder
>
> 1/2 teaspoon salt or Vege-Sal
>
> 1 cup small-curd cottage cheese
>
> 2 tablespoons grated horseradish

1. Preheat the oven to 350°F. Spray a 6-cup casserole with nonstick cooking spray, or butter it generously.

2. Use a food processor with the S blade in place to grind the ham, Cheddar, green pepper, and mushrooms together until finely chopped (no chunks of pepper or ham bigger than, say, a 1/2-inch cube).

3. In a large bowl, beat the eggs well. Add the soy or protein powder, baking powder, and salt, and beat well again.

4. Beat in the cottage cheese and horseradish, and then add the chopped ham mixture.

5. Pour the egg mixture into the casserole. Bake for about 40 minutes, or until it is puffy and set but still jiggles a bit in the middle when you shake it.

Yield: 4 servings, each with 10 grams of carbohydrates and 2 grams of fiber, for a total of 8 grams of usable carbohydrates and 29 grams of protein.

🍓 The carb analysis of your recipe may vary from mine, depending on the ham, Cheddar, and cottage cheese you use. As always, you can trim this carb count by using the lowest-carbohydrate ingredients you can find. And watch out when you buy your horseradish: I had to read a lot of labels to find one that didn't add sugar.

↻ Turkey Club Puff

Disguise your Friday-after-Thanksgiving leftovers in this delicious puff.

> 5 eggs
>
> 1/4 cup soy powder or unflavored protein powder
>
> 1/2 teaspoon salt
>
> 1/2 teaspoon baking powder
>
> 1 cup cottage cheese
>
> 1/2 pound Swiss cheese, cubed
>
> 1/4 cup melted butter
>
> 3/4 cup cubed turkey
>
> 6 slices bacon, cooked until crisp

1. Preheat the oven to 350°F. Spray a 6-cup casserole with nonstick cooking spray, or butter generously.

2. Break the eggs into a bowl, and beat them with a whisk. Whisk in the soy powder, salt, and baking powder, mixing very well.

3. Beat in the cottage cheese, Swiss cheese, melted butter, cubed turkey and crumbled bacon. Pour the whole thing into the greased casserole. Bake for 35 to 40 minutes, or until set.

Yield: 5 servings, each with 5 grams of carbohydrates, a trace of fiber, and 33 grams of protein.

Sausage, Egg, and Cheese Bake

> 1 pound pork sausage (hot or mild, as you prefer)
> 1/2 cup diced green pepper
> 1/2 cup diced onion
> 8 eggs
> 1/4 teaspoon pepper
> 1 cup shredded Cheddar cheese
> 1 cup shredded Swiss cheese

1. Preheat the oven to 350°F.

2. In a large, heavy, oven-proof skillet, start browning and crumbling the sausage over medium heat.

3. When some grease has cooked out of the sausage, add the green pepper and the onion, and continue cooking, stirring frequently, until the sausage is no longer pink.

4. In a large bowl, beat the eggs and pepper together, and stir in the Cheddar and Swiss cheeses.

5. Spread the sausage and vegetables evenly on the bottom of the skillet, and pour the egg and cheese mixture over it. Bake for 25 to 30 minutes, or until mostly firm but still just a little soft in the center.

Yield: 6 servings, each with 4 grams of carbohydrates, a trace of fiber, and 26 grams of protein.

Ꭷ Eggs Florentine

This is a great quick-and-simple supper for a tired night.

> 1 batch Creamed Spinach (see page 186)
> 4 eggs

1. Make Creamed Spinach according to the directions. After you've stirred in the cream and Parmesan cheese, spread the spinach on the bottom of your skillet in an even layer.

2. Using the back of a spoon, make four evenly spaced hollows in the spinach, and break an egg into each one. Turn the burner to low, and cover the skillet.

3. Cook until the eggs are done (about 5 minutes). Divide into four sections with a spatula to make serving easier.

Yield: 2 generous servings, each with 8 grams of carbohydrates and 4 grams of fiber, for a total of 4 grams of usable carbs and 20 grams of protein.

↻ Fried Mush

This idea would never have occurred to me, but it did occur to my friend Diana Lee: Ricotta cheese has a texture that's remarkably similar to that of cooked cornmeal. Based on that, she came up with this breakfast recipe, which she's allowed me to reprint from her book *Bread and Breakfast: Baking Low Carb II.*

> 4 large eggs
>
> 1/2 cup ricotta cheese
>
> 1/4 cup heavy cream
>
> 2 tablespoons Splenda
>
> 1/2 teaspoon cinnamon
>
> 1/4 teaspoon nutmeg
>
> 1 teaspoon oil

1. Preheat the oven to 350°F. Coat an 8 x 8-inch baking dish with nonstick cooking spray.

2. Mix all the ingredients together, and pour the mixture into the prepared baking dish.

3. Bake for 20 to 30 minutes, until a knife inserted in the middle comes out clean. Cut into quarters.

4. Heat the oil in a skillet, and fry the four pieces until they're brown on both sides. Serve with your favorite topping.

Yield: 4 servings, each with 2 grams of carbohydrates, a trace of fiber, and 9 grams of protein.

◌ Yogurt

When I tell people I make my own yogurt, they react as if I'd said I could transmute base metals into gold. But as you'll see, it's easy to make and considerably cheaper than buying the commercial stuff. "Officially," plain yogurt has 12 grams of carbohydrates per cup, but Dr. Goldberg and Dr. O'Mara point out in *The GO-Diet* that most of the lactose (milk sugar) is converted to lactic acid, leaving only about 4 grams per cup. So if you like yogurt, enjoy!

> 1 tablespoon plain yogurt
> 1 1/2 to 2 cups instant dry milk, or a 1-quart envelope

1. Fill a clean, 1-quart, snap-top container half full with water.

2. Put in the plain yogurt in the water, and stir. Add the powdered milk, and whisk until the lumps are gone.

   🍓 For your first batch, you'll use store-bought plain yogurt as a starter, but after that you can use a spoonful from the previous batch. Every so often it's good to start over with fresh, store-bought yogurt, though.

3. Fill the container to the top with water, whisk it one last time, and put the lid on.

4. Put your yogurt-to-be in a warm place. I use a bowl lined with an old electric heating pad set on low, but any warm spot will do, such as inside an old-fashioned gas oven with a pilot light, on the stove top directly over the pilot light, or even near a heat register in winter.

5. Let your yogurt sit for 12 hours or so. It should be thick and creamy by then, but if it's still a little thin, give it a few more hours. When it's ready, stick it in the refrigerator and use it just like store-bought plain yogurt. Or flavor it with vanilla or lemon extract and some Splenda or stevia/FOS blend. You can also stir in a spoonful of sugar-free preserves, or mash a few berries with a fork and stir them in.

Regarding those two different amounts of dry milk: Using the full 2 cups will give you richer, creamier yogurt, with more protein and more calcium, but with a couple extra grams of carbohydrates, as well. It's up to you. If you'd like, you can add 1/4 cup of heavy cream in place of 1/4 cup of the water, to make a higher-fat "whole milk" yogurt.

You can also, if you prefer, make your yogurt from liquid milk, but it's a pain. You have to scald the milk first and then cool it again before adding the "starter" yogurt, which seems like a lot of bother to me.

One last useful tidbit: If you find you use a lot of buttermilk—for example, if you decide you really enjoy low-carb muffins and such—you can make your own buttermilk exactly the same way you'd make yogurt. Simply substitute a couple of tablespoons of commercial buttermilk for a "starter" instead of the yogurt.

CHAPTER FOUR

Breads, Muffins, Cereals, and Other Grainy Things

Baked goods and other grain products, such as bread, cereal, pancakes, waffles, and so on, are among the foods that new low-carb dieters miss most. They are also among the foods that sell best for the low-carb specialty merchants. Many of these products are quite good, but they're often very pricey. With these recipes, you can make your own far more cheaply than you could buy them, and they'll often taste even better than the premade varieties available. When you know you can have a slice of toast or a grilled cheese sandwich now and then, your worries about your ability to stay low carb for the long haul will fade.

About Low-Carb Bread

If you're regularly buying commercially made low-carbohydrate bread, it's time you bought a bread machine! Given the price of low-carb specialty products, you'll make your money back in no time.

All of the recipes below are designed for a 1-pound bread machine, for the simple reason that that's the size I own. If you own a 1 1/2-pound or a 2-pound machine, you can simply multiply the ingredients by one and a half or two, respectively. If your machine has "quick" and "regular" cycles, use "regular." If it has "white" and "whole wheat" cycles, use "whole wheat."

If you're an experienced bread baker who doesn't own a bread machine but wants to try to make these recipes by hand, you certainly may, although I don't have all the instructions for you. What I can tell you is that tripling these quantities should give you the right amount for two regular-size handmade loaves.

All of these breads will be far easier to slice evenly if you wait until they cool and use a good, sharp, serrated bread knife. But don't be surprised if the smell of freshly baked bread makes it impossible to wait!

One other note: As mentioned in Chapter 1, these recipes all use plain old activated yeast—not "bread machine" or rapid rise yeast. I can't guarantee the results if you use another sort of yeast.

↻ White Bread

This bread has a firm, fine texture and a great flavor.

  1 cup water

  1/4 cup oat bran

  2 tablespoons psyllium husks

  3/4 cup vital wheat gluten

  1/2 cup vanilla-flavored whey protein powder

  1/3 cup rice protein powder

  1 teaspoon salt

  1 tablespoon oil

  1 tablespoon Splenda

  2 teaspoons yeast

Put the ingredients in your bread machine in the order given, and run the machine. Remove the loaf from the machine and bread case promptly to cool.

Yield: About 10 slices, each with 5 grams of carbohydrates and 1 gram of fiber, for a total of 4 grams of usable carbs and 24 grams of protein.

↷ "Whole Wheat" Bread

Slice this extra-thin so you can "afford" two slices, and it makes a great grilled cheese sandwich.

$1/2$ cup warmwater

$1/2$ cup heavy cream

1 tablespoon soft butter

1 egg

1 teaspoon salt

$3/4$ cup vital wheat gluten

2 tablespoons raw wheat germ

2 tablespoons wheat bran

$1/4$ cup psyllium husks

$1/2$ cup oat flour

$1/2$ cup vanilla-flavored whey protein powder

2 teaspoons yeast

Put the ingredients in your bread machine in the order given, and run the machine. Remove the loaf from the machine and bread case promptly to cool.

Yield: About 10 slices, each with 13 grams of carbohydrates and 7.5 grams of fiber, for a total of 5.5 grams of usable carbs and 19 grams of protein (more than two eggs!).

↻ Seed Bread

Nutty and filling! Make sure you chop your sunflower seeds, though, or they'll mostly sink to the bottom of your loaf.

1/2 cup warm water

1/2 cup heavy cream

1 tablespoon oil

1 egg

1/2 teaspoon salt

3/4 cup vital wheat gluten

1/2 cup oat bran

1/3 cup ground almonds

1/3 cup sunflower seeds, coarsely chopped

1/4 cup rice protein powder

2 tablespoons flaxseed

1/2 teaspoon blackstrap molasses

1 teaspoon Splenda

2 teaspoons yeast

Put the ingredients in your bread machine in the order given, and run the machine. Remove the loaf from the machine and bread case promptly to cool.

Yield: About 10 slices, each with 8 grams of carbohydrates and 2 grams of fiber, for a total of 6 grams of usable carbs and 21 grams of protein.

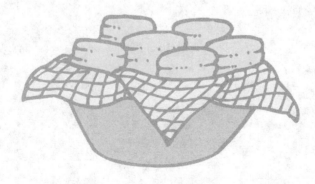

☌ Mom's Oatmeal Molasses Bread

My de-carbed version of the bread that won my mom first prize at the county fair. This has the best texture of any low-carb bread I know!

1/4 cup rolled oats

2 tablespoons raw wheat germ

2/3 cup boiling water

1 tablespoon blackstrap molasses

1 tablespoon Splenda

1 tablespoon soft butter

1 teaspoon salt

1/2 cup ground almonds

3/4 cup vital wheat gluten

1/4 cup vanilla-flavored whey protein powder

2 tablespoons water

2 teaspoons yeast

1. Put the rolled oats and wheat germ in the bread case of your bread machine. Pour the boiling water over them, and let them sit for at least 15 minutes.

2. Add everything else in the order given, and run the machine. Remove the loaf from the machine and bread case promptly to cool.

Yield: 8 slices, each with 5.5 grams of carbohydrates and 0.5 gram of fiber, for a total of 5 grams of usable carbs and 25 grams of protein.

↷ Sesame Seed Bread

I like to eat this toasted, along with a bowl of soup.

> 1 cup warm water
> 1/4 cup oat bran
> 1/4 cup wheat bran
> 1/4 cup sesame seeds
> 1/4 cup vanilla-flavored whey protein powder
> 1 cup vital wheat gluten
> 1 1/4 teaspoons salt
> 1 tablespoon blackstrap molasses
> 2 teaspoons yeast

Put the ingredients in your bread machine in the order given, and run the machine. Remove the loaf from the machine and bread case promptly to cool.

Yield: 12 slices, each with 6.5 grams of carbohydrates and 1.7 grams of fiber, for a total of 4.8 grams of usable carbs and 18 grams of protein.

↷ Rye Bread

I love rye bread, and it's so nice to be able to have it again! Leave out the caraway if you don't like it, but to many of us, it's just not proper rye bread without it.

> 1 cup warm water
> 1/2 cup wheat bran
> 1/2 cup whole grain rye flour
> 1/4 cup rice protein powder
> 3/4 cup vital wheat gluten
> 1 teaspoon salt
> 1 tablespoon oil
> 1 tablespoon caraway seeds
> 1 1/2 teaspoons yeast

Put the ingredients in your bread machine in the order given, and run the machine. Remove the loaf from the machine and bread case promptly to cool.

Yield: 12 slices, each with 6.8 grams of carbohydrates and 2 grams of fiber, for a total of 4.8 grams of usable carbs and 14 grams of protein.

◑ Cinnamon Raisin Bread

Sweet and cinnamony! Have a slice of this toasted and slathered with butter for breakfast, and you'll never know you're on a low-carb diet!

3/4 cup plus 2 tablespoons warm water

1/4 cup oat bran

1/2 cup ground almonds

1/3 cup vanilla-flavored whey protein powder

1 1/2 teaspoons cinnamon

3/4 cup plus 3 tablespoons vital wheat gluten

1/4 cup Splenda

1 tablespoon oil

1 teaspoon salt

2 teaspoons yeast

2 tablespoons raisins, each snipped in half

Put the ingredients in your bread machine in the order given, and run the machine. Remove the loaf from the machine and bread case promptly to cool.

Yield: 12 slices, each with 6 grams of carbohydrates and 0.6 grams of fiber, for a total of 5.4 grams of usable carbs and 19 grams of protein.

🍓 The reason you cut the raisins in half is to let them distribute more evenly throughout the bread; even so, there aren't a lot of them, I'll admit. That's because the raisins are the highest-carb part of this bread. If you want, you can leave them whole so each one will be more noticeable.

↻ Heart-y Bread

So named because both rice bran and flax are known to lower cholesterol. Want more good news? This bread tastes as good as it is good for
you.

> 1 cup plus 2 tablespoons water
>
> 1/3 cup rice bran
>
> 1/3 cup flaxseed meal
>
> 1 cup vital wheat gluten
>
> 1/3 cup vanilla-flavored whey protein powder
>
> 2 teaspoons blackstrap molasses
>
> 1 teaspoon salt
>
> 1 tablespoon oil
>
> 2 teaspoons yeast

Put the ingredients in your bread machine in the order given, and run the machine.
Remove the loaf from the machine and bread case promptly to cool.

Yield: 11 slices, each with 6.7 grams of carbohydrates and 2.6 grams of fiber, for a
total of 4.1 grams of usable carbs and 19 grams of protein.

☞ French Toast

Make this for breakfast some lazy weekend morning, and the family will think you're cheating on your diet!

> 4 eggs
> 1/2 cup heavy cream
> 1/2 cup water
> 1 teaspoon vanilla extract (optional)
> 6 slices low-carb bread of your choice (white, "whole wheat,"
>   cinnamon raisin, and oatmeal molasses are all good choices)
> Butter

1. Beat together the eggs, heavy cream, water, and vanilla extract (if using), and place the mixture in a shallow dish, such as a pie plate.

2. Soak the slices of bread in the mixture until they're well saturated; you'll have to do them one or two at a time. Let each slice soak for at least 5 minutes, turning once.

3. Fry each soaked piece of bread in plenty of butter over medium heat in a heavy skillet or griddle. Brown well on each side.

4. Serve with sugar-free syrup, cinnamon and Splenda, or sugar-free preserves, as you choose.

Yield: 6 servings. The carb count will vary with the type of bread you use, but the egg and cream add only 2 grams of carbs, no fiber, and 4 grams of protein per slice.

☌ English Muffins

Yes, you can make your own low-carb English Muffins. The yogurt is what gives them that characteristic, mildly sour taste.

1/2 cup warm water

1/2 cup yogurt

1 teaspoon salt

2/3 cup vital wheat gluten

1/4 cup psyllium husks

2 tablespoons raw wheat germ

1/4 cup wheat bran

1/2 cup oat flour

1/2 cup vanilla-flavored whey protein powder

1 1/2 teaspoons yeast

1. Put the ingredients in your bread machine in the order given, and run until the end of the "rise" cycle. Remove the dough from the machine.

2. Using just enough oat flour on your work surface to keep the dough from sticking, pat the dough out so it's 1/2 inch thick.

3. Using a tin can with both ends removed as a cutter (a tuna can works well), cut rounds from the dough. Cover them with a clean cloth, set them aside in a warm place, and let them rise for about 1 hour, or until they've doubled in bulk.

4. Heat a heavy skillet or griddle over medium-low heat. Scatter the surface lightly with wheat germ to prevent sticking, and place as many muffins in the skillet as will fit easily. Let the muffins bake for about 6 minutes per side, or until they're browned. Eat these just like you would regular English muffins—split them, toast them, and butter them.

Yield: About 6 muffins, or 12 servings, each with 13 grams of carbohydrates and 6.5 grams of fiber, for a total of 6.5 grams of usable carbs and 14 grams of protein.

ʒ Crunchy Protein Waffles

1/2 cup raw wheat germ

1 cup soy powder

1/2 cup vanilla-flavored whey protein powder

1/2 teaspoon salt

1 tablespoon Splenda

1/2 cup sesame seeds

3 eggs

3/4 cup heavy cream

1/2 cup water

4 to 6 tablespoons oil or melted butter

1. Preheat a waffle iron.

2. Combine the wheat germ, soy powder, whey protein powder, salt, Splenda, and sesame seeds in a large bowl.

3. Separate the eggs, reserving the yolks. Whip the whites until they're stiff, and set aside.

4. Whisk the cream, water, and oil together with the egg yolks, and pour them into the dry ingredients. Mix well, and gently fold in the egg whites.

5. Use a cup to pour the batter onto your waffle iron, and bake until they're golden brown and crispy. Serve with butter and sugar-free syrup, sugar-free jam or jelly, cinnamon and Splenda, or—my favorite—thawed, frozen strawberries and whipped cream.

Yield: This depends on the size of your waffle iron; mine makes rectangular waffles, and I get about 10 servings, each with 8 grams of carbohydrates and 2 grams of fiber, for a total of 6 grams of usable carbs and 10 grams of protein.

☌ Kim's Dutch Baby

A Dutch Baby is a big, puffy, eggy, baked pancake, and my sister Kim adores them, so I came up with this recipe for her. It's great for Sunday brunch.

2 tablespoons butter

1/3 cup low-carb bake mix

1/3 cup rice protein powder

1/4 cup Splenda

1/2 teaspoon salt

1/2 teaspoon cinnamon

4 eggs

1 cup half-and-half

2 teaspoons canola or other vegetable oil

1 teaspoon vanilla extract

1. Preheat the oven to 425°F. It is essential that the oven be up to temperature before putting your Dutch Baby in, so don't combine the wet and dry ingredients until the oven is ready.

2. Spray a large, cast-iron skillet or a 10-inch pie pan with nonstick cooking spray, and melt the butter in the bottom. Set aside.

3. In a bowl, combine the bake mix, protein powder, Splenda, salt, and cinnamon.

4. In a separate bowl, beat together the eggs, half-and-half, canola oil, and vanilla extract, and whisk it vigorously for a couple of minutes. (Beating air into it will make the Dutch Baby puff more.)

5. Beat in the dry ingredients just until well-mixed, and pour the batter into the prepared pan.

6. Bake for 20 minutes; reduce the temperature to 350°F, and bake for another 3 to 5 minutes.

Yield: 2 big servings, or 4 small ones (if you serve 4, you'll want some sausage or something along with it, I think). Depending on the brand of low-carb bake mix and protein powder you use, figure 20 to 25 grams of carbohydrates in the whole Dutch Baby and 3 to 4 grams of fiber. 2 servings would each have about 10 grams of usable carbs and about 38 grams of protein.

🍓 Your Dutch Baby will come out gloriously puffed, but it will quickly sink in the middle. That's okay—it's supposed to. It will be crunchy around the edges, and soft in the middle.

The traditional accompaniment for a Dutch Baby is a sprinkle of lemon juice and confectioner's sugar, but lemon and Splenda works great. You could also try cinnamon and Splenda, plain Splenda, some thawed frozen berries, or sugar-free jam or jelly. Yummy!

⏳ Granola

This isn't super-low in carbs, and it's really more for eating during maintenance than during weight loss. But it's far lower in carbs than standard granola, high in protein, very filling, and best of all, it tastes like real cereal!

2 1/2 cups rolled oats

3/4 cup sunflower seeds

3/4 cup sesame seeds

2/3 cup wheat germ

3/4 cup flaked, unsweetened coconut

1/2 cup chopped walnuts

1/2 cup slivered almonds

1/2 cup wheat bran

1/4 cup flaxseeds

1 teaspoon cinnamon

1/2 cup Splenda

3/4 cup vanilla-flavored whey protein powder

1/4 teaspoon blackstrap molasses

1/2 cup canola oil

1. Preheat the oven to 250°F.

2. In a large, shallow roasting pan, combine the rolled oats, sunflower seeds, sesame seeds, wheat germ, coconut, walnuts, almonds, bran, flaxseeds, cinnamon, Splenda, and protein powder, mixing them very well.

3. Stir the molasses into the canola oil; it won't really blend with it, but it will help the molasses get distributed evenly. Pour the mixture over the dry ingredients, and stir until it's uniformly distributed.

4. Place in the oven and toast for an hour, stirring once or twice. Store in a tightly covered container. Serve topped with cream or half-and-half.

Yield: Makes about 16 servings of 1/2 cup, each with 21.8 grams of carbohydrates and 6 grams of fiber, for a total of 15.8 grams of usable carbs and 11.6 grams of protein.

⌒ Evelyn's Granola

From reader Evelyn Nordahl, a much lower-carbohydrate granola recipe.

  1 cup Textured Vegetable Protein granules (available at health food stores)

  1 teaspoon cinnamon

  2 tablespoons Splenda

  1/2 cup unsweetened coconut flakes

  1/2 cup chopped pecans

  1/2 cup chopped, sliced, or slivered almonds

1. Combine the Textured Vegetable Protein granules, cinnamon, and Splenda in a plastic or glass container large enough to hold all the ingredients.

2. Spread the coconut, pecans, and almonds on a cookie sheet and toast under the broiler just until the coconut starts to brown. Remove from the oven and cool.

3. Add the toasted nuts to the granule mixture, attach the lid, and shake to mix.

Yield: About 10 servings of 1/4 cup, each with 9 grams of carbohydrates and 6 grams of fiber, for a total of 3 grams of usable carbs and 17 grams of protein.

  Evelyn eats this granola topped with about 2 tablespoons of water and 2 tablespoons of heavy cream, and she says it's "satisfying, crunchy and delicious."

⌒ Almond Pancake and Waffle Mix

This makes nice, tender pancakes and waffles that have a nutty taste and a texture similar to cornmeal pancakes and waffles.

> 2 cups almond meal
>
> 1/2 cup oat bran
>
> 1/2 cup vanilla-flavored whey protein powder
>
> 1/2 cup rice protein powder
>
> 2 tablespoons wheat bran
>
> 2 tablespoons raw wheat germ
>
> 2 tablespoons vital wheat gluten
>
> 2 1/2 tablespoons baking powder
>
> 1 1/2 teaspoons salt

1. Assemble all the ingredients in a food processor with the S blade in place. Run the processor for a minute or so, stopping once or twice to shake it so everything will be well combined.

2. Store the mix in an airtight container in the refrigerator.

Yield: Makes about 4 servings of 1 cup, each with 33 grams of carbohydrates and 3 grams of fiber, for a total of 30 grams of usable carbs and 36 grams of protein.

⌒ Pancakes from Almond Mix

I like to eat these topped with sugar-free grape jelly, but you could also serve them with sugar-free syrup, sugar-free jam, thawed sugar-free frozen fruit, or Splenda and cinnamon.

> 2 cups Almond Pancake and Waffle Mix (see page 132)
>
> 2 eggs
>
> 1 cup water
>
> 1 tablespoon canola, peanut, or sunflower oil

1. Spray a skillet or griddle with nonstick cooking spray, and set it over medium heat.

2. Mix all the ingredients with a whisk, and drop the batter by the tablespoonful onto the griddle or skillet. Cook as you would regular pancakes, turning to brown lightly on each side. Stir the batter between batches to prevent it from settling.

Yield: About 16 pancakes, each with 4 grams of carbohydrates, a trace of fiber, and 6 grams of protein.

🍓 For a little added flavor, melt a little butter on the griddle or skillet before you cook the batter.

ꙮ Waffles from Almond Mix

These remind me a lot of cornmeal waffles, and they're really good with bacon on the side.

> 1 cup Almond Pancake and Waffle Mix (see page 132)
>
> 1 teaspoon Splenda
>
> 1/2 cup half-and-half
>
> 1 egg
>
> 1/4 cup oil

1. Preheat a waffle iron.
2. In a mixing bowl, stir together the mix and Splenda.
3. In a separate bowl, stir together the half-and-half, egg, and oil, and pour the mixture into the dry ingredients. Stir only until everything is wet, and there are no big lumps of dry mix.
4. Bake in the waffle iron according to the machine's directions. Serve with butter and sugar-free syrup, cinnamon and Splenda, sugar-free jam or jelly, or another low-carb topping of your choice.

Yield: In my waffle iron, this makes 6 servings, each with 5 grams of carbohydrates, a trace of fiber, and 6 grams of protein.

ꙮ Perfect Protein Pancakes

These taste just like mom used to make—you'd never guess they were low carb.

> 2 eggs
>
> 1/2 cup ricotta cheese
>
> 1/4 cup vanilla-flavored whey protein powder
>
> 1/2 teaspoon baking powder
>
> 1/8 teaspoon salt

1. Spray a heavy skillet or griddle with nonstick cooking spray and place it over medium heat.
2. In a mixing bowl, whisk together the eggs and ricotta until quite smooth. Whisk in the whey protein powder, baking powder, and salt, only mixing until well combined.

3. Drop batter onto the skillet or griddle by the tablespoonful. When the bubbles on the surface of the pancakes are breaking and staying broken, flip them and cook the other side.

4. Serve with butter and sugar-free syrup, sugar-free jelly, Splenda and cinnamon, or a few mashed berries sweetened with Splenda.

Yield: 14 "silver dollar" pancakes, each with about 0.6 grams of carbohydrates, no fiber, and 2.5 grams of protein.

🍓 I'd call five of these tiny pancakes a "serving," so double or triple your batches accordingly. Even better, make extras to freeze, and you can warm them up in the toaster oven for a healthy breakfast on a hurried morning.

Zucchini Pancakes

I know the name sounds strange, but if you like zucchini bread you should really try Vicki Cash's pancakes.

3 eggs (or 2 eggs and 2 egg whites)
2 tablespoons half-and-half
1/4 cup canola oil
2/3 cup low-carb bake mix
1 teaspoon cinnamon
1/2 teaspoon salt
1/2 teaspoon nutmeg
1 small zucchini, shredded (1 to 1 1/2 cups)

1. Mix the eggs, half-and-half, canola oil, bake mix, cinnamon, salt, and nutmeg together until no longer lumpy. Mix in the zucchini, and let the batter sit for 5 minutes.

2. While the batter sits, spray a nonstick griddle or skillet with canola cooking spray, and place it over medium-high heat.

3. Pour the batter onto the griddle about 1/4 cup at a time. Flip the pancakes when their edges are slightly brown, and cook thoroughly on both sides. Serve with butter or pureed berries or peaches.

Yield: 3 servings. The carb count will vary with the brand of low-carb bake mix you use, but figure about 5 grams of usable carbs and about 20 grams of protein.

ᔕ Cheese Popovers

These are from *Lo-Carb Cooking*, by Debra Rowland, and they are tasty!

      1 cup almond flour

      1/2 teaspoon salt

      1 cup cream

      2 eggs

      1 tablespoon melted butter

      1/4 cup shredded Cheddar cheese

1. Preheat the oven to at 425°F.

2. Beat the flour, salt, cream, eggs, and butter until smooth. Stir in the cheese.

3. Spoon the mixture into 8 muffin cups. Bake for 15 minutes, reduce heat to 350°F, and bake for 25 additional minutes, or until golden brown. Serve immediately.

Yield: 8 servings, each with 6 grams of carbohydrates, a trace of fiber, and 10 grams of protein.

⑤ Buttermilk Bran Muffins

Tender, moist, sweet, and perfumed with cinnamon. And, using the GO-Diet's figure of 4 grams of carbohydrates per cup of buttermilk, not a bad deal, carbohydrates-wise.

> 2/3 cup wheat bran
>
> 3/4 cup plus 2 tablespoons vanilla-flavored whey protein powder
>
> 2 tablespoons vital wheat gluten
>
> 1/4 teaspoon salt
>
> 1 teaspoon baking soda
>
> 1/4 cup Splenda
>
> 1/2 teaspoon cinnamon
>
> 1/2 cup chopped walnuts or pecans (optional)
>
> 1 cup buttermilk
>
> 1 egg
>
> 3 tablespoons oil
>
> 1 tablespoon blackstrap molasses

1. Preheat the oven to 350°F.
2. In a mixing bowl, combine the wheat bran, protein powder, wheat gluten, salt, baking soda, Splenda, cinnamon, and nuts, and stir until well combined.
3. In a measuring cup, stir together the buttermilk, egg, oil, and molasses.
4. Spray 10 cups of a muffin tin well with nonstick cooking spray.
5. Give the wet ingredients one last stir, and pour them into the dry ingredients. With a spoon, stir just long enough to moisten all the dry ingredients. Do not over-mix! The batter should look rough, and a few lumps are fine.
6. Spoon into the prepared muffin cups, dividing the mixture evenly (the muffin cups should be about 2/3 full).
7. Bake for 20 to 25 minutes, and then turn out of the muffin cups onto a wire rack to cool.

Yield: 10 muffins, each with 13.5 carbohydrates and 6 grams of fiber, for a total of 7.5 grams of usable carbs and 9 grams of protein.

🍓 Try doubling this recipe and freezing the leftovers. Thaw the muffins a few at a time to grab on those mornings when you need a fast and nutritious breakfast.

↻ Sour Cream, Lemon, and Poppy Seed Muffins

1 cup almond meal

1 cup vanilla-flavored whey protein powder

1 1/2 teaspoons baking powder

1/2 teaspoon salt

1/3 cup Splenda

1 teaspoon baking soda

2 tablespoons poppy seeds

1 cup sour cream

2 eggs

2 tablespoons water

2 teaspoons lemon extract

Grated rind of 1 lemon

1. Preheat the oven to 400°F.

2. In a mixing bowl, combine the almond meal, protein powder, baking powder, salt, Splenda, baking soda, and poppy seeds, and stir until well combined.

3. In a separate bowl, combine the sour cream, eggs, water, lemon extract, and lemon rind, and whisk together well.

4. When your oven is up to temperature, spray 16 muffin tins well with nonstick cooking spray. (You can use paper liners, if you prefer.)

5. Pour the sour cream mixture into the dry ingredients, and stir together with just a few strokes—just enough to make the mixture evenly moist. Do not over-mix.

6. Spoon the batter evenly into muffin cups, and bake for 20 minutes.

Yield: Makes 16 muffins, each with 5.25 grams of carbohydrates and 1 gram of fiber, for a total of 4.25 grams of usable carbs and 7.75 grams of protein.

↻ Sour Cream Coffee Cake

Here's a coffee cake for you, from Diana Lee's invaluable *Baking Low Carb*. Notice that this has enough protein to be a satisfying breakfast all by itself.

Cake

1 cup sour cream

2/3 cup oil

1/2 cup water

3 eggs

2 teaspoons almond extract

1 1/4 cups vanilla-flavored whey protein powder

1/4 cup oat flour

2 tablespoons vital wheat gluten

1 teaspoon baking soda

1 tablespoon baking powder

2 teaspoons cinnamon

1/2 cup Splenda

1 tablespoon liquid saccharine sweetener (such as Sweet 'n Low liquid)

Topping

1/2 cup chopped nuts

2 tablespoons Splenda

1/4 teaspoon cinnamon

1. Preheat the oven to 350°F, and grease a springform pan.

2. Combine the sour cream, oil, water, eggs, and almond extract. Mix these ingredients together well.

3. Add the protein powder, oat flour, vital wheat gluten, baking soda, baking powder, cinnamon, Splenda, and liquid saccharine. Mix until blended, and pour into the prepared pan.

4. Combine the nuts, Splenda, and cinnamon to make the topping, and sprinkle it over the batter in the springform pan. Bake for 30 to 35 minutes.

Yield: 12 slices, each with 9 grams of carbohydrates and 1 gram of fiber, for a total of 8 grams of usable carbs and 24 grams of protein.

ᔕ "Corn Bread"

This low-carb alternative comes from Debra Rowland's *Lo-Carb Cooking*.

> 1 cup butter, softened
>
> 2 teaspoons Splenda
>
> 5 eggs
>
> 1 1/2 cups almond flour
>
> 1/2 cup hazelnut flour
>
> 1 teaspoon baking powder
>
> 2 teaspoons butter extract

1. Preheat the oven to 350°F.

2. Cream butter and Splenda well. Add the eggs one at a time, beating well after each.

3. Mix the almond and hazelnut flours with baking powder, and add this dry mixture to the egg mixture a little at a time while continuously beating.

4. Mix in the butter extract, and pour the batter into a 9-inch springform or cake pan. Bake for 50 to 55 minutes.

> 🍓 If you're like Debra Rowland, you're lucky enough to have access to store-bought almond and hazelnut flours to make this recipe with. I'm not so lucky. I have made this recipe with almonds and hazelnuts I ground in my food processor, though, and it worked fine, so don't be afraid to try it "from scratch."

♋ Hot Almond Cereal

Here's a recipe for all of you who miss hot cereal in the morning. Loaded with fiber, it's a great way to get the benefits of flax—not to mention that it's really, really tasty.

> 1 cup flaxseeds
> 1 cup ground almonds
> 1/2 cup oat bran
> 1 1/4 cups wheat bran
> 1 cup vanilla-flavored whey protein powder

1. Preheat the oven to 300°F.

2. Grind your flaxseeds in a food processor with the S blade in place. Flaxseeds take a while to grind up, so you may have to run the processor for several minutes. (You can buy flaxseed meal if you prefer, but flaxseed oil spoils pretty quickly after the seeds are ground, so I much prefer to grind my own.)

3. While the food processor is running, lightly toast your ground almonds by putting them in a shallow baking pan in the oven for 5 minutes or so.

4. When the flaxseeds are ground and the almonds are toasted, combine them with the oat bran, wheat bran, and protein powder, and store in an airtight container.

5. To make a bowl of cereal, put 1/2 cup of the mixture in a bowl and add 3/4 cup of boiling water and a pinch of salt. Stir, and let your cereal sit for a few minutes before eating.

Yield: About 9 servings, each with about 16 grams of carbohydrates and 9 grams of fiber, for a total of 7 grams of usable carbs and 11 grams of protein.

🍓 Try this with a little Splenda and cream, or even a little cinnamon. Personally, I like to add just a drop or two of blackstrap molasses to give it a brown-sugar flavor without many extra carbs.

⌒ Cinnamon Hot Cereal

For those of you who used to eat your oatmeal with cinnamon and sugar. Add Splenda and cream to taste.

> 1 cup ground flaxseeds
>
> 1 cup ground almonds
>
> 1/2 cup oat bran
>
> 1 1/2 cups wheat bran
>
> 1/2 cup vanilla-flavored whey protein powder
>
> 2 teaspoons cinnamon

1. Combine all the ingredients well, and store in an airtight container.

2. To make a bowl of cereal, put 1/2 cup of the mixture in a bowl, and add 3/4 cup boiling water and a pinch of salt. Stir, and let your cereal sit for a few minutes before eating.

Yield: About 5 servings, each with 15 grams of carbohydrates and 9.5 grams of fiber, for a total of 5.5 grams of usable carbs and 11 grams of protein.

⌒ Hot Chocolate Bran Cereal

Remember Cocowheats? Here's a chocolate hot cereal for the kid in you, from Diana Lee's *Bread and Breakfast: Baking Low Carb II.*

> 1/4 cup toasted wheat bran
>
> 1 envelope low-carb, sugar-free hot chocolate mix
>
> 1/4 cup vanilla-flavored whey protein powder
>
> 1 tablespoon ground almonds
>
> 1/3 cup water

1. Whisk the bran, hot chocolate mix, whey protein, and almonds together. Add the water, and mix until combined.

2. Microwave on full power for 30 seconds, and stir. Microwave for another 30 seconds (if you want this thicker, microwave it longer), and serve with cream.

Yield: 1 serving. With the lowest-carb cocoa mix, this has 17 grams of carbohydrates and 9 grams of fiber, for a total of 8 grams of usable carbs and 20 grams of protein.

About Making Low-Carb Crackers

To make all these cracker recipes, you will need a roll of nonstick baking parchment, available at housewares stores everywhere, or Teflon pan liners, available at really good cookware stores. My roll of baking parchment cost me all of $3. Do not try to simply make these crackers on a cookie sheet, no matter how well greased: As you stand at your sink, endlessly, laboriously chipping your crackers off the cookie sheet, you will be very sorry.

⟲ Sunflower Parmesan Crackers

These have a great, crunchy texture and a wonderful flavor.

    1 cup raw, shelled sunflower seeds
    1/2 cup grated Parmesan cheese
    1/4 cup water

1. Preheat the oven to 325°F.

2. Put the sunflower seeds and Parmesan in a food processor with the S blade in place, and process until the sunflower seeds are a fine meal with almost a flour consistency. Add the water, and pulse the processor until the dough is well blended, soft, and sticky.

3. Cover your cookie sheet with a piece of baking parchment. Turn the dough out onto the parchment, tear off another sheet of parchment, and put it on top of the dough.

4. Through the top sheet of parchment, use your hands to press the dough into as thin and even a sheet as you can. Take the time to get the dough quite thin—the thinner, the better, so long as there are no holes in the dough. Peel off the top layer of parchment, and use a thin, sharp, straight-bladed knife or a pizza cutter to score the dough into squares or diamonds.

5. Bake for about 30 minutes, or until evenly browned. Peel off the parchment, break along the scored lines, and let the crackers cool. Store them in a container with a tight lid.

Yield: How many carbs per cracker? It will vary with the size and thickness of your crackers. I get about 6 dozen, each with just a trace of carbohydrates, a trace of fiber, and 1 gram of protein. But you can eat the whole batch for just 13 grams of usable carbohydrates, so who's counting?

↷ Sunflower Sesame Crackers

      1 cup raw, shelled sunflower seeds

      1/2 cup sesame seeds

      1/2 teaspoon salt

      1/4 cup water

1. Preheat the oven to 325°F.

2. In a food processor with the S blade attached, grind the sunflower seeds to a fine meal.

3. Add the sesame seeds and salt, and pulse the food processor just long enough to combine. (You want the sesame seeds to stay whole.) Add the water, and pulse to make a dough.

4. Cover your cookie sheet with a piece of baking parchment. Turn the dough out onto the parchment, tear off another sheet of parchment, and put it on top of the dough.

5. Through the top sheet of parchment, use your hands to press the dough into as thin and even a sheet as you can. Take the time to get the dough quite thin—the thinner, the better, so long as there are no holes in the dough. Peel off the top layer of parchment and use a thin, sharp, straight-bladed knife or a pizza cutter to score the dough into squares or diamonds. If you like, you could sprinkle a little salt over the surface and gently press it into the dough before scoring the crackers.

6. Bake for about 30 minutes, or until they're a light golden color. Peel off the parchment, break along the scored lines, and let the crackers cool. Store them in a container with a tight lid.

Yield: About 6 dozen small crackers, each with 1 gram of carbohydrates and about 0.5 gram of fiber, for a total of 0.5 gram of usable carbs and 1 gram of protein.

Sunflower Cheddar Crackers

Miss Cheese Nips? Try these.

>   1 1/2 cups raw, shelled sunflower seeds
>
>   1 1/2 cups grated Cheddar cheese
>
>   1/2 teaspoon salt, plus additional for sprinkling
>
>   1/4 cup water

1. Preheat the oven to 325°F.

2. In a food processor with the S blade attached, grind the sunflower seeds to a fine meal.

3. Add the Cheddar and salt, and pulse the processor six to eight times to blend. Add the water, and pulse until a dough ball forms.

4. Cover your cookie sheet with a piece of baking parchment. Turn the dough out onto the parchment, tear off another sheet of parchment, and put it on top of the dough.

5. Through the top sheet of parchment, use your hands to press the dough into as thin and even a sheet as you can. Take the time to get the dough quite thin—the thinner, the better, so long as there are no holes in the dough. Peel off the top layer of parchment. Sprinkle a little salt over the surface and gently press it in into place. Use a thin, sharp, straight-bladed knife or a pizza cutter to score the dough into squares or diamonds.

6. Bake for about 30 minutes. Peel off the parchment, break along the scored lines, and let the crackers cool. Store them in a container with a tight lid.

Yield: About 6 dozen crackers, each with 1 gram of carbohydrates and 0.5 gram of fiber, for a total of 0.5 gram of usable carbs and 1 gram of protein.

🍓 Thanks to the cheese, these crackers come with a bonus: 21 milligrams of calcium!

⌒ Bran Crackers

Tired of paying through the nose for fiber crackers? These are similar to Fiber Rich or Bran-a-Crisp, except that they're thinner, crispier, lower-carb—and a whole lot cheaper. Plus they're great with dips, patés, and tuna or egg salad.

    1 1/2 cups wheat bran
    1/2 cup rice protein powder
    1 teaspoon salt
    1 1/2 cups water

1. Preheat the oven to 350°F.

2. Combine the wheat bran, protein powder, and salt, stirring them together well. Stir in the water, making sure everything is wet, and let the mixture sit for about 5 minutes.

3. Cover a cookie sheet with baking parchment and turn the dough out onto the parchment (the dough will be very soft). Using the back of a spoon, pat and smooth this out into a thin, even, unbroken sheet.

4. Bake for 10 minutes, and use a pizza cutter or a knife with a thin, sharp blade to score the sheet of dough into crackers. Put the sheet back in the oven, and bake for another 20 minutes.

5. Turn the oven to its lowest temperature, and let the crackers sit in the warm oven for at least 3 hours, until they're good and dry and crisp. Break apart, and store in an airtight container.

    Yield: 3 dozen crackers, each with just over 2 grams of carbohydrates and 1 gram of fiber, for a total of about 1 gram of usable carbs and just a trace of protein.

Pizza

A big thank you to Jennifer Eloff at sweety.com for this recipe from *Splendid Low-Carbing!* To make these pizza crusts, you first have to make her Almond Whey Bake Mix #1:

☽ Almond Whey Bake Mix #1

1 1/3 cups ground almonds

3/4 cup natural whey protein powder

1/2 cup unbleached spelt flour or 1/2 cup unbleached all-purpose flour

1 tablespoon vital wheat gluten

In a medium bowl, combine all the ingredients and stir well. Store in an airtight container at room temperature.

Whey Pizza Crusts

Now, use the bake mix to make your Pizza Crusts.

> 3/4 cup water, less 1 tablespoon
>
> 2 tablespoons olive oil
>
> 1 1/2 cups Almond Whey Bake Mix #1 (see page 147)
>
> 2/3 cup vital wheat gluten
>
> 1/2 cup wheat bran
>
> 1/3 cup natural whey protein powder
>
> 2 tablespoons Splenda
>
> 1 tablespoon spelt flour or all-purpose flour
>
> 1 tablespoon sugar
>
> 1 tablespoon skim milk powder
>
> 1 tablespoon bread machine yeast
>
> 1 teaspoon salt

1. Preheat the oven to 375°F, and warm the water in the microwave for 30 seconds.
2. Place the water, olive oil, Bake Mix #1, wheat gluten, wheat bran, protein powder, Splenda, flour, sugar, skim milk powder, yeast, and salt in the bread machine.
3. Program the bread machine for pizza dough, or knead and first rise.
4. When the dough is ready, remove it from the machine and divide it in half. On a lightly floured surface, roll out each ball of dough as far as possible. Cover with a towel, and allow to sit for 10 to 20 minutes. Grease two 12-inch pizza pans.
5. Roll the dough again. Place it on the pizza pans, and roll it out to fit each pan, using a small rolling pin or another small cylindrical object.
6. Cover the crusts with pizza sauce, toppings, and grated cheese. Bake on lowest oven rack for 20 to 25 minutes, or until the crusts are browned.

Yield: 2 pizzas with 12 slices each, or 24 servings. The carb count of your toppings will vary, depending on what you use, but the crust will add just 2.6 grams of carbohydrates, no fiber, and 6 grams of protein.

🍓 A convection oven bakes pizza evenly and more quickly, so be sure to adjust your baking time accordingly.

Tortillas

Yet another great recipe from *Splendid Low-Carbing* by Jennifer Eloff at sweety.com. Again, you start this recipe by making a bake mix:

Almond Whey Bake Mix #2

- 1 1/3 cup ground almonds
- 3/4 cup spelt flour
- 1/2 cup natural whey protein powder
- 1/4 cup vital wheat gluten

In a medium bowl, combine all ingredients. Mix with a wooden spoon until well combined. Store in an airtight container.

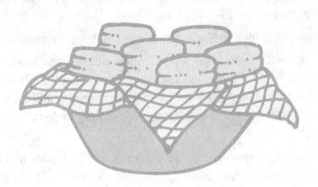

ꗬ Whey Tortillas

Jen Eloff at sweety.com says, "These, in my humble opinion, taste better than the regular, almost tasteless white flour tortillas we used to buy."

3/4 cup warm water (105° to 115°F; this will feel warm, but not hot, on your wrist)

1 tablespoon sugar

1 tablespoon yeast

2 tablespoons olive oil

1 1/3 cups Almond Whey Bake Mix #2 (see page 155)

2/3 cup vital wheat gluten

1/2 cup wheat bran

1/3 cup spelt flour or all-purpose flour

2 tablespoons Splenda

1 tablespoon sugar

1 tablespoon skim milk powder

1 teaspoon salt

1. Preheat the oven to 200°F.

2. Pour the warm water in a large electric mixer bowl. Dissolve the sugar in the water, and then sprinkle yeast over the water's surface.

3. Allow the mixture to sit for 3 to 5 minutes, then stir to dissolve completely.

4. Add the olive oil, Almond Whey Bake Mix #2, wheat gluten, wheat bran, flour, Splenda, sugar, skim milk powder, and salt. Using a dough hook attachment on an electric mixer, mix, scraping the sides of the bowl occasionally, until the dough is moist and elastic. (If you don't have an electric mixer, you can do this by hand, with a wooden spoon.)

5. On a lightly floured surface, knead the dough briefly, and then place it in a greased bowl. Cover loosely with foil and place it in the oven. Turn the oven off, and allow the dough to double in size (this will take about 1 hour).

6. When the dough has risen, remove, punch down, and break into 20 small balls. Cover the dough balls with a clean dishtowel to keep them from drying out.

7. Roll each dough ball into a paper-thin circle on a lightly floured surface.

8. In a dry, nonstick skillet, cook each dough round briefly on both sides, until brown spots appear. Place your tortillas in a plastic bag to keep them supple, or refrigerate or freeze for longer storage.

Yield: 20 tortillas, each with 4.4 grams of carbohydrates, no fiber. and 6.2 grams of protein.

CHAPTER FIVE

Hot Vegetable Dishes

When folks first go low-carb, they suddenly don't know what to serve for side dishes. The answer is vegetables. If you're used to thinking of vegetables as something that sits between the meat and the potato, usually being ignored, read this chapter and think again!

Here, right up front, are three recipes that every low-carber needs:

ᘒ Cauliflower Purée (a.k.a. "Fauxtatoes")

This is a wonderful substitute for mashed potatoes if you want something to put a fabulous sour cream gravy on! Feel free, by the way, to use frozen cauliflower instead; it works quite well here.

> 1 head fresh or 1 1/2 pounds frozen cauliflower
>
> 4 tablespoons butter
>
> Salt and pepper

1. Steam or microwave the cauliflower until it's soft.
2. Drain it thoroughly, and put it through the blender or food processor until it's well pureed. Add the butter and salt and pepper to taste.

Yield: 6 generous servings, each with 5 grams of carbohydrates and 2 grams of fiber, for a total of 3 grams of usable carbs and 2 grams of protein.

ᔕ Fauxtatoes Deluxe

This extra-rich fauxtatoes recipe comes from Adele Hite, and it is the basis for the "grits" part of her Low-Carb Shrimp and Grits recipe. (See page 298)

> 1 large head cauliflower
> 1/3 cup cream
> 4 ounces cream cheese
> 1 tablespoon butter
> Salt and pepper

1. Simmer the cauliflower in water with the cream added to it. (This keeps the cauliflower sweet and prevents it from turning an unappetizing gray color.) When the cauliflower is very soft, drain thoroughly.

2. Put the still-warm cauliflower in a food processor with the cream cheese, butter, and salt and pepper to taste, and process until smooth. (You may have to do this in more than one batch.)

Yield: 6 generous servings, each with 6 grams of carbohydrates and 2 grams of fiber, for a total of 4 grams of usable carbs and 4 grams of protein.

> Give your fauxtatoes a little zing by adding a few cloves of sliced garlic to the cooking water or some roasted garlic to the food processor when blending the cauliflower with the other ingredients. Each clove of garlic added will add just 1 gram of carbohydrates to the carb count for the batch.

ᔕ Cauliflower Rice

Many thanks to Fran McCullough! I got this idea from her book *Living Low Carb*, and it's served me very well.

> 1/2 head cauliflower

Simply put the cauliflower through your food processor using the shredding blade. This gives the cauliflower a texture that's remarkably similar to rice. You can steam, microwave, or even sauté it in butter. Whatever you do, though, don't overcook it!

Yield: About 3 cups, or 3 servings, each with 5 grams of carbohydrates and 2 grams of fiber, for a total of 3 grams of usable carbs and 2 grams of protein.

◌ Cauliflower Rice Deluxe

This is higher-carb than plain Cauliflower Rice, but the wild rice adds a grain flavor that makes it quite convincing. Plus, wild rice has about 25 percent less carbohydrates than most other kinds of rice. I only use this for special occasions, but it's wonderful.

> 3 cups Cauliflower Rice (see page 159)
>
> 1/4 cup wild rice
>
> 3/4 cup water

1. Cook your cauliflower rice as desired (I steam mine when making this), taking care not to overcook it to mushiness, but just until it's tender.

2. Put the wild rice and water in a saucepan, cover it, and set it on a burner on lowest heat until all the water is gone (at least one-half hour, maybe a bit more).

3. Toss together the cooked cauliflower rice and wild rice, and season as desired.

Yield: 4 cups, or 8 servings, each with 6 grams of carbohydrates and 1 gram of fiber, for a total of 5 grams of usable carbs and 2 grams of protein.

◌ Company Dinner "Rice"

This is my favorite way to season the cauliflower–wild rice blend above. It's a big hit at dinner parties!

> 1 small onion, chopped
>
> 1 stick butter, melted
>
> 4 cups Cauliflower Rice Deluxe (see above)
>
> 6 strips bacon, cooked until crisp, and crumbled
>
> 1/4 teaspoon salt or Vege-Sal
>
> 1/4 teaspoon pepper
>
> 1/2 cup grated Parmesan cheese

Sauté the onion in the butter until it's golden and limp. Toss the Cauliflower Rice Deluxe with the sautéed onion and the bacon, salt, pepper, and cheese. Serve.

Yield: 8 servings, each with 8 grams of carbohydrates and 2 grams of fiber, for a total of 6 grams of usable carbs and 5 grams of protein.

⌒ Sautéed Mushrooms

What could be better with a steak? Feel free to play with this recipe—use all butter or all olive oil, throw in a clove of garlic, try a few variations until you find what you like.

> 2 tablespoons butter
>
> 2 tablespoons olive oil
>
> 8 ounces mushrooms, thickly sliced
>
> Salt and pepper

1. Melt the butter and heat the olive oil over medium-high heat in a heavy skillet.

2. Add the mushrooms and sauté, stirring frequently, for 5 to 7 minutes, or until the mushrooms are limp and brown. Salt and pepper lightly, and serve.

Yield: 3 generous servings, each with 4 grams of carbohydrates and 1 gram of fiber, for a total of 3 grams of usable carbs and 2 grams of protein.

🍓 Try this recipe with mushrooms other than the familiar "button" 'shrooms. Criminis and portobellos are both delicious prepared this way, for instance. Avoid shitakes, however; they are much higher in carbohydrates.

Mushrooms in Sherry Cream

This is rich and flavorful, and best served with a simple roast or the like.

8 ounces small, very fresh mushrooms

1/4 cup dry sherry

1/4 teaspoon salt or Vege-Sal, divided

1/2 cup sour cream

1 clove garlic

1/8 teaspoon pepper

1. Wipe the mushrooms clean, and trim the woody ends off the stems.

2. Place the mushrooms in a small saucepan with the sherry, and sprinkle with 1/8 teaspoon of salt.

3. Bring the sherry to a boil, turn the burner to low, cover the pan, and let the mushrooms simmer for just 3 to 4 minutes, shaking the pan once or twice while they're cooking.

4. In another saucepan over very low heat, stir together the remaining 1/8 teaspoon salt, sour cream, garlic, and pepper. You want to heat the sour cream through, but don't let it boil, or it will separate.

5. When the mushrooms are done, pour off the liquid into a small bowl. As soon as the sour cream is heated through, spoon it over the mushrooms, and stir everything around over medium-low heat. If it seems a bit thick, add a teaspoon or two of the reserved liquid.

6. Stir the mushrooms and sour cream together for 2 to 3 minutes, again making sure that the sour cream does not boil, and serve.

Yield: 3 servings, each with 4 grams carbohydrates and 1 gram of fiber, for a total of 3 grams of usable carbs and 2 grams of protein.

↻ Slice of Mushroom Heaven

Rich enough to give Dean Ornish fits, and oh-so-good. Thanks to my friend Kay for the name!

4 tablespoons butter

1 pound mushrooms, sliced

1/2 medium onion, finely chopped

1 clove garlic, crushed

1/4 cup dry white wine

1 teaspoon lemon juice

1 1/2 cups half-and-half

3 eggs

1 teaspoon salt or Vege-Sal

1/4 teaspoon pepper

3 cups shredded Gruyère cheese (a little more than 1/2 pound)

1. Preheat the oven to 350°F.

2. Melt the butter in a heavy skillet over medium heat, and begin frying the mushrooms, onion, and garlic. When the mushrooms are limp, turn the heat up a bit and boil off the liquid. Stir in the white wine, and cook until that's boiled away, too.

3. Stir in the lemon juice and turn off the heat. Transfer the mixture to a large mixing bowl, and stir in the half-and-half, eggs, salt, pepper, and 2 cups of the cheese.

4. Spray an 8 x 8-inch baking pan with nonstick cooking spray, and spread the mixture from step 3 evenly over the bottom. Sprinkle the rest of the cheese on top, and bake for 50 minutes, or until the cheese on top is golden.

Yield: 9 generous servings, each with 5 grams of carbohydrates and 1 gram of fiber, for a total of 4 grams of usable carbs and 13 grams of protein.

🍓 This dish is good hot, but I actually like it better cold—plus, when it's cold, it cuts in nice, neat squares. I think it makes a nice breakfast or lunch, and it's definitely a fine side dish. It would even make a good vegetarian main course.

Kolokythia Krokettes

These are rapidly becoming one of our favorite side dishes. They're Greek, and very, very tasty. A terrific side dish with roast lamb or Greek roasted chicken.

> 3 medium zucchini, grated
>
> 1 teaspoon salt or Vege-Sal
>
> 3 eggs
>
> 1 cup crumbled feta
>
> 1 teaspoon dried oregano
>
> 1/2 medium onion, finely diced
>
> 1/8 teaspoon pepper
>
> 3 tablespoons soy powder or rice protein powder
>
> Butter

> Shave some time preparing the ingredients for this dish by running the zucchini and the onion through a food processor.

1. Mix the grated zucchini with the salt in a bowl, and let it sit for an hour or so. Squeeze out and drain the liquid.

2. Mix in the eggs, feta, oregano, onion, pepper, and soy powder, and combine well.

3. Spray a heavy skillet with nonstick cooking spray, add a healthy tablespoon of butter, and melt over medium heat. Fry the batter by the tablespoonful, turning once. Add more butter between batches, as needed, and keep the cooked krokettes warm. The trick to these is to let them get quite brown on the bottom before trying to turn them, or they tend to fall apart. If a few do fall apart, don't sweat it; the pieces will still taste incredible.

Yield: 6 servings, each with 6 grams of carbohydrates and 2 grams of fiber, for a total of 4 grams usable carbs and 8 grams of protein.

Zucchini With Sour Cream
For People Who Don't Love Zucchini

Marilee Wellersdick sends this recipe. My sister, who tested it, says the name is no joke—it went over well with nonzucchini-loving in-laws.

    4 tablespoons butter
    1 medium onion, chopped
    8 small zucchini, sliced about 1/8 inch thick
    Salt and pepper
    1 cup sour cream

1. Melt the butter in a large, preferably nonstick skillet. Add the onion and zucchini, and salt and pepper to taste.

2. Cover and cook on medium heat, stirring occasionally, until the zucchini is translucent (15 to 20 minutes).

3. Remove from the heat, and stir in the sour cream. Serve.

Yield: 6 servings, each with 11 grams of carbohydrates and 3 grams of fiber, for a total of 8 grams of usable carbs and no protein.

⌒ Zucchini Casserole

Jodee Rushton, who contributed this recipe, says, "Since each serving has protein as well as vegetable, it's great as part of a lunch with some other veggies. It's also a great snack."

    2 tablespoons butter

    1 1/2 pounds zucchini, unpeeled, washed, and sliced

    2 eggs, beaten

    1 tablespoon unbleached flour

    1/2 teaspoon dry mustard

    1/2 teaspoon ground nutmeg

    1/2 teaspoon salt

    Pepper

    1 packet Splenda

    1 cup heavy cream

    6 ounces sharp Cheddar cheese, shredded

1. Preheat the oven to 325°F, and spray a large casserole with nonstick cooking spray.

2. Melt the butter in a large, heavy skillet. Add the sliced zucchini, and sauté over medium-high heat until tender, stirring frequently. When done, remove from the heat and let cool until lukewarm. Place in the prepared casserole.

3. Combine the eggs, flour, mustard, nutmeg, salt, pepper to taste, and Splenda in a large mixing bowl; whisk together well. Add the heavy cream and Cheddar, and mix well.

4. Add the egg mixture to the cooled zucchini, and mix well. Place in the oven, and bake for 30 minutes or until set. Cool and serve.

Yield: 6 servings, each with 6 grams of carbohydrates and 1 gram of fiber, for a total of 5 grams of usable carbs and 11 grams of protein.

Zucchini-Crusted Pizza

This is like a somewhat-more-substantial quiche on the bottom, and pizza on top.

3 1/2 cups shredded zucchini

3 eggs

1/3 cup rice protein powder or soy powder

1 1/2 cups shredded mozzarella

1/2 cup grated Parmesan cheese

A pinch or two of dried basil

1/2 teaspoon salt

1/4 teaspoon pepper

Oil

1 cup sugarless pizza sauce

Toppings as desired (sausage, pepperoni, peppers, mushrooms, or whatever you like)

1. Preheat the oven to 350°F.

2. Sprinkle the zucchini with a little salt, and let it sit for 15 to 30 minutes. Put it in a strainer and press out the excess moisture.

3. Beat together the strained zucchini, eggs, protein powder, 1/2 cup of mozzarella, Parmesan, basil, salt, and pepper.

4. Spray a 9 x 13-inch baking pan with nonstick cooking spray, and spread the zucchini mixture in it.

5. Bake for about 25 minutes, or until firm. Brush it with a little oil, and broil it for about 5 minutes, until it's golden.

6. Next, spread on the pizza sauce, then add the remaining 1 cup of mozzarella and other toppings.

   If you're using vegetables as toppings, you may want to sauté them a bit first.

7. Bake for another 25 minutes, then cut into squares and serve.

   Yield: 4 generous servings, each with 14 grams of carbohydrates and 2 grams of fiber, for a total of 12 grams of usable carbs and 22 grams of protein. (Analysis does not include toppings.)

Eggplant Parmesan Squared

When you use Parmesan cheese instead of breadcrumbs to "bread" the eggplant slices, it becomes Eggplant Parmesan Squared! This takes a little doing, but it's delicious, and it's easily filling enough for a main dish.

1/2 cup low-carb bake mix or unflavored protein powder

2 or 3 eggs

1 1/4 to 1 3/4 cups Parmesan cheese

1 large eggplant, sliced no more than 1/4-inch thick

Olive oil for frying

1 clove garlic, cut in half

1 1/2 cups sugar-free spaghetti sauce

8 ounces shredded mozzarella

🍓 How many eggs and how much cheese you will need depends on how big your eggplant is.

1. Preheat the oven to 350°F.

2. Put the bake mix on a plate, break the eggs into a shallow bowl and beat well, and put 1 to 1 1/2 cups of Parmesan on another plate.

3. Dip each eggplant slice in the bake mix so each side is well dusted.

4. Dip each "floured" slice of eggplant in the beaten egg and then in the Parmesan so that each slice has a good coating of the cheese. Refrigerate the "breaded" slices of eggplant for at least half an hour, or up to an hour or two.

5. Pour 1/8 inch of olive oil in the bottom of a heavy skillet over medium heat. Add the garlic, letting it sizzle for a minute or two before removing. Now fry the refrigerated eggplant slices until they're golden brown on both sides (you'll have to add more olive oil as you go along.)

6. Spread 1/2 cup of spaghetti sauce in the bottom of a 9 x 11-inch roasting pan. Arrange half of the eggplant slices to cover bottom of pan. Cover with the mozzarella, and top with the remaining eggplant. Pour the rest of the spaghetti sauce on, and sprinkle the remaining 1/4 cup of Parmesan on top.

7. Bake for 30 minutes.

Yield: 6 servings, each with 13 grams of carbohydrates and 4.5 grams of fiber, for a total of 8.5 usable carbs and 24 grams of protein.

↻ Cauliflower-Green Bean Casserole

Reader Honey Ashton says her family loves this. It makes a great holiday side dish.

> 2 bags (1 pound each) frozen cauliflower
>
> 1 cup crosscut green beans
>
> 1 cup mayonnaise
>
> 1 cup butter
>
> 1/4 small yellow or white onion, finely sliced
>
> 1 cup freshly cooked, crumbled bacon
>
> 1 cup shredded mixture Mozzarella and Cheddar cheeses

1. Preheat the oven to 300°F.
2. Follow the package directions to cook the cauliflower; add the beans to cook with cauliflower. Drain after cooking.
3. Place the cooked veggies in a large casserole, and stir in the mayonnaise, butter, onion, and bacon; mix thoroughly.
4. Top the casserole with the cheese. Bake for 20 minutes or until the cheese has melted, and serve immediately.

Yield: 8 servings, each with 10 grams of carbohydrates and 4 grams of fiber, for a total of 6 grams of usable carbs and 11 grams of protein.

↺ Cauliflower Kugel

A kugel is a traditional Jewish casserole that comes in both sweet and savory varieties. This savory kugel makes a nice side dish with a simple meat course. It could also be served as a vegetarian main dish.

2 packages (10 ounces each) frozen cauliflower, thawed

1 medium onion, chopped

1 cup cottage cheese

1 cup shredded Cheddar cheese

4 eggs

$1/2$ teaspoon salt or Vege-Sal

$1/4$ teaspoon pepper

Paprika

1. Preheat the oven to 350°F.

2. Chop the cauliflower into $1/2$-inch pieces. Combine with the onion, cottage cheese, Cheddar, eggs, salt, and pepper in a large mixing bowl, and mix very well.

3. Spray an 8 x 8-inch baking pan with nonstick cooking spray, and spread the cauliflower mixture evenly on the bottom. Sprinkle paprika lightly over the top, and bake for 50 to 60 minutes, or until the kugel is set and lightly browned.

Yield: 9 servings, each with 5 grams of carbohydrates and 2 grams of fiber, for a total of 3 grams of usable carbs and 10 grams of protein.

↷ Smoky Cauliflower and Sausage

Holly Holder, who sent this recipe, says, "My kids, who wouldn't touch cauliflower, loved this recipe. They had no idea what it was—and my lips are sealed!"

  1 medium head cauliflower or 1 bag (1 pound) frozen cauliflower

  1 package (8 ounces) cream cheese, softened

  1/2 pound bulk sausage, cooked and crumbled

  4 ounces smoked Gruyère, Swiss, or any other smoked cheese,
    cut into thin slices

  Salt and pepper

1. Preheat the oven to 350°F.

2. Cut up the cauliflower, and steam or microwave it until tender. Mash with a potato masher, and mix in the cream cheese and sausage.

3. Spread half the cauliflower mixture in a 2-quart casserole. Top with half of the cheese slices.

4. Add the remaining cauliflower and top with the remaining cheese. Bake until bubbly (about 30 minutes).

Yield: 6 servings, each with 5 grams of carbohydrates and 2 grams of fiber, for a total of 3 grams of usable carbs and 13 grams of protein.

  🍓 Don't be fooled into overcooking your casserole: Smoked Gruyère will not look melted, but it will be very creamy when dished out.

᠗ Green Beans Almondine

My girlfriend Tonya always though that this was a terribly complicated dish because it's elegant and delicious. As if! It's child's play.

1 bag (1 pound) frozen French-cut green beans

1/2 cup slivered almonds

4 tablespoons butter

1. Steam or microwave the beans according to the package directions.

2. While the beans are cooking, sauté the almonds in the butter over medium heat, stirring frequently.

3. When the beans are done and the almonds are golden, drain the water off of the beans and pour the almonds and butter over them; use a scraper to get all the butter. Toss the mixture, and serve.

Yield: 4 servings, each with 12 grams of carbohydrates and 4 grams of fiber, for a total of 8 grams of usable carbs and 6 grams of protein.

Green Beans Pecandine. Make this exactly as you would Green Beans Almondine, only substitute 1/2 cup of chopped pecans for the slivered almonds. Just as good!

Yield: 4 servings, each with 11 grams of carbohydrates and 4 grams of fiber, for a total of 7 grams of usable carbs and 3 grams of protein.

Cashew Green Beans. This tasty twist comes from a reader known only as Starrc—thanks, whoever you are! Make as you would Green Beans Almondine, but substitute 1/2 cup of raw cashew pieces for the almonds.

Yield: 4 servings, each with 13 grams of carbohydrates and 4 grams of fiber, for a total of 9 grams usable carbs and 5 grams of protein.

↻ Lemon Pepper Beans

I think this makes a particularly good side dish with chicken or fish.

> 1 bag (1 pound) frozen green beans, French cut or crosscut, thawed
>
> 1/4 cup olive oil
>
> 1 clove garlic, crushed
>
> 1 tablespoon lemon juice
>
> 1/4 teaspoon pepper

Over high heat, stir-fry the beans in the olive oil until they're tender-crisp. Stir in the garlic, lemon juice, and pepper. Cook just another minute, and serve.

Yield: 4 servings, each with 9 grams of carbohydrates and 3 grams of fiber, for a total of 6 grams of usable carbs and 2 grams of protein.

↻ Herbed Green Beans

> 3 tablespoons butter
>
> 1 bag (1 pound) frozen, crosscut green beans, thawed
>
> 1/4 cup finely diced celery
>
> 1/4 cup finely diced onion
>
> 1 clove garlic, crushed
>
> 1/2 teaspoon dried rosemary, slightly crushed
>
> 1/2 teaspoon dried basil, slightly crushed
>
> Salt

1. Melt the butter in a heavy skillet over medium heat. Add the beans, celery, onion, and garlic to the skillet, and sauté until the beans are tender-crisp.

2. Stir in the rosemary and basil, and sauté another minute or so. Salt to taste, and serve.

Yield: 4 servings, each with 10 grams of carbohydrates and 4 grams of fiber, for a total of 6 grams of usable carbs and 2 grams of protein.

ꙮ Italian Bean Bake

If you're having a roast, simplify your life by serving this dish—it can cook right alongside the meat.

> 1 bag (1 pound) frozen Italian green beans, thawed
>
> 2 cans (8 ounces) tomato sauce
>
> 1/4 small onion, minced
>
> 1 clove garlic, crushed
>
> 1 teaspoon spicy brown or Dijon mustard
>
> Pepper
>
> 1/2 cup shredded mozzarella

1. Preheat the oven to 350°F.
2. Put the beans in an 8-cup casserole.
3. Combine the tomato sauce, onion, garlic, mustard, and a dash of pepper in a mixing bowl; stir into the beans.
4. Bake for 1 hour, or until the beans are tender, and then top with mozzarella and bake for another 3 to 5 minutes, or until the cheese is melted. Serve.

Yield: 4 servings, each with 12 grams of carbohydrates and 4 grams of fiber, for a total of 8 grams of usable carbs and 6 grams of protein.

🍓 If you're not serving a roast and you'd like to slice a half-hour off the baking time for this dish, microwave the beans until they're tender-crisp before you combine them with the sauce.

∽ Greek Beans

 2 tablespoons olive oil

 1/2 small onion, finely minced

 1 clove garlic, crushed

 1 bag (1 pound) frozen, cut green beans, thawed

 1/2 cup diced canned tomatoes

 1/4 cup beef broth or bouillon

 1/4 cup dry white wine

1. Heat the oil in a large, heavy skillet over medium heat. Add the onion and garlic, and sauté for a minute or two.

2. Drain the beans and add them to the skillet, stirring to coat. Sauté the beans for 6 to 7 minutes, adding another tablespoon of oil if the skillet starts to get dry.

3. Stir in the tomatoes, broth, and wine. Turn up the heat to medium-high, and let everything simmer until the beans are just tender-crisp and most of the liquid has cooked off (about 5 minutes).

Yield: 4 servings, each with 11 grams of carbohydrates and 3 grams of fiber, for a total of 8 grams of usable carbs and 3 grams of protein.

∽ Green Beans Vinaigrette

 1 bag (1 pound) frozen, cut green beans, thawed

 4 tablespoons butter

 4 tablespoons Italian Vinaigrette Dressing (see page 232, or use bottled)

Sauté the green beans in the butter in a large, heavy skillet set over medium-high heat. When they're not quite tender-crisp, stir in the dressing, and simmer for another 5 to 7 minutes. Serve.

Yield: 4 servings, each with 9 grams of carbohydrates and 3 grams of fiber, for a total of 6 grams of usable carbs and 2 grams of protein.

⟳ Green Beans a la Carbonara

Bacon, cheese, and garlic—if these three things won't get your family to eat green beans, nothing will. Another great recipe from the *Low Carb Success Calender* by Vicki Cash, this has enough protein to be a main dish.

7 to 10 thick strips of bacon

1 teaspoon olive oil

1/2 small onion, chopped

1 clove garlic, minced

1 bag (1 pound) frozen green beans

6 eggs

3 tablespoons cream

1/2 teaspoon red pepper flakes

1/4 teaspoon nutmeg

Salt and pepper

3/4 cup grated Parmesan cheese

1. Fry the bacon slices in a large, nonstick skillet over medium heat until they're not quite crisp. Drain on paper towels, and sauté the onion and garlic in the remaining bacon grease until brown.

2. Place the green beans in a 2-quart microwave-safe bowl with 1 tablespoon of water. Cover and microwave on high for 10 minutes, turning halfway through cooking.

3. While the beans are cooking, dice the bacon and add it to the onion and garlic. Keep the skillet over a warm burner. Beat together the eggs, cream, pepper flakes, nutmeg, and salt and pepper to taste, as if you were preparing scrambled eggs.

4. Turn the heat under the skillet up to medium. Add the egg mixture, hot green beans, and Parmesan to the skillet, stirring until the eggs are thoroughly cooked. Serve immediately.

Yield: 4 servings, each with 12 grams of carbohydrates and 3 grams of fiber, for a total of 9 grams of usable carbs and 27 grams of protein.

↻ Fried Brussels Sprouts

We've served these to company many times, and they're always a hit, even with people who think they don't like brussels sprouts. We didn't think we liked brussels sprouts, either, until our dear friends John and Judy Horwitz served them to us this way—and suddenly we were addicted.

> 1 pound brussels sprouts (fresh is best, but frozen will do)
> Olive oil
> 3 or 4 cloves garlic, crushed

1. If you're using fresh brussels sprouts, remove any bruised, wilted, or discolored outer leaves, and trim the stems. If you're using frozen brussels sprouts, just thaw them.

2. In a heavy-bottomed pot or skillet, heat 1/2 inch of olive oil over a medium flame. Add the brussels sprouts and fry them, stirring occasionally, until they are very dark brown all over—you really want them just about burned.

3. For the last minute or so, add the garlic and stir it around well. Remove the skillet from the heat and serve the sprouts before the garlic burns. Unbelievable!

Yield: Technically 4 servings, but my husband and I can easily eat a pound of these between the two of us. Assuming you can bring yourself to share with 3 other people, you'll each get 10 grams of carbohydrates with 4 grams of fiber per serving, for a total of 6 grams of usable carbs and 4 grams of protein.

↻ Simple Sprouts

> 1 pound brussels sprouts
> 3 to 4 tablespoons butter

1. Trim the stems of your brussels sprouts, and remove any wilted or yellowed leaves. Thinly slice the sprouts using the slicing blade of a food processor.

2. Melt the butter in a heavy skillet, and sauté the brussels sprouts over medium-high heat until they're tender but not mushy (about 7 to 10 minutes). They should be getting a few brown spots around the edges. Serve.

Yield: 4 servings, each with 9 grams of carbohydrates and 4 grams of fiber, for a total of 5 grams of usable carbs and 4 grams of protein.

Nutty Brussels Sprouts

> 1 pound brussels sprouts
>
> 1/2 cup hazelnuts
>
> 6 tablespoons butter
>
> 4 slices bacon
>
> 1/4 teaspoon salt or Vege-Sal
>
> 1/8 teaspoon pepper

1. Trim the stems of your brussels sprouts, and remove any wilted or yellowed leaves. Thinly slice your brussels sprouts using the slicing blade of a food processor.

2. Chop the hazelnuts to a medium texture in a food processor.

3. Melt 2 tablespoons of the butter in a heavy skillet over medium heat, and add the hazelnuts. Sauté, stirring frequently, for about 7 minutes or until golden. Remove from the skillet, and set aside.

4. Cook the bacon, either using a separate skillet or the microwave. While the bacon is cooking, melt the remaining 4 tablespoons of butter over medium-high heat in the same skillet you used for the hazelnuts. Add the sliced brussels sprouts, and sauté, stirring frequently, for 7 to 10 minutes, or until tender.

5. Stir in the toasted hazelnuts and the seasonings, and transfer to a serving dish. Drain the bacon, crumble it over the top, and serve.

Yield: 4 servings, each with 12 grams of carbohydrates and 5 grams of fiber, for a total of 7 grams of usable carbs and 8 grams of protein.

ᔕ 'Baga Fries

I'll bet you've never tried a rutabaga, and you're just guessing you're not going to like them. Well, everyone who tries these likes them.

2 pounds rutabaga

3 to 4 tablespoons butter

1. Peel your rutabaga and cut it into strips the size of big steak fries, using a good, big, heavy knife with a sharp blade.

2. Steam the "fries" over boiling water in a pan with a tight lid until they're easily pierced with a fork but not mushy (about 10 to 15 minutes). You want them still to be al dente.

3. Melt the butter in a heavy-bottomed skillet over medium-high heat, and fry the strips of rutabaga until they're browned on all sides. Salt and serve.

Yield: 6 servings, each with 12 grams of carbohydrates and 4 grams of fiber, for a total of 8 grams of usable carbs and 2 grams of protein.

ᔕ Glazed Turnips

These make wonderful substitute for potatoes with a roast.

3 cups chopped turnips, cut into small chunks

2 tablespoons butter

1/2 small onion

1 teaspoon Splenda

1/2 teaspoon liquid beef bouillon concentrate

1/8 teaspoon paprika

1. Steam or microwave the turnip chunks until tender (I steam mine in the microwave for about 7 minutes on High), then drain.

2. Melt the butter in a heavy skillet over medium heat. Add the turnips and onion, and sauté until the onion is limp.

3. Stir in the Splenda, bouillon concentrate, and paprika, coating all the turnips, and sauté for just another minute or two.

Yield: 6 servings, each with 12 grams of carbohydrates and 3 grams of fiber, for a total of 9 grams of usable carbs and 2 grams of protein.

↷ Mashed Garlic Turnips

Great with a steak, a roast, or chops.

> 2 pounds turnips, peeled and cut into chunks
>
> 8 cloves garlic, peeled and sliced
>
> 2 tablespoons butter
>
> 2 tablespoons prepared horseradish
>
> 1 teaspoon salt or Vege-Sal
>
> 1/2 teaspoon pepper
>
> 1/8 teaspoon ground nutmeg
>
> 3 tablespoons chopped fresh chives

1. Place the turnips and the garlic in a saucepan with a tight-fitting lid. Add water to fill about halfway, cover, and place over medium-high heat. Bring to a boil, turn down the burner, and simmer until quite soft (about 15 minutes). Drain the turnips and garlic very well.

2. Using a potato masher, mash the turnips and garlic together. Stir in the butter, horseradish, salt, pepper, and nutmeg, and mix well. Just before serving, stir in the chives.

Yield: 6 servings, each with 10 grams of carbohydrates and 2 grams of fiber, for a total of 8 grams of usable carbs and 2 grams of protein.

↻ Turnips Au Gratin

This is sublime with top-quality Vermont Cheddar cheese, but you can make it with any good, sharp Cheddar.

> 2 pounds turnips, peeled and thinly sliced
>
> 1 cup heavy cream
>
> 1 cup half-and-half
>
> 3 cups shredded sharp Cheddar cheese
>
> 2 teaspoons prepared horseradish
>
> 1/4 teaspoon ground nutmeg
>
> 1/2 medium onion, sliced
>
> Salt and pepper

1. Preheat the oven to 350°F.

2. Steam the turnips until they're just tender (I steam mine in the microwave for 7 minutes on High).

3. While the turnips are cooking, combine the heavy cream and half-and-half in a saucepan over very low heat. Bring to a simmer.

4. When the cream is up to temperature, whisk in 2 2/3 cups of the cheese, a couple of tablespoons at a time. Stir each addition until it's completely melted before adding more. When all of the cheese is melted into the sauce, whisk in the horseradish and nutmeg. Turn off the burner.

5. Spray an 8 x 8-inch glass baking dish with nonstick cooking spray. Put about one-third of the turnips in the dish, and scatter half of the sliced onion over it. Add another layer of one-third of the turnips, half of the onions, and the final third of the turnips on top. Pour the cheese sauce over the whole thing, and scatter the last 1/3 cup of cheese over the top. Bake for 30 to 40 minutes, or until golden.

Yield: 6 servings, each with 12 grams of carbohydrates and 2 grams of fiber, for a total of 10 grams of usable carbs and 17 g of protein.

ᔕ Indian Cabbage

Good with anything curried. This combination of seasonings works
well with green beans, too.

> Oil or butter
>
> 1 teaspoon black mustard seed
>
> 1 teaspoon turmeric
>
> 4 cups shredded cabbage
>
> 1 teaspoon salt or Vege-Sal

1. Put a heavy skillet over medium heat. Add a few tablespoons of oil or butter (I like to use coconut oil), and then the mustard seed and the turmeric. Sauté together for just a minute.

2. Stir in the cabbage, add the salt or Vege-Sal, and stir-fry for a few minutes, combining the cabbage well with the spices.

3. Add a couple of tablespoons of water, cover, and let the cabbage steam for a couple more minutes, until it is tender-crisp.

Yield: 4 servings, each with 4 grams of carbohydrates and 2 grams of fiber, for a total of 2 grams of usable carbs and 1 gram of protein.

ᔕ Sweet-and-Sour Cabbage

> 3 slices bacon
>
> 4 cups shredded cabbage
>
> 2 tablespoons cider vinegar
>
> 2 teaspoons Splenda

1. In a heavy skillet, cook the bacon until crisp. Remove and drain.

2. Add the cabbage to the bacon grease, and sauté it until tender-crisp.

3. Stir in the vinegar and Splenda, crumble in the bacon, and serve.

Yield: 4 servings, each with 4 grams of carbohydrates and 2 grams of fiber, for a total of 2 grams of usable carbs and 2 grams of protein.

꩜ Thai Stir-Fried Cabbage

This exotic and tasty dish cooks lightening-fast, so make sure you have everything cut up, mixed up, and ready to go before you start stir-frying.

> 2 tablespoons lime juice
>
> 2 tablespoons Thai fish sauce (nam pla)
>
> 2/3 teaspoon red pepper flakes
>
> Peanut, canola, or coconut oil
>
> 6 cups finely shredded napa cabbage
>
> 6 scallions, sliced
>
> 2 cloves garlic, crushed
>
> 1/3 cup unsweetened, flaked coconut
>
> 1/4 cup chopped, dry-roasted peanuts

1. Mix together the lime juice, fish sauce, and red pepper flakes. Set aside.

2. In a wok or heavy-bottomed skillet, heat a few tablespoons of oil over high heat. Add the cabbage, scallions, and garlic, and stir-fry for no more than 5 minutes, or just until the cabbage is hot through.

3. Add the step 1 mixture to the cabbage, and stir to coat. Let it cook just another minute, and stir in the coconut. Serve topped with peanuts.

Yield: 4 servings, each with 13 grams of carbohydrates and 4 grams of fiber, for a total of 9 grams of usable carbs and 5 grams of protein.

◯ Ratatouille

You pronounce this oh-so-French dish "rat-a-TOO-ee."

3/4 cup olive oil

3 cups chopped eggplant, cut into 1-inch cubes

3 cups sliced zucchini

1 medium onion, sliced

2 green peppers, cut into strips

3 cloves garlic

1 can (14 1/2 ounces) sliced tomatoes

1 can (4 ounces) sliced black olives, drained

1 1/2 teaspoons dried oregano

1/2 teaspoon salt

1/4 teaspoon pepper

1. Heat the oil in a heavy skillet over medium heat. Add the eggplant, zucchini, onion, peppers, and garlic.

2. Sauté for 15 to 20 minutes, turning with a spatula from time to time so it all comes in contact with the olive oil. Once the vegetables are all starting to look about half-cooked, add the tomatoes (including the liquid), olives, oregano, salt, and pepper.

3. Stir it all together, cover, turn the burner to low, and let the whole thing simmer for 40 minutes or so.

Yield: 8 servings, each with 11 grams of carbohydrates and 3 grams of fiber, for a total of 8 grams of usable carbs and 2 grams of protein.

🍓 You want to use your largest skillet for this dish—possibly even your wok, if you have one. This amount of veggies will cause even a 10-inch skillet to nearly overflow. And don't be afraid to toss in a little more olive oil if you need it while sautéing.

↻ Zucchini-Mushroom Skillet

       1 large or 2 medium zucchini

       8 ounces mushrooms

       1 medium onion

       1/2 cup olive oil

       2 cloves garlic, crushed

       1/2 teaspoon oregano

       Salt

1. Halve the zucchini lengthways, then cut into 1-inch sections. Wipe the mushrooms clean with a damp cloth, then quarter them vertically. Halve the onion, and cut it into slices about 1/4 inch thick.

2. Heat the olive oil in a heavy skillet over medium-high heat. Add the zucchini, mushrooms, onion, and garlic, and stir-fry until the zucchini and mushrooms are just barely tender and the onion is tender-crisp (about 10 minutes).

3. Stir in the oregano, salt to taste, and serve.

Yield: 4 servings, each with 7 grams of carbohydrates and 2 grams of fiber, for a total of 5 grams of usable carbs and 2 grams of protein.

↻ Snow Peas, Mushrooms, and Bean Sprouts

The combination of flavors here is magical, somehow; these three vegetables seem to be made for each other.

       3 tablespoons peanut oil

       4 ounces fresh snow peas

       4 ounces fresh mushrooms, sliced

       4 ounces fresh bean sprouts

       1 teaspoon soy sauce

1. Heat the oil in a wok or heavy skillet over high heat. Add the snow peas and mushrooms, and stir-fry until the snow peas are almost tender-crisp (3 to 4 minutes).

2. Add the bean sprouts, and stir-fry for just another 30 seconds to 1 minute.

3. Stir in the soy sauce, and serve.

Yield: 3 servings, each with 7 grams of carbohydrates and 2 grams of fiber, for a total of 5 grams of usable carbs and 3 grams of protein.

↻ Buttered Snow Peas

If you've only had snow peas in Chinese food, try them this way.
They're really wonderful.

> 4 tablespoons butter
>
> 12 ounces fresh snow peas

1. Melt the butter in a heavy skillet over medium-high heat.
2. Add the snow peas, and sauté just until tender-crisp.

Yield: 3 servings, each with 9 grams of carbohydrates and 3 grams of fiber, for a total of 6 grams of usable carbs and 3 grams of protein.

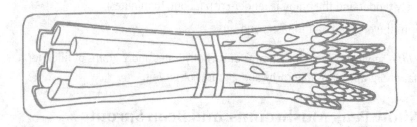

About Cooking Asparagus

Asparagus is divine if cooked correctly, and mushy and nasty if overcooked—and it's way too easy to overcook. If you're cooking it on the stove top, the best way, believe it or not, is standing up in an old stove top coffee perker with the guts removed. This lets the tougher ends boil while the tender tips steam. I put my asparagus in the coffee pot, add about 3 inches of water, and put on the lid. Set it over a medium-high burner, and bring the water to a boil. Once it's boiling, 5 minutes is plenty!

If you don't have a coffee perker (or an asparagus pot, for that matter, which lets you do the same thing), I'd recommend that you microwave your asparagus. Place the stems in a microwave-safe casserole or glass pie plate. If you're using a pie plate or a round casserole, arrange the asparagus with the tips toward the center. (I've microwaved asparagus in a rectangular casserole, and it's come out fine.) Add a tablespoon or two of water, and cover with plastic wrap or a lid, if your casserole has one. Microwave it on High for 5 to 6 minutes, then remove the plastic wrap or lid immediately, or the trapped steam will keep cooking your asparagus.

One more asparagus note: Believe it or not, the proper way to eat asparagus is with your fingers, dipping it in whatever sauce may be provided. This is according to Miss Manners, Amy Vanderbilt, and all other etiquette authorities. It's definitely more fun than using a fork—the kids may even take to asparagus this way—and it's amusing to see people look at you, thinking, "With her fingers?" knowing all along that you are correct and they are incorrect.

Asparagus with Lemon Butter

To me, this is the taste of springtime.

>   1 pound asparagus
>   1/4 cup butter
>   1 tablespoon lemon juice

1. Break the ends off the asparagus where they snap naturally. Steam or microwave the asparagus until just barely tender-crisp.

2. While the asparagus is cooking, melt the butter and stir in the lemon juice. Put the lemon butter in a pretty little pitcher, and let each diner pour a pool of it onto his or her plate for dipping.

   Yield: 4 servings, each with 5 grams of carbohydrates and 2 grams of fiber, for a total of 3 grams of usable carbs and 3 grams of protein.

Asparagus with Aioli and Parmesan

Cold asparagus, dipped in garlic sauce and cheese…yum.

> 2 pounds asparagus
> Aioli (see page 408)
> 1/2 cup grated Parmesan cheese

1. Break the ends off the asparagus where they snap naturally. Steam or microwave the asparagus for a bare 3 to 4 minutes, or just until the color brightens. (You want these even less done than tender-crisp.) Chill the asparagus.

2. At dinnertime, give each diner a couple of tablespoons of aioli and a little hill of Parmesan. Dip each asparagus stalk in the aioli, then in the Parmesan, and eat.

Yield: 4 servings, each with 6 grams of carbohydrates and 2 grams of fiber, for a total of 4 grams of usable carbs and 5 grams of protein.

Asparagus Pecandine

I never thought anything could be as good with asparagus as lemon butter is—and then I tried this.

> 5 tablespoons butter
> 1/2 cup chopped pecans
> 1 1/2 teaspoons tarragon vinegar
> 1 pound asparagus, steamed just until tender-crisp

1. Melt the butter in a heavy skillet over medium-high heat. Stir in the pecans and sauté, stirring frequently, for 5 to 7 minutes, or until the pecans are golden and crisp through. Stir in the tarragon vinegar.

2. Place the asparagus on serving plates, and spoon the sauce over it. Serve immediately.

Yield: 4 servings, each with 8 grams of carbohydrates and 4 grams of fiber, for a total of 4 grams of usable carbs and 4 grams of protein.

Garlic Asparagus

> 1 pound fresh asparagus
> 1/4 cup olive oil
> 2 cloves garlic, crushed

1. Break the ends off the asparagus where they snap naturally. Cut asparagus on the diagonal into 1-inch lengths.

2. Heat the olive oil in a heavy skillet over medium-high heat. Add the asparagus, and sauté, stirring occasionally, until it is tender-crisp (6 to 8 minutes).

3. Stir in the garlic, sauté 1 minute more, and serve.

Yield: 4 servings, each with 6 grams of carbohydrates and 2 grams of fiber, for a total of 4 grams of usable carbs and 3 grams of protein.

Fried Artichokes

This is one of the fastest ways I know to cook artichokes.

> 1 large artichoke
> Olive oil
> Lemon wedges
> Salt

1. Cut about 1 inch off the top of your artichoke, trim the stem, and pull off the bottom few rows of leaves. Now slice it vertically down the center. You'll see the "choke"—the fuzzy, inedible part at the center. Using the tip of a spoon, scrape every last bit of this out (it pulls off of the yummy bottom part of the artichoke quite easily).

2. In a large, heavy skillet, heat 1 inch of olive oil over medium-high heat. When the oil is hot, add your cleaned artichoke, flat side down. Fry for about 10 minutes, turning over halfway through. It should be tender, and just starting to brown a bit. Drain on paper towels or a brown paper bag.

3. Serve the artichoke halves with lemon wedges to squeeze over them and salt to sprinkle on them to taste.

Yield: 1 serving, with 13 grams of carbohydrates and a whopping 7 grams of fiber, for a total of 6 grams of usable carbs (a couple of teaspoons of lemon juice add just 1 more gram) and 4 grams of protein.

🍓 If you've never encountered a fresh artichoke, you'll probably be surprised
to find that they're sort of fun to eat: You peel off the leaves, one by one,
and drag the base of each one between your teeth, scraping off the little bit
of edible stuff and the bottom of each leaf. When you've finished doing
that and you have a big pile of artichoke leaves on your plate, use a fork
and knife to eat the delectable heart.

↻ Artichokes with Aioli

Artichokes with a rich, garlicky sauce—what's not to like?

> 6 artichokes
> Salt
> 1 batch Aioli (see page 408)

1. Cut about 1 inch off the top of each artichoke, trim the stems, and pull off the
   bottom few rows of leaves.

2. Put enough water to cover the artichokes in a good-size kettle, and bring it to a boil.
   Add a couple of teaspoons of salt, and drop in your artichokes.

3. Turn the burner down, and let the artichokes simmer until they're tender.
   Depending on how big they are, this could take anywhere from 15 to 45 minutes.
   When the artichokes are done, drain them well.

4. Divide the aioli between four small dishes, and put a dish of aioli and an artichoke
   on each serving plate.

Yield: 6 servings, each with 15 grams of carbohydrates and 7 grams of fiber, for a
total of 8 grams of usable carbs and 5 grams of protein.

🍓 Peel off the leaves, one by one, and dip the tender, edible bottom ends
in the aioli, then scrape them between your teeth. Each diner will need
to cut or scrape off the fuzzy "choke" after eating all the leaves. They can
then use a knife and fork to cut up the artichoke's heart and dip it in the
remaining aioli.

↻ Stir-Fried Spinach

Spinach originated in Asia, so stir-frying it is a very traditional way of preparing it.

> 1/4 cup peanut oil
>
> 2 pounds fresh spinach, washed and dried
>
> 2 cloves garlic, crushed

Heat the oil in a heavy skillet or wok over high heat. Add the spinach and garlic, and stir-fry for only a minute or two, then serve.

Yield: 6 servings, each with 6 grams of carbohydrates and 4 grams of fiber, for a total of 2 grams of usable carbs and 4 grams of protein.

↻ Sicilian Spinach

> 3 tablespoons butter
>
> 2 pounds fresh spinach, washed and dried
>
> 1 clove garlic, crushed
>
> 1 or 2 anchovy fillets, finely chopped

1. Heat the butter in a heavy skillet. Add the spinach and garlic, and sauté until the spinach is just limp.

2. Stir in the anchovies, and serve.

Yield: 6 servings, each with 5 grams of carbohydrates and 4 grams of fiber, for a total of just 1 gram of usable carbs and 5 grams of protein.

> 🍓 Not everyone likes anchovies, and if you're among those who don't, just leave them out.

Creamed Spinach

    1 package (10 ounces) frozen, chopped spinach, thawed

    1/4 cup heavy cream

    1/4 cup grated Parmesan cheese

    1 clove garlic, crushed

Put all the ingredients in a heavy-bottomed saucepan over medium-low heat, and simmer for 7 to 8 minutes.

Yield: 3 servings, each with 5 grams of carbohydrates and 3 grams of fiber, for a total of 2 grams of usable carbs and 6 grams of protein.

Greek Spinach

    1 tablespoon butter

    1/4 small onion, minced

    1 package (10 ounces) frozen, chopped spinach, thawed

    1/4 cup crumbled feta cheese

    1/4 cup cottage cheese

1. Melt the butter in a heavy skillet over medium heat. Add the onion, and let it sizzle for just a minute. Add the spinach and sauté, stirring now and then, for 5 to 7 minutes.

2. Add in the cheeses and stir until they start to melt. Let the spinach cook for another minute or so, then serve.

Yield: 3 servings, each with 6 grams of carbohydrates and 3 grams of fiber, for a total of 3 grams of usable carbs and 7 grams of protein.

⌒ Sag Paneer

With cottage cheese, this isn't totally authentic, but it's mighty tasty.

> 2 tablespoons butter
>
> 1 teaspoon curry powder
>
> 1 package (10 ounces) frozen, chopped spinach, thawed
>
> 1 teaspoon salt or Vege-Sal
>
> 1/3 cup small-curd cottage cheese
>
> 2 teaspoons sour cream

1. Melt the butter in a heavy skillet over low heat, and stir in the curry powder. Let the curry powder cook in the butter for 3 to 4 minutes.

2. Stir in the spinach and the salt. Cover the skillet, and let the spinach cook for 4 to 5 minutes, or until heated through.

3. Stir in the cottage cheese and sour cream, and cook, stirring, until the cheese has completely melted.

Yield: 3 servings, each with 5 grams of carbohydrates and 3 grams of fiber, for a total of 2 grams of usable carbs and 6 grams of protein.

About Cooking Broccoli

If you're using fresh broccoli, cut it up and peel the stems. If you've been discarding the stems, you'll be startled to discover that they're the best part of the broccoli once you've peeled off the tough skin.

Broccoli is another vegetable that's great when it's cooked just barely enough, but revolting when it's overcooked. I often think that the reason there are so many broccoli-haters in the world is because they've only been exposed to mushy, sulfurous, gray, overcooked broccoli. So above all, don't overcook your broccoli!

You can steam or microwave broccoli interchangeably. If you're steaming, start timing after the water comes to a boil. Fresh broccoli needs about 7 minutes and frozen broccoli (assuming you start with it still frozen) needs 10 or 11 minutes. If you're microwaving your broccoli (my favorite way to cook it), put it in a microwave-safe casserole, add a tablespoon or two of water, and cover with plastic wrap or a lid. Microwave on High for about 5 minutes for fresh broccoli or closer to 10 minutes for frozen, stirring halfway through to make sure it cooks evenly. However you cook your broccoli, uncover it as soon as it reaches the degree of doneness you prefer, or it will continue to cook and end up mushy.

⟲ Broccoli with Lemon Butter

I'm always bemused when I see frozen broccoli with lemon butter at the grocery store. I mean, how hard is it to add butter and lemon juice to your broccoli?

> 1 pound frozen broccoli or 1 large head fresh broccoli
>
> 4 tablespoons butter
>
> 1 tablespoon lemon juice

Steam or microwave your broccoli. When it's cooked, drain off the water, and toss the broccoli with the butter and lemon juice until the butter is melted. That's it!

Yield: 4 servings, each with 6 grams of carbohydrates and 3 grams of fiber, for a total of 3 grams of usable carbs and 3 grams of protein.

↻ Broccoli Piquant

This is a country-style dish that's good with pork chops.

    1 bag (1 pound) frozen broccoli "cuts"
    4 slices bacon
    1 clove garlic, crushed
    3 tablespoons cider vinegar

1. Steam or microwave the broccoli until just tender-crisp.

2. While the broccoli is cooking, fry the bacon until crisp, remove from the pan, and drain. Pour off all but a couple of tablespoons of the fat.

3. When the broccoli is cooked, drain and add it to the bacon fat in the skillet. Add the garlic and vinegar, and stir over medium heat for a minute or two.

4. Crumble the bacon over the broccoli, stir for another minute or so, and serve.

Yield: 4 servings, each with 7 grams of carbohydrates and 3 grams of fiber, for a total of 4 grams of usable carbs and 5 grams of protein.

↻ Ginger Stir-Fry Broccoli

    2 to 3 tablespoons peanut oil or other bland oil
    2 cloves garlic, crushed
    1 bag (1 pound) frozen broccoli "cuts," thawed
    1 tablespoon grated fresh ginger
    1 tablespoon soy sauce

1. Heat the peanut oil in a wok or heavy skillet over high heat. Add the garlic and the broccoli, and stir-fry for 7 to 10 minutes, or until the broccoli is tender-crisp.

2. Stir in the ginger and soy sauce, stir-fry for just another minute, and serve.

Yield: 4 servings, each with 7 grams of carbohydrates and 3 grams of fiber, for a total of 4 grams of usable carbs and 4 grams of protein.

About Cooking Spaghetti Squash

If you've never cooked a spaghetti squash, you may be puzzled as to how to go about it, but it's really easy: Just stab it several times (to keep it from exploding), and put it in your microwave on High for 12 to 15 minutes. Then slice it open, and scoop out and discard the seeds. Now take a fork and start scraping at the "meat" of the squash. You will be surprised and charmed to discover that it separates into strands very much like spaghetti, only yellow-orange in color.

Spaghetti squash is not a terribly low-carb vegetable, but it's much lower-carb than spaghetti, so it's a useful substitute in many recipes—especially casseroles. If you only need half of your cooked spaghetti squash right away, the rest will live happily in a zipper-lock bag in your fridge for 3 to 4 days until you do something else with it.

⌒ Spaghetti Squash Alfredo

We love this! My husband is an Alfredo fiend, so by using spaghetti squash instead of pasta, he gets his fix without all those additional carbs.

    2 cups cooked spaghetti squash

    3 tablespoons butter

    3 tablespoons heavy cream

    1 clove garlic, crushed

    1/4 cup grated or shredded Parmesan cheese

Simply heat up your squash, and stir in everything else. Stir until the butter is melted, and serve!

Yield: 4 servings, each with 4 grams of carbohydrates, a trace of fiber, and 3 grams of protein.

🍓 This makes a very nice side dish with some chicken sautéed in olive oil and garlic.

↻ Spaghetti Squash Carbonara

This makes a very filling side dish.

>8 slices bacon
>
>4 eggs
>
>3/4 cup grated Parmesan cheese
>
>3 cups cooked spaghetti squash
>
>1 clove garlic, crushed

1. Fry the bacon until it's crisp. Remove from pan, and pour off all but a couple tablespoons of grease.

2. Beat the eggs with the cheese, and toss with the spaghetti squash. Pour the squash mixture into the hot fat in the skillet, and add the garlic. Toss for 2 to 3 minutes.

3. Crumble in the bacon, toss, and serve.

Yield: 6 servings, each with 6 grams of carbohydrates and 1 gram of fiber, for a total of 5 grams of usable carbs and 11 grams of protein.

🍓 You can make this dish higher in protein by using a cup or two of diced, leftover ham in place of the bacon. Brown the ham in olive oil, remove from the pan, cook the squash mixture in the oil, and then toss in the ham just before serving.

Spicy Sesame "Noodles" with Vegetables

This isn't terribly low-carb, but it sure can pull you out of the hole when you've got vegetarians coming to dinner.

    3 cups cooked spaghetti squash
    1/4 cup water
    3 tablespoons soy sauce
    5 tablespoons tahini
    1 1/2 tablespoons rice vinegar
    1/2 teaspoon red pepper flakes
    1 tablespoon sesame seeds
    2 to 3 tablespoons peanut oil or other bland oil
    1 1/2 cups mushrooms, thickly sliced
    2/3 cup diced green pepper
    1/2 cup diced celery
    1/2 cup chopped onion
    1/4 pound snow peas, cut into 1-inch lengths
    2 tablespoons grated fresh ginger
    2 cloves garlic, crushed
    1/2 cup cooked shrimp or diced leftover chicken, pork,
        or ham per serving (optional)

1. Place the spaghetti squash in a large mixing bowl.

2. In a separate bowl, combine the water, soy sauce, tahini, rice vinegar, and pepper flakes, mixing well. Pour over the spaghetti squash, and set aside.

3. Place your sesame seeds in a small, heavy skillet over high heat, and shake the skillet constantly until the seeds start to "pop." They won't pop like popcorn, but they will make little popping sounds and jump in the skillet. When that happens, immediately turn off the heat and shake the seeds out onto a small plate to cool. Set aside.

4. Just before you're ready to serve the dish, heat the oil in a large skillet or wok. Add the mushrooms, pepper, celery, onion, snow peas, ginger, and garlic, and stir-fry over high heat for 7 to 10 minutes or until tender-crisp.

5. When the vegetables are done, add them to the large mixing bowl with the spaghetti squash mixture, and toss until well combined.

6. Pile the veggies and "noodles" on serving plates. Top the meat-eaters' servings with the shrimp, chicken, pork, or ham (if using), and scatter sesame seeds over each serving.

Yield: 4 servings, each with 19 grams of carbohydrates and 4 grams of fiber, for a total of 15 grams of usable carbs and 7 grams of protein. (Analysis does not include optional meat.)

🍓 This is a great dish to make for guests, because so much of it can be done ahead of time: You can prepare the noodles (step 2) and the garnish (step 3) before your company arrives, and then just stir-fry the veggies and garnish the plates when it's time to eat.

CHAPTER SIX

Side Dish Salads

I'm hard-pressed to think of a food that is more ill-done-by than salad. Way too many people dump some "iceberg mix" in a bowl, throw in some pink, mealy winter tomatoes, slosh some gooey bottled dressing on top, and then wail that their families show no enthusiasm for salad.

Made with just a little attention, salad is one of the most delicious, exciting foods imaginable. It is, of course, one of the most nutritious, as well, so learn to pay attention to your salads.

First of all, ditch the iceberg lettuce; not only is it the least-nutritious lettuce on the market, it's also the blandest. Try all sorts of other green and leafy things, such as romaine, Boston lettuce, butterhead, radicchio, frizzee, fresh spinach, or whatever else you can find. Try making some fresh dressings, too. And unless all the members of your family have violently opposing opinions on salad dressing, try actually tossing your salad with the dressing, instead of just sloshing it on top. I think you'll be surprised at the difference it makes in the end product.

The dressings, by the way, are at the end of this chapter. But let's get to the salads themselves right now.

↻ Greek Salad

This is a wonderful, filling, fresh-tasting salad we never get tired of.

> 1 large head romaine lettuce
>
> 1 cup chopped fresh parsley
>
> 1/2 cucumber, sliced
>
> 1 green pepper, sliced
>
> Greek Lemon Dressing (see page 233)
>
> 1/4 sweet red onion, thinly sliced into rings
>
> 12 to 15 Greek olives
>
> 2 ripe tomatoes, cut into wedges
>
> 4 to 6 ounces feta cheese, crumbled
>
> Anchovy fillets packed in olive oil (if desired)

1. Wash and dry your romaine, and break or cut it into bite-size pieces. Cut up and add the parsley, cucumber, and green pepper.

    🍓 You can do step 1 ahead of time, if you like, which makes this salad very doable on a weeknight.

2. Just before serving, pour on the Greek dressing, and toss the salad like crazy.

3. Arrange the onions, olives, and tomatoes artistically on top, and sprinkle the crumbled feta in the middle. You can also add the anchovies at this point, if you know that everybody likes them, but I prefer to make them available for those who like them to put on their individual serving.

Yield: 4 servings, each with 16 grams of carbohydrates and 6 grams of fiber, for a total of 10 grams of usable carbs and 11 grams of protein.

ꙅ Autumn Salad

The flavor contrasts in this salad are lovely, and I've kept the pear to a quantity that won't add too many carbs.

> 2 tablespoons butter
>
> 1/2 cup chopped walnuts
>
> 10 cups loosely packed assorted greens (romaine, red leaf lettuce, and fresh spinach)
>
> 1/4 sweet red onion, thinly sliced
>
> 1/4 cup olive oil
>
> 2 teaspoons wine vinegar
>
> 2 teaspoons lemon juice
>
> 1/4 teaspoon spicy brown or Dijon mustard
>
> 1/8 teaspoon salt
>
> 1/8 teaspoon pepper
>
> 1/2 ripe pear, chopped
>
> 1/3 cup crumbled blue cheese

1. Melt the butter in a small, heavy skillet over medium heat. Add the walnuts, and let them toast in the butter, stirring occasionally, for about 5 minutes.

2. While the walnuts are toasting—and make sure you keep an eye on them and don't burn them—wash and dry your greens, and put them in salad bowl with the onion. Toss with the oil first, then combine the vinegar, lemon juice, mustard, salt, and pepper, and add that to the salad bowl. Toss until everything is well covered.

3. Top the salad with the pear, the warm toasted walnuts, and the crumbled blue cheese; serve.

Yield: 4 generous servings, each with 13 grams of carbohydrates and 6 grams of fiber, for a total of 7 grams of usable carbs and 10 grams of protein.

◌ Arugula-Pear Salad

An extraordinary combination of flavors. If you've never tried arugula, you'll be surprised: It tastes almost as if it's been roasted. You could use grated Parmesan cheese, but I think the bigger pieces of thinly sliced Parmesan make a difference in the salad's flavor.

> 3 1/2 to 4 cups washed, dried, torn-up arugula
>
> 1/2 ripe pear, cut in small chunks or slices
>
> 3 tablespoons extra-virgin olive oil
>
> Juice of 1 lemon
>
> Salt and pepper
>
> 2 tablespoons very thinly sliced bits of Parmesan cheese

Combine the arugula and pear in a salad bowl. Add the olive oil, and toss well. Add the lemon juice, salt and pepper lightly, and toss again. Top with Parmesan, and serve.

Yield: 2 generous servings, each with 9 grams of carbohydrates and 2 grams of fiber, for a total of 7 grams of usable carbs and 3 grams of protein.

◌ Spinach Pecan Salad

> 2 pounds fresh spinach
>
> Salt or Vege-Sal
>
> 10 scallions, thinly sliced, including about 2 inches of the green sprout
>
> 1/4 cup extra-virgin olive oil
>
> 1/4 cup lemon juice
>
> 1/4 pound toasted, salted pecans, chopped

1. Wash and dry the spinach until you're absolutely sure it's clean—spinach can hold a lot of grit! When you're sure it's clean and dry, put it in a salad bowl, and sprinkle it with a little salt—maybe a teaspoonful—and squeeze the leaves gently with your hands. You'll find that the spinach "deflates," or sort of gets a bit limp and reduces in volume. Add the scallions to the bowl.

2. Pour on the olive oil, and toss the salad thoroughly. Add the lemon juice, and toss again. Top with the pecans, and serve.

Yield: 6 servings, each with 12 grams of carbohydrates and 6 grams of fiber, for a total of 6 grams of usable carbs and 6 grams of protein.

Classic Spinach Salad

4 cups fresh spinach

1/8 large, sweet red onion, thinly sliced

3 tablespoons oil

2 tablespoons apple cider vinegar

2 teaspoons tomato paste

1 1/2 teaspoons Splenda

1/4 small onion, grated

1/8 teaspoon dry mustard

Salt and pepper

2 slices bacon, cooked until crisp, and crumbled

1 hard-boiled egg, chopped

1. Wash the spinach very well, and dry. Tear up larger leaves. Combine with the onion in a salad bowl.

2. In a separate bowl, mix up the oil, vinegar, tomato paste, Splenda, onion, mustard, and salt and pepper to taste. Pour the mixture over the spinach and onion, and toss.

3. Top the salad with the bacon and egg, and serve.

Yield: 2 generous servings, each with 7 grams of carbohydrates and 2 grams of fiber, for a total of 5 grams of usable carbs and 2 grams of protein.

Summer Treat Spinach Salad

Worried about where you'll get your potassium now that you're not eating bananas? Each serving of this salad has more potassium than three bananas!

2 pounds raw spinach

1 ripe avocado

1/4 cantaloupe

1/2 cup alfalfa sprouts

2 scallions, sliced

French Vinaigrette Dressing (see page 232)

1. Wash the spinach very well, and dry. Tear up larger leaves.

2. Cut the avocado in half, remove the pit and the peel, and cut into chunks.

3. Peel and chunk the cantaloupe, or, if you want to be fancy, use a melon baller.

4. Add the avocado and cantaloupe to the spinach, along with the alfalfa sprouts and scallions. Toss with the vinaigrette right before serving.

   Yield: 6 servings, each with 11 grams of carbohydrates and 5 grams of fiber, for a total of 6 grams of usable carbs and 5 grams of protein.

ꙮ **Mixed Greens with Warm Brie Dressing**

This elegant dinner party fare is a carbohydrate bargain with lots of flavor.

> 1 1/2 quarts torn romaine lettuce, washed and dried
> 1 1/2 quarts torn red leaf lettuce, washed and dried
> 2 cups torn radicchio, washed and dried
> 1 cup chopped fresh parsley
> 4 scallions, thinly sliced, including the crisp part of the green shoot
> 1/2 cup extra-virgin olive oil
> 1/2 small onion, minced
> 3 cloves garlic, crushed
> 6 ounces Brie, rind removed, cut into small chunks
> 1/4 cup sherry vinegar
> 1 tablespoon lemon juice
> 1 1/2 teaspoons Dijon mustard

1. Put the lettuce, radicchio, parsley, and scallions in a large salad bowl, and keep cold.

2. Put the olive oil in a heavy-bottomed saucepan over medium-low heat. Add the onion and garlic, and let them cook for 2 to 3 minutes.

3. Melt in the Brie, one chunk at a time, continuously stirring with a whisk. (It'll look dreadful at first, but don't sweat it.)

4. When all the cheese is melted in, whisk in the sherry vinegar, lemon juice, and Dijon mustard. Let it cook for a few minutes, stirring all the while, until your dressing is smooth and thick. Pour over the salad and toss.

   Yield: 6 servings, each with 7 grams of carbohydrates and 3 of fiber, for a total of 4 grams of usable carbs and 8 grams of protein.

ᴐ Bayside Salad

This is my version of a fantastic salad I had at a restaurant called *The Bayside Grill*, down near the Gulf Coast. The combination of greens isn't vital—you can change it some, as long as you make sure to include some bitter greens, such as endive.

2 tablespoons butter

1/4 cup chopped pecans

2 cups torn romaine

1 cup torn radicchio

1 cup torn frizee

1 cup torn Boston lettuce

1 cup torn curly endive

1/4 sweet red onion, thinly sliced

Raspberry Vinaigrette (see page 237)

1/4 cup crumbled blue cheese

4 slices bacon, cooked until crisp

1. Melt the butter in a heavy skillet. Add the pecans and toast them over medium heat, stirring for 5 minutes or so, until brown and crisp.

2. Toss the romaine, radicchio, frizee, Boston lettuce, curly endive, and onion with the Raspberry Vinaigrette.

3. Pile the salad on 4 serving plates, and top each with 1 tablespoon of pecans, 1 tablespoon of blue cheese, and 1 crumbled slice of bacon.

Yield: 4 servings, each with 6 grams of carbohydrates and 2 grams of fiber, for a total of 4 grams of usable carbs and 2 grams of protein.

ꙮ Caesar Salad

This is the salad that made Tijuana restaurateur Caesar Cardini famous. If you've only had that wilted stuff that passes for Caesar salad on salad bars and buffets, you have to try this.

> 1 large head romaine lettuce
> Caesar Dressing (see page 239)

Wash, dry, and tear up an entire head of romaine lettuce. Toss it with the dressing. That's it!

Yield: 6 servings, each with 5 grams of carbohydrates and 2 grams of fiber, for a total of 3 grams of usable carbs and 6 grams of protein.

🍓 If you're feeling particularly spiffy and you have some low-carb bread on hand, you could dice up a couple of slices, put them in a pan with 1/4 cup of olive oil and a couple of cloves of garlic, and sauté them for a few minutes, until they're brown and crispy. But me, I'd only bother with that for company.

ꕥ Our Favorite Salad

We've served this salad over and over, and we never tire of it. This dressing tastes a lot like Caesar, but it's less trouble, and there's no blender to wash afterwards.

1 clove garlic

1/2 cup extra-virgin olive oil

1 head romaine

1/2 cup chopped fresh parsley

1/2 green pepper, diced

1/4 cucumber, quartered and sliced

1/4 sweet red onion

2 to 3 tablespoons lemon juice

2 to 3 teaspoons Worcestershire sauce

1/4 cup Parmesan cheese

1 medium ripe tomato, cut into thin wedges

1. Crush the clove of garlic in a small bowl, cover it with the olive oil, and set it aside.

2. Wash and dry your romaine, break it up into a bowl, and add the parsley, pepper, cucumber, and onion. Pour the garlic-flavored oil over the salad, and toss until every leaf is covered.

3. Sprinkle on the lemon juice, and toss again. Then sprinkle on the Worcestershire sauce, and toss again. Finally, sprinkle on the Parmesan, and toss one last time. Top with the tomatoes, and serve.

Yield: 6 servings, each with 7 grams of carbohydrates and 3 grams of fiber, for a total of 4 grams of usable carbs and 4 grams of protein.

Update Salad

This recipe went around in the 1960s, using curly endive instead of this mixture of bitter greens, and of course, using sugar in the dressing. I like to think I've brought it into the 21st century—hence the name.

Salad

2 medium green peppers, cut in smallish strips

1 large bunch parsley, chopped

$2/3$ cup torn radicchio

$2/3$ cup chopped curly endive

$2/3$ cup chopped frizee

3 tomatoes, each cut in 8 lengthwise wedges

$1/8$ of a large, sweet red onion, thinly sliced

2 tablespoons chopped black olives

Dressing

$1/4$ cup water

$1/2$ cup tarragon vinegar

$1/2$ teaspoon salt or Vege-Sal

1 $1/2$ tablespoons lemon juice

1 tablespoon Splenda

$1/8$ teaspoon blackstrap molasses

Topping

6 tablespoons sour cream

1. Put the peppers, parsley, radicchio, endive, frizee, tomatoes, onion, and olives in a big bowl, and set aside.

2. In a separate bowl, combine the water, vinegar, salt, lemon juice, Splenda, and molasses. Pour it all over the salad, and toss.

3. Stick the whole thing in the refrigerator, and let it sit there for a few hours, stirring it now and then if you think of it.

4. To serve, put a 1-tablespoon dollop of sour cream on each serving.

Yield: 6 servings, each with 9 grams of carbohydrates and 2 grams of fiber, for a total of 7 grams of usable carbs and 2 grams of protein.

Parsley Salad

If you've always thought of parsley as a garnish, it's time to start thinking of it as a food. It's delicious, and very, very nutritious.

> 3 tomatoes, diced
>
> 1 cucumber, peeled (if desired) and diced
>
> 3 scallions, sliced
>
> 1 bunch of parsley, stems removed, leaves chopped
>
> 1/4 cup fresh lemon juice
>
> 1/2 cup extra-virgin olive oil
>
> Salt and pepper
>
> 1 small can sliced black olives

1. Combine the tomatoes, cucumber, scallions, and parsley; chill.

2. Combine the lemon juice, olive oil, and salt and pepper to taste, and toss with the vegetables.

3. Top with the olives, and serve.

Yield: 4 servings, each with 10 grams of carbohydrates and 3 grams of fiber, for a total of 7 grams of usable carbs and 2 grams of protein.

ᐣ California Salad

    4 cups torn romaine lettuce
    4 cups torn red leaf lettuce
    1 ripe, black avocado
    3 tablespoons extra-virgin olive oil
    2 tablespoons lemon juice
    Salt and pepper
    1/2 cup alfalfa sprouts

1. Combine the romaine and red leaf lettuces in a salad bowl, then peel the avocado and cut it into small chunks. (It's easiest just to scoop out bits with a spoon.) Add the avocado to the bowl.

2. Toss the salad first with the oil, then the lemon juice, then finally with salt and pepper to taste. Top with the sprouts, and serve.

Yield: 4 servings, each with 12 grams of carbohydrates and 5 grams of fiber, for a total of 7 grams of usable carbs and 4 grams of protein.

🍓 If you're thinking about substituting a green avocado for the black one called for, remember that the little black avocados are substantially lower in carbs.

ᐣ Tomatoes Basilico

This is a simple, elegant summer classic, but you shouldn't even bother trying it with second-rate tomatoes.

    4 medium size, ripe tomatoes
    1/2 cup fresh, coarsely chopped basil

Slice the tomatoes and arrange them on a platter. Sprinkle the basil over them, and let the salad sit for a half-hour or so before serving.

Yield: 4 generous servings, each with 6 grams of carbohydrates and 2 grams of fiber, for a total of 4 grams of usable carbs and 1 gram of protein.

↺ Tomato-Mozzarella Plate

It's hard to know whether this is a salad or an appetizer. All that really matters is that it's good, and remarkably easy. The tomatoes you use must be superb, and you must use fresh mozzarella, not the cheap kind sold for pizza. Look for it in a tub of water in the fancy cheese case.

> 1/2 cup fresh, finely chopped basil
> 1/4 cup extra-virgin olive oil
> 1 pound fresh mozzarella
> 3 ripe tomatoes, sliced
> Fresh ground or coarsely ground pepper

1. Mix the basil with the olive oil, and set aside.

2. Cut 18 slices of mozzarella and tomatoes (6 slices from each tomato). Arrange three slices of tomato and three slices of mozzarella on each serving plate.

3. Spoon a couple of teaspoons of the basil and olive oil over each plate. Scatter just a tiny bit of pepper over each plate, and serve.

Yield: 6 servings, each with 5 grams of carbohydrates and 1 gram of fiber, for a total of 4 grams of usable carbs and 17 grams of protein.

↺ Melon with Prosciutto

Another dish that's hard to classify, this one is an Italian classic.

> 1 ripe cantaloupe
> 12 very thin slices prosciutto (6 to 8 ounces)

Cut your melon into 12 wedges, removing seeds and rind. Wrap each melon wedge in a slice of prosciutto. Serve and enjoy!

Yield: 12 servings, each with 4 grams of carbohydrates, a trace of fiber, and 6 grams of protein.

> 🍓 If you can't get real Italian prosciutto, you could use any good, thinly sliced deli ham.

↻ Melon Prosciutto Salad

  ¹/₂ ripe cantaloupe
  ¹/₂ ripe honeydew
  8 ounces prosciutto

1. Seed and peel the melons, and cut them into 1-inch chunks (or use a melon baller).
2. Chop the prosciutto, toss everything together, and serve.

  Yield: 10 servings, each with 8 grams of carbohydrates and 1 gram of fiber, for a total of 7 grams of usable carbs and 7 grams of protein.

Make-Ahead Salads

I just love deli-style salads—you know, the kind you can make ahead and just pull out of the refrigerator when you want them. There are so many varieties and they are so, so convenient. I like to make them in big batches. That way I have fast, easy vegetables for a few days.

Our first several make-ahead salads feature cucumbers—not only because cucumbers are delicious, but also because they're about the lowest-carb vegetable around!

○ Sour Cream and Cuke Salad

> 1 green pepper
>
> 2 cucumbers, scrubbed but not peeled
>
> 1/2 large, sweet red onion
>
> 1/2 head cauliflower
>
> 2 teaspoons salt or Vege-Sal
>
> 1 cup sour cream
>
> 2 tablespoons vinegar (apple cider vinegar is best, but wine vinegar will do)
>
> 2 rounded teaspoons dried dill weed

1. Slice the pepper, cucumbers, onion, and cauliflower as thinly as you possibly can. The slicing blade on a food processor works nicely, and it saves you mucho time, but I've also done it with a good, sharp knife.

2. Toss the vegetables well with the salt, and chill them in the refrigerator for an hour or two.

3. In a separate bowl, mix the sour cream, vinegar, and dill, combining well.

4. Remove the veggies from the fridge, drain off any water that has collected at the bottom of the bowl, and stir in the sour cream mixture.

Yield: 10 servings, each with 4 grams of carbohydrates and 1 gram of fiber, for a total of 3 grams of usable carbs and 1 gram of protein.

🍓 You can eat this right away and it will be great, but it improves overnight.

↻ Monica's In-Laws' Cucumber Salad

Monica is a reader who didn't send me her last name, but she did send me this great salad recipe.

>3 medium cucumbers, thinly sliced
>
>3 teaspoons salt
>
>1/4 cup Splenda
>
>1/4 cup vinegar
>
>1 cup sour cream
>
>1/2 cup finely chopped onion
>
>1 teaspoon chopped fresh dill weed
>
>Salt and pepper

1. Put the cukes in a large bowl, and sprinkle with the salt. Refrigerate for 1 to 2 hours.

2. Drain off any water that has collected at the bottom of the bowl, rinse, and drain again.

3. Dissolve the Splenda in the vinegar, whisk in the sour cream, onion, and dill, and fold the mixture into the cukes. Salt and pepper to taste, and serve.

Yield: 8 servings, each with 7 grams of carbohydrates and 1 gram of fiber, for a total of 6 grams of usable carbs and 2 grams of protein.

↻ Gorkensalad

From reader Heather Firth, who says this is "a really amazing cucumber salad. The cucumbers are limp but still crunchy."

   4 peeled cucumbers, thinly sliced

   1 1/2 tablespoons salt

   1/4 cup water

   3 tablespoons cider vinegar

   3 tablespoons oil

   2 tablespoons Splenda

   Pepper

1. Peel and slice the cucumbers. Put them in a large bowl and sprinkle the salt over them. Stir the salt into the cucumbers, cover, and refrigerate overnight.

2. An hour or so before serving, remove the cucumbers from the refrigerator and squeeze the water out of them, using your hands and working in small batches. The slices will go from kind of stiff and opaque to limp and almost translucent. Pour off the resulting water.

3. Mix together the water, vinegar, oil, and Splenda, and salt and pepper to taste. This is the "dressing"—it should be light, tangy, and just slightly sweet. Pour this over the cucumbers, and mix them up. Chill until ready to serve.

Yield: 10 servings, each with 4 grams of carbohydrates and 1 gram of fiber, for a total of 3 grams of usable carbs and 1 gram of protein.

Thai Cucumber Salad

Sweet and hot and so good! This, by the way, is one of those magnificent recipes that is low-carb, low-fat, low-calorie, okay for vegetarians, and tastes great.

   1/2 small red onion

   1 small, fresh jalapeño, seeds removed

   3 medium cucumbers

   2 or 3 cloves fresh garlic, crushed

   2 tablespoons grated fresh ginger

   1/2 cup rice vinegar

   1/2 teaspoon salt

   1/4 teaspoon pepper

   2 tablespoons Splenda

1. Using a food processor with the S blade in place, put the onion and jalapeño in the food processor, and pulse until they are both finely chopped.

2. Remove the S blade and put on the slicing disk. Quarter the cucumbers lengthwise, then run them through processer.

   🍓 If you're not using a food processor, you'll want to dice the onion and mince the jalapeño, then slice the cucumber as thin as you can.

3. Put the onion, jalapeño, and cucumbers in a big bowl. In a separate bowl, thoroughly combine the garlic, ginger, vinegar, salt, pepper, and Splenda. Pour over the vegetables, and mix well.

4. Chill for a few hours before serving, for the best flavor.

   Yield: 8 generous servings, each with 6 grams of carbohydrates and 1 gram of fiber, for a total of 5 grams of usable carbs and 1 gram of protein.

↩ Broccoli Salad

   1/2 cup olive oil

   1/4 cup vinegar

   1 clove garlic, crushed

   1/2 teaspoon Italian seasoning herb blend

   1/2 teaspoon salt or Vege-Sal

   1/8 teaspoon pepper

   4 cups frozen broccoli "cuts"

1. Whisk the olive oil, vinegar, garlic, herbs, salt, and pepper together.

2. Don't even bother to thaw the broccoli—just put it in a bowl, and pour the olive oil mixture on top of it. Mix well, and let it sit for several hours in the fridge. Stir it now and then if you think of it, and serve as is or on greens.

Yield: 6 servings, each with 7 grams of carbohydrates and 4 grams of fiber, for a total of 3 grams of usable carbs and 4 grams of protein.

🍓 Of course, if you prefer, you can use fresh broccoli to make this salad. You'll have to peel the stems, cut it up, and steam it for about 5 minutes first. And at that point, it will be very much like thawed frozen broccoli! Personally, I take the easy route.

↻ Parmesan Bean Salad

This salad is filling enough to make a nice light lunch.

　　　1 pound bag frozen, crosscut green beans

　　　1/2 cup minced red onion

　　　4 tablespoons extra-virgin olive oil

　　　5 tablespoons cider vinegar

　　　1/2 teaspoon salt or Vege-Sal

　　　1/2 teaspoon paprika

　　　1/4 teaspoon dried ginger

　　　3/4 cup grated Parmesan cheese

1. Steam or microwave the green beans until they're tender-crisp.

2. Let the beans cool a bit, then stir in the onion, oil, vinegar, salt, paprika, and ginger, then finally the Parmesan cheese. Chill well, and serve.

Yield: 4 servings, each with 12 grams of carbohydrates and 4 grams of fiber, for a total of 8 grams of usable carbs and 9 grams of protein.

↻ Low-Carb Rosy Radish Salad

This looks very pretty, and tastes surprisingly mild.

　　　1 bag (1 pound) frozen crosscut green beans

　　　4 slices bacon, cooked until crisp, and crumbled

　　　1 small onion, chopped

　　　1 cup sliced radishes

　　　3 tablespoons cider vinegar

　　　1 1/2 tablespoons Splenda

　　　3/4 teaspoon salt or Vege-Sal

　　　1/4 teaspoon pepper

1. Steam or microwave the beans until they're tender-crisp.

2. Combine the beans, bacon, onion, and radishes in a mixing bowl. In a separate bowl, combine the vinegar, Splenda, salt, and pepper.

3. Pour the mixture over the salad, toss, and serve.

Yield: 5 servings, each with 10 grams of carbohydrates and 3 grams of fiber, for a total of 7 grams of usable carbs and 4 grams of protein.

Colorful Bean Salad

 1 can (14 $1/2$ ounces) cut green beans
 1 can (14 $1/2$ ounces) cut wax beans
 $1/2$ cup chopped sweet red onion
 $3/4$ cup Splenda
 1 teaspoon salt
 $1/2$ teaspoon pepper
 $1/2$ cup canola oil
 $2/3$ cup cider vinegar

1. Drain the green and wax beans, and combine them in a bowl with the onion.

2. In a separate bowl, combine the Splenda, salt, pepper, oil, and vinegar; pour the mixture over the vegetables.

3. Let it marinate for several hours at least; overnight won't hurt. Drain off the marinade, and serve.

Yield: 4 generous servings. If you were to eat all of the marinade, this would have 17 grams of carbohydrates per serving, but since you don't, each serving actually has about 10 grams of carbohydrates and 4 grams of fiber, for a total of 6 grams of usable carbs and 2 grams of protein.

   If you like, you can make this with 1 $1/2$ cups each of frozen green and wax beans, cooked tender-crisp. This is certainly preferable to pouring the vitamins down the sink, the way you do with canned beans. Sadly, though, frozen wax beans aren't available in my neck of the woods. You could do it with fresh beans, too, but again, fresh wax beans are thin on the ground around here.

↷ Dilled Beans

Hard to say if this is a salad or a pickle, but whatever you call it, it's tasty.

> 1 bag (1 pound) frozen crosscut green beans
>
> 1/2 cup wine vinegar
>
> 1/2 cup water
>
> 1 clove garlic
>
> 2 teaspoons salt
>
> 2 teaspoons red pepper flakes
>
> 3 tablespoons dried dill weed

1. Steam or microwave the beans until they're tender-crisp.

2. While the beans are cooking, combine the vinegar, water, garlic, salt, pepper flakes, and dill in a small saucepan, and bring to a boil.

3. Drain the beans, and put them in a jar with a tight-fitting lid. Pour the vinegar mixture over the beans, and cover. Refrigerate for a day or two, shaking the jar whenever you think of it. Serve cold.

Yield: 8 servings, each with 6 grams of carbohydrates and 2 grams of fiber, for a total of 4 grams of usable carbs and 1 gram of protein.

ᔕ Sesame Asparagus Salad

This is from Jennifer Eloff's wonderful cookbook *Splendid Low-Carbing*.
Jen, of sweety.com, says it's simple, yet it has an eye-catching presentation.

> 1 pound fresh asparagus
>
> 5 cups water
>
> 4 teaspoons soy sauce
>
> 2 teaspoons sesame or olive oil
>
> 1 tablespoon sesame seeds

1. Break off the tough ends of the asparagus by bending each stalk back until it snaps.

2. Bring the water to a boil in a large saucepan, and drop the asparagus stalks into the rapidly boiling water. Parboil for 5 minutes, drain immediately, and rinse in cold water. Pat dry with paper towels.

3. Combine the soy sauce and oil in a small bowl. Lay the asparagus stalks in a casserole, and toss with the soy sauce mixture.

4. Sprinkle with the sesame seeds, and chill in the refrigerator for an hour or two before serving.

Yield: 6 servings, each with 2 grams of carbohydrates and 1 gram of fiber, for a total of 1 gram of usable carbs and 1 gram of protein.

ᔕ Coleslaw

This is my standard coleslaw recipe, and it always draws compliments.
The tiny bit of onion really sparks the flavor.

> 1 head green cabbage
>
> 1/4 sweet red onion
>
> Coleslaw Dressing (see page 240)

1. Using a food processor's slicing blade or a sharp knife, reduce your cabbage to little bitty shreds, and put those shreds in a great big bowl.

2. Mince the onion really fine, and put that in the bowl, too.

3. Pour on the dressing, and toss well.

Yield: 10 servings, each with 1 gram of carbohydrates, a trace of fiber, and 1 gram of protein.

🍓 Just get invited to a picnic, and short on time for making something that'll feed a crowd? This recipe makes a veritable bucketful, and it's a wonderful side dish to almost any plain meat, including chops and chicken. If you like, you could even use bagged coleslaw from the grocery store and just add my dressing; I promise not to tell!

ᔕ Coleslaw for Company

The colors in this slaw are so intense, it's almost too beautiful to eat.

> 1 head red cabbage
> 1 small carrot, shredded
> 1/4 sweet red onion, finely minced
> Coleslaw Dressing (see page 240)

1. Using a food processor's slicing blade or a sharp knife, shred your cabbage and put it in a big bowl.
2. Add the carrot and onion, and toss with the dressing. Admire, and enjoy.

Yield: 10 servings, each with 2 grams of carbohydrates, a trace of fiber, and 1 gram of protein.

ᔕ Coleslaw Italiano

My sister makes this recipe, and it's quite good.

> 4 cups shredded cabbage
> 1/2 cup Italian Vinaigrette Dressing (see page 232 or use bottled)

Toss the cabbage with the Italian dressing, and serve.

Yield: 8 servings, each with 3 grams of carbohydrates and 1 gram of fiber, for a total of 2 grams of usable carbs and 1 gram of protein.

Asian Ginger Slaw

Even my slaw-hating husband likes this! A very different texture and flavor than your standard slaw.

4 cups finely shredded napa cabbage

1/4 cup shredded carrot

2 scallions, thinly sliced

1/4 cup pale, inner celery stalk, thinly sliced

1/4 cup mayonnaise

1 teaspoon grated fresh ginger

2 tablespoons rice vinegar

1 teaspoon soy sauce

1 teaspoon Splenda

1. Combine the cabbage, carrot, scallions, and celery in a salad bowl.

2. In a separate bowl, combine the mayonnaise, ginger, vinegar, soy sauce, and Splenda. Beat together until smooth, pour over the vegetables, toss, and serve.

Yield: 8 servings, each with 4 grams of carbohydrates and 1 gram of fiber, for a total of 3 grams of usable carbs and 1 gram of protein.

↻ Confetti UnSlaw

This may be a raw cabbage salad, but it's not much like coleslaw. Plus, it's utterly gorgeous on the plate.

> 2 cups shredded green cabbage
>
> 2 cups shredded red cabbage
>
> 1/2 sweet red pepper, chopped
>
> 1/2 green pepper, chopped
>
> 4 scallions, sliced, including the crisp part of the green
>
> 1/3 cup grated carrot
>
> 1 small celery rib, thinly sliced
>
> 2 tablespoons minced fresh parsley
>
> Creamy Garlic Dressing (see page 238)

Just cut up and combine all these vegetables, and toss with the Creamy Garlic Dressing.

Yield: 8 servings, each with 6 grams of carbohydrates and 2 grams of fiber, for a total of 4 grams of usable carbs and 1 gram of protein.

↻ Cauliflower-Olive Salad

Unusual, and unusually good.

     1/2 head cauliflower, broken into small florets

     1/2 cup diced red onion

     1 can (2 1/4 ounces) sliced ripe olives, drained

     1/2 cup chopped fresh parsley

     1/4 cup lemon juice

     1/4 cup olive oil

     1/4 cup mayonnaise

     1/2 teaspoon salt or Vege-Sal

     About a dozen cherry tomatoes

     Lettuce (optional)

1. Combine the cauliflower, onion, olives, and parsley in a bowl.

2. Combine the lemon juice, olive oil, mayonnaise, and salt in a separate bowl. Pour over the veggies, and toss well.

3. Chill for at least an hour—a whole day wouldn't hurt a bit. When you're ready to serve the salad, cut the cherry tomatoes in half and add them to the salad. Serve on a bed of lettuce if you wish, but it's wonderful alone, too.

Yield: 4 servings, each with 7 grams of carbohydrates and 2 grams of fiber, for a total of 5 grams of usable carbs and 1 gram of protein.

↻ UnPotato Salad

You are going to be so surprised; this is amazingly like potato salad.

> 1 large head of cauliflower, cut into small chunks
>
> 2 cups diced celery
>
> 1 cup diced red onion
>
> 2 cups mayonnaise
>
> 1/4 cup cider vinegar
>
> 2 teaspoons salt or Vege-Sal
>
> 2 teaspoons Splenda
>
> 1/2 teaspoon pepper
>
> 4 hard-boiled eggs, chopped

1. Put the cauliflower in a microwave-safe casserole, add just a tablespoon or so of water, and cover. Cook it on High for 7 minutes, and let it sit, covered, for another 3 to 5 minutes. You want your cauliflower tender, but not mushy. (And you may steam it, if you prefer.)

2. Drain the cooked cauliflower, and combine it with the celery and onions. (You'll need a big bowl.)

3. Combine the mayonnaise, vinegar, salt, Splenda, and pepper. Pour the mixture over the vegetables, and mix well. Mix in the chopped eggs last, and only stir lightly, to preserve some small hunks of yolk. Chill and serve.

Yield: 12 servings, each with 3 grams of carbohydrates and 1 gram of fiber, for a total of 2 grams of usable carbs and 3 grams of protein.

🍓 Use the time while the cauliflower cooks to dice your celery and onions.

Bacon, Tomato, and Cauliflower Salad

This recipe originally called for cooked rice, so I thought I'd try it with cauliflower "rice." I liked it so much, I made it again the very next day.

  1/2 head cauliflower

  1/2 pound bacon, cooked until crisp, and crumbled

  2 medium tomatoes, chopped

  10 to 12 green onions, sliced, including all the crisp part of the green

  1/2 cup mayonnaise

  Salt and pepper

  Lettuce (optional)

1. Put the cauliflower through a food processor with the shredding disk. Steam or microwave it until it's tender-crisp.

2. Combine the cooked cauliflower with the bacon, tomatoes, onions, and mayonnaise in a big bowl. Salt and pepper to taste, and mix.

   🍓 This salad holds a molded shape really well, so pack it into a custard cup and unmold it on a plate lined with lettuce; it looks quite pretty served this way.

Yield: 5 servings, each with 6 grams of carbohydrates and 2 grams of fiber, for a total of 4 grams of usable carbs and 15 grams of protein.

Cauliflower-Mozzarella Salad Basilico

Just like the Bacon, Tomato, and Cauliflower Salad, this originally called for rice, but it works great with cauliflower. Make your own pesto or use store-bought, whichever you prefer.

1/2 head cauliflower, run through the shredding blade of a food processor (about 4 cups)

15 cherry tomatoes, halved

15 strong black olives, pitted and coarsely chopped

1/3 pound mozzarella, cut in 1/2-inch cubes

1 tablespoon finely minced sweet red onion

2 tablespoons olive oil

1/4 cup Tootsie's Pesto (see page 418)

1 tablespoon wine vinegar

1/2 teaspoon salt

1/4 teaspoon pepper

1. Cook the cauliflower "rice" until tender-crisp (about 5 minutes on high in a microwave). Let it cool.

2. When the "rice" is cool, add the tomatoes, olives, mozzarella, and onion, and toss well.

3. Whisk together the olive oil, pesto, vinegar, salt, and pepper. Pour the mixture over the salad, and toss.

4. Let the salad sit for at least a half an hour for the flavors to blend; overnight wouldn't hurt.

Yield: 5 servings, each with 6 grams of carbohydrates and 1 gram of fiber, for a total of 5 grams of usable carbs and 9 grams of protein.

ᕲ Avocado-Lime Salad

When avocados are in season, there is no easier or more-nutritious salad than this.

> 2 big lettuce leaves
>
> 1 ripe, black avocado
>
> 2 teaspoons lime juice
>
> Salt

Simply place a lettuce leaf on a salad plate, slice the avocado, and arrange the avocado slices attractively on the lettuce. Sprinkle a teaspoon of lime juice over each serving, and salt lightly.

Yield: 2 servings, each with 8 grams of carbohydrates and 3 grams of fiber, for a total of 5 grams of usable carbs and 2 grams of protein. This is also loaded with healthy, monounsaturated fats, and potassium.

ᕲ Guacamatoes

So pretty, and just wonderful served with a simple grilled steak.

> 6 ripe, smallish tomatoes
>
> Lettuce leaves or other greenery
>
> 1 batch Guacamole (see page 51)

1. Cut the stems out of the tomatoes, leaving the skin intact at the very bottom. Slice each tomato into eight wedges, being careful not to cut through the tomato skin at the very bottom of the stem.

2. Place a lettuce leaf or some other greenery on each salad plate, and put a tomato on top, spreading the wedges out to look like a flower.

3. Spoon 2 to 3 heaping tablespoons of guacamole into the middle of the tomato flower, and serve.

Yield: 6 servings. Depending on the size of your tomatoes, each will have about 17 grams of carbohydrates and 5 grams of fiber, for a total of 12 grams of usable carbs and 4 grams of protein.

> 🍓 Don't have a family of six? Why not halve the recipe and use the rest of the guacamole for omelets or something? With over 1,000 mg of potassium in a serving, you're going to want to find a way to serve Guacamatoes often.

⌒ Mayonnaise

If you have a blender, making your own sugar-free mayonnaise is a snap. If you're on a paleo diet or an antiyeast diet, use 3 tablespoons of lemon juice and omit the vinegar. (Don't feel, by the way, that the presence of this recipe means that jarred mayonnaise is off-limits for most low-carbers; it isn't. I just thought you ought to know how easy and good it is when made from scratch.)

> 1 egg
> 1 teaspoon dry mustard
> 1 teaspoon salt
> Dash of Tabasco
> 1 1/2 tablespoons vinegar
> 1 1/2 tablespoons lemon juice
> 1/2 to 2/3 cup olive or other vegetable oil

1. Place the egg, mustard, salt, Tabasco, vinegar, and lemon juice in the blender. Have the oil ready in a measuring cup.

2. Turn on the blender, and let it run for a second. With the blender running, pour in oil in a very thin stream—no thicker than a pencil lead. The mayonnaise will start to thicken before your eyes. When it gets thick enough that the "whirlpool" disappears and oil starts to collect on top, stop adding oil and turn off the blender.

3. Store your mayo in a tightly covered jar in the refrigerator, and keep in mind that homemade mayonnaise does not have the shelf life that the commercial kind does.

Yield: A little over 1 cup, with just a trace of carbohydrates, fiber, and protein—it's mostly healthy fat!

Dressings

These dressings are a great place to use homemade mayonnaise, although jarred is fine, too. Some of these recipes will give you leftovers that you should store in your refrigerator, but not for as long as you would a commercial dressing. And my general rule is this: 6 servings is about what I'd put on a large, family-size salad. So if you see "12 servings," figure that you can get two salads out of it if you're a family of 6, more if you have a smaller family.

⟡ French Vinaigrette Dressing

No, this is not that sweet, tomatoey stuff that somehow has gotten the name "French dressing." No Frenchman would eat that stuff on a bet! This is a classic vinaigrette dressing.

> 1/2 teaspoon salt
>
> 1/4 teaspoon pepper
>
> 1/4 to 1/3 cup wine vinegar
>
> 1/2 teaspoon Dijon mustard
>
> 3/4 cup extra-virgin olive oil

Put all the ingredients in a container with a tight lid, and shake well. Shake again before pouring over salad and tossing.

Yield: 12 servings, each with only a trace of carbohydrates, fiber, and protein.

🍓 The French Vinaigrette and Italian Vinaigrette Dressing recipes make approximately enough for two big, family-size salads, but feel free to double them and keep them in the fridge.

⟡ Italian Vinaigrette Dressing

Add a little zip to the French Vinaigrette, and you've got Italian Vinaigrette.

> 1/3 cup wine vinegar
>
> 2 cloves garlic, crushed
>
> 1/2 teaspoon oregano
>
> 1/4 teaspoon basil
>
> 1 or 2 drops Tabasco
>
> 2/3 cup extra-virgin olive oil

Put all the ingredients in a container with a tight-fitting lid, and shake well.

Yield: 12 servings, each with 1 gram of carbohydrates, a trace of fiber, and a trace of protein.

Creamy Italian Dressing. This is a simple variation on the Italian Vinaigrette. Just add 2 tablespoons of mayonnaise to the Italian Vinaigrette Dressing and whisk until smooth.

Yield: 12 servings, each with 1 gram of carbohydrates, a trace of fiber, and a trace of protein.

◯ Greek Lemon Dressing

The use of lemon juice in place of vinegar in salad dressings is distinctively Greek.

> 3/4 cup extra-virgin olive oil
>
> 1/4 cup lemon juice
>
> 2 tablespoons dried oregano, crushed
>
> 1 clove garlic, crushed
>
> Salt and pepper

Put all the ingredients in a container with a tight-fitting lid, and shake well.

🍓 This is best made at least a few hours in advance, but don't try to double the recipe and keep it around. Lemon juice just doesn't hold its freshness the way vinegar does.

Yield: 12 servings, each with 1 gram of carbohydrates, a trace of fiber, and a trace of protein.

Blue Cheese Dressing

2 cups mayonnaise

1/2 cup buttermilk

1/2 cup small-curd cottage cheese

1/2 teaspoon Worcestershire

1 clove garlic, crushed

1 teaspoon salt or Vege-Sal

3 ounces crumbled blue cheese

Whisk together the mayonnaise, buttermilk, cottage cheese, Worcestershire, garlic, and salt, mixing well. Gently stir in the blue cheese, to preserve some chunks. Store in a container with a tight-fitting lid.

Yield: Makes roughly 3 cups. A 2-tablespoon serving has 1 gram of carbohydrates, a trace of fiber, and 2 grams of protein.

Balsamic-Parmesan Dressing

3 tablespoons balsamic vinegar

1/3 cup extra-virgin olive oil

1 tablespoon mayonnaise

2 cloves garlic, crushed

1 teaspoon grated onion

1/4 teaspoon salt or Vege-Sal

1/4 teaspoon pepper

1 teaspoon spicy brown or Dijon mustard

1 tablespoon grated Parmesan cheese

Whisk all the ingredients together until smooth. Store in a container with a tight-fitting lid, and shake or whisk again before tossing with salad.

Yield: 6 servings, each with 1 gram of carbohydrates, a trace of fiber, and a trace of protein.

⟳ Doreen's Dressing

My friend Doreen made this up, and told me about it when I told her I was writing a cookbook. So I tried it and discovered that it's simple and wonderful.

> 1/2 cup mayonnaise
>
> 3 tablespoons balsamic vinegar
>
> 1 clove garlic, crushed

Simply combine all ingredients, and store in container with a tight-fitting lid.

Yield: 6 servings, each with 1 gram of carbohydrates, a trace of fiber, and a trace of protein.

⟳ Ranch Dressing

> 1 cup mayonnaise
>
> 1 cup buttermilk
>
> 2 tablespoons finely chopped green onions
>
> 1/4 teaspoon onion powder
>
> 2 tablespoons minced fresh parsley
>
> 1 clove garlic, crushed
>
> 1/4 teaspoon paprika
>
> 1/8 teaspoon cayenne powder or a few drops of Tabasco
>
> 1/4 teaspoon salt
>
> 1/4 teaspoon black pepper

Combine all ingredients well, and store in the refrigerator, in a container with a tight-fitting lid.

Yield: Makes about 24 servings, each with 1 gram of carbohydrates, a trace of fiber, and 1 gram of protein.

Tangy "Honey" Mustard Dressing

You know that honey, despite being "natural," is pure sugar, right? Make this instead.

> 1/4 cup canola oil
>
> 2 tablespoons apple cider vinegar
>
> 2 tablespoons spicy brown or Dijon mustard
>
> 1 tablespoon plus 2 teaspoons Splenda
>
> 1/8 teaspoon pepper
>
> 1/8 teaspoon salt

Combine all ingredients, and store in a container with a tight-fitting lid.

Yield: 6 servings, each with 1 gram of carbohydrates, a trace of fiber, and a trace of protein.

> This makes a little over 1/2 cup, or just enough for one big salad, but feel free to double, or even quadruple, this recipe.

Mellow "Honey" Mustard Dressing

> 1 1/4 cup mayonnaise
>
> 1/4 cup spicy brown mustard
>
> 1/3 cup Splenda
>
> 4 tablespoons water
>
> 1 teaspoon salt

Combine all ingredients, and store in the refrigerator, in a container with a tight-fitting lid.

Yield: 12 servings, each with 1 gram of carbohydrates, a trace of fiber, and 1 gram of protein.

↻ Raspberry Vinegar

Commercial raspberry vinegar has as much as 4 grams of carbohydrates per tablespoon, so keep a batch of this on hand.

>   1/2 cup white vinegar
>   1/4 teaspoon raspberry cake flavoring (this is a highly concentrated oil in a teeny little bottle)
>   3 tablespoons Splenda

Just combine these ingredients, and store in a container with a tight-fitting lid.

Yield: About 1/2 cup, with 11.5 grams of carbohydrates in the whole batch or 1.5 grams of carbohydrates per tablespoon, no fiber, and no protein.

↻ Raspberry Vinaigrette Dressing

Sweet and tangy, raspberry vinaigrette is a favorite you'll get to enjoy more often once you're making your own low-carb variety.

>   1/4 cup Raspberry Vinegar (see above)
>   1/4 cup canola or other bland oil
>   3 tablespoons plus 1 teaspoon mayonnaise
>   1 teaspoon spicy brown or Dijon mustard
>   Pinch salt and pepper

Blend all the ingredients, and store in the refrigerator, in a container with a tight-fitting lid.

Yield: 6 servings, each with a trace of carbohydrates, fiber, and protein.

Parmesan Peppercorn Dressing

    2 tablespoons olive oil

    3 tablespoons mayonnaise

    2 tablespoons wine vinegar

    3 tablespoons grated Parmesan cheese

    1 teaspoon freshly ground black pepper (coarse-cracked pepper will do,
        if you don't have a pepper mill.)

Blend all the ingredients, and store in the refrigerator, in a container with
a tight-fitting lid.

Yield: 6 servings, each with 1 gram of carbohydrates, a trace of fiber,
and 1 gram of protein.

Creamy Garlic Dressing

Look at all that garlic! If you plan to get kissed, make sure you share
this salad with the object of your affections.

    1/2 cup mayonnaise

    Pinch each of pepper and salt

    8 cloves garlic, crushed

    2 tablespoons olive oil

    2 tablespoons wine vinegar

Combine all the ingredients well, and store in the refrigerator, in a container with a
tight-fitting lid.

Yield: 6 servings, each with 2 grams of carbohydrates, a trace of fiber, and a trace
of protein.

This is only enough for one big salad, but I wouldn't double it; I'd make this
one fresh so the garlic flavor will be better.

⌒ Caesar Dressing

If you're afraid of raw eggs, you could use Egg Beaters or check your grocery store for pasteurized eggs. Me, I just use an egg. This is far better than any bottled Caesar dressing I've found, if it's not quite as wonderful as what I had on my honeymoon in Mexico—although I suspect that the atmosphere had something to do with that.

4 tablespoons lemon juice

1/4 cup olive oil

1 teaspoon pepper

1 1/2 teaspoons Worcestershire sauce

1 clove garlic, peeled and smashed

1/2 teaspoon salt or Vege-Sal

1 raw egg

1/2 cup grated Parmesan

2 inches anchovy paste (you could use an anchovy fillet or two if you prefer, but anchovy paste is handier, and it keeps forever in the fridge)

Put everything in a blender, run it for a minute, and toss with one really huge Caesar salad—dinner-party-sized—or a couple of smaller ones. Use it up pretty quickly, and keep it refrigerated because of the raw egg.

🍓 If you'd like this a little thicker, you could add 1/4 teaspoon of guar or xanthan to the mix.

Yield: 8 servings, each with 1 gram of carbohydrates, a trace of fiber, and 3 grams of protein.

◯ Coleslaw Dressing

Virtually all commercial coleslaw dressing is simply full of sugar, which is a shame, since cabbage is a very low-carb vegetable. I just love coleslaw, so I came up with a sugar-free dressing.

> 1/2 cup mayonnaise
> 1/2 cup sour cream
> 1 to 1 1/2 tablespoons apple cider vinegar
> 1 to 1 1/2 teaspoons prepared mustard
> 1/2 to 1 teaspoon salt or Vege-Sal
> 1/2 to 1 packet artificial sweetener, or 1 teaspoon of Splenda

Combine all the ingredients well, and toss with coleslaw. (See the recipes on page 222.)

🍓 You may, of course, vary these proportions to taste. Also, a teaspoon or so of celery seed can be nice in this, for a little variety. I use this much dressing for a whole head of cabbage. If you're used to commercial coleslaw, which tends to be simply swimming in dressing, you may want to double this, or use this recipe for half a head.

Yield: 12 servings, each with 1 gram of carbohydrates, with a trace of fiber, and a trace of protein.

CHAPTER SEVEN

Chicken and Turkey

Around here we eat chicken no fewer than a couple of times a week, and many other families do the same. After all, chicken is inexpensive, and it's always tasty. It also lends itself to infinite variation, as this chapter will prove. A useful tip to keep in mind: If a recipe calls for a cut up broiler-fryer, as many of these recipes do, feel free to substitute the chicken parts you prefer. I often use just legs and thighs, both because I like dark meat best and because they're often dirt-cheap.

Ground turkey is also good to have on hand, and it's a nice change from ground beef. You'll find some interesting ways to use it in this chapter.

Ranchhouse Chicken

> 1 cut up broiler-fryer
> 1/4 cup Ranch Dressing (see page 235)

1. Preheat the oven to 375°F.
2. Arrange the chicken in a roasting pan, and spoon the dressing over it, smearing it a bit with the back of the spoon to cover each piece. Roast for 75 to 90 minutes.

Yield: 4 servings, each with 1 gram of carbohydrates, no fiber, and 44 grams of protein. (The dressing adds maybe 3 grams of carbs to the whole batch.)

↱ Tarragon Chicken

    1 cut up broiler-fryer

    2 tablespoons butter

    1 teaspoon salt or Vege-Sal

    Pepper

    3 tablespoons dried tarragon

    1 clove garlic, crushed

    1/2 cup dry white wine

1. If your chicken is in quarters, cut the legs from the thighs and the wings from the breasts. (It will fit in your skillet more easily this way.)

2. Melt the butter in a heavy skillet over medium-high heat, and brown the chicken, turning it once or twice, until it's golden all over.

3. Pour off most of the fat, and sprinkle the chicken with the salt and just a dash of pepper. Scatter the tarragon over the chicken, crushing it a little between your fingers to release the flavor, then add the garlic and the wine.

4. Cover the skillet, turn the burner to low, and simmer for 30 minutes, turning the chicken at least once. Spoon a little of the pan liquid over each piece of chicken when serving.

Yield: 4 servings, each with 2 grams of carbohydrates, a trace of fiber, and 44 grams of protein.

∽ Curried Chicken

4 or 5 chicken quarters, cut up and skinned

1 medium onion

1 tablespoon butter

1 rounded tablespoon curry powder

1 cup heavy cream

3 or 4 cloves of garlic, crushed

1/2 cup water

1. Preheat the oven to 375°F.

2. Arrange the chicken in a shallow baking pan. Chop the onion, and scatter it over the chicken.

3. Melt the butter in a small, heavy skillet, and sauté the curry powder in it for a couple of minutes—just until it starts to smell good.

4. Mix together the cream, garlic, water, and sautéed curry powder, and pour this over the chicken. Bake it, uncovered, for 1 hour to 1 hour and 20 minutes, turning the chicken over every 20 to 30 minutes so that the sauce flavors both sides.

5. To serve, arrange the chicken on a platter. Take the sauce in the pan (it will look dreadful, sort of curdled up, but it will smell like heaven) and scrape it all into your blender. Blend it with a little more water or cream, if necessary, to get a nice, rich, golden sauce. Pour it over the chicken and serve.

Yield: 4 generous servings, each with 6 grams of carbohydrates and 1 gram of fiber, for a total of 5 grams of usable carbs and 42 grams of protein.

🍓 Ahem. Take a look at the first ingredient in this recipe—the chicken is skinned, right? Now, that's not because you can't have chicken skin on a low-carb diet, it's because cooking chicken with the skin on in a recipe like this only results in flabby, uninteresting chicken skin. Do you like crispy chicken skin? I sure do. Check out Chicken Chips (page 244) to find out what I do with the skin I pull off that chicken.

↻ Chicken Chips

> Chicken skin
> Salt

1. Preheat the oven to 375°F.

2. Take any and all chicken skin you have on hand—chunks of chicken fat will work, too—and spread them out as flat as you can on the broiler rack.

3. Bake for 10 to 15 minutes, or until the skin gets brown and crunchy (thicker pieces take longer than thinner ones). Sprinkle with salt and eat like chips—these are not to be believed!

Yield: This will totally depend on how much chicken skin you bake, but here's the info that really matters: There's no carbohydrates here at all.

↻ Pizza Chicken

This recipe is basically a skillet cacciatore, except for the mozzarella—that's what makes it Pizza Chicken.

> 3 chicken quarters, either legs or thighs
> 1 to 2 tablespoons olive oil
> 1 can (8 ounces) plain tomato sauce
> 1 can (4 ounces) mushrooms, drained
> 1/2 cup dry red wine
> 1 green pepper, chopped
> 1 small onion, chopped
> 1 or 2 cloves garlic, crushed, or 1 to 2 teaspoons jarred chopped garlic in oil
> 1 to 1 1/2 teaspoons dried oregano
> 3 ounces shredded mozzarella cheese
> Parmesan cheese (optional)

1. Strip the skin off the chicken, and cut leg and thigh quarters in two at the leg joint.

2. Warm the olive oil in a big, heavy skillet, and brown the chicken in it over medium heat.

3. Pour in the tomato sauce, mushrooms, and wine. Add the green pepper, onion, garlic, and oregano. Cover the whole thing, turn the burner to its lowest setting, and forget about it for 45 minutes to 1 hour.

4. When the chicken is cooked through, remove the pieces from the skillet, and put them on the serving plates. If the sauce isn't good and thick by now, turn up the burner to medium-high, and let the sauce boil down for a few minutes.

5. While the sauce is thickening, sprinkle the shredded mozzarella over the chicken, and warm each plate in the microwave for 20 to 30 seconds on 50 percent power to melt the cheese. (Your microwave may take a little more or a little less time.)

6. Spoon the sauce over each piece of chicken, and serve. Sprinkle a little Parmesan over your Pizza Chicken, if you like.

Yield: 3 servings, each with 16 grams of carbohydrates and 4 grams of fiber, for a total of 12 grams of usable carbs and 49 grams of protein.

☊ Looed Chicken

Traditionally looing is done on the stove, but this makes a terrific slow cooker recipe.

> 1 cut-up broiler-fryer (about 3 1/2 pounds), 4 or 5 chicken quarters,
>   or 4 or 5 boneless, skinless chicken breasts
>
> 1 batch Looing Sauce (see page 413)
>
> Scallions, sliced
>
> Toasted sesame oil

1. Put your chicken in your slow cooker, pour the looing sauce over it, cover the slow cooker, set it to Low, and forget about it for 8 to 9 hours.

2. At dinnertime, remove the chicken from the looing sauce, put each piece on a serving plate, scatter a few sliced scallions over each serving, and top with a few drops of toasted sesame oil.

Yield: 4 or 5 servings. The looing sauce adds no more than a gram or so of carbohydrates and no fiber, and each 4 ounces of meat will have 28 grams of protein.

◯ Roast Chicken with Balsamic Vinegar

Wonderfully crunchy skin, with a sweet-and-tangy sauce to dip bites of chicken in.

> Bay leaves
>
> 1 cut up broiler-fryer
>
> Salt or Vege-Sal
>
> Pepper
>
> 3 to 4 tablespoons olive oil
>
> 3 to 4 tablespoons butter
>
> 1/2 cup dry white wine
>
> 3 tablespoons balsamic vinegar

1. Preheat the oven to 350°F.

2. Tuck a bay leaf or two under the skin of each piece of chicken. Sprinkle each piece with salt and pepper, and arranged them in a roasting pan.

3. Drizzle the chicken with olive oil, and dot them with the same amount of butter. Roast in the oven for 1 1/2 hours, turning each piece every 20 to 30 minutes. (This makes for gloriously crunchy, tasty skin.)

4. When the chicken is done, put it on a platter and pour off the fat from the pan. Put the pan over a burner set on medium, and pour in the wine and balsamic vinegar. Stir this around, dissolving the tasty brown stuff stuck to the pan to make a sauce. Boil this for just a minute or two, pour into a sauceboat or a pitcher, and serve with the chicken.

Yield: 4 servings, each with 2 grams of carbohydrates, a trace of fiber, and 44 grams of protein.

Spicy Peanut Chicken

This takes 10 minutes to put together, and only another 15 to cook. It's hot and spicy, quasi-Thai.

> 1 teaspoon ground cumin
>
> 1/2 teaspoon ground cinnamon
>
> 2 or 3 boneless, skinless chicken breasts
>
> 2 to 3 tablespoons olive or peanut oil for sautéing (I think peanut is better here)
>
> 1/2 smallish onion, thinly sliced
>
> 1 can (14 1/2 ounces) diced tomatoes
>
> 2 tablespoons natural peanut butter
>
> 1 tablespoon lemon juice
>
> 2 cloves garlic, crushed
>
> 1 fresh jalapeño, cut in half and seeded

1. On a saucer or plate, stir the cumin and cinnamon together, then rub into both sides of chicken breasts.

2. Put 2 to 3 tablespoons of oil in a heavy skillet over medium heat, and add the chicken and sliced onion. Brown the chicken a bit on both sides.

3. While that's happening, put all the liquid and half the tomatoes from the can of tomatoes in a blender or food processor, along with the peanut butter, lemon juice, garlic, and jalapeño. (Wash your hands after handling that hot pepper, or you'll be sorry the next time you touch your eyes!) Blend or process until smooth.

4. Pour this rather thick sauce over the chicken (which you've turned at least once by now, right?), add the rest of the canned tomatoes, cover, turn the burner to Low, and let it sit for 10 to 15 minutes, or until the chicken is cooked through.

Yield: About 3 servings, each with 14 grams of carbohydrates and 1 gram of fiber, for a total of 13 grams of usable carbs and 26 grams of protein.

🍓 Some like it hot, and some like it a little bit less so. So when you're buying your ingredients, choose a little jalapeño or a big one, depending on how hot you like your food. I use a big one, and it definitely makes this dish hot. And don't forget, there's no law against using only half a jalapeño.

↻ Skillet Chicken Florentine

My husband took one bite of this and said, "This is going to get you a lot of new readers!" I know of no other dish that's so quick and easy, yet so incredibly good.

Olive oil

2 or 3 boneless, skinless chicken breasts

1 package (10 ounces) frozen chopped spinach, thawed

2 cloves garlic, crushed

1/4 cup heavy cream

1/4 cup grated Parmesan cheese

1. Warm a little olive oil in a heavy skillet, and brown the chicken breasts over medium heat to the point where they just have a touch of gold. Remove the chicken from the skillet.

2. Add a couple more tablespoons of olive oil, the spinach, and the garlic, and stir for 2 to 3 minutes. Stir in the cream and cheese, and spread the mixture evenly over the bottom of the skillet. Place the chicken breasts on top, cover, turn the burner to low, and let simmer for 15 minutes.

3. Serve chicken breasts with the spinach on top.

Yield: 3 servings, each with 5 grams of carbohydrates and 3 grams of fiber, for a total of 2 grams of usable carbs and 33 grams of protein.

↺ Those Chicken Things

Kate Sutherland sends this recipe, and says this works best on a gas grill.

>   1 bunch scallions (about 10)
>   1 package (8 ounces) cream cheese, softened
>   8 boneless, skinless chicken breasts
>   16 to 24 slices bacon

1. Clean, trim, and chop the scallions, including a generous portion of the green. Mix the scallions into the cream cheese, and set aside.

2. Butterfly the chicken breasts from the thinnest edge in toward the thickest. (This thickest edge will be the middle of the breast once it is opened up) Working one piece at a time, open the breast up, and put it in a heavy zipper-lock bag. Seal the bag, and with a rolling pin, hammer, dumbbell, or whatever else you can find, pound the chicken breast until it is 1/4-inch thick all over. Repeat with the remaining chicken breasts.

3. Once all 8 breasts have been flattened, place an equal amount of the cream cheese and scallion mixture on each. Wrap the chicken meat around the cheese mix so that it is completely enclosed.

4. Wrap a strip of bacon around the ball of chicken, stretching it a bit to provide maximum overlap. Then wrap a second piece of bacon around the still exposed portion of the chicken, again giving it a bit of a stretch. Secure with a few tooth-picks. (Depending on the size of the chicken breasts, you may need a third piece of bacon. Most of the chicken should be covered by the bacon strips.)

5. Refrigerate for several hours or overnight. They should be well chilled before they go on the grill.

6. Cover the barbecue rack with a sheet of aluminum foil, and spray it with nonstick cooking spray. (The foil helps prevent flare-ups from the bacon fat and also helps the chicken cook evenly.) Preheat the grill to High.

7. Place the chicken on the covered rack, reduce the heat to Medium, and close the lid. Turn about every 5 minutes, until all sides are nicely browned. When the cheese starts to ooze out in a few places, they are done. (Depending on the size of the pieces and the overall temperature of your barbecue, this should take 20 to 30 minutes.) Remove the toothpicks and serve.

Yield: 8 servings, each with 1 gram of carbohydrates, a trace of fiber, and 36 grams of protein.

↻ Chicken and Artichoke Skillet

This is quick and easy enough for a weeknight, but elegant enough for company.

3 tablespoons butter

4 boneless, skinless chicken breasts

1 can (14 ounces) quartered artichoke hearts, drained

1/2 red bell pepper, cut into strips

1 medium onion, sliced

1 clove garlic, crushed

1/4 cup dry white wine

1 teaspoon dried thyme

1. Melt 2 tablespoons of butter in a heavy skillet over medium heat, and sauté the chicken breasts until they're golden (5 to 7 minutes per side). Remove from the skillet.

2. Melt the remaining tablespoon of butter, and toss the artichoke hearts, pepper, onion, and garlic into the skillet. Sauté for 3 minutes or so, stirring frequently.

3. Pour the wine and sprinkle the thyme over the vegetables. Place the chicken breasts over the vegetables, turn the heat to medium low, cover, and simmer for 10 minutes.

Yield: 4 servings, each with 8 grams of carbohydrates and 4 grams of fiber, for a total of 4 grams of usable carbs and 26 grams of protein.

↻ Teriyaki Chicken

4 to 6 boneless, skinless chicken breasts

1 batch Teriyaki Sauce (see page 411)

1. Put your chicken breasts in a large zipper-lock bag, and pour the teriyaki sauce over them. Stick the bag in the refrigerator, and let the breasts marinate for at least 1 hour. (More time won't hurt; if you do this in the morning, you can cook as soon as you come home at night.)

2. When you're ready to cook, pour off the marinade into a small saucepan. Grill or broil your chicken for 5 to 7 minutes per side, checking doneness by cutting into one breast to see if it's done. Don't overcook, or your chicken will be dry.

3. While your chicken is cooking, bring the marinade to a boil for a few minutes. It will then be safe to pour a little on each piece of chicken before serving.

Yield: 4 to 6 servings (depending on the number of breasts you cook), each with 2 grams of carbohydrates, a trace of fiber, and 26 grams of protein.

↻ Satay without a Stick

Here's a recipe for boneless, skinless chicken breasts that reminds me of satay, the popular Asian kebabs.

> 1 tablespoon oil
> 1 clove garlic, crushed
> 1 teaspoon curry powder
> 1 boneless, skinless chicken breast
> Not-Very-Authentic Peanut Sauce (see page 402)

1. Put a heavy skillet over medium heat. Add the oil, garlic, and curry powder, and stir for a few seconds to flavor the oil.

2. Add the chicken breasts, and sauté for about 7 minutes on each side, or until done through.

3. Serve with the peanut sauce, warming it first, if desired.

Yield: 1 serving, with 2 grams of carbohydrates, with a trace of fiber, and 28 grams of protein. (Analysis includes a serving of sauce.)

↻ Picnic Chicken

> 2/3 cup apple cider vinegar
> 3 tablespoons oil
> 2 teaspoons salt
> 1/4 teaspoon pepper
> 1 cut up broiler-fryer

1. Combine the vinegar, oil, salt, and pepper, and pour over the chicken in a large zipper-lock bag. Marinate for at least an hour; more time wouldn't hurt.

2. Preheat the broiler to High. Take the chicken out of the marinade and broil it about 8 inches from the flame. Baste it with the marinade every 10 to 15 minutes while cooking. Give it about 25 minutes per side, or until done through. (Pierce it to the bone; the juices should run clear, not pink.) You may need to rearrange the chicken pieces on your broiler rack to get them to cook evenly, so they're all ready at the same time.

Yield: 4 servings, each with 3 grams of carbohydrates per serving if you consumed all the marinade, but of course you don't, so each serving has less than 1 gram of carbohydrates, no fiber, and 44 grams of protein.

🍓 You may be wondering why this is called Picnic Chicken—it's because come summer, if you really were going on a picnic, you could bring the bag of chicken and marinade along in the cooler and grill it at the park or the beach. What a treat! But make sure you don't continue basting the chicken with the marinade once you're done cooking it: If you do, you're risking food poisoning.

Middle Eastern Skillet Chicken

3 boneless, skinless chicken breasts

3 tablespoons olive oil

1 medium onion, chopped

1/2 teaspoon ground coriander

1 teaspoon ground cumin

1/4 teaspoon ground cinnamon

1/2 teaspoon turmeric

1/4 teaspoon black pepper

1 tablespoon freshly grated ginger

1 can (14 1/2 ounces) diced tomatoes

2 cloves garlic, crushed

1 cup chicken broth

1. Cut the chicken breasts into cubes. Heat the olive oil over medium heat in a heavy skillet, and add the chicken and onions.

2. Sauté for a couple of minutes, then stir in the coriander, cumin, cinnamon, turmeric, and pepper. Cook until the chicken is white all over.

3. Add the ginger, tomatoes, garlic, and broth; stir. Cover, turn the burner to Low, and simmer for 15 minutes.

Yield: 3 servings, each with 14 grams of carbohydrates and 1 gram of fiber, for a total of 13 grams of usable carbs and 26 grams of protein.

↻ Chicken Paprikash

Making my Paprikash with real sour cream is one of the great joys of low-carbing!

> 3 tablespoons butter
> 1 cut-up broiler-fryer
> 1 small onion
> 2 tablespoons paprika
> 1/2 cup chicken broth
> 1 cup sour cream
> Salt or Vege-Sal and pepper

1. Melt the butter in a heavy skillet, and brown the chicken and onions over medium-high heat.

2. In a separate bowl, stir the paprika into the chicken broth. Pour the mixture over the chicken.

3. Cover the skillet, turn the burner to low, and let it simmer for 30 to 45 minutes.

4. When the chicken is tender and cooked through, remove it from the skillet and put it on a serving platter. Stir the sour cream into the liquid left in the pan, and stir until smooth and well blended. Heat through, but do not let it boil, or it will curdle. Salt and pepper to taste, and serve this gravy with the chicken.

Yield: 4 servings, each with 7 grams of carbohydrates and 1 gram of fiber, for a total of 6 grams of usable carbs and 53 grams of protein.

🍓 Be sure to serve plenty of Cauliflower Purée (see page 158) with it, to smother in the extra gravy!

☞ Homestyle Turkey Loaf

If you haven't eaten a lot of ground turkey, you may find it's a nice change from meatloaf made from ground beef.

> 1 pound ground turkey
>
> 1/2 cup crushed pork rinds
>
> 1 rib celery, finely chopped
>
> 1 small onion, finely chopped
>
> 1/2 cup finely chopped apple
>
> 1 1/2 tablespoons Worcestershire sauce
>
> 2 teaspoons poultry seasoning
>
> 1 teaspoon salt or Vege-Sal
>
> 1 egg

1. Preheat the oven to 350°F.
2. Combine all the ingredients in a big bowl and—with clean hands—squeeze it together until it's very well combined.
3. Spray a loaf pan with nonstick cooking spray, and pack the turkey mixture into the pan. Bake for 50 minutes.

Yield: 5 servings, each with 5 grams of carbohydrates and 1 gram of fiber, for a total of 4 grams of usable carbs and 32 grams of protein.

↻ Curried Turkey Loaf

This has a good, rich curry flavor, and it's great with Cranberry Chutney. (See page 414)

> 2 pounds ground turkey
>
> 1 medium onion, chopped fairly fine
>
> 2 eggs
>
> 2 cloves garlic, crushed
>
> 1 to 2 tablespoons curry powder
>
> 1 tablespoon salt or Vege-Sal
>
> 1 teaspoon pepper

1. Preheat the oven to 350°F.
2. Combine all the ingredients in a big bowl and—with clean hands—squeeze it together until it's very well combined.
3. Spray a loaf pan with nonstick cooking spray, and pack the turkey mixture into the pan. Bake for 60 to 75 minutes.

   Yield: 6 servings, each with 4 grams of carbohydrates and 1 gram of fiber, for a total of 3 grams of usable carbs and 29 grams of protein.

Low-Carb Microwave Pasticchio

This has become my sister's standby recipe for potlucks and other casserole occasions.

Pasticchio

1/2 medium onion, chopped

1 clove garlic, crushed

1 pound ground turkey

3/4 teaspoon ground cinnamon

1/8 teaspoon ground nutmeg

1 cup ricotta cheese

1/4 cup chopped fresh parsley

1/4 teaspoon salt or Vege-Sal

1/8 teaspoon pepper

Sauce

2 tablespoons butter

1/2 teaspoon salt or Vege-Sal

1 1/2 cups heavy cream

1/2 cup Parmesan cheese

2 cups cooked spaghetti squash

1. In a microwave-safe casserole, combine the onion and garlic; place the turkey on top. Microwave this, uncovered, for 5 minutes at full power. Stir it up a bit, breaking up the ground turkey in the process. Microwave the turkey and onion mixture for another 3 minutes, or until the turkey is done through.

2. Break up the turkey some more—you want it well crumbled—and drain off the fat. Stir in the cinnamon and nutmeg, and microwave it for just another minute, to blend the flavors. Transfer the turkey mixture to a bowl.

3. In a separate bowl, combine the ricotta cheese, parsley, and salt and pepper.

4. In yet another bowl or a measuring cup (okay, you need both a microwave and a dishwasher for this to be a convenient recipe!) combine the butter, sauce, cream, and cheese to make the sauce.

5. Spray your microwave-safe casserole with nonstick cooking spray. In the dish, layer half of the spaghetti squash, then half the turkey mixture, then half the

ricotta mixture, then half the sauce. Repeat the layers, ending with the sauce.

6. Microwave the pasticchio at full power for 6 to 8 minutes, or until it's bubbly and hot clear through. Let it sit for 5 minutes or so, and serve.

Yield: 6 servings, each with 7 grams of carbohydrates, a trace of fiber, and 22 grams of protein.

ᘒ Asian Turkey Burgers

Ground turkey is handy, but by itself it can be bland. Here's a good way to liven it up.

        1 pound ground turkey

        1/4 cup minced onion

        3 tablespoons chopped fresh parsley

        2 tablespoons Worcestershire

        2 tablespoons minced green bell pepper

        1 tablespoon soy sauce

        1 tablespoon cold water

        1 tablespoon grated fresh ginger

        1/4 teaspoon pepper

        2 cloves garlic, crushed

1. Combine all the ingredients in a big bowl and—with clean hands—squeeze it together until it's very well combined.

2. Divide into three equal portions, and form into burgers about 3/4 inch thick.

3. Spray a skillet with nonstick cooking spray, and place over medium-high heat. Cook the burgers for about 5 minutes per side, until done through.

Yield: 3 servings, each with 5 grams of carbohydrates and 1 gram of fiber, for a total of 4 grams of usable carbs and 27 grams of protein.

↻ Saltimbocca

Who says all Italian food involves pasta?

 4 boneless, skinless chicken breasts

 1/4 pound prosciutto or good boiled ham, thinly sliced

 40 leaves fresh or dry sage (fresh is preferable)

 2 tablespoons butter

 2 tablespoons olive oil

 1/2 cup dry white wine

1. Place a chicken breast in a large, heavy, zipper-lock bag and, using a hammer, meat tenderizer, or what-have-you, pound it until it's 1/4 inch thick. Repeat with the remaining chicken breasts.

2. Once all your chicken breasts are pounded thin, place a layer of the prosciutto on each one, scatter about 10 sage leaves over each one, and roll each breast up. Fasten with toothpicks.

3. Melt the butter with the olive oil in a heavy skillet over medium heat. Add the chicken rolls and sauté, turning occasionally, until golden all over.

4. Add the wine to the skillet, turn the burner to low, cover the skillet, and simmer for 15 minutes.

5. Remove the rolls to a serving plate, and cover to keep warm. Turn the burner up to High, and boil the liquid in the skillet hard for 5 minutes, to reduce. Spoon over rolls, and serve.

Yield: 4 servings, each with 2 grams of carbohydrates, no fiber, and 37 grams of protein.

⟳ Saltimbocca Gruyère

I couldn't decide which version I liked best, so I included both!

> 4 boneless, skinless chicken breasts
>
> 1/4 pound prosciutto or good boiled ham, thinly sliced
>
> 1 cup shredded Gruyère cheese
>
> 2 tablespoons butter
>
> 2 tablespoons olive oil
>
> 1/2 cup dry white wine

1. Place a chicken breast in a large, heavy, zipper-lock bag and, using a hammer, meat tenderizer, or what-have-you, pound it until it's 1/4 inch thick. Repeat with the remaining chicken breasts.

2. Once all your chicken breasts are pounded thin, place a layer of the prosciutto followed by some shredded Gruyère over each one, and then roll each breast up. Fasten with toothpicks.

3. Melt the butter with the olive oil in a heavy skillet over medium heat. Add the chicken rolls, and sauté, turning occasionally, until golden all over.

4. Add the wine to the skillet, turn the burner to low, cover the skillet, and simmer for 15 minutes.

5. Remove the rolls to a serving plate, and cover to keep warm. Turn the burner up to high, and boil the liquid in the skillet hard for 5 minutes, to reduce. Spoon over rolls, and serve.

Yield: 4 servings, each with just a trace of carbohydrates, no fiber, and 45 grams of protein.

ᕗ Key Lime Chicken

An unusual—and good!—combination of flavors.

1 cut-up broiler-fryer
1/2 cup lime juice
1/2 cup olive oil
1 tablespoon grated onion
2 teaspoons tarragon
1 teaspoon seasoned salt
1/4 teaspoon pepper

1. Arrange the chicken pieces on the broiler rack, skin side down.
2. In a bowl, combine the lime juice, oil, onion, tarragon, salt, and pepper, and brush the chicken well with the mixture.
3. Broil the chicken about 8 inches from the flame for 45 to 50 minutes, turning the chicken and basting with more lime mixture every 10 minutes or so.

Yield: 4 servings, each with 4 grams of carbohydrates, a trace of fiber, and 44 grams of protein.

ᕗ Deviled Chicken

4 tablespoons butter
1/2 cup Splenda
1/4 cup spicy brown mustard
1 teaspoon salt
1 teaspoon curry powder
1 cut-up broiler-fryer

1. Preheat the oven to 375°F.
2. Melt the butter in a shallow roasting pan. Add the Splenda, mustard, salt, and curry powder, and stir until well combined.
3. Roll the chicken pieces in the butter mixture until coated, then arrange them skin side up in the pan. Bake for 1 hour.

Yield: 4 servings, each with 5 grams of carbohydrates, a trace of fiber, and 44 grams of protein.

↻ Jerk Chicken

This hot-and-sweet Jamaican chicken is great for a special barbecue, but you have to remember to begin marinating the chicken the day before.

   1 batch Jerk Marinade (see page 412)
   1 cut-up broiler-fryer

1. Smear the jerk marinade all over your chicken—even up under the skin. Coat it well, and put the chicken in a zipper-lock bag.

2. Wash your hands! You don't want the hot peppers to stay on them.

3. Let the chicken sit in the refrigerator overnight. When dinnertime comes, preheat the oven to 375°F.

4. Pull your chicken out of the bag, but do not wipe the marinade off. Roast your chicken for about 40 minutes, then finish on the grill. (This prevents the chicken from drying out and scorching.)

Yield: 4 servings, each with 4 grams of carbohydrates and 1 gram of fiber, for a total of 3 grams usable carbs and 44 grams of protein.

↻ Tasty Roasted Chicken

> 1 whole chicken (about 5 pounds)
>
> 1 heaping tablespoon mayonnaise
>
> Salt
>
> Pepper
>
> Paprika
>
> Onion powder

1. Preheat the oven to 375°F.

2. If your chicken was frozen, make sure it's completely thawed. (If it's still a bit icy in the middle, run some hot water inside it until it's not icy anymore.) Take out the giblets.

   🍓 If you've never cooked a whole chicken before and you're wondering where the heck the giblets are, you'll find them in the body cavity.

3. Dry your chicken, and put it on a plate. Scoop the mayo out of the jar (being careful not to get raw chicken germs in the mayonnaise jar), and use it to give your chicken a massage. That's right, just rub every inch of that chicken's skin with the mayonnaise.

4. Sprinkle the chicken liberally with equal parts salt, pepper, paprika, and onion powder, on all sides. Put the chicken on a rack in a shallow roasting pan, and put it in the oven.

5. Roast for 1 1/2 hours, or until the juices run clear when you stick a fork in where the thigh joins the body. Remove the chicken from the oven, and let it sit for 10 to 15 minutes before carving, to let the juices settle.

Yield: 5 generous servings, each with a trace of carbohydrates, a trace of fiber, and 52 grams of protein.

Chicken Taco Filling

This is easy, versatile, and likely to be popular with the family.

1 pound boneless, skinless chicken breasts, or 1 1/2 to 2 pounds chicken parts

1 cup chicken broth

2 tablespoons Taco Seasoning (see page 404)

1. If you're using chicken parts (I like to make this with leg and thigh quarters), skin them first. Put your chicken in either a large, heavy-bottomed saucepan, or in your slow cooker.

2. Mix together the chicken broth and the taco seasoning, and pour the mixture over the chicken. If you're cooking this on the stove top, simply cover the pot, put it over low heat, and let it simmer for about 1 1/2 hours. If you're using a slow cooker, set the pot on Low, and leave it for 6 to 8 hours.

3. With either method, when the chicken is done, use two forks to tear it into largish shreds. If you've used bone-in chicken parts, this is the time to remove the bones, as well. If you've cooked this on the stove top, most of the liquid will have cooked away, but if you've used a slow cooker, there will be quite a lot of liquid, so turn the pot up to High, leave the cover off, and let the liquid cook down. Stir the chicken back into the reduced seasoning liquid, and it's ready to serve.

Yield: 4 servings, each with 1 gram of carbohydrates, a trace of fiber, and 26 grams of protein.

Don't know what to do with your taco filling? See Cheesy Bowls and Taco Shells (page 83), Taco Salad (page 372), and Taco Omelet (page 92).

Chicken Piccata

Meat cooked "piccata" is traditionally floured first, but with all this flavor going on, who'll miss it?

> 4 boneless, skinless chicken breasts
> 1/4 cup olive oil
> 1 clove garlic, crushed
> 1 tablespoon lemon juice, or the juice of 1/2 lemon
> 1/2 cup dry white wine
> 1 tablespoon capers, chopped
> 3 tablespoons fresh parsley, chopped

1. Place a chicken breast in a large, heavy, zipper-lock bag and, using a hammer, meat tenderizer, or what-have-you, pound it until it's 1/4 inch thick. Repeat with the remaining chicken breasts.

2. Heat the olive oil in a large, heavy skillet over medium-high heat. Add the chicken; if it doesn't all fit at the same time, cook it in two batches, keeping the first batch warm while the second batch is cooking. Cook the chicken until it's done through (3 to 4 minutes per side).

3. Remove the chicken from the pan. Add the garlic, lemon juice, white wine, and capers to the pan, stirring it all around to get the tasty little brown bits off the bottom of the pan. Boil the whole thing hard for about 1 minute, to reduce it a little.

4. Put the chicken back in the pan for another minute, sprinkle the parsley over it, and serve.

Yield: 4 servings, each with 1 gram of carbohydrates, a trace of fiber, and 29 grams of protein.

Pork Piccata. Make this variation just like Chicken Piccatta, only substitute 4 good, big pork steaks, or chops, or thinly sliced pork butt (1 to 1 1/2 pounds of meat total) for the chicken breasts. (Cut the bones out of the pork steaks or chops, if using, and discard.)

Yield: 4 servings, each with 1 gram of carbohydrates, a trace of fiber, and 26 grams of protein.

↻ Chicken-Almond Stir-Fry

Serve this tasty stir-fry over brown rice for the carb-eaters in your family, and enjoy yours straight.

    2 tablespoons soy sauce

    4 tablespoons dry sherry

    1 clove garlic, smashed

    1 inch or so fresh gingerroot, grated

    1/4 teaspoon guar (optional)

    Peanut oil (canola or coconut oil would work, too)

    1/3 cup slivered almonds

    1 1/2 cups snow peas, cut in half

    1 1/2 cups mushrooms, sliced

    15 scallions, cut into pieces about 1 inch long

    1/4 cup sliced water chestnuts (optional; they up the carb count,
        but they're tasty)

    3 large boneless, skinless chicken breasts, cut into 1/2-inch cubes

> 🍓 There's one hard-and-fast rule with stir-fries: Make sure all your ingredients are chopped, sliced, and grated before you begin cooking.

1. Stir together the soy, sherry, garlic, and ginger. (If you're using the guar, put these seasonings through the blender with the guar.)

2. Heat a couple of teaspoons of the peanut oil in a wok or large, heavy skillet over high heat. Add the almonds, and stir-fry them until they're light golden. Remove, and set aside.

3. Heat another couple of tablespoons of oil in the pan, and add the snow peas, mushrooms, scallions, and water chestnuts (if using) to the pan. Stir-fry for about 5 minutes, or until just barely tender-crisp. Remove from the pan and set aside.

4. Heat another couple of tablespoons of oil in the pan, and add the chicken. Stir-fry for 5 to 7 minutes, or until done; there should be no pink left.

5. Return the vegetables to the skillet, and add the soy sauce/sherry mixture from step 1. Toss everything together well. Cover and simmer for 3 to 4 minutes. Top with the almonds, and serve.

Yield: 3 servings, each with 18 grams of carbohydrates and 6 grams of fiber, for a total of 12 grams of usable carbs and 36 grams of protein.

ᔐ Lemon-Pepper Chicken and Gravy

  1 cut-up broiler-fryer

  1 1/4 teaspoons lemon pepper

  1 1/4 teaspoons onion powder

  1 teaspoon salt

  1/4 cup chicken broth

  1/2 cup heavy cream

  1 1/2 teaspoons spicy brown or Dijon mustard

1. Preheat the oven to 375°F.

2. Sprinkle the chicken pieces with 1 teaspoon of lemon pepper, 1 teaspoon of onion powder, and the salt. Arrange in a roasting pan, and roast, basting once or twice, for about 1 hour or until the juices run clear when the chicken is pierced.

3. Remove the chicken from the roasting pan and skim off the excess fat, leaving just the brown drippings. Place the roasting pan over a low burner, add the chicken broth to the pan, and stir, scraping up the tasty brown bits off the bottom of the pan. When the broth is simmering, add the cream, the rest of the lemon pepper and onion powder, and the mustard. Stir well, heat through, and pour over the chicken.

Yield: 4 servings, each with 2 grams of carbohydrates, a trace of fiber, and 44 grams of protein.

ᔐ Thai-ish Chicken Basil Stir-Fry

If all you've had are Chinese stir-fries, you'll find this an interesting change.

  2 tablespoons Thai fish sauce (nam pla)

  2 tablespoons soy sauce

  1 teaspoon Splenda

  1/4 teaspoon guar or xanthan

  2 teaspoons dried basil

  1 1/2 teaspoons red pepper flakes

  Peanut, canola, or coconut oil

  2 cloves garlic, crushed

  3 boneless, skinless chicken breasts cut into 1/2-inch cubes

1 small onion, sliced

1 1/2 cups frozen, crosscut green beans, thawed

1. Combine the fish sauce, soy sauce, Splenda, and guar in a blender. Blend for several seconds, then turn off the blender and add the basil and red pepper flakes, and set aside.

2. Heat a few tablespoons of oil in a wok or heavy skillet over high heat. When the oil is hot, add the garlic, chicken, and onion, and stir-fry for 3 to 4 minutes. Add the green beans, and continue to stir-fry until the chicken is done through.

3. Stir the blended seasoning mixture into the stir-fry, turn the burner to medium, cover, and let it simmer for 2 to 3 minutes (the beans should be tender-crisp).

Yield: 3 servings, each with 13 grams of carbohydrates and 3 grams of fiber, for a total of 10 grams of usable carbs and 31 grams of protein.

↻ Sautéed Sesame Chicken Breasts

Try serving this with a salad, a broccoli dish, or both.

4 boneless, skinless chicken breasts

1/4 cup sesame seeds

Salt

3 tablespoons peanut oil

1. Place a chicken breast in a large, heavy, zipper-lock bag and, using a hammer, meat tenderizer, or what-have-you, pound it until it's 1/4 inch thick. Repeat with the remaining chicken breasts.

2. Sprinkle each side of each breast evenly with 1/2 tablespoon of sesame seeds, and lightly salt.

3. Heat the peanut oil in a heavy skillet over medium heat. Add the chicken breasts and sauté for about 5 minutes each side, or until lightly golden. (You may have to do this in two batches; keep the first batch warm on an oven-proof plate in the oven, on its lowest temperature setting.) Serve.

Yield: 4 servings, each with 2 grams of carbohydrates and 1 gram of fiber, for a total of 1 gram of usable carbs and 30 grams of protein.

⌒ Stewed Chicken with Moroccan Seasonings

This is almost a Moroccan "tangine," but all the recipes I've seen call for some sort of starch. So I ditched the starch and just kept the seasonings, which are exotic and delicious.

   1/4 cup olive oil

   3 1/2 to 4 pounds chicken, cut up

   1 medium onion, thinly sliced

   2 cloves garlic, crushed

   3/4 cup chicken broth

   1/2 teaspoon ground coriander

   1/2 teaspoon ground cinnamon

   1/2 teaspoon paprika

   1/2 teaspoon ground cumin

   1 teaspoon ground ginger

   1/2 teaspoon pepper

   1/4 teaspoon cayenne

   1 tablespoon Splenda

   1 tablespoon tomato paste

   1 teaspoon salt or Vege-Sal

1. Heat the oil in a Dutch oven over medium heat, and brown the chicken in the oil.

2. When the chicken is golden all over, remove it from the Dutch oven, and pour off the fat. Put the chicken back in the Dutch oven, and scatter the onion and garlic over it.

3. Combine the garlic, broth, coriander, cinnamon, paprika, cumin, ginger, pepper, cayenne, Splenda, tomato paste, and salt, and whisk together well. Pour over the chicken, cover the Dutch oven, and turn the burner to low. Let the whole thing simmer for a good 45 minutes.

4. Uncover the chicken and let it simmer for another 15 minutes or so, to let the juices concentrate a bit. Serve each piece of chicken with some of the onion and juices spooned over it.

Yield: 4 generous servings, each with 6 grams of carbohydrates and 1 gram of fiber, for a total of 5 grams of usable carbs and 58 grams of protein.

⌒ Greek Roasted Chicken

Many carry-out places do a brisk business in chickens roasted Greek-style, and it's no wonder why—they're terrific. But the best-kept secret about those roasters is that they're as easy as can be to make at home.

3 to 4 pounds of chicken (whole, split in half, cut-up broiler-fryer, or cut-up parts of your choice)

1/4 lemon juice

1/2 cup olive oil

1/2 teaspoon salt

1/4 teaspoon pepper

1. Wash your chicken, and pat it dry with paper towels.

2. Combine the lemon juice, olive oil, salt, and pepper, and stir them together well. If you're using a whole chicken, rub it all over with some of this mixture, making sure to rub plenty inside the body cavity, as well. If you're using cut-up chicken, put it in a large zipper-lock bag, pour the marinade over it, and seal the bag.

3. Let the chicken marinate for at least an hour, or as long as a day.

4. At least 1 hour before you want to serve the chicken, pull it out of the bag. You can either grill your chicken or you can roast it in a 375°F oven for about 1 hour. Either way, cook it until the juices run clear when it's pierced to the bone.

Yield: 5 servings, each with less than 1 gram of carbohydrates, a bare trace of fiber, and 52 grams of protein.

🍓 If you have a rotisserie, this is a terrific dish to cook in it. Follow the instructions that come with your unit for cooking times.

↻ Chicken Liver and "Rice" Casserole

I'm a big fan of chicken livers, and they're highly nutritious. No, the liver does not contain every toxin eaten by the animal during its life. The liver processes and removes this stuff, it doesn't just hold on to it forever.

1 stick butter

1 small onion, chopped

1 rib celery, including leaves, diced

1 bay leaf, crumbled fine

1/2 teaspoon dried thyme

1/2 teaspoon salt or Vege-Sal

1/2 teaspoon seasoned salt

1 pound chicken livers, cut into bite-size pieces

4 cups Cauliflower Rice Deluxe (see page 160)

1/4 cup grated Parmesan cheese

1. Preheat oven to 375°F.

2. Melt the butter in a heavy skillet over medium heat, and sauté the onion, celery, bay leaf, thyme, salt, and seasoned salt.

3. When the onion is golden, add the chicken livers, and cook for another 5 minutes, stirring frequently. Toss the vegetables and livers together with the Cauliflower Rice Deluxe.

4. Spray a good-size casserole (10 cups or so) with nonstick cooking spray, and dump the liver and "rice" mixture into the casserole. Sprinkle the top with the Parmesan, and bake the whole thing, uncovered, for 15 minutes.

Yield: 5 servings, each with 16 grams of carbohydrates and 3 grams of fiber, for a total of 13 grams usable carbs and 21 grams of protein.

◯ Chicken with Camembert and Almonds

4 boneless, skinless chicken breasts

6 tablespoons butter

8 ounces Camembert

1/3 cup slivered almonds

4 scallions, thinly sliced

1. Place a chicken breast in a large, heavy, zipper-lock bag and, using a hammer, meat tenderizer, or what-have-you, pound it until it's 1/4 inch thick. Repeat with the remaining chicken breasts.

2. Melt 4 tablespoons of the butter in a heavy skillet over medium heat. Sauté the chicken until it's golden on the first side.

3. While the first side of the chicken is cooking, divide the cheese into four equal portions, peel off the white rind, and thinly slice each portion.

4. Flip the chicken and lay a portion of cheese over each chicken breast.

5. Melt the remaining 2 tablespoons of butter in a small skillet, and add the almonds. Stir until they're lightly golden.

6. When the second side of the chicken is golden and the cheese is melted, place each breast on a serving plate, and divide the almonds evenly over them. Scatter a sliced scallion over each breast, and serve.

Yield: 4 servings, each with 4 grams of carbohydrates and 2 grams of fiber, for a total of 2 grams of usable carbs and 43 grams of protein.

🍓 If you're the type of person who likes to multitask, this recipe is for you. If you can slice and peel the cheese while the first side of the chicken cooks and get the almonds toasting, you should be able to get the almonds done just in time to move hot almonds onto just-done chicken breasts.

CHAPTER EIGHT

Fish

Of all the good things that can be said about fish, this is the one that is likely to appeal to the greatest number of people: Fish is very quick to cook. Unlike the poultry, beef, and lamb and pork chapters, this is a chapter where the vast majority of the recipes take no more than 15 minutes to get on the table. With today's jammed schedules, that's a good thing to keep in mind. The tighter your time is, the better the idea of eating fish becomes.

Of course, it's a good idea for another excellent reason: Fish is really, really good for you. In particular, if you're in the minority whose total cholesterol levels have gone up since starting your low-carb diet, you'll want to eat fish frequently, especially salmon, with its heart-healthy EPA oils.

You'll see it noted again and again in this chapter, and I'll say it here, too: Most mild, white fishes are interchangeable in recipes. They'll taste a bit different and have slightly different textures, but the same recipes that work for tilapia will work for sole; the same recipes that work for orange roughy will work for cod. By the way, if you haven't tried tilapia, you ought to check it out. It's a mild, white fish that is being farmed more widely. Because tilapia is farmed, it tends to be less expensive than fish that has to be caught, so look for it.

ꙍ The Simplest Fish

Not only is this simple, it's lightening-quick, too.

> 1 tablespoon butter
> 1 fillet (about 6 ounces) mild white fish
> 1 tablespoon minced fresh parsley
> Wedge of lemon

1. Melt the butter in a heavy-bottomed skillet over low heat. Add the fish fillets, and sauté for 5 minutes on each side, or until the fish is opaque and flakes easily, turning carefully.

2. Transfer to serving plates, top with the minced parsley, and serve with a wedge of lemon.

   Yield: 1 serving, with a trace of carbohydrates, no fiber, and 31 grams of protein.

ꙍ Unbelievably Easy Shrimp

Want cold, cooked shrimp for dipping? Here's how to get them perfect, every time.

> 2 quarts water
> 1 tablespoon salt
> 1 pound shelled, deveined raw shrimp

1. Put the water in a large saucepan, put the salt in the water, and put the saucepan over high heat. When the water is boiling, dump in your shrimp.

2. Bring the water just back up to the boil, and turn off the burner. Let the shrimp sit another minute if they're tiny, or 2 to 3 minutes if they're big.

3. Drain them in a colander, and run them under some cold water. Chill them, and serve with cocktail sauce, aioli, or mustard-mayonnaise.

   Yield: 4 generous servings, each with 1 gram of carbohydrates, no fiber, and 23 grams of protein.

ᲘᲘ Scampi!

> 1/2 cup butter
>
> 1/4 cup olive oil
>
> 3 cloves garlic, crushed
>
> 1 pound raw shrimp in the shell
>
> 1/4 cup dry white wine
>
> 1/4 cup minced fresh parsley

1. Melt the butter with the olive oil in a heavy skillet over medium-low heat. Add the garlic, and stir it around.

2. Add the shrimp to the skillet. If they're room temperature, they'll take 2 to 3 minutes per side; frozen shrimp will take 4 to 5 minutes per side. Be careful not to overcook them.

3. Add the wine, and simmer for another 1 to 2 minutes. Serve garnished with the parsley, and put out plenty of napkins!

Yield: 3 servings, each with 3 grams of carbohydrates, a trace of fiber, and 31 grams of protein.

> 🍓 Feel free to increase this recipe to however much your skillet can hold. This makes a great fast-and-easy company dinner; just add a salad and some crusty bread for the carb-eaters, and call it a party.

ᲘᲘ Obscenely Rich Shrimp

This is a bit of trouble, and it's not cheap, so you'll probably only want to make it for company—but wow.

> 2 packages (10 ounces each) frozen chopped spinach
>
> 3 tablespoons butter
>
> 1 pound mushrooms, sliced
>
> 1 small onion, diced
>
> 1 bag (14 ounces) frozen, cooked, shelled shrimp (the little ones are best)
>
> 2 teaspoons liquid beef bouillon concentrate
>
> 1 1/2 cups heavy cream
>
> 1 cup sour cream

1 cup grated Parmesan cheese

1 cup unsweetened flaked coconut

1. Preheat the oven to 350°F.

2. Cook the spinach; I put mine in a glass casserole, cover it, and microwave it on High for 7 minutes.

3. Melt the butter in a heavy skillet over medium heat, and start sautéing the mushrooms and onions. When they're starting to get limp, break up your frozen shrimp a bit, and add them to the skillet.

4. When the shrimp are thawed and the onions are quite limp and translucent, scoop out the veggies and shrimp with a slotted spoon, and put them aside in a bowl. Turn up the burner to medium-high. A fair amount of liquid will have accumulated in the bottom of the skillet; add the beef bouillon concentrate to it, and boil the liquid until it's reduced to about one-third of its original volume.

5. Turn the burner back down to low, stir in the heavy cream, sour cream, and Parmesan, and just heat it through (don't let it boil). Stir the shrimp and vegetables back into this sauce.

6. Rescue your spinach from the microwave, and drain it well by putting it in a strainer and pressing it with the back of a spoon, to make sure all the liquid is removed.

7. Spray a 10-cup casserole with nonstick cooking spray, and spread half of the spinach in the bottom of it. Put half of the shrimp mixture over that. Repeat the layers with the rest of the spinach and the rest of the sauce.

8. Top with the coconut and bake for a 1 1/2 hours.

Yield: 6 servings, each with 15 grams of carbohydrates and 5 grams of fiber, for a total of 10 grams of usable carbs and 26 grams of protein. (Not to mention outrageous amounts of fat, but that doesn't bother us!)

Scallops on Spinach with Walnut Sauce

From the kitchen of Tanya Rachfal.

Walnut Sauce

2 cups water

1/4 cup chopped walnuts

2 tablespoons lemon juice

1 teaspoon grated lemon rind

4 tablespoons extra-virgin olive oil

1/2 teaspoon salt

1/2 teaspoon freshly ground black pepper

Remaining Ingredients

1 pound turkey bacon

12 ounces large sea scallops (16 to 20)

Peanut oil

1 pound spinach

1. Bring the water to a boil in a small saucepan. Add the walnuts and boil for 30 seconds, then drain. Put the walnuts in a bowl, and combine with the lemon juice, lemon rind, olive oil, salt, and pepper. Mix well, and set aside.

2. Cut the slices of turkey bacon in half. Wrap a piece of bacon around a scallop and slip onto a skewer. Baste the scallops with the peanut oil.

3. Wash the spinach leaves thoroughly, and cook over high heat until done. Broil the scallops for 5 minutes, turn, baste, and broil the other side for 5 minutes. Serve the scallops over spinach and top with the sauce.

Yield: 4 servings, each with 10 grams of carbohydrates and 4 grams of fiber, for a total of 6 grams of usable carbs and 37 grams of protein.

Baked Orange Roughy

1 1/2 pounds orange roughy fillets, cut into serving-size pieces

1 teaspoon salt or Vege-Sal

Pepper

1/4 medium onion, very thinly sliced

Juice of 1 lemon, or 2 tablespoons bottled lemon juice

1/4 cup butter, melted

Paprika

Minced fresh parsley (optional)

1. Preheat the oven to 325°F. Spray a shallow baking dish with nonstick cooking spray.

2. Arrange the fish in the prepared pan, and sprinkle with salt and pepper to taste. Scatter the onion over the fish.

3. In a small bowl, combine the lemon juice and butter, and pour over the fish and onions. Sprinkle with paprika.

4. Bake, uncovered, for 30 minutes. Sprinkle with parsley (if using), and serve.

Yield: 4 servings, each with 2 grams of carbohydrates, a trace of fiber, and 25 grams of protein.

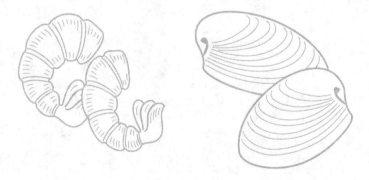

↶ Fish Baked in a Bed of Rock Salt

Maureen Bernardis sends this recipe all the way from Trieste, Italy, and says, "I have never been a fish eater, unless it was 'not fishy' fish. After discovering this recipe I am a total convert, and we now have fresh fish at least once a week."

> Fresh whole fish, about 2 pounds
> Rock salt (enough to cover the fish)
> Salt and pepper
> Olive oil

1. Preheat the oven to 350°F.

2. Clean the fish, leaving the scales and heads on. (Your fish market may do this for you, if you ask.)

3. Line the bottom of a pan with a layer of rock salt, place the fish on the salt, and cover it completely with more rock salt. Bake for 40 minutes.

4. Remove from the oven and break away the salt. Open the fish and season with salt, pepper, and olive oil to taste. Serve hot.

Yield: 4 generous servings, each with no carbohydrates, no fiber, and 35 to 40 grams of protein.

🍓 You can also put a lemon slice, a bay leaf, sage, or rosemary inside the fish before you cook it, for a different flavored dish every time you cook. Don't be afraid to experiment.

↻ Orange Roughy Bonne Femme

This is my favorite fish recipe, and it's very, very simple to make. Kids will probably like it, too.

 1/4 cup low-carb bake mix
 Pinch of salt or Vege-Sal
 3 to 4 tablespoons butter
 1 1/2 pounds orange roughy fillets

1. Mix the bake mix with the pinch of salt (about 1/8 teaspoon). Dip the fillets in the bake mix, covering them lightly all over.

2. Melt the butter in a heavy skillet over medium heat. Sauté the "floured" fillets in the butter for 5 to 7 minutes per side, or until golden brown. Serve just as it is, or with a squeeze of lemon juice.

   Yield: 4 servings, each with 1 gram of carbohydrates, no fiber, and 25 grams of protein.

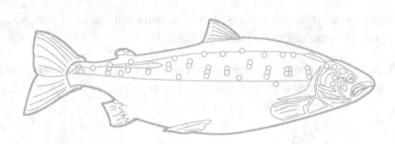

↻ Wine and Herb Tilapia Packets

A simple company fish dish.

> 1 1/2 pounds tilapia fillets, cut into 4 portions
>
> 4 tablespoons butter
>
> 1/2 cup dry white wine
>
> 1/4 cup minced fresh herbs (chives, basil, oregano, thyme, or a combination of these)
>
> Salt

1. Preheat the oven to 350°F.

2. Tear a piece of aluminum foil about 18 inches square for each fillet. Place a fillet in the center of the foil square, and curl the edges up a little. Put 1 tablespoon of butter, 2 tablespoons of wine, a tablespoon of minced herbs, and just a little salt on the filet.

3. Fold the foil up around the fish, rolling the edges down in the middle and at the ends, so the packet won't leak in the oven. Repeat for all 4 servings.

4. Place the packets right on the oven shelf—there's no need for a pan—and bake for 35 minutes.

Yield: 4 servings, each with 2 grams of carbohydrates and 1 gram of fiber, for a total of 1 gram of usable carbs and 31 grams of protein.

> 🍓 When it's time to serve dinner, simply place a packet on each plate, and let diners open their own. That way, no one loses a drop of the yummy butter, wine, and herb sauce the fish cooked in.

⌒ Tilapia on a Nest of Vegetables

Quite beautiful to look at, and a fast one-dish dinner. You could substitute green pepper for either the red or the yellow, if you like.

> 3 tablespoons olive oil
>
> 1 cup red pepper, cut into thin strips
>
> 1 cup yellow pepper, cut into thin strips
>
> 1 1/2 cups zucchini, cut in matchstick strips
>
> 1 1/2 cups yellow squash, cut in matchstick strips
>
> 1 cup sweet red onion, thinly sliced
>
> 1 clove garlic, crushed
>
> 1 pound tilapia fillets
>
> Salt and pepper
>
> 1/4 teaspoon guar or xanthan
>
> Lemon wedges (optional)

1. Heat the olive oil in a heavy skillet over medium-high heat, and sauté the peppers, zucchini, squash, onion, and garlic for just 2 to 3 minutes, stirring frequently.

2. Sprinkle the tilapia fillets lightly on either side with the salt and pepper, and lay them over the vegetables in the skillet. Cover, turn the burner to medium-low, and let the fish steam in the moisture from the vegetables for 10 minutes, or until it flakes easily.

3. With a spatula, carefully transfer the fish to a serving platter, and use a slotted spoon to pile the vegetables on top of the fish. Pour the liquid that has accumulated in the skillet into a blender, and add the guar. Run the blender for a few seconds, then pour the thickened juices over the fish and vegetables. To serve, spoon a mound of the vegetables onto each diner's plate, and place a piece of the fish on top. A few lemon wedges are nice with this, but hardly essential.

Yield: 4 servings, each with 11 grams of carbohydrates and 2 grams of fiber, for a total of 8 grams of usable carbs and 22 grams of protein.

ᑐ Ranch Fish

Karen Andrews sends this easy and delicious recipe.

>   2 pounds white fish fillets
>   1 package (1 ounce) dry Ranch dressing mix
>   1/3 cup lemon juice
>   2 tablespoons olive oil
>   3 tablespoons white wine

1. Spray a cookie sheet with nonstick cooking spray. Arrange the filets on the cookie sheet.

2. Combine the dressing mix, lemon juice, oil, and wine, and pour over fish. Broil for 9 to 12 minutes, or until done.

    Yield: 4 servings, each with 2 grams of carbohydrates, a trace of fiber, and 41 grams of protein.

ᑐ Tuna Melt Casserole

Hey, we all grew up on tuna casserole. Here's one with no noodles, for the low-carb grownups we've become.

>   1 teaspoon oil
>   1 can (6 ounces) albacore tuna, drained and mashed
>   1 cup shredded Cheddar cheese
>   3 slices (1 1/2 ounces) processed American cheese
>   3 eggs
>   3 tablespoons ground flaxseed meal or 3 tablespoons low-carbohydrate bake mix
>   1 teaspoon garlic powder
>   1/2 to 1 teaspoon salt

1. Preheat the oven to 400°F, and grease a 9-inch pie plate with the oil.

2. In a large bowl, combine the tuna, cheeses, eggs, flaxseed meal, garlic, and salt. Mix well.

3. Pour the tuna mixture into the prepared pie plate, pat down firmly, and bake for approximately 30 minutes, or until browned and bubbly.

Yield: 3 servings, each with 5 grams of carbohydrates and 3 grams of fiber, for a total of 2 grams of usable carbs and 38 grams of protein.

ᔕ Crispy Parmesan Fish

This comes from Dona Crawford, who says she first tried it on a retreat in Sun Valley, Idaho.

> 1 pound cod fillets
> 2 1/2 tablespoons mayonnaise
> 1 teaspoon Dijon mustard
> 1 teaspoon Worcestershire sauce
> 1 tablespoon minced onion
> 1 ounce grated Parmesan cheese

1. Preheat the oven to 350°F, and spray a shallow baking dish with nonstick cooking spray. Place the fish in the prepared baking dish.
2. In a small bowl, combine the mayonnaise, mustard, Worcestershire, and onion, and spread evenly over fillets.
3. Sprinkle the filets with the Parmesan, and bake uncovered for 30 minutes, or until crispy.

Yield: 3 servings, each with 1 gram of carbohydrates, a trace of fiber, and 31 grams of protein.

🍓 This combination of seasonings tastes great on chicken, too.

ᔣ Broiled Marinated Whiting

With a big salad and some crusty bread for the carb-eaters, this makes
a nice, simple supper.

> 1/2 cup olive oil
>
> 3 tablespoons wine vinegar
>
> 1 tablespoon lemon juice
>
> 1 teaspoon Dijon mustard
>
> 1 clove garlic, crushed
>
> 1/2 teaspoon dried basil
>
> 1/4 teaspoon salt
>
> 1/4 teaspoon pepper
>
> 6 whiting fillets

1. Combine the oil, vinegar, lemon juice, mustard, garlic, basil, salt, and pepper, and mix well.

2. Place the fillets in a large, zipper-lock bag, and pour in the oil mixture. Refrigerate for several hours, turning the bag over from time to time.

3. Remove the fish from the marinade. Broil about 8 inches from the heat, for 4 to 5 minutes per side, or cook on a stove top grill.

4. While the fish is cooking, put the leftover marinade in a saucepan and boil it briefly, then served it as a sauce.

Yield: 3 servings, each with just over 1 gram of carbohydrates, no fiber, and 34 grams of protein.

🍓 If you're in a hurry or you just don't have all the ingredients to make this dish, use 3/4 cup of store-bought vinaigrette dressing, instead.

ꙑ Salsa Fish

 1 fillet (about 6 ounces) firm-fleshed white fish, such as cod or sole

 2 tablespoons salsa

1. Preheat the oven to 350°F.

2. Place the fish in a shallow baking pan, cover with the salsa, and bake for 30 to 40 minutes, or until the fish flakes easily.

 Yield: 1 serving, with 2 grams of carbohydrates and 1 gram of fiber, for a total of 1 gram of usable carbs and 31 grams of protein.

ꙑ Salmon with Lemon-Dill Butter

A classic flavor combination, and after you make this, you'll understand why.

 4 tablespoons butter, softened

 1 tablespoon lemon juice

 1 teaspoon dry dill weed or 1 tablespoon snipped fresh dill

 4 salmon steaks, each 1 inch thick

 Olive oil

1. Put the butter, lemon juice, and dill in a food processor with the S blade in place. Pulse until well combined, scraping down the sides once or twice if necessary. (If you don't have a food processor, you can simply beat these things together by hand.) Chill.

2. About 15 minutes before dinner, rub each salmon steak on both sides with olive oil. Arrange the steaks on the broiler rack, and broil 8 inches from high heat for 5 to 6 minutes per side, or until the salmon flakes easily.

3. Place on the serving plates, top each steak with a tablespoon of the lemon-dill butter, and serve.

 Yield: 4 very generous servings, each with only a trace of carbohydrates, a trace of fiber, and about 34 grams of protein.

↻ Feta-Spinach Salmon Roast

I saw something like this being sold for outrageous amounts of money in the fish case at the local grocery store, and I thought, "I can do that!"

> 3 ounces cream cheese, softened
> 3/4 cup crumbled feta
> 2 scallions, thinly sliced, including the crisp part of the green
> 1/2 cup fresh spinach, chopped
> 2 skinless salmon fillets of roughly equal size and shape, totaling 3/4 pound
> Olive oil

1. Preheat the oven to 350°F.

2. Combine the cream cheese and feta, mashing and stirring with a fork until well blended. Add the scallions and spinach, and combine well.

3. Spread the mixture evenly over one salmon fillet. (The filling will be about 3/4 inch thick.) Top with the second salmon fillet. Brush both sides with olive oil, turning the whole thing over carefully with a spatula.

4. Place the loaf on a shallow baking pan, and bake for 20 minutes. Slice carefully with a sharp, serrated knife.

Yield: 2 servings, each with 5 grams of carbohydrates, a trace of fiber, and 45 grams of protein.

Orange Salmon Packets

$1/4$ cup plain yogurt

2 tablespoons mayonnaise

$1/4$ teaspoon orange extract

1 tablespoon Splenda

1 tablespoon lemon juice

2 scallions, finely minced

1 tablespoon parsley, finely minced

1 pound salmon fillets

1. Preheat the oven to 425°F.

2. Combine the yogurt, mayonnaise, orange extract, Splenda, lemon juice, scallions, and parsley. Set aside.

3. If your salmon fillets have skin on them, remove it, and cut the fish into 4 serving-size pieces.

4. Tear 4 large squares of heavy-duty aluminum foil. Place each piece of salmon in the center of a square of foil, and spoon 2 tablespoons of the sauce over it. Fold the foil up over the salmon, bringing the edges together, and roll the edges to make a tight seal. Roll up each end, as well.

5. When all your salmon fillets are snug in their own little packets, bake them for 15 minutes.

    You can put your salmon packets in a roasting pan, if you're afraid they'll spring a leak, but I just put mine right on the oven rack.

6. Place on individual serving plates, cut open, and serve. If you have a little sauce left over, serve it on the side.

Yield: 4 servings, each with less than 2 grams of carbohydrates, a trace of fiber, and 24 grams of protein.

꧂ Mustard-Glazed Salmon

     1 salmon fillet (5 ounces)

     1 tablespoon Mellow "Honey" Mustard Dressing (see page 236)

     1 scallion, finely minced

     1/2 teaspoon dried thyme

1. Preheat the oven to 350°F.

2. If there's skin on your salmon, remove it. Place the fillet on a baking tray.

3. In a small bowl, mix together the dressing, scallion, and thyme; spread it evenly over the fish. Bake for 12 to 15 minutes, or until the fish flakes easily.

Yield: 1 serving, with 4 grams of carbohydrates and 1 gram of fiber, for a total of 3 grams of usable carbs and 29 grams of protein.

🍓 Don't be too squeamish about buying salmon with skin on it. It actually peels off quite easily, and it adds almost no time to the preparation process.

꧂ Aioli Fish Bake

     1 fillet (about 6 ounces) of mild, white fish

     2 tablespoons Aioli (see page 408)

     1 tablespoon grated Parmesan cheese

1. Preheat the oven to 350°F.

2. Spray a shallow baking pan (a jelly roll pan is ideal) with nonstick cooking spray. Working right on the baking pan, spread a fillet thickly with Aioli, and sprinkle 1/2 tablespoon of Parmesan over that. Turn carefully, and spread Aioli and sprinkle Parmesan on other side. Bake for 20 minutes, and serve.

Yield: 1 serving, with 1 gram of carbohydrates, a trace of fiber, and 32 grams of protein.

ꙩ Panned Swordfish Steaks
with Garlic and Vermouth

Simple, fast, and elegant. And do you know how much you'd pay for this at a restaurant?

> 1 pound swordfish steaks
> Salt and pepper
> 1 tablespoon olive oil
> 1/4 cup water
> 1/4 cup dry vermouth
> 2 or 3 cloves garlic, crushed
> 3 to 4 tablespoons minced parsley

1. Sprinkle the swordfish steaks lightly on both sides with salt and pepper.

2. Place a heavy skillet over high heat, and add the olive oil. When the oil is hot, add the swordfish and sear on both sides (about 1 to 1 1/2 minutes per side). Then add the water, vermouth, and garlic, and turn down the heat to medium. Cover, and let the fish simmer for 10 minutes.

3. Remove to a serving platter or individual serving plates, and keep warm. Turn the heat under the skillet to high, and boil the pan juices hard for a minute or two, until they're reduced to 1/4 cup or so. Pour over the fish, and top with parsley.

Yield: 3 servings, each with 2 grams of carbohydrates, no fiber, and 32 grams of protein.

Noodleless Shrimp Pad Thai

This isn't terribly low in carbs—it's a maintenance dish, really—but I know that there are a lot of Thai food fans out there and that Pad Thai is the most popular Thai dish. So this is a lot lower-carb than Pad Thai with noodles, plus it's fast and incredibly tasty.

2 tablespoons Thai fish sauce (nam pla)

1 tablespoon Splenda

2 tablespoons peanut oil or other bland oil

2 cloves garlic, smashed

12 cooked, peeled shrimp

2 eggs, beaten slightly

3 cups cooked spaghetti squash

1 1/2 cups bean sprouts

2 tablespoons dry-roasted peanuts, chopped

4 scallions, sliced

2 tablespoons cilantro, chopped

1 lime, cut into wedges

1. Mix the fish sauce and Splenda, and set the mixture aside.

2. Put the oil in a heavy skillet over medium-high heat, and sauté the garlic for a minute. Add the shrimp, and sauté for another minute. Add the fish sauce mixture.

3. Pour the beaten eggs into the skillet, let them set for 15 to 30 seconds, and then scramble. Stir in the spaghetti squash and bean sprouts, mixing with the shrimp and egg mixture. Cook until just heated through.

4. Place on serving plates. Top each serving with chopped peanuts, scallions, and cilantro, and serve with a wedge of lime on the side.

Yield: 3 servings, each with 19 grams of carbohydrates and 2 grams of fiber, for a total of 17 grams of usable carbs and 13 grams of protein.

🍓 If this carb count sounds way too high to you, keep in mind that regular Pad Thai usually has over 60 grams of carbohydrates per serving, making this dish quite a bargain, carb-wise.

ꙅ Sautéed Seafood and Red Pepper

This outstanding recipe comes from Alix Sudlow, who says that the leftovers are delicious for lunch the next day.

> 2 tablespoons olive oil
> 2 salmon fillets (about 6 ounces each)
> 1 red bell pepper, deseeded and thickly sliced
> 8 ounces large fresh shrimp, shelled and deveined
> 8 ounces sea scallops, rinsed and patted dry
> 4 cloves of garlic, peeled and chopped
> 1 tablespoon fresh lemon or lime juice (optional)
> 1/2 teaspoon ground red pepper or dried hot red pepper flakes, or a dash of hot pepper sauce
> Salt and black pepper
> 2 tablespoons fresh cilantro and/or parsley, finely chopped

1. Heat the olive oil in a large skillet—do not crowd the ingredients—over medium heat. Put the salmon fillets in the skillet, skin side down. Scatter the red pepper slices around. Cook for about 6 minutes on a medium heat, turning once halfway through.

2. Add the shrimp, scallops, garlic, lemon juice (if using), red pepper, salt, and pepper. Fry for 2 to 3 minutes more, until the shrimp and scallops are opaque.

3. Move to serving dishes. Scatter the cilantro over it, and serve.

Yield: 4 servings, each with 5 grams of carbohydrates and 1 gram of fiber, for a total of 4 grams of usable carbs and 38 grams of protein.

↷ Shrimp and Andouille Jambalaya

If you can't find andouille, just substitute the lowest-carb smoked sausage you can find.

> 12 ounces andouille sausage, sliced 1/2 inch thick
> 1/4 cup olive oil
> 1 1/3 cups chopped onion
> 2 cloves garlic, crushed
> 1 large green pepper, diced
> 1 can (14 1/2 ounces) diced tomatoes, including liquid
> 1 cup chicken broth
> 1 teaspoon dried thyme
> 6 cups Cauliflower Rice (about one good-size cauliflower; see page 159)
> 2 cups shelled, deveined, medium-size shrimp
> Salt and pepper
> Tabasco

1. In a Dutch oven, start browning the andouille in the olive oil. When it's lightly golden on both sides, add the onion, garlic, and green pepper. Sauté the vegetables until the onion is becoming translucent.

2. Add the tomatoes, chicken broth, and thyme, and bring to a simmer. Let it simmer for 20 minutes or so, uncovered, to blend the flavors.

3. Add the "rice" and simmer for another 15 minutes, or until the cauliflower is starting to get tender.

4. Add the shrimp, and simmer for another 5 minutes or so—just long enough to cook the shrimp. Add salt, pepper, and Tabasco to taste, and serve.

Yield: 6 servings, each with 12 grams of carbohydrates and 4 grams of fiber, for a total of 8 grams of usable carbs and 32 grams of protein.

↶ Salmon Patties

These are quick, easy, and from-the-pantry-shelf convenient. If you don't have scallions in the refrigerator, use a tablespoon or so of finely minced onion.

> 1 can (14 3/4 ounces) salmon
> 1/4 cup oat bran
> 1 egg
> 2 scallions, finely sliced
> 3 tablespoons butter

1. Drain the salmon, place it in a mixing bowl, and mash it well. (Don't worry about any skin that may be in there, just mash it right in.)

2. Add the oat bran, egg, and scallions, and mix everything well. Form into 4 patties.

3. Melt the butter in a heavy skillet over medium heat. Sauté the patties in the butter, turning carefully, until they're quite golden on both sides (7 to 10 minutes per side).

Yield: 2 servings, each with 9 grams of carbohydrates and 2 grams of fiber, for a total of 7 grams usable carbs and 47 grams of protein.

🍓 Not only do these patties have lots of healthy fish oils, they also contain half your day's requirement of calcium.

↷ Tequila Lime Grilled Shrimp

Tired of burgers and chicken at your cookouts? Try this, instead.

> 2 pounds really large, raw shrimp in their shells (about 30 shrimp)
> 1 batch Tequila Lime Marinade (see page 411)

1. Put your shrimp in a big zipper-lock bag, pour the marinade over them, squeeze out the air, and seal the bag. Put the bag in the refrigerator, and let the shrimp marinate for at least a few hours, turning the bag now and then.

2. When it's time for dinner, drain off the marinade into a saucepan, and grill or broil your shrimp (3 to 4 minutes per side should do it; you want them pink all the way through, of course).

3. While the shrimp is cooking, boil the marinade hard for a few minutes. This kills the germs so you can serve it as a dipping sauce.

Yield: It should be 6 servings (but you know how appetites can be at barbecues), each with 3 grams of carbohydrates, a trace of fiber, and 31 grams of protein.

Teriyaki Shrimp. Most people only use teriyaki on steak or chicken, but it's just as good on shrimp. Just follow the directions for the Tequila Lime Grilled Shrimp, but use Teriyaki Sauce (see page 411) instead of Tequila Lime Marinade.

Yield: 6 servings, each with 4 grams of carbohydrates, a trace of fiber, and 32 grams of protein.

ᕲ Instant Shrimp Stir-Fry

 ¼ cup peanut oil

 15 medium-size, frozen, cooked, peeled shrimp

 1 cup frozen "stir-fry blend" vegetables

 1 ½ tablespoons Stir-Fry Sauce (see page 402)

1. Heat the oil in a skillet or wok over high heat. Put the shrimp and vegetables, both still frozen, in the skillet. Stir-fry for 3 to 5 minutes, or until the shrimp are hot through and the vegetables are tender-crisp.

2. Stir in the stir-fry sauce, and serve. If you want to make 2 servings, double everything but the oil.

Yield: 1 serving, with 9 grams of carbohydrates and 3 grams of fiber, for a total of 6 grams of usable carbs and 21 grams of protein.

ᕲ Cajun Skillet Shrimp

I threw this together when my husband brought a friend home for a quick lunch. This takes no more than 10 minutes, and it was a big hit.

 3 tablespoons olive oil

 2 cups shelled, deveined shrimp (cooked or uncooked)

 1 clove garlic, crushed

 1 small onion, sliced

 ½ green pepper

 ½ yellow pepper

 1 teaspoon Cajun seasoning

1. Heat the oil in a heavy skillet over medium-high heat. If your shrimp are uncooked, throw them in now, along with the garlic, onion, and peppers, and stir-fry the lot together until the shrimp are pink clear through and the vegetables are just tender-crisp. If you're using cooked shrimp, sauté the vegetables first, then add the shrimp and cook just long enough to heat them through. (I threw mine in still frozen, and they were thawed and hot in just 4 to 5 minutes.)

2. Sprinkle the Cajun seasoning over everything. Stir it in, and serve.

Yield: 2 servings, each with 11 grams of carbohydrates and 2 grams of fiber, for a total of 9 grams of usable carbs and 28 grams of protein.

Shrimp Alfredo

I invented this for my Alfredo-obsessed husband, and he loves it.

> 2 cups frozen broccoli "cuts"
>
> 3 tablespoons butter
>
> 3 cloves garlic, crushed
>
> 2 cups thawed small, frozen shrimp, cooked, shelled, and deveined
>
> 3/4 cup heavy cream
>
> 1/4 teaspoon guar or xanthan
>
> 1 cup grated Parmesan cheese

1. Steam or microwave the broccoli until tender-crisp.

2. Melt the butter in a heavy skillet over medium heat, and stir in the garlic. Add the broccoli, drained, and the shrimp, and stir to coat with garlic butter.

3. While the shrimps are heating through, put the cream in the blender, turn it to a low speed, and add the guar. Turn the blender off quickly, so you don't make butter.

4. Pour the cream into the skillet, and stir in the Parmesan. Heat to a simmer, and serve.

Yield: 3 servings, each with 11 grams of carbohydrates and 4 grams of fiber, for a total of 7 grams of usable carbs and 30 grams of protein.

Parmesan Shrimp

This recipe comes from reader Karen Nichols, who says: "This is a beautiful dish served with steamed asparagus alongside, and it's also good presented over baked fish fillets. The shrimp can go further this way and serve more people."

2 tablespoons butter

1 tablespoon finely chopped onion

1 clove garlic, crushed

1/4 teaspoon salt

1/4 teaspoon ground red pepper

1/4 teaspoon white pepper

1 1/2 cups heavy cream

3 tablespoons grated Parmesan cheese

3 tablespoons low-carb ketchup

1 pound cooked shrimp, peeled and deveined

Fresh chopped chives for garnish (optional)

1. Melt the butter in a medium saucepan, and sauté the onion in it until tender, but not browned. Add the garlic, salt, and red and white peppers. Stir in the cream, Parmesan cheese, and low-carb ketchup.

2. Bring to a boil, then reduce heat and simmer, uncovered, stirring occasionally, until the sauce thickens (15 to 20 minutes).

3. Stir in the cooked shrimp. Move to a serving plate, and garnish with chopped chives, if using.

Yield: 4 servings, each with 4.5 grams of carbohydrates, a trace of fiber, and 27 grams of protein.

Low-Carb Shrimp and Grits

Here's one for you Southerners, from Adele Hite of Durham, North Carolina. My recipe tester—Kay, an Alabaman—loved this, and said the grits were great all by themselves, too.

Grits

1 recipe Fauxtatoes Deluxe (see page 159)

4 ounces cream cheese

1 cup white Cheddar cheese

1 cup grated Parmesan cheese

1 teaspoon black pepper

Shrimp

2 tablespoons butter

2 ounces chopped bacon

1 cup sliced mushrooms

2 ounces very thinly sliced oil-packed sun-dried tomatoes (about 4 tomatoes)

2 teaspoons lemon juice

1 teaspoon minced garlic

1/2 cup dry white wine

1/2 pound peeled, deveined shrimp

1/2 cup chopped green onions

1. Combine the Fauxtatoes, cream cheese, Cheddar, Parmesan, and black pepper in a saucepan. Stir over low heat until smooth.

2. Put the butter in a skillet, and add the chopped bacon. Brown the bacon slightly, and add the mushrooms, tomatoes, lemon juice, garlic, and wine. Simmer until the mushrooms are cooked.

3. Add the shrimp, and cook until they're just done. Toss with green onions, and serve over the grits.

Yield: 5 servings, each with about 18 grams of carbohydrates and 5 grams of fiber, for a total of 13 grams of usable carbs and 33 grams of protein.

🍓 If you want to follow Kay's suggestion and serve the "cheese grits" by themselves as a side dish, figure on 6 servings, each with 7 grams of carbohydrates and 2 grams of fiber, for a total of 5 grams of usable carbs and 15 grams of protein.

☓ Fried Catfish

I admit that without cornmeal this is somewhat inauthentic, but my catfish-loving spouse thought it was great. Catfish is among the least expensive fish, too, so this is a bargain to serve.

> 1/4 cup finely ground almonds
>
> 1/4 cup finely ground hazelnuts
>
> 2 tablespoons rice protein powder
>
> 1 1/2 teaspoons seasoned salt
>
> 1 egg
>
> 1 tablespoon water
>
> 1 pound catfish fillets
>
> Oil for frying (peanut, canola, or sunflower)
>
> Lemon wedges

1. On a plate, combine the almonds, hazelnuts, protein powder, and seasoned salt, stirring well.

2. In a shallow bowl, beat the egg with the water.

3. Wash and dry the catfish fillets. Dip each one in the egg, then in the nut mixture, pressing it well into the fish.

4. If you have a deep fryer, by all means use it to fry your fish until it's a deep gold color (7 to 10 minutes). If you don't, use a large, heavy skillet. Pour 1 inch of oil into the skillet, and put it over medium-high heat. Let it heat for at least 5 minutes; you don't want to put your fish in until the oil is up to temperature.

    🍓 To test the oil, carefully put in one drop—no more—of water. It should sizzle, but not make the oil spit. If the oil spits, it's too hot. Turn the burner down and wait for it to cool a bit.

5. When the oil is hot, put in your fish, and fry it until it's a deep gold in color. If the oil doesn't completely cover the fish, you'll have to carefully turn it after about 5 minutes. (Figure 7 to 10 minutes total frying time.) Serve with lemon wedges.

Yield: Serves 3, unless one of them is my husband, in which case it may only serve 2. Assuming my husband isn't at your house (and if he is, I'd like to hear about it), each serving has 4 grams of carbohydrates and 1 gram of fiber, for a total of 3 grams of usable carbs and 30 grams of protein.

CHAPTER NINE

Beef

There seems to be no end to the ways we can use beef—by itself, in casseroles, and in sandwiches, sauces, and pizzas, beef is a delicious way to get plenty of protein for no carbs at all. This chapter gives you some low-carb editions of high-carb favorites, as well as showing you some ways to use beef that you may never have even considered before. So read on.

Hamburgers

Let's talk about hamburgers for a moment. There is much to be said in favor of the humble hamburger—it's cheap, it's quick, it's easy, and just about everybody likes it. Rarely will you hear the kids complain, "Oh, no. Hamburgers again?" Furthermore, it's a food that is easy to make for both the "normal" eaters and the low-carbers: Just leave the bun off of yours!

On the other hand, plain hamburgers, without a bun, can become just a wee bit boring to the adult palate over time. What follows are some recipes to help you vary your burgers. All the carb and protein analyses are based on burgers that weigh $1/3$ pound before cooking.

↺ Bleu Burger

    1 hamburger patty

    1 tablespoon crumbled blue cheese

    1 teaspoon finely minced sweet red onion

Cook your burger by your preferred method. When it's almost done to your liking, top with the bleu cheese and let it melt. Remove from the heat, put it on plate, and top with onion.

Yield: 1 serving, with only a trace of carbohydrates, no fiber, and 27 grams of protein.

↺ Smothered Burgers

Mmmmushrooms and onions!

    4 hamburger patties

    2 tablespoons butter or olive oil

    1/2 cup sliced onion

    1/2 cup sliced mushrooms

    Dash of Worcestershire sauce

Cook your burgers by your preferred method. While the burgers are cooking, melt the butter or heat the oil in a small, heavy skillet over medium-high heat. Add the onion and mushrooms, and sauté until the onions are translucent. Add a dash of Worcestershire sauce, stir, and spoon over burgers.

Yield: 4 servings, each with just 2 grams of carbohydrates, at least a trace of fiber, and 27 grams of protein.

ᘓ Mexiburgers

    1 hamburger patty

    1 ounce jalepeño Jack or Monterey Jack cheese

    1 tablespoon salsa

Cook your burger by your preferred method. When it's almost done to your liking, melt the cheese over the burger. Top with salsa and serve.

Yield: 1 serving, with 2 grams of carbohydrates, a trace of fiber, and 27 grams of protein.

ᘓ Poor Man's Poivrade

A real peppery bite—not for the timid!

    1 hamburger patty

    1 tablespoon coarse cracked pepper

    1 tablespoon butter

    2 tablespoons dry white wine, dry sherry, or dry vermouth

1. Roll your raw hamburger patty in the pepper until it's coated all over.

2. Fry the burger in the butter over medium heat, until it's done to your liking.

3. Remove the burger to a plate. Add the wine to the skillet, and stir it around for a minute or two, until all the nice brown crusty bits are scraped up. Pour this over the hamburger, and serve.

Yield: 1 serving, with between 4 and 6 grams of carbohydrates per serving (depending on whether you use wine, sherry, or vermouth—wine is lowest, vermouth is highest) and 2 grams of fiber, for a total of 2 to 4 grams of usable carbs and 27 grams of protein.

↻ Pizza Burger

    1 hamburger patty

    1 tablespoon sugar-free jarred pizza sauce

    2 tablespoons shredded mozzarella cheese

Cook the burger by your preferred method. When it's almost done to your liking, top with pizza sauce, then mozzarella. Cook until the cheese is melted, and serve.

Yield: 1 serving, with (depending on your brand of pizza sauce), no more than 2 grams of carbohydrates, no fiber, and 28 grams of protein.

🍓 One of the lowest-carb nationally distributed brands of spaghetti sauce is Hunt's Classic. It has 7.5 grams of carbs per 1/2-cup serving, of which 4 g is fiber, for an effective carb count of just 3.5 grams.

↻ Ellen's Noodleless Lasagne

Ellen Radke sent this recipe for all you folks who miss lasagne! My dear friend Maria, who tested it on her husband and five kids, was asked if she would make this again. Her answer? An enthusiastic "Yes!"

> 1 pound ground beef
>
> 1 cup low-carb spaghetti sauce
>
> 1 can (4 ounces) sliced mushrooms
>
> 1 cup ricotta cheese
>
> 1 egg, beaten
>
> 1 1/2 cups shredded mozzarella cheese
>
> 1/2 tablespoon Italian seasoning
>
> 20 to 25 slices pepperoni

1. Preheat the oven to 350°F.

2. Brown the ground beef in a frying pan, and drain off the oil. Add the spaghetti sauce and mushrooms, and simmer 10 minutes.

3. In a small bowl, mix the ricotta, egg, 1/4 cup mozzarella, and Italian seasoning. Beat well with a fork.

4. Grease an 8 x 8-inch glass baking dish with nonstick cooking spray. Spread the beef mixture in the bottom of the dish. Spread the ricotta mixture on top of the beef mixture. Lay half the pepperoni slices on top of the ricotta mixture. Put remaining 1 cup of the shredded mozzarella over the pepperoni slices, and lay the remaining pepperoni on top of the cheese. Bake until bubbly (about 20 minutes).

Yield: 4 servings, each with 9 grams of carbohydrates and 3 grams of fiber, for a total of 6 grams of usable carbs and 43 grams of protein.

🍓 Recipe-tester Ellen adds: "Next time, I'll try mixing in some Parmesan cheese with the ricotta, and maybe adding a layer of spinach."

Ultra Meat Sauce

Spaghetti without the spaghetti, as it were.

> 1 1/2 pounds of ground beef
>
> 1 small onion, diced
>
> 1 clove garlic crushed
>
> 1 green pepper, diced
>
> 1 can (4 ounces) mushrooms, drained
>
> 2 cups low-carb spaghetti sauce

1. Brown and crumble the ground beef in a large, heavy skillet. As the grease starts to collect in the skillet, add the onion, garlic, green pepper, and mushrooms. Continue cooking until pepper and onion are soft.

2. Pour off the excess grease. Stir in the spaghetti sauce, and serve.

Yield: 5 servings, with (if you use the lowest-carbohydrate spaghetti sauce) 11 grams of carbohydrates and 4.6 grams of fiber, for a total of 6.4 grams of usable carbs and 25 grams of protein.

This is a good supper for the family, because, again, it's easy to add carbs for those who want them—you eat your very meaty meat sauce with a good sprinkling of Parmesan, and you let the carb-eaters have theirs over spaghetti. Serve a big salad with it, and there's dinner.

◯ Skillet Stroganoff

I pound ground beef

1 medium onion, diced

1 clove garlic, crushed

1 can (4 ounces) mushrooms, drained

1 teaspoon liquid beef broth concentrate

2 tablespoons Worcestershire sauce

1 teaspoon paprika

3/4 cup sour cream

Salt or Vege-Sal and pepper to taste

1. Brown and crumble the ground beef in a heavy skillet over medium heat. Add the onion and garlic as soon as there's a little grease in the bottom of the pan, and cook until all pinkness is gone from the ground beef.

2. Drain the excess grease. Add the mushrooms, broth concentrate, Worcestershire, and paprika. Stir in the sour cream, then add salt and pepper to taste. Heat through, but don't let it boil. This is great as-is, but you may certainly serve it over noodles for the non-low-carb set.

Yield: 3 servings, each with 9 grams of carbohydrates and 2 grams of fiber, for a total of 7 grams of usable carbs and 28 grams of protein.

↻ Ground Beef "Helper"

When your family starts agitating for the "normal" food of yore, whip up this recipe.

> 1 pound lean ground beef or ground turkey
>
> 1/2 cup chopped green pepper
>
> 1/2 cup chopped onion
>
> 1/2 cup diced celery
>
> 2 cans (8 ounces each) tomato sauce
>
> 2 cloves garlic, crushed; 1 teaspoon minced garlic;
>   or 1/2 teaspoon garlic powder
>
> 1/2 teaspoon Italian seasoning
>
> 2 cups shredded Cheddar or Monterey Jack cheese
>
> 1 box (about 1 3/4 ounces) low-carb pasta
>
> 1/3 cup water
>
> Salt and pepper to taste

1. In a large, oven-safe skillet, brown the meat with the pepper, onion, and celery. Drain off the grease.

2. Add the tomato sauce, garlic, seasoning, 1 cup of the cheese, pasta, water, and salt and pepper to taste. Cover and simmer over low heat for 10 minutes. Turn on broiler to preheat during last the few minutes of cooking time.

3. Stir well. Spread the remaining 1 cup of cheese over the top, and broil until the cheese starts to brown.

Yield: 6 servings, each with 11 grams of carbohydrates and 2 grams of fiber, for a total of 9 grams of usable carbs and 36 grams of protein.

⌒ Mexican Meatballs

Marilee Wellersdick sends this easy, South-of-the-Border skillet meal.

> 1 pound ground beef or ground turkey
>
> 2 eggs
>
> 1 medium onion, finely chopped
>
> 3 cloves garlic, minced
>
> 2 teaspoons ground coriander
>
> 1/2 teaspoon salt
>
> 2 tablespoons oil
>
> 1 can (14 1/2 ounces) cut or crushed tomatoes
>
> 1 can (8 ounces) tomato sauce
>
> 1 tablespoon chili powder
>
> 1/2 teaspoon ground cumin

1. Mix together the ground beef, eggs, half of the onion, two-thirds of the garlic, coriander, and salt. Shape the mixture into 2-inch balls.

2. Heat the oil in a large skillet. Add the meatballs and brown them. Add the tomatoes, tomato sauce, the remaining half of the onion, the remaining third of the garlic, chili powder, and cumin to the skillet. Cover and simmer over medium-low heat for 45 minutes.

Yield: 4 servings, each with 15 grams of carbohydrates and 3 grams of fiber, for a total of 12 grams of usable carbs and 24 grams of protein.

෮ Ground Beef Stir-Fry

This looks like a lot of instructions, but it actually goes together rather quickly. It's good when you're missing Chinese food, which is generally full of added sugar and starch.

    2 tablespoons soy sauce

    3 tablespoons dry sherry

    1 or 2 cloves garlic, crushed

    1 pound ground beef

    Peanut oil or other bland oil for stir-frying

    1/2 cup coarsely chopped walnuts

    2 cups frozen crosscut green beans, thawed, or 2 cups frozen broccoli
      "cuts," thawed

    1 medium onion, sliced

    1 1/2 teaspoons grated fresh ginger

1. In a bowl, combine 1 tablespoon soy sauce, 4 1/2 teaspoons sherry, and the garlic. Add the ground beef and, with clean hands, mix the flavorings into the meat.

    🍓 Remember the Law of Stir-Frying: Have everything chopped, thawed, sliced, and prepped before you start cooking!

2. Heat 2 to 3 tablespoons oil in a wok or large, heavy skillet over high heat. Put the walnuts in the skillet and fry for a few minutes, until crispy. Drain and put aside.

3. Using the same oil, stir-fry bite-size chunks of the ground beef mixture until done through. Lift out the beef, and drain.

4. Pour the oil and fat out of the skillet, and put a few tablespoons of fresh oil in. Heat it up over high heat, and add the green beans, onion, and ginger. Stir-fry until the vegetables are tender-crisp.

5. Add the beef back to the pan, and stir everything up. Stir in the remaining soy sauce and sherry, and another clove of crushed garlic if you like.

6. Serve without rice for you and on top of rice for the carb-eaters in the family. Sprinkle the toasted walnuts on top of each serving, and pass the soy sauce at the table for those who like more.

Yield: 3 servings, each with 19 grams of carbohydrates and 6 grams of fiber, for a total of 13 grams of usable carbs and 34 grams of protein.

Burger Scramble Florentine

The only name I have to attribute this to is "Dottie," which is too bad, because my sister, who tested this recipe, says it's great.

> 1 1/2 pounds lean ground beef
>
> 1/2 cup onion, finely diced
>
> 10 ounces frozen spinach, thawed and drained
>
> 1 package (8 ounces) cream cheese, softened
>
> 1/2 cup heavy cream
>
> 1/2 cup shredded Parmesan cheese
>
> Salt and pepper

1. Preheat the oven to 350°F. Spray a large casserole with nonstick cooking spray.

2. In a large skillet, brown the ground beef and onion. Add the spinach and cook until the meat is done.

3. In a bowl, combine the cream cheese, heavy cream, Parmesan, and salt and pepper to taste. Mix well.

4. Combine the cream cheese mixture and the meat mixture, and spoon into the prepared casserole. Bake, uncovered, for 30 minutes or until bubbly and browned on top.

Yield: 6 servings, each with 5 grams of carbohydrates and 2 grams of fiber, for a total of 3 grams of usable carbs and 28 grams of protein.

Garden Burger Scramble. Substitute a 10-ounce package of frozen green beans for the spinach, and use Garden Vegetable Cream Cheese instead of plain.

Yield: 6 servings, each with 6 grams of carbohydrates and 2 grams of fiber, for a total of 4 grams of usable carbs and 28 grams of protein.

↶ Green Bean Spaghetti

This recipe comes from *Lowcarbezine!* reader Marcia McCance, and it's a great dish if you're craving Italian food. If you use French cut green beans, they'll remind you more of spaghetti.

> 1 package (12 ounces) frozen green beans
>
> 2 to 3 tablespoons olive oil
>
> 1 small onion, chopped
>
> 1 green pepper, diced
>
> 4 or 5 medium mushrooms, sliced
>
> 1 pound ground beef, turkey, or chicken
>
> Salt
>
> 1 can (4 ounces) plain tomato sauce
>
> 1 tablespoon Italian seasoning
>
> Parmesan cheese

1. Cook the green beans according to package directions.

2. While the beans are cooking, put the olive oil in a large, heavy skillet over medium heat and sauté the onion, green pepper, and mushrooms until the onion is translucent.

3. Add the ground beef, cook, and stir, crumbling the meat until all pinkness is gone. Salt to taste.

4. Add the tomato sauce and the Italian seasoning. Bring to a boil, reduce to a simmer, and cook for about 5 minutes. Do not overcook.

5. Drain your green beans, pour the meat sauce over them, top with Parmesan, and serve.

Yield: 4 servings, each with 19 grams of carbohydrates and 5 grams of fiber, for a total of 14 grams of usable carbs and 26 grams of protein.

ᕫ Meatza!

Here's a dish for all you pizza-lovers, and I know you are legion. Just add a salad, and you have a supper that will please the whole family.

1 1/2 pounds ground beef or 3/4 pound ground beef mixed with 3/4 pound Italian-style sausage

1 small onion, finely chopped

1 clove garlic, crushed

1 teaspoon dried oregano or Italian seasoning (optional)

8 ounces sugar-free pizza sauce

Parmesan or Romano cheese (optional)

8 ounces shredded mozzarella

Toppings (peppers, onions, mushrooms, or whatever you like)

Olive oil (optional)

1. Preheat the oven to 350°F.

2. In a large bowl and with clean hands, combine the meat with the onion and garlic, and a teaspoon of oregano or Italian seasoning (if using). Mix well.

3. Pat the meat mixture out in an even layer in a 9 x 12-inch baking pan. Bake for 20 minutes.

4. When the meat comes out, it will have shrunk a fair amount, because of the grease cooking off. Pour off the grease and spread the pizza sauce over the meat. Sprinkle the Parmesan on the sauce (if using), and then distribute the shredded mozzarella evenly over the sauce.

5. Top with whatever you like: green peppers, banana peppers, mushrooms, olives, anchovies. I love broccoli on pizza, and thawed frozen broccoli "cuts" work perfectly. You could also use meat toppings, such as sausage and pepperoni, but they seem a little redundant, since the whole bottom layer is meat.

6. Drizzle the whole thing with a little olive oil (if using; it's really not necessary).

7. Put your Meatza! 4 inches below a broiler set on High. Broil for about 5 minutes, or until the cheese is melted and starting to brown.

Yield: 6 servings, each with about 5 grams of carbohydrates per serving, only a trace of fiber, and 27 grams of protein. (Based on using sugar-free pizza sauce, and only cheese, no veggies.)

🍓 If you haven't been able to find a pizza sauce that doesn't have sugar, you might combine an 8-ounce can of tomato sauce with a crushed clove of garlic and some oregano.

↻ Joe

Our favorite one-dish skillet supper. It's flexible, too; don't worry if you use a little less or a little more burger, or one more or one fewer egg. It'll still come out great.

> 1 ¹/2 pounds ground beef
>
> 1 package (10 ounces) frozen chopped spinach
>
> 1 medium onion, chopped
>
> 1 or 2 cloves garlic, crushed
>
> 5 eggs
>
> Salt and pepper

1. In a heavy skillet over a medium flame, begin browning the ground beef.

2. While the beef is cooking, cook the spinach according to the package directions (or 5 to 7 minutes on high in the microwave should do it).

3. When the ground beef is half done, add the onion and garlic, and cook until the beef is completely done. Pour off the extra fat.

4. Drain the spinach well—I put mine in a strainer and press it with the back of a spoon—and stir it into the ground beef.

5. Mix up the eggs well with a fork, and stir them in with the beef and spinach. Continue cooking and stirring over low heat for a few more minutes, until the eggs are set. Salt and pepper to taste, and serve.

Yield: 6 servings, each with 4 grams of carbohydrates and 2 grams of fiber, for a total of 2 grams of usable carbs and 25 grams of protein.

🍓 My sister likes a little Parmesan cheese sprinkled over her Joe, and I surely wouldn't argue about a little thing like that!

↻ Sloppy José

So easy it's almost embarrassing, and the kids will probably like it. Different brands of Salsa vary a lot in their carb contents, so read labels carefully.

 1 pound ground beef

 1 cup salsa (mild, medium, or hot, as you prefer)

 1 cup shredded Mexican-style cheese

1. In a large skillet, crumble and brown the ground beef, and drain off the fat.

2. Stir in the salsa and cheese, and heat until the cheese is melted.

Yield: About 4 servings, each with 4 grams of carbohydrates and 1 gram of fiber, for a total of 3 grams of usable carbs and 27 grams of protein.

Mega Sloppy José. Try adding another 1/2 cup salsa and another 1/2 cup cheese.

Yield: 4 servings, each with 6 grams of carbohydrates and 2 grams of fiber, for a total of 4 grams of usable carbs and 30 grams of protein.

🍓 This is good with a salad, or even on a salad. Of course, if you have carb-eaters around, they'll love the stuff on some corn tortillas.

◌ All-Meat Chili

Some folks consider tomatoes in chili to be anathema, but I like it this way. Don't look funny at that cocoa powder, by the way. It's the secret ingredient!

2 pounds ground beef

1 cup chopped onion

3 cloves garlic, crushed

1 can (14 $1/2$ ounces) tomatoes with green chilies

1 can (4 ounces) plain tomato sauce

4 teaspoons ground cumin

2 teaspoons dried oregano

2 teaspoons unsweetened cocoa powder

1 teaspoon paprika

1. Brown and crumble the beef in a heavy skillet over medium-high heat. Pour off the grease, and add the onion, garlic, tomatoes, tomato sauce, cumin, oregano, cocoa, and paprika. Stir to combine.

2. Turn the burner to low, cover, and simmer for 30 minutes. Uncover and simmer for another 15 to 20 minutes, or until the chili thickens a bit. Serve with grated cheese, sour cream, chopped raw onion, or other low-carb toppings.

Yield: 6 servings, each with 7 grams of carbohydrates and 2 grams of fiber, for a total of 5 grams of usable carbs and 27 grams of protein.

🍓 It's easy to vary this recipe to the tastes of different family members. If some people like beans in their chili, just heat up a can of kidney or pinto beans, and let them spoon their beans into their own serving. If you like beans in your chili, buy a can of black soybeans at a health food store; there are only a couple of grams of usable carbs in a couple of tablespoons. And of course, if you like your chili hotter than this, just add crushed red pepper, cayenne, or hot sauce to take things up a notch.

Mexicali Meat Loaf

    1 pound ground beef

    1 pound mild pork sausage

    1 cup crushed plain pork rinds

    1 can (4 1/2 ounces) diced mild green chilies

    1 medium onion, finely chopped

    8 ounces Monterey Jack cheese, cut into 1/4- to 1/2-inch cubes or shredded

    3/4 cup salsa (mild, medium, or hot, as desired)

    1 egg

    2 or 3 cloves garlic, crushed

    2 teaspoons dried oregano

    2 teaspoons ground cumin

    1 teaspoon salt or Vege-Sal

1. Preheat the oven to 350°F.

1. Combine all these ingredients in a really big bowl, and then, with clean hands, knead it all until it's thoroughly blended.

2. Dump it out on a clean broiler rack, and form into a loaf—it'll be a big loaf—about 3 inches thick. Bake for 1 1/2 hours.

   Do chop the onion quite fine for your meat loaves. If it's in pieces that are too big, it tends to make the loaf fall apart when you cut it. The Mexicali Meat Loaf may crumble a bit anyway, because it's quite tender.

Yield: 8 servings, each with 5 grams of carbohydrates and 1 gram of fiber, for a total of 4 grams of usable carbs and 28 grams of protein.

○ Low-Carb Swiss Loaf

I adapted this from a recipe that had a whole pile of bread crumbs and a cup of milk in it. I simply left them out, and I've never missed them.

> 2 1/2 pounds ground beef
>
> 5 ounces Swiss cheese, diced small or grated
>
> 2 eggs, beaten
>
> 1 medium onion, chopped
>
> 1 green pepper, chopped
>
> 1 small rib celery, chopped
>
> 1 teaspoon salt or Vege-Sal
>
> 1/2 teaspoon pepper
>
> 1/2 teaspoon paprika

1. Preheat the oven to 350°F.

2. With clean hands, combine all the ingredients in a large bowl, until the mixture is well blended.

3. Pack the meat into one large loaf pan or two small ones. Bake a large loaf for 1 1/2 to 1 3/4 hours. Bake two small loaves for 1 1/4 hours.

   🍓 I turn the loaf out of the pan and onto the broiler rack, and I bake it there so the excess fat runs off—not because I'm afraid of fat, but because I like it better that way. If you like, though, you could bake yours right in the pan, and it would probably be a bit more tender.

Yield: 8 servings, each with 3 grams of carbohydrates and 1 gram of fiber, for a total of 2 grams of usable carbs and 30 grams of protein.

Zucchini Meat Loaf Italiano

The inspiration for this meat loaf was a recipe in an Italian cookbook. The original recipe was for a "zucchini mold," and it had only a tiny bit of meat in it. I thought to myself, "How could adding more ground beef be a problem here?" And I was right; it's very moist and flavorful.

3 tablespoons olive oil

2 medium zucchini, chopped (about 1 1/2 cups)

1 medium onion, chopped

2 or 3 cloves garlic, crushed

1 1/2 pounds ground beef

2 tablespoons snipped fresh parsley

1 egg

3/4 cup grated Parmesan cheese

1 teaspoon salt

1/2 teaspoon pepper

1. Preheat the oven to 350°F.

2. Heat the olive oil in a skillet and sauté the zucchini, onion, and garlic in it for 7 to 8 minutes.

3. Let the veggies cool a bit, then put them in a big bowl with the beef, parsley, egg, cheese, salt, and pepper. Using clean hands, mix thoroughly.

4. Take the rather soft meat mixture and put it in a big loaf pan, if you like, or form the loaf right on a broiler rack so the grease will drip off. (Keep in mind if you do it this way, your loaf won't stand very high, it'll be about 2 inches thick.)

5. Bake for 75 to 90 minutes, or until the juices run clear but the loaf is not dried out.

Yield: 5 servings, each with 3 grams of carbohydrates and 1 gram of fiber, for total of 2 grams of usable carbs and 29 grams of protein.

My Grandma's Standby Casserole

Okay, my grandma used egg noodles instead of spaghetti squash, but it tastes good this way, too. This is handy for potlucks and such.

> 1 pound ground beef
>
> 2 tablespoons butter
>
> 1 clove garlic, crushed
>
> 1 teaspoon salt
>
> Dash pepper
>
> 2 cans (8 ounces each) plain tomato sauce
>
> 6 scallions
>
> 3 ounces cream cheese
>
> 1 cup sour cream
>
> 3 cups cooked spaghetti squash
>
> 1/2 cup shredded Cheddar cheese

1. Preheat the oven to 350°F.

2. Brown the ground beef in the butter. Pour off the grease, and stir in the garlic, salt, pepper, and tomato sauce.

3. Cover, turn the burner to low, and simmer for 20 minutes.

4. While the meat is simmering, slice the scallions, including the crisp part of the green, and combine with the cream cheese and sour cream. Blend well.

5. In the bottom of a 6-cup casserole, layer half the spaghetti squash, half the scallion mixture, and half the tomato-beef mixture; repeat the layers. Top with the Cheddar, and bake for 20 minutes.

Yield: 5 servings, each with 15 grams of carbohydrates and 2 grams of fiber, for a total of 13 grams of usable carbs and 23 grams of protein.

⌒ Beef Taco Filling

      1 pound ground beef

      2 tablespoons Taco Seasoning (see page 404)

      1/4 cup water

1. Brown and crumble the ground beef in a heavy skillet over medium-high heat.

2. When the meat is cooked through, drain the grease and stir in the seasoning and water. Let it simmer for about 5 minutes, and serve.

Yield: 4 servings, each with less than 1 gram of carbohydrates, no fiber, and 19 grams of protein.

🍓 Use in the Taco Omelets (see page 92), Taco Salads (see page 372), Cheesy Bowls and Taco Shells (see page 83) and Tortillas (see page 156).

⌒ Reuben Casserole

Another great recipe from Vicki Cash. Thanks, Vicki!

      4 small summer squash or zucchini

      2 tablespoons water

      1 can (27 ounces) sauerkraut, drained

      1 tablespoon caraway seeds

      2 tablespoons Dijon mustard

      8 ounces shaved corned beef or pastrami

      4 ounces grated Swiss cheese

1. Slice the squash into bite-size pieces. Place the pieces in a 2-quart microwave-safe casserole, and add the water. Cover and microwave on High for 3 minutes.

2. Add the sauerkraut, caraway seeds, mustard, and meat, mixing well. Cover and microwave on High for 6 minutes, stirring halfway through.

3. Stir in the cheese, and microwave for 3 to 5 more minutes, or until the cheese is melted.

Yield: 4 servings, each with 16 grams of carbohydrates and 8 grams of fiber, for a total of 8 grams of usable carbs and 21 grams of protein.

↷ Beef Fajitas

This is my take on a recipe sent to me by Carol Vandiver. You can serve these with low-carb tortillas, if you like, but I just pile mine on a plate, top them with salsa, sour cream, and guac, and eat 'em with a fork.

1/2 cup lite beer

1/2 cup oil

2 tablespoons lime juice

1/2 small onion, thinly sliced

1 teaspoon red pepper flakes

1/4 teaspoon ground cumin

1/4 teaspoon pepper

1 1/2 pounds skirt steak

1 tablespoon oil

1 medium onion, thickly sliced

1 green pepper, cut into strips

Low-carb tortillas, purchased, or homemade (see page 156)

Guacamole (see page 51)

Salsa

Sour cream

1. Mix together the beer, oil, lime juice, onion, pepper flakes, cumin, and pepper; this is your marinade.

2. Place the skirt steak in a large zipper-lock bag, and pour the marinade over it. Seal the bag, pressing out the air, and put it in the fridge. Let your steak marinate for a minimum of several hours.

3. When you're ready to cook, remove your steak from the bag, reserving a couple of tablespoons of the marinade. Slice your steak quite thin, across the grain.

4. Add the oil to a large, heavy skillet over high heat, and tilt to coat the bottom. When the skillet is good and hot, add the steak slices, onion, and pepper. Stir-fry them until the meat is done through and the vegetables are crisp-tender.

5. Stir in the reserved marinade, and serve, with or without low-carb tortillas, topped with guacamole, salsa, and sour cream.

Yield: 4 servings, each with about 5 grams of carbohydrates and 1 gram of fiber, for a total of 4 grams of usable carbs and 34 grams of protein. (Analysis does not include guacamole, sour cream, salsa, or low-carb tortillas).

↻ Steakhouse Steak

Ever wonder why steak is better at a steakhouse than it is at home?
Part of it is that the best grades of meat are reserved for the restaurants,
but it's also the method: quick grilling, at very high heat, very close to
the flame. Try it at home, with this recipe.

> Olive oil
> 1 1/2 to 2 pounds well-marbled steak (sirloin, rib eye, or the like),
>   1 to 1 1/2 inches thick

1. Rub a couple of teaspoons of olive oil on either side of the steak.

2. Arrange your broiler so you can get the steak so close that it's almost, but not quite,
   touching the broiling element. (I have to put my broiler pan on top of a skillet
   turned upside down to do this.) Turn the broiler to high, and get that steak in there.
   Leave the oven door open—this is crucial. For a 1-inch-thick steak, set the oven
   timer for 5 to 5 1/2 minutes; for a 1 1/2-inch-thick steak, you can go up to 6 minutes.

3. When the timer beeps, quickly flip the steak, and set the timer again. Check at this
   point to see if your time seems right. If you like your steak a lot rarer or more well-
   done than I do, or if you have a different brand of broiler, you may need to adjust
   how long you broil the second side for.

4. When the timer goes off again, get that steak out of there quickly, put it on a serving
   plate, and season it any way you like.

Yield: The number of servings will depend on the size of your steak, but what you
really need to know is that there are no carbs here at all.

∿ Southwestern Steak

I adore steak, I adore guacamole, and the combination is fantastic.

> Olive oil
> 1 1/2 to 2 pounds well-marbled steak (sirloin, rib eye, or the like),
>   1 to 1 1/2 inches thick
> Guacamole (see page 51)
> Salt and pepper

Prepare the Steakhouse Steak (see page 322) to your preferred degree of doneness. Spread each serving of steak with a heaping tablespoon of guacamole, and salt and pepper to taste.

Yield: The number of servings will depend on the size of your steak, but the guacamole will add 4 grams of carbohydrates and 1 gram of fiber, for a total of 3 grams of usable carbs. You'll also get 275 milligrams of potassium.

∿ Cajun Steak

> 2 to 3 teaspoons Cajun Seasoning
> 1 pound sirloin steak, 1 inch thick

Simply sprinkle Cajun seasoning over both sides of your steak. Then either pan-broil it (cook in on a very hot, ungreased, heavy skillet) or cook it on a stove top grill over maximum heat. Either way, cook it just 6 1/2 minutes per side.

Yield: 3 or 4 servings; the Cajun seasoning adds a bare trace of carbohydrates to each.

⌒ Steak Vinaigrette

You don't have to make a batch of homemade vinaigrette every time you want a steak; store-bought will work just as well here.

> Steak, in your preferred cut and quantity
>
> 1/2 cup vinaigrette dressing for each pound of steak

1. Put your steak in a 1-quart zipper-lock bag, and pour the vinaigrette dressing over it. Let the steak marinate for at least 15 minutes, or leave it all day, if you have the time.

2. When you're ready to cook your steak, remove it from the bag, discard the marinade, and broil or grill it, as you prefer (see page 322).

   Yield: Assume 1 pound of steak is 2 servings, each with about 1 gram of carbohydrates, maximum, no fiber, and 33 grams of protein.

⌒ Blue Cheese Steak Butter

This is one of those recipes that would have horrified me back in my low-fat days—and it's so good! If you don't have a food processor, you can make this by hand; it will just take some vigorous mixing.

> 1/2 pound blue cheese, crumbled
>
> 3/4 cup softened butter
>
> 1 or 2 cloves garlic, crushed
>
> 1 tablespoon spicy brown mustard
>
> 2 or 3 drops Tabasco

1. Put all the ingredients in your food processor, and run it until it's well blended and smooth. Taste it—do you want a bit more mustard? A little salt and pepper? A dash more Tabasco? Go ahead and add it.

2. When it's so good you want to cry, put it in a pretty dish and chill it. Then drop a good, rounded tablespoonful over each serving of freshly grilled or broiled steak.

   Yield: Roughly 12 tablespoons, each with 1 gram of carbohydrates, only a trace of fiber, and 4 grams of protein.

   🍓 If you have some steak-loving people on your Christmas list—and hey, who doesn't?—a ball of Blue Cheese Steak Butter wrapped in foil makes a nice present.

ꙅ Platter Sauce for Steak

Make this with the drippings when you're pan-broiling a steak (cooking it in a hot, dry skillet).

>   2 tablespoons butter
>   1 teaspoon dry mustard
>   1/2 teaspoon Worcestershire
>   1/2 teaspoon salt or Vege-Sal
>   1/2 teaspoon pepper

1. After pan-broiling a steak, pour off most of the grease. Melt the butter in the pan, then stir in the mustard, Worcestershire, salt, and pepper, stirring it around so you scrape up the nice brown bits from the pan.
2. Let it bubble a minute, pour it over the hot steak, and serve.

   Yield: This is about enough for a 1-pound steak and will add only 1 gram of carbohydrates, no fiber, and no protein.

ꙅ Garlic Butter Steak

And you thought garlic butter was only good on bread.

>   4 tablespoons butter, softened
>   1 or 2 cloves garlic, crushed
>   1 1/2 pound steak

1. Blend the butter with the garlic. (A food processor is good for this, but not essential.)
2. Broil or grill your steak, as you prefer(see page 320). Melt a tablespoon of garlic butter over each serving.

   Yield: 4 servings, each with less than 1 gram of carbohydrates, no fiber, and 25 grams of protein.

↻ Marinated Sirloin

    1 cup water

    1/2 cup soy sauce

    3 tablespoons Worcestershire sauce

    1/2 medium onion, finely minced

    1 1/2 tablespoons balsamic vinegar

    1/2 tablespoon wine vinegar

    1 1/2 tablespoons lemon juice

    1 tablespoon spicy brown or Dijon mustard

    2 cloves garlic, crushed

    1 1/2 to 2 pounds sirloin steak, 1 inch thick

1. Combine the water, soy sauce, Worcestershire, onion, balsamic vinegar, wine vinegar, lemon juice, mustard, and garlic in a large measuring cup or bowl with a pouring lip. This is your marinade.

2. Place the steak in a large, zipper-lock bag, pour in the marinade, and seal the bag. Place it in a flat pan (in case the bag springs a leak), and stick the whole thing in the fridge for at least several hours, or overnight if you have the time.

3. About 15 minutes before you're ready to cook, remove your steak from the bag, and broil or grill it to your liking (see page 322).

    Yield: Figure at least 4 servings from a 1 1/2-pound steak, and 5 or 6 servings from a 2-pounder. There are a few grams of carbs in the marinade, but since you discard most of it, there's less than 1 gram of carbohydrates added to each serving, no fiber, and no protein. Each serving of steak has no carbohydrates, no fiber, and about 25 grams of protein.

↻ Teriyaki Steak

2 pounds of thinly cut, lean, boneless steak (such as London broil or flank steak)

    1 batch Teriyaki Sauce (see page 411)

1. Put your steak in a large zipper-lock bag, and pour the sauce over it. Squeeze out the extra air, seal the bag, and let the steak marinate for at least a half an hour, or overnight if you have the time.

2. When you're ready to cook the steak, pour the marinade into a small saucepan. Grill or broil (see page 322) the steak quickly with high heat.

3. While the steak is cooking, boil the marinade hard for a few minutes.

4. When the steak is done, slice it thin, across the grain. Serve with the boiled marinade.

Yield: 6 servings. The marinade has 3 grams of carbohydrates per tablespoon; however, if you don't spoon any over your steak, you'll get only a fraction of a gram, no fiber, and no protein. Each serving of steak has no carbohydrates, no fiber, and 23 grams of protein.

ꙮ Steak Au Poive with Brandy Cream

For pepper lovers only!

> 3/4 pound tender, well marbled steak (such as rib eye or sirloin),
>   1/2 to 3/4 inch thick
> 4 teaspoons coarse cracked pepper
> 1 tablespoon butter
> 1 tablespoon olive oil
> 2 tablespoons brandy
> 2 tablespoons heavy cream
> Salt

1. Place your steak on a plate, and sprinkle 2 teaspoons of the pepper evenly over it. Using your hands or the back of a spoon, press the pepper firmly into the steak's surface. Turn the steak over, and do the same thing to the other side.

2. Add the butter and oil to a large, heavy skillet over high heat. When the skillet is hot, add your steak. For a 1/2-inch-thick steak, 4 1/2 minutes per side is about right; go maybe 5 1/2 minutes for a 3/4-inch-thick steak.

3. When the steak is done on both sides, turn off the burner, pour the brandy over it, and light it on fire.

4. When the flames die down, remove the steak to a serving platter, and pour the cream into the skillet. Stir it around, dissolving the meat juices and brandy into it. Salt lightly, and pour it over the steak.

Yield: 2 servings, each with 3 grams of carbohydrates and 1 gram of fiber, for a total of 2 grams of usable carbs and 25 grams of protein.

↻ Basil Beef Stir-Fry

Basil in stir-fries is a Thai touch, but this isn't hot, as most Thai food is.

> 1 pound boneless chuck
>
> ¹/2 cup peanut oil or other bland oil
>
> 6 scallions, including the crisp part of the green, cut into 1-inch lengths
>
> 2 teaspoons dried basil or 2 tablespoons chopped fresh basil
>
> 1 tablespoon soy sauce
>
> ¹/4 teaspoon Splenda
>
> Pepper

1. Thinly slice the beef across the grain.

2. Put the oil in a wok or heavy skillet over high heat. When it's hot, add the beef and stir-fry for a minute or two. Add the scallions, and stir-fry for another 3 to 4 minutes, or until all the pink is gone from the beef.

3. Add the basil, soy sauce, Splenda, and pepper to taste, and toss with the beef, cooking just another minute or so.

Yield: 3 servings, each with 3 grams of carbohydrates and 1 gram of fiber, for a total of 2 grams of usable carbs and 25 grams of protein.

Beef Burgundy

A handy one-dish company meal. Put it together on a Saturday morning, and it will cook happily by itself all afternoon.

1/4 cup olive oil

2 pounds boneless beef round or chuck, cut into 2-inch cubes

1 cup dry red wine

3/4 teaspoon guar or xanthan

1 1/2 teaspoons salt or Vege-Sal

1 teaspoon paprika

1 teaspoon dried oregano

1 big onion, sliced

8 ounces mushrooms, wiped clean with a damp cloth

2 green peppers, cut into chunks

1. Preheat the oven to 250°F.

2. Put the oil in a heavy skillet over medium-high heat, and brown the beef in the oil.

3. Put the browned beef in a 10-cup casserole with a lid.

4. Combine the wine and guar in the blender, blending for 10 seconds or so, and then pour the mixture over the beef.

5. Add the salt, paprika, oregano, onion, mushrooms, and green peppers to the casserole, and give it a quick stir. Cover and put it in the oven for 5 hours. When it comes out, you can boil down the liquid a bit in a saucepan to make it thicker, if you like, but it's quite nice just like this.

Yield: 6 generous servings, each with 8 grams of carbohydrates and 3 grams of fiber, for a total of 5 grams of usable carbs and 25 grams of protein.

Regarding Slow Cookers

Slow cookers are tremendously useful for folks who work all day, but it can be hard to find the time to assemble everything before you get out of the house in the morning. Here's the solution: Put together your slow-cooker recipe the night before. If your slow cooker is like mine, it has a removable crockery liner. Just plunk all of your ingredients into this, cover it, and stick it in the refrigerator. When you get up in the morning, slip that crockery liner into your microwave—I have to turn the lid upside down to make mine fit—and nuke it on half-power for about 10 minutes to take off the chill. Slip the crockery liner back into the base unit, set the slow cooker, and you're good to go.

If you can't fit your crockery liner in your microwave, figure an extra hour of slow cooking to make up for the chill. And you know not to take the lid off of your slow cooker while it's cooking, right? Every time you do this, you slow down the cooking by about one-half hour! Just figure that your food hasn't disappeared or anything, and leave it alone until dinnertime.

Good Low-Carb Slow-Cooked Short Ribs

     1 can (8 ounces) plain tomato sauce

     3/4 cup water

     2 tablespoons wine or cider vinegar

     4 tablespoons soy sauce

     2 teaspoons Splenda

     3 to 4 pounds beef short ribs

     1 large onion

1. In a bowl, mix together the tomato sauce, water, vinegar, soy sauce, and Splenda.

2. Put the ribs in the slow cooker. (It's okay if they're frozen, you don't have to bother thawing them.) Slice the onion, and place it on top of the ribs. Pour the sauce over the onion and ribs.

3. Set the slow cooker on Low, and cook for 8 to 9 hours. (If you put the ribs in thawed, cut about 1 hour off the cooking time.)

Yield: 5 servings from 3 pounds of ribs, 7 servings from 4 pounds, each with about 7 grams of carbohydrates and 1 gram of fiber, for a total of 6 grams of usable carbs and 41 grams of protein. (Total carbs will vary with how much of the sauce you eat, since most of the carbs are in there.)

This recipe gives you tremendously tasty ribs in a thin but flavorful sauce— it's more like a broth. If you'd like, you could put about 1 cup of the sauce through the blender with 3/4 teaspoon or so of guar or xanthan to thicken it, but I rather like it as is.

New England Boiled Dinner

This is our traditional St. Patrick's Day dinner, but it's a simple, satisfying one-pot meal on any chilly night. If you have carb-eaters in the family, you can add a few little red boiling potatoes, still in their jackets, to this.

> 6 small turnips (golf ball to tennis ball size)
>
> 2 big ribs celery, cut into chunks
>
> 2 medium onions, cut into chunks
>
> 1 corned beef "for simmering" (about 3 pounds)
>
> 1/2 head cabbage
>
> Spicy brown mustard
>
> Horseradish
>
> Butter

This is easy, but it takes a long time to cook. Do yourself a favor, and assemble it ahead of time.

1. Peel the turnips and throw them in into the slow cooker, along with the celery and the onions. Set your corned beef on top, and add water to cover.

2. There will be a seasoning packet with your corned beef—dump it into the slow cooker. Put the lid on the slow cooker, set it on Low, and leave it alone for 10 to 12 hours. (You can cut the cooking time down to 6 to 8 hours if you set the slow cooker on High, but the Low setting yields the most tender results.)

3. When you come home from work all those hours later, remove the corned beef from the cooker with a fork or some tongs, put the lid back on the slow cooker to retain heat, put the beef on a platter, and keep it someplace warm. Cut your cabbage into big wedges, and drop it into the slow cooker with the other vegetables.

4. Re-cover the slow cooker, and turn it up to High. Have a green beer (lite beer, of course) while the cabbage cooks for 1/2 hour.

5. With a slotted spoon, remove all the vegetables and pile them around the corned beef on a platter. Serve with the mustard and horseradish as condiments for the beef and butter for the vegetables.

Yield: 8 servings (and of course, you don't need a thing with it), each with 9 grams of carbohydrates and 2 grams of fiber, for a total of 7 grams of usable carbs and 26 grams of protein.

Beef in Beer

The tea, the beer, and the long, slow cooking make this as tender as can be.

> 1/4 cup soy powder or low-carb bake mix
>
> Salt and pepper
>
> 2 pounds boneless beef round roast
>
> Olive oil
>
> 1 medium onion, sliced
>
> 1 can (8 ounces) plain tomato sauce
>
> 1 can (12 ounces) lite beer
>
> 1 teaspoon instant tea powder
>
> 1 can (4 ounces) mushrooms, drained
>
> 2 cloves garlic, crushed

1. Combine the soy powder with a little salt and pepper, and dredge the beef in it.

2. Heat a few tablespoons of oil in a heavy skillet over medium-high heat, and sear the meat until it's brown all over. Place the meat in a slow cooker.

3. In the oil left in the skillet, fry the onion for a few minutes, and add that to the slow cooker, too.

4. Now pour the tomato sauce and beer over the beef. Sprinkle the instant tea over it, and throw in the mushrooms and garlic. Put the lid on the slow cooker, set it on Low, and let it cook for 8 to 9 hours. Good served with pureed cauliflower.

Yield: 6 servings, each with 8 grams of carbohydrates and 1 gram of fiber, for a total of 7 grams of usable carbs and 31 grams of protein.

To keep the carbs super-low, use the lowest-carb lite beer available: Miller Lite or Milwaukee's Best Light.

Peking Slow-Cooker Pot Roast

Sounds nuts, but tastes great! This takes starting ahead, but it's not a lot of work.

　　　　3 to 5 pound beef roast (round, chuck, or rump)

　　　　5 or 6 cloves garlic

　　　　8 ounces cider vinegar

　　　　8 ounces water

　　　　1 small onion

　　　　1 1/2 cups strong coffee (instant works fine)

　　　　1 teaspoon guar or xanthan

　　　　Salt and pepper

1. At least 24 to 36 hours before you want to actually cook your roast, stick holes in the meat with a thin-bladed knife, cut your garlic cloves into slices, and insert a slice into each hole. Put your garlicked roast in a big bowl, and pour the vinegar and the water over it. Put it in the fridge, and let it sit there for a day or so, turning it over when you think of it so the whole thing marinates.

2. On the morning of the day you want to serve your roast, pour off the marinade and put your roast in your slow cooker. Thinly slice your onion, and put it on top of the roast. Pour the coffee over the roast and onion, put on the lid, set the cooker on Low, and leave it alone for 8 hours for a smaller roast or up to 10 hours for a larger one.

3. When you're ready to eat, remove your roast from the cooker carefully, because it will now be so tender it's likely to fall apart.

4. Scoop out 2 cups of the liquid and some of the onions, and put them in the blender with the guar. Blend for few seconds, then pour into a saucepan set over high heat. Boil this sauce hard for about 5 minutes, to reduce it a bit. Salt and pepper the sauce to taste (it's amazing the difference the salt and pepper make, here; I didn't like the flavor of this sauce until I added the salt and pepper, and then I liked it a lot), and slice and serve your roast with this sauce.

Yield: If you use a 4 pound, boneless roast, you'll get 12 servings, each with 3 grams of carbohydrates, a trace of fiber, and 34 grams of protein.

　　Warning: Do not try to make this with a tender cut of beef! This recipe will tenderize the toughest cut; a tender one will practically dissolve. Use inexpensive, tough cuts, and prepare to be amazed at how fork-tender they get.

Ruben Corned-Beef Casserole

This recipe comes from my pal Diana Lee, of *Baking Low Carb* fame.

> 8 ounces fresh corned beef, shredded
>
> 2 eggs
>
> 1/2 cup mayonnaise
>
> 1/2 cup heavy whipping cream
>
> 1 teaspoon dehydrated onion
>
> 1/2 teaspoon dry mustard
>
> 2 teaspoons caraway seeds
>
> 2/3 cup sauerkraut
>
> 2 cups shredded Swiss cheese

1. Preheat the oven to 375°F.

2. Grease a 6-cup casserole, and place the corned beef in the bottom of it.

3. In a bowl, combine the eggs, mayonnaise, whipping cream, onion, dry mustard, and caraway seeds. Drain and rinse the sauerkraut, and add it to the mayonnaise mixture.

4. Pour the mayo mixture over the corned beef, and sprinkle the cheese on top. Bake covered for 30 minutes, then uncover for an additional 15 minutes.

Yield: 4 servings, each with 6 grams of carbohydrates and 1 gram of fiber, for a total of 5 grams of usable carbs and 29 grams of protein.

Anglo-Saxon Soul Food, a.k.a. Roast Beef and Yorkshire Pudding

For those of us of English descent, this is the taste of the Sunday dinners of our childhood. These three recipes will impress the heck out of your family and friends.

The Noble Beef

From the price of prime rib these days, I suspect they're feeding the steers pure gold. Still, this will cost you just a little more than buying one slice of prime rib in a restaurant.

> 4 pounds beef standing rib roast
> 1/4 cup oil

1. Preheat the oven to 550°F.

2. Have the beef at room temperature, and rub it all over with the oil. Put it on a rack in a roasting pan, fatty side up. Stick a meat thermometer in it, deep in the center, but not touching a bone.

3. Put the roast in the oven, and immediately turn the heat down to 350°F. Beef generally takes about 20 minutes per pound to come out medium-rare, so figure on about 1 hour and 20 minutes to cook this roast. Check that meat thermometer, though; I've had a roast surprise me more than once. When the thermometer reads between 140° (rare) and 160°F (almost well-done), take it out, put it on a platter in a warm place, and let it sit for a bit while you bake the Yorkshire pudding.

Yield: Enough to serve 6 people quite handsomely, and of course, there's no carbohydrates here.

⟲ Yorkshire Pudding

For the uninitiated, this is just a big popover flavored with beef drippings. Have the wet and dry ingredients assembled and ready to go when your beef comes out of the oven, or your roast will cool while you're making this.

> 1/4 cup beef drippings (both the fat and the nice brown juice, mixed)
>
> 1/3 cup low-carb bake mix
>
> 1/3 cup rice protein powder
>
> 1 teaspoon salt or Vege-Sal
>
> 4 eggs
>
> 2 teaspoons oil
>
> 1 cup half-and-half

1. Preheat the oven to 425°F.

   🍓 It is essential that the oven be all the way up to temperature before you put in your Yorkshire pudding, or it won't puff up the way it should, so turn up the oven when you're taking out the roast.

2. Spray a large, cast-iron skillet or a 10-inch pie pan with nonstick cooking spray, then put the beef drippings in it and tilt the pan to cover the whole bottom. Set aside.

3. In a bowl, combine the bake mix, protein powder, and salt, stirring them together.

4. In a separate bowl, combine the eggs, oil, and half-and-half.

5. When the oven is up to temperature, whisk the liquid ingredients well for at least 1 minute; 2 wouldn't hurt. Add the dry ingredients, and whisk just until everything is well combined.

6. Pour the mixture into the prepared pan, and bake for 20 minutes. Turn the oven down to 350°F, and give it another 5 minutes or so. Cut into wedges, and serve with Beef Gravy (see page 338).

Yield: 8 servings, each with 3 grams of carbohydrates and 1 gram of fiber, for a total of 2 grams of usable carbs and 9.5 grams of protein.

↻ Beef Gravy

Faced with leftover roast beef, and no gravy, I came up with this, and it's as good as any beef gravy I've ever had. If you have any nice, brown beef juices from your roast, they can only improve it further, but be sure to skim off the fat before adding them, as it will ruin the texture.

1 can (14 1/2 ounces) beef broth

2 tablespoons dry red wine

1 teaspoon liquid beef bouillon concentrate

1 tablespoon finely minced onion

1 small clove garlic, crushed

3/4 teaspoon guar or xanthan

1/3 cup heavy cream

1/4 teaspoon Gravy Master or similar gravy seasoning/coloring liquid

Salt and pepper

1. In a heavy saucepan, combine the broth, wine, bouillon concentrate, onion, and garlic. Bring this to a boil over medium heat, and let it boil until reduced to one-third the original volume. (This will take at least 15 to 20 minutes.)

2. When the mixture is reduced, pour it into a blender (if you're not sure your blender will take the heat, let it cool for 5 to 10 minutes first), turn it on, and add the guar. Blend for 15 seconds or so. Pour it back into the saucepan, turn the heat back on to low, and whisk in the cream and the gravy seasoning liquid. Salt and pepper to taste, heat through, and serve.

Yield: Makes 8 servings of 2 tablespoons, each with less than 2 grams of carbohydrates and 1 gram of fiber, for a total of just under 1 gram of usable carbs and 3 grams of protein.

↻ Ginger Beef

This is my favorite thing to do with a pot roast. It has a bright flavor full of tomato, fruit, and ginger.

> 3 tablespoons olive oil
>
> 3- to 4-pound boneless chuck or round roast, about 2 inches thick
>
> 1 small onion
>
> 1 clove garlic, crushed
>
> 1 can (14 1/2 ounces) diced tomatoes
>
> 1 tablespoon Splenda
>
> 1 teaspoon ground ginger
>
> 1/4 cup cider vinegar

1. Place the oil in a large, heavy skillet, and brown the roast in it over medium-high heat. When both sides are well-seared, add the onion, garlic, and tomatoes.

2. In a bowl, stir the Splenda and ginger into the vinegar, and add that mixture to the skillet, stirring to combine.

3. Cover the skillet, turn the burner to low, and let the whole thing simmer for about 1 1/4 hours. Serve with the vegetables piled on top.

Yield: 3 pound roast should yield at least 6 servings, each with 6 grams of carbohydrates and 1 gram of fiber, for a total of 5 grams of usable carbs and 47 grams of protein.

⟳ Yankee Pot Roast

This old-time favorite is just as good as you remember.

> 1/4 cup olive oil
>
> 2 1/2- to 3-pound boneless chuck roast
>
> 1 3/4 cup water
>
> 1 medium onion, sliced
>
> 1 large rib celery, sliced
>
> 2 small turnips, cut into chunks
>
> 1 medium carrot, sliced
>
> 1/2 cup chopped fresh parsley
>
> 4 ounces mushrooms, thickly sliced
>
> 1 teaspoon liquid beef bouillon concentrate
>
> 1/2 teaspoon guar or xanthan gum

1. Put the oil in a Dutch oven over medium heat, and sear the roast in the oil until it's dark brown all over. Remove the roast from the Dutch oven.

2. Put 1/4 cup of the water and the sliced onions in the Dutch oven, and place the roast directly on top of the onions. Cover the Dutch oven, set the burner to low, and forget about it for 1 1/2 to 2 hours.

3. Remove the roast again—it'll be very tender and may break a bit—and add 1 cup of the water and the celery, turnips, carrot, parsley, and mushrooms. Put the roast back in, on top of the veggies, and cover the Dutch oven. Let it simmer for another 30 to 45 minutes, or until the turnip and carrot are soft.

4. Remove the roast to a serving platter, and use a slotted spoon to pile the vegetables over the roast or in a separate bowl, as you prefer.

5. Put the last 1/2 cup of water in your blender with the bouillon and guar, and blend for 15 seconds or so, or until all the thickener is dissolved. Scrape the mixture into the Dutch oven, and stir it around to thicken the gravy. Pour the gravy over the roast, or put it in a gravy boat or pitcher, and serve.

Yield: 6 to 8 servings, depending on the size of your roast. A 3-pound roast has 8 servings, each with 5 grams of carbohydrates and 1 gram of fiber, for a total of 4 grams of usable carbs and 28 grams of protein.

CHAPTER TEN

Pork and Lamb

Americans eat more chicken and beef than any other meats, but pork is still quite popular, and with good reason: It's tasty and inexpensive. If you still think of pork as being very fatty, think again. The low-fat craze has dramatically affected pork breeding and feeding, and most pork is now very lean. This means you'll want to take care not to overcook your pork, or it may well end up dry. It also means that most pork is less flavorful than the pork of yore, you'll want to season it well. This chapter will show you how.

As for lamb, I've never understood why it isn't very popular in this country. It's one of the most widely eaten meats in the rest of the world. I grew up eating lamb, and I adore it. If you haven't tried it, you simply must. Unfortunately, because so little lamb is eaten in the United States, it is something of a specialty item, and the prices reflect this. If you love lamb—or learn to love it—keep an eye out for sales. Every now and then I'll find the same grade boneless leg of lamb that usually runs $4.99 a pound for just $1.99. That's when I buy three, and stock the freezer. I also watch for lamb chops and steaks on special.

↻ Pork Chops with Mustard Cream Sauce

Something good to do with pork chops, now that you're not breading them. For each serving you'll need:

> Salt or Vege-Sal
>
> Pepper
>
> 1 pork chop, 1 inch thick
>
> 1 tablespoon olive oil
>
> 1 tablespoon dry white wine
>
> 1 tablespoon heavy cream
>
> 1 tablespoon spicy brown mustard or Dijon mustard

1. Salt and pepper the chop on both sides.

2. Heat the oil in a heavy skillet over medium heat. Sauté the chop until they're browned on both sides and done through (depending on the size of your skillet, this may take a couple of batches). Put the chop on a serving platter, and keep it warm.

3. Put the wine in the skillet, and stir it around, scraping all the tasty brown bits off the pan as you stir. Stir in the cream and mustard, blend well, and cook for a minute or two. Pour over the chop and serve.

Yield: 1 serving, with 2 grams of carbohydrates, a trace of fiber, and about 20 grams of protein.

↻ Italian Herb Pork Chops

For each serving you'll need:

> 1 clove garlic, crushed
>
> 1 pork chop, 1 inch thick
>
> 1/2 teaspoon dried, powdered sage
>
> 1/2 teaspoon dried, powdered rosemary
>
> Salt or Vege-Sal
>
> 2 tablespoons dry white wine

1. Rub the crushed garlic into both sides of your pork chop.

2. In a bowl, mix the sage and rosemary together, and sprinkle this evenly over both sides of the pork chop, as well. Sprinkle lightly with the salt.

3. Place the chops in a heavy skillet (if you're feeding several people, you may well need two skillets), and add water just up to the top edge of the pork chop. Cover the skillet, turn the burner to low, and let the chop simmer for about 1 hour, or until the water has all evaporated.

4. Once the water is gone, the chop will start to brown. Turn it once or twice to get it browned on both sides. (The pork chop will be very tender, so use a spatula and be careful, but if it breaks a little, it will still taste great.)

5. Remove the porkchop to a serving platter, and pour the wine into the skillet. Turn up the burner to medium-high, and stir the wine around, scraping up the stuck-on brown bits from the pan. Bring this to a boil, and let it boil hard for a minute or two to reduce it just a little. Pour this sauce over the pork chop, and serve.

Yield: 1 serving, with 2 grams of carbohydrates, a trace of fiber, and about 23 grams of protein.

↻ Pork Chops and Sauerkraut

3 slices bacon

3 pork chops, 1 inch thick

1 small onion, chopped

1 can (14 1/2 ounces) sauerkraut, drained

2 tablespoons Splenda

1/4 teaspoon dry mustard

2 tablespoons dry white wine

1/4 teaspoon blackstrap molasses

1. Fry the bacon until just barely crisp in a heavy skillet over medium heat. Drain and set aside.

2. Pour off all but about 2 tablespoons of the grease, and brown the chops in it over medium heat. (You want them to have just a little color on each side.) Remove from the skillet, and set aside.

3. Put the onion, sauerkraut, Splenda, mustard, wine, and molasses in the skillet, and stir for a moment to blend. Crumble in the bacon and stir again, just for a moment. Place the chops on top of the sauerkraut mixture, turn the burner to low, and cover the pan. Simmer for 45 minutes.

Yield: 3 servings, each with 11 grams of carbohydrates and 4 grams of fiber, for a total of 7 grams of usable carbs and 27 grams of protein.

Apple-Glazed Pork Chops

Pork and apples are a great combination. Ever since I stopped eating apple sauce, I've been looking for a way to have this combination of flavors again!

> 2 tablespoons olive oil
>
> 2 pork chops, 1 inch thick (about 8 ounces each)
>
> 1/4 cup cider vinegar
>
> 1 1/2 tablespoons Splenda
>
> 1/2 teaspoon soy sauce
>
> 1 small onion, thinly sliced

1. Put the oil in a heavy skillet, and brown the pork chops in the oil.

2. When both sides are brown, stir together the vinegar, Splenda, and the soy sauce, and pour the mixture over the chops. Scatter the onion on top.

3. Cover, and turn the burner to low. Let the chops simmer, turning at least once, for 45 minutes or until the pan is almost dry. Serve the chops with the onions, and scrape all the nice, syrupy pan liquid over them.

Yield: 2 servings, each with 8 grams of carbohydrates and 1 gram of fiber, for a total of 7 grams of usable carbs and 36 grams of protein.

Pork Chops with Garlic and Balsamic Vinegar

The balsamic vinegar gives these a tangy-sweet flavor.

> 2 tablespoons olive oil
>
> 2 or 3 pork rib chops, 2 inches thick
>
> 3/4 cup chicken broth
>
> 3 tablespoons balsamic vinegar
>
> 3 cloves garlic, crushed
>
> 1/4 teaspoon guar or xanthan

1. Put the oil in a large, heavy skillet over medium-high heat, and sear the chops in the oil until well-browned on both sides. Add the broth, vinegar, and garlic.

2. Cover the skillet, turn the burner to low, and let the chops simmer for 1 hour. Remove the chops to a serving platter or serving plates, and put the liquid from the pan into a blender. Add the guar or xanthan, run the blender for a few moments, and pour the thickened sauce over the chops.

Yield: 2 or 3 servings, each with 2 grams of carbohydrates, a trace of fiber, and 36 grams of protein.

Artichoke-Mushroom Pork

This is wonderful, and it cooks quite quickly because you pound the pork thin.

> 1 1/2 pounds boneless pork loin, cut into 4 slices across the grain
>
> 4 tablespoons butter
>
> 1 small onion, sliced
>
> 1 clove garlic, crushed
>
> 8 ounces sliced mushrooms
>
> 1 can quartered artichoke hearts, drained
>
> 1/2 cup chicken broth
>
> 2 teaspoons Dijon or spicy brown mustard

1. Put a piece of pork into a heavy zipper-lock bag, and pound until it is 1/4 inch thick. Repeat for the remaining pieces of pork.

2. Melt 2 tablespoons of the butter in a large, heavy skillet over medium heat, and brown the meat on both sides, (about 4 minutes per side). You'll have to do them one or two at a time. Set the browned pork on a plate, and keep it warm.

3. Add the rest of the butter to the skillet, and add the onion, garlic, and mushrooms. Sauté until the mushrooms and onion are limp. Add the artichokes, chicken broth, and mustard, and stir around to dissolve the tasty brown bits on the bottom of the skillet.

4. Add the pork back into the skillet (you'll have to stack it a bit), cover, and let simmer for about 5 minutes. Serve the pork with the vegetables spooned over the top.

Yield: 4 servings, each with 6 grams of carbohydrates and 2 grams of fiber, for a total of 4 grams of usable carbs and 25 grams of protein.

If you prefer, you can make this out of 4 pork chops with the bones cut out.

↻ Looed Pork

This is a great way to add a lot of flavor to the usually bland boneless pork loin.

> 1 1/2 pounds boneless pork loin, sliced about 1 1/2 inch thick
> 1 batch Looing Sauce (see page 413)
> Scallions, sliced
> Toasted sesame oil

1. Put the pork in a slow cooker, pour the looing sauce over it, cover the cooker, and set it to Low. Forget about it for 8 to 9 hours.

2. At dinnertime, remove the pieces of pork from the looing sauce. Put each piece on a serving plate, scatter a few sliced scallions over each serving, and top with a few drops of toasted sesame oil.

Yield: 4 generous servings with no more than 1 gram of carbohydrates, no fiber, and 35 grams of protein.

↻ Mu Shu Pork

I hear from lots of people that they miss Chinese food, so here's a Chinese restaurant favorite, de-carbed. Low-carb tortillas stand in here for mu shu pancakes, and they work fine. If you want to de-carb this even further, just eat it with a fork and forget the tortillas.

> 3 eggs, beaten
> Peanut oil
> 1/2 cup slivered mushrooms
> 8 ounces boneless pork loin, sliced across the grain and then
>   cut into matchsticks
> 1 cup shredded napa cabbage
> 3 scallions, sliced
> 1 cup bean sprouts
> 3 tablespoons soy sauce
> 2 tablespoons dry sherry
> 4 low-carb tortillas
> Hoisin Sauce (see page 403)

🍓 Make sure you have everything cut up and ready to go before you cook a thing, and this recipe will be a breeze.

1. First, in a wok or heavy skillet over high heat, scramble the eggs in a few table-spoons of the peanut oil until they're set but still moist. Remove and set aside.

2. Wipe the wok out if there's much egg clinging to it. Add another 1/4 cup or so of peanut oil, and heat. Add the pork, and stir-fry until it's mostly done. Add the cab-bage, scallions, and sprouts, and stir-fry for 3 to 4 minutes. Add the eggs back into the wok, and stir them in, breaking them into small pieces. Now add the soy sauce and sherry, and stir.

3. To serve, take a warmed, low-carb tortilla, and smear about 2 teaspoons of hoisin sauce on it. Put about a quarter of the stir-fry mixture on the tortilla, and wrap it up.

Yield: 2 servings, each with 11 grams of carbohydrates and 3 grams of fiber, for a total of 8 grams of usable carbs and 27 grams of protein (Analysis does not include low-carb tortillas or hoisin sauce.)

↷ Robinsky's Cabbage & Sausage

Robin Wilkins says this makes a great one-plate meal. Just make sure you read the labels on the kielbasa carefully, as they vary widely in carb count.

> 2 to 3 tablespoons butter
>
> 1 medium onion, chopped
>
> 1 pound Polska Kielbasa or similar low-carb sausage, sliced
>
> 1 head cabbage, chopped

1. Divide the butter between two skillets. Sauté the onion and sausage in one and sauté the cabbage in the other. The cabbage will overwhelm your frying pan at first, but it will reduce in volume as it fries.

2. When cooked to the texture you like (I like mine tender-crisp), combine the contents of both skillets, and toss.

Yield: 3 servings. The carb content of this depends completely on the sausage used. Using a low-carb sausage, each serving has 8 grams of carbohydrates and 1 gram of fiber, for a total of 7 grams of usable carbs and 21 grams of protein.

↻ Country Sausage Skillet Supper

>   1 pound bulk pork sausage, hot or mild
>   1 small onion, chopped
>   3/4 cup shredded Cheddar cheese

1. Crumble the sausage in a heavy skillet over medium heat. As the grease starts to cook out of it, add the onion.

2. Cook until the sausage is no longer pink and the onion is translucent. Pour off the grease, spread the sausage mixture evenly in the pan, and scatter the Cheddar over the top. Cover and return to the heat for a minute or two, until the cheese is melted, and serve.

Yield: 3 servings, each with 5 grams of carbohydrates and 1 gram of fiber, for a total of 4 grams of usable carbs and 25 grams of protein.

🍓 Feel free to substitute turkey sausage, if you prefer it.

↻ Kielbasa and Brussels Sprouts

My sister, who tested this recipe, just loved it. Sadly, this is the one recipe sent in by a *Lowcarbezine!* reader that I can't credit—the original email is lost. My apologies to the inventor, and my thanks.

>   1 pound frozen brussels sprouts
>   1 pound kielbasa, sliced into 1-inch pieces

1. Preheat the oven to 350°F. Spray an 8 x 8-inch glass baking dish with nonstick cooking spray.

2. Place the frozen sprouts on the bottom of the prepared baking dish. Arrange the kielbasa over the sprouts, to let the juices flow over them. Cover with foil and bake for 40 minutes. Remove the cover and bake for 15 additional minutes, if you like your kielbasa browned.

Yield: 3 servings, each with 15 grams of carbohydrates and 5 of fiber, for a total of 10 grams of usable carbs and 25 grams of protein. (This was analyzed for the average kielbasa, so you could knock off a few extra grams by choosing the lowest-carb kielbasa available.)

⌒ **Polynesian Pork**

> 4 or 5 large pork chops, 1 to 1 1/2 inches thick
>
> 1/2 cup soy sauce
>
> 4 cloves garlic, crushed
>
> 1/3 cup Splenda
>
> 1/2 teaspoon blackstrap molasses
>
> 1 1/2 teaspoons grated fresh ginger

1. Preheat the oven to 325°F.

2. Put the pork chops in a large zipper-lock bag.

3. Combine the soy sauce, garlic, Splenda, molasses, and ginger, mixing them in a blender for a second or two, if possible.

4. Pour the mixture into the bag with the pork. Seal the bag, and let it sit for 20 minutes or so, turning once.

5. Remove the pork from the marinade, reserving the marinade in a small bowl. Place the chops in a shallow roasting pan, and bake for 60 to 90 minutes, or until done through. Brush once or twice with the leftover marinade while cooking.

Yield: 4 or 5 servings. If you were to eat all the marinade, each serving would have 7 grams of carbohydrates, but you don't, so figure 2 or 3 grams of carbohydrates, a trace of fiber, and 25 grams of protein.

🍓 This marinade works well with a pork roast, too, but of course it will take longer to roast.

↻ Sausage Skillet Mix-Up

    1 pound bulk pork sausage, hot or mild

    1 small onion, chopped

    2 ribs celery, chopped

    1 green pepper, chopped

    1 cup chicken broth

    2 teaspoons chicken bouillon powder

    2 tablespoons Worcestershire sauce

    1/2 teaspoon pepper

    3 cups Cauliflower Rice (see page 159)

1. Brown and crumble the sausage in a heavy skillet over medium-high heat. When the sausage is no longer pink, pour off the grease, add the remaining ingredients, and give the mixture a stir.

2. Turn the burner to low, cover the skillet, and let it simmer for 15 to 20 minutes, or until the cauliflower is tender.

Yield: 3 servings, each with 16 grams of carbohydrates and 4 grams of fiber, for a total of 12 grams of usable carbs and 22 grams of protein.

↻ Cocido de Puerco

This Mexican-style pork stew is simply marvelous. Do use bony cuts of meat, as they're more flavorful—and cheaper, too.

    3 pounds bony cuts of pork (meaty pork neck bones are ideal)

    2 tablespoons olive oil

    1 clove garlic, crushed

    1 large onion, sliced

    1 large green pepper, diced

    2 medium zucchini, cut into chunks

    1 can (14 1/2 ounces) diced tomatoes

    2 teaspoons cumin

    2 teaspoons dried oregano

    1/2 teaspoon red pepper flakes (optional)

1. In a heavy skillet over medium-high heat, sear the pork bones in the oil until they're brown all over.

2. Turn the heat to low, and add the garlic, onion, pepper, zucchini, tomatoes, cumin, oregano, and pepper flakes. Cover the skillet, and let it simmer for 1 hour.

Yield: About 6 servings, depending on how meaty your bones are, each with 13 grams of carbohydrates and 4 grams of fiber, for a total of 9 grams of usable carbs and about 35 grams of protein.

Ham Slice with Mustard Sauce

2 to 3 tablespoons oil

Ham steak, about 2 pounds

1/2 cup water

3 tablespoons prepared mustard

3 tablespoons Splenda

1/4 teaspoon blackstrap molasses

Salt and pepper

1. Put the oil in a heavy skillet over medium heat, and fry the ham steak until it is golden on both sides. Remove the ham from the skillet, set it on a platter, and keep it warm.

2. Pour the water into the skillet and stir it around, scraping up all the brown bits from the ham. Stir in the mustard, Splenda, molasses, and salt and pepper to taste. Pour over the ham, and serve.

Yield: 5 servings, each with 2 grams of carbohydrates, a trace of fiber, and 36 grams of protein.

☾ Jerk Pork

    1 recipe Jerk Marinade (see page 412)

    6 pork chops, 1 inch thick (about 8 ounces each)

1. Smear jerk marinade all over the chops, put the chops in a large zipper-lock bag, and refrigerate. Now wash your hands—that marinade is hot! Let the chops marinate for at least several hours, or overnight.

2. When you're ready to cook, grill these chops slowly, well above a low charcoal fire or a gas grill set on Low. Broil them only if you must.

Yield: 6 servings, each with 3 grams of carbohydrates and 1 gram of fiber, for a usable carb count of 2 grams (that's assuming you eat all the marinade, but of course some will fall off in the cooking process) and 42 grams of protein.

☾ Winter Night Lamb Stew

On a raw winter's night, sometimes you just want stew. Here's one with no potatoes, and you can make it in your big skillet.

    3 tablespoons olive oil

    1 1/2 pounds lean lamb stew meat, cut into chunks

    1 cup chopped onion

    1 1/2 cup diced turnip

    1 1/2 cup diced rutabaga

    3/4 cup beef broth

    1/2 teaspoon guar or xanthan

    1/2 teaspoon salt or Vege-Sal

    1/4 teaspoon pepper

    1 bay leaf

    3 cloves garlic, crushed

1. Put the oil in a heavy skillet over medium-high heat, and brown the lamb in the oil. Add the onion, turnip, and rutabaga.

2. Put the beef broth and guar in a blender, and blend for a few moments. Pour the mixture into the skillet. (If you choose not to use a thickener, just add the broth directly to the skillet.) Add the salt, pepper, bay leaf, and garlic, and stir.

3. Cover, turn the burner to low, and let simmer for 1 hour.

   Yield: 4 servings, each with 12 grams of carbohydrates and 3 grams of fiber, for a total of 9 grams of usable carbs and 38 grams of protein.

↻ Quick Curried Lamb

I invented this for a quick lunch for my husband one day when there just happened to be a hunk of lamb in the fridge that needed to be used. It was so good, I decided it was worth repeating.

> 3 tablespoons butter
> 1 tablespoon curry powder
> 1 clove garlic
> 1 large onion
> 1 pound lean lamb, cut in 1/2-inch cubes
> Salt and pepper

1. Melt the butter in a heavy skillet over medium heat. Add the curry powder, and stir for a minute or so.

2. Add the garlic, onion, and lamb. Sauté, stirring frequently, for 7 minutes or so, or until the lamb is done through. Salt and pepper to taste, and serve.

   Yield: 3 servings, each with 5 grams of carbohydrates and 1 gram of fiber, for a total of 4 grams of usable carbs and 31 grams of protein.

◌ Lamb Kebabs

Very simple and very Greek. Add a Greek salad, and there's dinner.

>   2 pounds lean lamb, cut into 1-inch cubes
>   1/2 cup olive oil
>   1/4 cup lemon juice
>   1 clove garlic, crushed
>   1/2 teaspoon dried oregano
>   2 small onions, quartered

1. Put the lamb cubes into a large, zipper-lock bag.

2. Mix together the olive oil, lemon juice, garlic, and oregano. Pour it over the lamb cubes in the bag, and refrigerate it for an hour or two (or overnight, if possible).

3. When it's time to cook dinner, pour off the marinade into a bowl, and set it aside. Thread your lamb chunks on skewers, alternating the pieces of meat with a "layer" or two of the onion. You can grill these, if you like, or broil them 8 inches or so from the broiler. Turn the kebabs while they're cooking, and brush once or twice with the reserved marinade, but only toward the beginning of the cooking time; you don't want to reintroduce raw meat germs to your cooked kebabs. Check for doneness by cutting into a chunk of meat after 10 minutes; they should be done within 15 minutes.

Yield: I get 6 skewers from this, each with 4 grams of carbohydrates and 1 gram of fiber, for a total of 3 grams of usable carbs and 31 grams of protein.

◌ Thyme-Perfumed Lamb Steaks

>   1 lamb steak (6 to 8 ounces)
>   2 teaspoons olive oil
>   2 teaspoons lemon juice
>   1 tablespoon fresh thyme leaves, stripped from their stems.

1. Rub the lamb steak with the olive oil and then the lemon juice. Cover the lamb with the thyme leaves, letting it sit for at least a couple of hours so the thyme flavor permeates the lamb.

2. Broil close to the heat for 4 to 5 minutes per side, or grill.

Yield: 1 serving, with 1 gram of carbohydrates, a trace of fiber, and 30 grams or so of protein.

Mediterranean Leg of Lamb

Lamb makes a wonderful Sunday dinner roast. If you don't want to roast a whole leg of lamb at once because it's a lot of meat, ask the butcher to cut one leg into two roasts. Make half now, and freeze the other half for another day.

> Leg of lamb, with or without the bone in.
>
> 1 cup dry red wine
>
> 1 cup olive oil
>
> 5 cloves garlic, crushed
>
> 3 tablespoons lemon juice
>
> 1 tablespoon dried rosemary
>
> 1 tablespoon dried oregano

1. Place your leg of lamb in a pan large enough to hold it.

2. Combine the wine, 1/2 cup of the olive oil, 3 cloves of the garlic, and the lemon juice, rosemary, and oregano. Pour this marinade over the lamb, and let the lamb sit in it for at least 5 to 6 hours, turning it from time to time.

3. When the time comes to cook your lamb, preheat the oven to 425°F. Remove the meat from the marinade and place it on a rack in a roasting pan. Leave the rosemary needles and bits of oregano clinging to it.

4. Combine the remaining olive oil and cloves of garlic, and spoon this mixture over the lamb, coating the whole leg. Position the leg with the fat side up and insert a meat thermometer deep into the center of the thickest part of the meat, but don't let it touch the bone.

5. When the oven is up to temperature, put your roast in and set the timer for 10 minutes. After 10 minutes, turn the oven down to 350°F, and roast for about 30 minutes per pound of meat, or until the meat thermometer registers 170° to 180°F. Remove the lamb from the oven, and let it sit for 15 to 20 minutes before carving.

Yield: 3 servings per pound, each with no carbohydrates or fiber to speak of, and about 21 grams of protein. (This sounds low, I know, but remember: Part of that weight is bone.)

🍓 Make Lamb Gravy (see page 358) to go with your roast lamb, and serve it with some Cauliflower Rice (see page 158).

↻ Lamb Gravy

Drippings from Mediterranean Leg of Lamb (see page 357)

1 cup chicken broth

3/4 teaspoon guar or xanthan

Salt and pepper to taste

1. Skim the fat off of the drippings from the roast. (Fat will ruin the texture of your gravy.)

2. Pour 1/2 cup of the chicken broth into the roasting pan with the skimmed drippings, and stir it around, scraping up the yummy browned bits from the rack and the bottom of the pan. When most of the stuck-on stuff is dissolved into the broth, put the roasting pan over medium-high heat.

3. Put the rest of the chicken broth in a blender with the guar or xanthan, and run the blender for a few seconds to dissolve all of the thickener. Pour the thickened broth into the roasting pan, and stir until all the gravy is thickened. (If it gets too thick, add a little more chicken broth; if it's not quite thick enough, let it simmer for a few minutes to cook down.)

4. Salt and pepper the gravy to taste, and serve with the leg of lamb.

Yield: The only carbohydrates in this gravy will be some fiber from the guar or xanthan, plus maybe 1 gram per serving from the herbs and wine.

🍓 The easiest way to skim drippings is to pour them into a large, heavy, zipper-lock bag. Seal the bag, and tip it so one corner points down over the roasting pan. Let it hang this way for a minute or so, until you see the fat float to the top and the good, flavorful, dark-colored pan juices at the bottom. Snip a tiny triangle off the bottom corner of the bag, and let the juices run out. Grab the corner of the bag to stop the flow before the fat runs into the pan, and throw the bag and the grease away.

CHAPTER ELEVEN

Main Dish Salads

I think main dish salads are one of the very best things for a low-carber to eat, because they offer infinite variety. Of course, they contain enough vegetables that you probably won't want to eat much else in the way of carbohydrates at that particular meal, but with all the flavor and eye appeal these salads offer, who needs anything else?

Chicken Waldorf Salad

Measure your apple carefully, as it's the main source of carbs here.

    1 1/2 cups diced cooked chicken
    1/2 cup diced apple
    2 big ribs celery, diced
    1/2 cup chopped walnuts
    1/3 cup mayonnaise

Combine all the ingredients, mix well, and serve.

Yield: 2 servings, each with 9 grams of carbohydrates and 3 grams of fiber, for a total of 6 grams of usable carbs and 40 grams of protein.

Cajun Chicken Salad

2 boneless, skinless chicken breasts

1 teaspoon Cajun Seasoning (store-bought, or see page 405)

1 sweet red pepper, cut into small strips

1 green pepper, cut into small strips

1/4 sweet red onion, thinly sliced

3 tablespoons tarragon vinegar

1 teaspoon spicy brown or Dijon mustard

1 clove garlic, crushed

1/3 cup olive oil

1 teaspoon dried tarragon

Salt and black pepper to taste

1. Place a chicken breast in a large, heavy zipper-lock bag, and pound with a meat tenderizer, hammer, or whatever you have available, until it's 1/4 inch thick. Repeat with the second breast.

2. Sprinkle both sides of each pounded chicken breast with the Cajun seasoning. Grill or sauté until cooked through.

3. Cut both chicken breasts in strips about 1/4 inch wide. Combine with the peppers and onion.

4. In a small bowl, combine the tarragon vinegar, mustard, garlic, oil, dried tarragon, and salt and pepper to taste; mix well. Pour over the chicken and vegetables, and toss. Serve right away, or let it sit for several hours for the flavors to blend.

Yield: 2 servings, each with 11 grams of carbohydrates and 3 grams of fiber, for a total of 8 grams of usable carbs and 29 grams of protein.

ℭ Dana's Tuna Salad

This is my lunchtime standby. With so many vegetables, this really is a tuna salad.

      2 large ribs celery, or 3 small ones

      1/2 green pepper

      1/4 medium, sweet red onion

      1 can chunk light tuna

      1/3 cup mayonnaise

1. Dice up the vegetables. I like them fairly chunky, so I get lots of crunchy texture. This should come to 1 1/2 to 2 cups of veggies.

2. Add the tuna and mayo, and mix it up. Sometimes I eat this with fiber crackers, or stuff it into a tomato, but it's awfully good just eaten with a fork, right out of the mixing bowl. (Hey, I'm home alone at lunchtime…I'm allowed to eat out of the mixing bowl.)

Yield: This could feed 2, but most of the time I treat it as 1 serving. If you're nice enough to share, each serving will have 5 grams of carbohydrates and 1 gram of fiber, for a total of 4 grams of usable carbs and 21 grams of protein.

↻ Classic Egg Salad

Here's your lunch for the week after Easter.

4 hard-boiled eggs, chopped

1 rib celery, diced

5 or 6 scallions, sliced

1/2 green pepper, diced

1/3 cup mayonnaise

1/2 teaspoon prepared mustard

Combine all the ingredients, and serve on lettuce.

Yield: 2 servings, each with 7 grams of carbohydrates and 2 grams of fiber, for a total of 5 grams of usable carbs and 14 grams of protein.

Not Quite So Classic Egg Salad. My mother has always liked olives in her egg salad, so I tried it, and it's surprisingly good. Just make Classic Egg Salad, but substitute 4 or 5 chopped green olives for the green pepper and leave out the mustard.

Yield: 2 servings, each with 6 grams of carbohydrates and 2 grams of fiber, for a total of 4 grams of usable carbs and 14 grams of protein.

↻ Chicken Pecan Salad

A good reason to cook an extra couple of pieces of chicken every time you're roasting some. This will keep you full for hours.

1 1/2 cups cooked chicken, diced

2 big ribs celery, diced

1/4 medium, sweet red onion, diced

1/4 cup chopped pecans

1/3 cup mayonnaise

Salt

Toss the chicken, celery, onion, pecans, and mayonnaise together. Salt to taste, and serve.

Yield: 2 servings, each with 5 grams of carbohydrates and 2 grams of fiber, for a total of 3 grams of usable carbs and 24 grams of protein.

Dilled Chicken Salad

1 1/2 cups cooked chicken, diced

1 large rib celery, diced

1/2 green pepper, diced

1/4 medium, sweet red onion, diced

3 tablespoons mayonnaise

3 tablespoons sour cream

1 teaspoon dried dill weed

Salt

1. Combine the chicken, celery, pepper, and onion in a bowl.

2. In a separate bowl, mix together the mayonnaise, sour cream, and dill. Pour the mixture over the chicken and veggies, toss, salt to taste, and serve.

Yield: 2 servings, each with 5 grams of carbohydrates and 1 gram of fiber, for a total of 4 grams of usable carbs and 24 grams of protein.

This is wonderful when made with leftover turkey, too.

Chef's Salad

    10 cups romaine, iceberg, red leaf, or any other favorite lettuce

    1/4 pound deli turkey breast

    1/4 pound deli ham

    1/4 pound deli roast beef

    1/4 pound Swiss cheese

    1 green pepper, cut into strips or rings

    1/2 sweet red onion, cut into rings

    4 hard-boiled eggs, halved or quartered

    2 ripe tomatoes, cut vertically into 8 wedges each

    Salad dressing

1. Make nice beds of the lettuce on 4 serving plates.

2. Cut the turkey, ham, roast beef, and Swiss cheese into strips. (It's nice, by the way, to get fairly thickly sliced meat and cheese for this.) Arrange all of this artistically on the beds of lettuce, and garnish with the pepper, onion, eggs, and tomatoes. Let each diner add his or her own dressing.

Yield: 4 servings, each with 13 grams of carbohydrates and 4 grams of fiber, for a total of 9 grams of usable carbs and 37 grams of protein. (Analysis does not include salad dressing.)

This salad is infinitely variable, of course; if you don't eat ham, hate roast beef, or love Swiss cheese, feel free to play around with these instructions. I only put down amounts so we could analyze the carb count and give you a guide to work from.

ᔕ Chicken Caesar Salad

> 1 boneless, skinless chicken breast
>
> 2 to 3 cups romaine lettuce, washed, dried, and broken up
>
> 2 tablespoons Caesar Dressing (bottled, or see page 239)
>
> 2 tablespoons Parmesan cheese, in thin slivers or grated

1. Grill the chicken breast. (I do mine in an electric tabletop grill for about 5 minutes, but you could sauté it, if you prefer.)

2. While the chicken cooks, put the lettuce in a bowl, pour the dressing over it, and toss well. Pile it on your serving plate.

3. Slice the cooked chicken breast into thin strips, and pile it on top of the lettuce. Scatter the Parmesan on top, and dig in.

Yield: 1 serving, with 5 grams of carbohydrates and 2 grams of fiber, for a total of 3 grams of usable carbs and 26 grams of protein.

Shrimp Caesar Salad. Make this just like Chicken Caesar Salad (above), but substitute 10 to 12 good-size cooked shrimp for the chicken breast. Frozen, precooked, shelled shrimp are handy for this because they thaw quickly, especially if you put them in a zipper-lock baggie and set them in warm tap water for a few minutes.

Yield: 5 grams of carbohydrates and 2 grams of fiber, for a total of 3 grams of usable carbs and 30 grams of protein.

↺ Souvlaki Salad

This skewered lamb is usually served as a sandwich in pita bread, but it makes a fabulous salad for a lot fewer carbs.

> 2 pounds lean lamb, cut into 1-inch cubes
>
> 1/2 cup olive oil
>
> 1 cup dry red wine
>
> 1 teaspoon salt
>
> 1/4 teaspoon pepper
>
> 1 teaspoon oregano
>
> 3 cloves garlic, crushed
>
> 1 head romaine lettuce
>
> 1/4 sweet red onion, sliced paper-thin
>
> 24 cherry tomatoes, halved
>
> 2/3 cup Greek Lemon Dressing (see page 233)
>
> 6 tablespoons plain yogurt or sour cream (the yogurt is more authentic)

1. Put the lamb cubes in a large, zipper-lock bag.

2. Combine the oil, wine, salt, pepper, oregano, and garlic. Pour the mixture over the lamb cubes in the bag. Let this marinate for at least a few hours.

3. When you're ready to cook the lamb, pour off the marinade and thread the cubes onto skewers. You can grill these or broil them 8 inches or so from the broiler. Turn the kebabs while they're cooking, and check for doneness by cutting into a chunk of meat after 10 minutes. They should be thoroughly cooked in 15 minutes.

   🍓 If you don't have any skewers, you can always just lay the lamb cubes on the broiler pan. They're a lot easier to turn over if they're on skewers, however.

4. While the meat is cooking, wash and dry your lettuce, and arrange it on serving plates.

5. Push the cooked meat off the skewers and onto the prepared beds of lettuce. Scatter some red onion over each plate, and arrange 8 cherry tomato halves on each. Drizzle each plate with a couple of tablespoons of dressing, and top each with a tablespoon of yogurt.

Yield: 6 servings, each with 11 grams of carbohydrates and 4 grams of fiber, for a total of 7 grams of usable carbs and 34 grams of protein.

↻ Sirloin Salad

I admit it: I copied this directly from a salad I had at Applebee's. It was so good and so easy, I just had to tell you about it.

    8 ounces sirloin steak, 1 inch thick
    2 cups romaine lettuce, washed, dried, and broken up
    1/2 medium, ripe tomato, cut into thin wedges
    1/8 sweet red onion, thinly sliced
    Salad dressing of your choice
       (vinaigrette and bleu cheese dressing are both good with this)

1. Grill or broil the steak to your preferred degree of doneness. While the steak is cooking, arrange the lettuce on a serving plate.

2. Cut the cooked steak into thin slices across the grain, and pile it on top of the lettuce. Arrange the tomato wedges around the edge, and scatter the onion over the top. Serve with the dressing of your choice.

Yield: 1 serving, with 7 grams of carbohydrates and 3 grams of fiber, for a total of 4 grams of usable carbs and 44 grams of protein. (Analysis does not include dressing.)

Asian Chicken Salad

This is an wonderful salad, different from any I've ever tried. Do use rice vinegar instead of another kind, and napa cabbage instead of regular. They may seem like small distinctions, but they make all the difference.

        2 tablespoons oil

        1/2 cup walnuts, chopped

        4 boneless, skinless chicken breasts

        3 cups thinly sliced bok choy

        3 cups thinly sliced napa cabbage

        1/4 cup grated carrots

        1 cucumber, thinly sliced

        1/2 cup sliced scallions

        1/2 cup chopped fresh cilantro

        1/3 cup soy sauce

        1/4 cup rice vinegar

        1 tablespoon lime juice

        2 tablespoons Splenda

        3 cloves garlic, crushed

        1/2 teaspoon red pepper flakes (or to taste)

1. Put the oil in a heavy skillet over medium heat and toast the walnuts, stirring for about 4 to 5 minutes or until they're brown and crisp. Set aside.

2. Grill your chicken breasts, and slice them into strips; I use my electric tabletop grill, but you can use whatever method you prefer.

3. Combine the bok choy, cabbage, carrots, cucumber, scallions, and cilantro in a big bowl.

4. In a separate bowl, combine the soy sauce, rice vinegar, lime juice, Splenda, garlic, and red pepper flakes. Pour about two-thirds of this dressing over the salad, and toss well, coating all the vegetables.

5. Heap the salad onto four serving plates, top each with a sliced chicken breast, and drizzle the rest of the dressing over them. Sprinkle with chopped walnuts, and serve.

Yield: 4 generous servings, each with 15 grams of carbohydrates and 4 grams of fiber, for a total of 11 grams of usable carbs and 36 grams of protein.

🍓 We generally only have 2 people to eat all this salad, so I set half of the vegetable mixture aside in a container in the refrigerator. Don't put dressing on the half you plan to reserve, just put the dry, shredded vegetables in a container in the fridge, save half of your dressing to go with it, and reserve some of the walnuts, as well. This is wonderful to have on hand for a quick, gourmet lunch—just grill a chicken breast, toss the salad with the dressing, and presto, lunch is served.

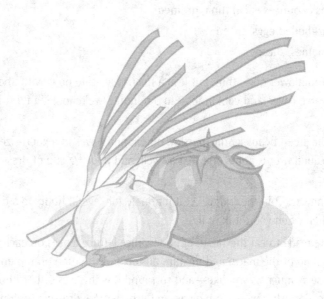

↶ Nicer Niçoise

Salad niçoise is traditionally made with green beans and cold, boiled potatoes, but of course, we're not going to be eating those potatoes. I thought I'd try it with cauliflower, and sure enough, it worked great!

1/3 head cauliflower

1 bag (1 pound) frozen, crosscut green beans, thawed but not cooked

1 clove garlic, crushed

1/4 to 1/2 cup fresh parsley, minced

1/4 medium, red onion, diced

8 to 10 olives, sliced (I used stuffed olives, but use whatever you like best.)

1/2 to 3/4 cup vinaigrette dressing (homemade or bottled)

Lettuce (to line plate)

3 cans (6 ounces each) tuna, drained

6 hard-boiled eggs, sliced

3 tomatoes, sliced

1. Slice your cauliflower quite thin. Put it in a microwave-safe bowl with about 1 tablespoon of water, cover, and cook it for 4 to 5 minutes (we're looking for it to be just tender).

2. Combine the green beans, garlic, parsley, onion, and olives in a good-size bowl. When the cauliflower is done, add that as well, and pour 1/2 cup of dressing over the whole thing.

3. Stir well, and stick it in the fridge. Let it marinate for several hours to a day, stirring now and then when you think of it.

4. When you're ready to eat the salad, put a few nice lettuce leaves on each plate, and spoon a mound of the marinated mixture on top. Put the tuna on top and in the middle—use as much as you like—and surround it with slices of hard-boiled egg and tomato. Garnish it with more olives and drizzle more dressing on top, if you like, and serve.

Yield: 6 servings, each with 12 grams of carbohydrates and 3 grams of fiber, for a total of 9 grams of usable carbs and 30 grams of protein.

ꙩ Dinner Salad Italiano

1 head romaine lettuce, washed, dried, and broken up

1 cup sliced fresh mushrooms

1/2 cucumber, sliced

1/4 sweet red onion, thinly sliced

1/2 pound sliced salami, cut into strips

1/2 pound sliced provolone, cut into strips

Italian or vinaigrette dressing (bottled, or see page 232)

2 ripe tomatoes, cut into wedges

Make a big tossed salad from the lettuce, mushrooms, cucumber, onion, salami, and provolone. Toss with bottled Italian or vinaigrette dressing, then add the sliced tomatoes and serve.

Yield: 3 servings, each with 17 grams of carbohydrates and 6 grams of fiber, for a total of 11 grams of usable carbs and 36 grams of protein.

↻ Taco Salad

A great summer supper. The wild card in this recipe is the ranch dressing—different brands vary tremendously in carb count. Choose a really, really low-carb one, and you'll drop the carb count below what's listed here.

> 2 quarts romaine or iceberg lettuce, washed, dried, and broken up
>
> 1 cup diced green pepper
>
> 1/2 medium cucumber, sliced
>
> 1 medium tomato, sliced into thin wedges, or 15 cherry tomatoes, halved
>
> 1/2 cup diced sweet red onion
>
> 1/2 ripe avocado, peeled, seeded, and cut into small chunks
>
> 1/2 cup cilantro, chopped (optional)
>
> 1 can (4 ounces) sliced black olives, drained (optional)
>
> 2/3 cup salsa plus additional for topping
>
> 1/2 cup ranch dressing
>
> 1 batch Chicken or Beef Taco Filling (see pages 263 and 320)
>
> 1 cup shredded Cheddar or Monterey Jack cheese
>
> Sour cream

1. Put the lettuce, pepper, cucumber, tomato, onion, avocado, cilantro (if using), and olives (if using) in a large salad bowl.

2. Stir together the 2/3 cup of salsa and the ranch dressing, pour it over the salad, and toss.

3. Divide the salad between the serving plates, and top each one with the taco filling and shredded cheese. Put the salsa and sour cream on the table, so folks can add their own.

Yield: 6 servings, each with 12 grams of carbohydrates and 4 grams of fiber, for a total of 8 grams of usable carbs and 22 grams of protein.

ᔕ Sweet 'n' Nutty Tuna Salad

Here's something a little different for when you get tired of your usual tuna salad. That's actually how I invented this recipe.

1 rib celery, diced

2 tablespoons chopped pecans, walnuts, or almonds

10 red, seedless grapes, quartered

2 tablespoons diced red onion

1 can (6 ounces) tuna

1/3 cup mayonnaise

Combine all the ingredients, and enjoy!

Yield: I eat the whole thing by myself, but then, I'm a glutton. This could easily be 2 servings, each with 7 grams of carbohydrates and 1 gram of fiber, for a total of 6 grams of usable carbs and 23 grams of protein.

ᔕ Mozzarella Salad

This is rich and filling. The texture is quite different, depending on whether you use shredded or cubed cheese, but they're both good.

1 1/2 cups shredded or diced mozzarella

1/4 cup sliced scallions

1/2 cup diced celery

1/4 cup mayonnaise

2 tablespoons wine vinegar

1/2 teaspoon oregano

1/2 teaspoon basil

1. Combine the mozzarella, scallions, and celery in a mixing bowl.
2. In a separate bowl, combine the mayonnaise, vinegar, oregano, and basil. Pour the mixture over the salad, stir to combine, and serve.

Yield: 2 servings, each with 6 grams of carbohydrates and 2 grams of fiber, for a total of 4 grams of usable carbs and 20 grams of protein.

Mediterranean Chicken and "Rice" Salad

2 cups Cauliflower Rice (see page 159)

1 clove garlic, crushed

3 tablespoons wine vinegar

2 tablespoons olive oil

1 tablespoon mayonnaise

1/4 teaspoon salt

1/4 teaspoon pepper

1 cup diced cooked chicken

1/3 cup diced sweet red onion

1/2 cup diced celery

1/2 cup diced green pepper

1/3 cup chopped fresh parsley

1. Steam your cauliflower "rice" until just tender; for this small amount, I put it in a bowl, add about 1 tablespoon of water, cover it, and microwave it on High for 5 minutes. Put it in the refrigerator to cool.

    🍓 Use the time while you wait for the cauliflower to cool to do all the dicing and chopping for the rest of the recipe.

2. Mix together the garlic, vinegar, oil, mayonnaise, salt, and pepper, and blend well.

3. Toss the chicken, onion, celery, pepper, and parsley with the cooled cauliflower. Pour the dressing on the mixture and toss. This is good served right away, but even better the next day.

Yield: 2 servings, each with 14 grams of carbohydrates and 5 grams of fiber, for a total of 9 grams of usable carbs and 24 grams of protein.

ꙅ Summer Tuna Salad

> 1 medium cucumber, cut into chunks
>
> 1/3 cup sweet red onion, sliced
>
> 1/3 cup chopped fresh parsley
>
> 1/2 large green pepper, cut into small strips
>
> 15 cherry tomatoes, quartered
>
> 1 can (6 ounces) tuna, drained
>
> 1/4 cup extra-virgin olive oil
>
> 2 tablespoons wine vinegar
>
> 1 clove garlic, crushed
>
> 1/4 teaspoon salt
>
> 1/8 teaspoon pepper

1. Put the cucumber, onion, parsley, pepper, tomatoes, and tuna in a salad bowl.

2. In a separate bowl, combine the oil, vinegar, garlic, salt, and pepper. Pour the mixture over the salad, toss, and serve.

Yield: 2 servings, each with 16 grams of carbohydrates and 4 grams of fiber, for a total of 12 grams of usable carbs and 25 grams of protein.

ꙅ Cottage Cheese Salad

This makes a nice, light lunch that would carry well in a snap-top container.

> 1 scallion, sliced, including the crisp part of the green
>
> 2 radishes, thinly sliced
>
> 1/2 cup cucumber, quartered lengthways and thinly sliced
>
> 1/2 cup cottage cheese
>
> 2 tablespoons sour cream
>
> A few lettuce leaves

Mix together the scallion, radishes, cucumber, cottage cheese, and sour cream. Place a few leaves of lettuce on a serving dish, and scoop the cottage cheese mixture onto it. Serve.

Yield: 1 serving, with 8 grams of carbohydrates and 1 gram of fiber, for a total of 7 grams of usable carbs and 17 grams of protein.

Tuna Egg Waldorf

2 large ribs celery, diced

1/2 cup diced red onion

1/2 cup diced red apple

1/2 cup chopped pecans

1 can (6 ounces) tuna, drained

3 hard-boiled eggs, chopped

3/4 cup mayonnaise

Salt

Lettuce

Put the celery, onion, apple, pecans, tuna, and hard-boiled eggs in a big bowl.
Toss with the mayonnaise until it's all coated. Salt to taste, and serve on a
lettuce-lined plate. (Or not; if you want to just eat it by itself, I won't tell.)

Yield: 3 servings, each with 10 grams of carbohydrates and 3 grams of fiber,
for a total of 7 grams of usable carbs and 23 grams of protein.

CHAPTER TWELVE

Soups

Everybody loves soup. Unfortunately, way too many people think of soup as something that comes out of a can or a packet, and the vast majority of packaged soups have added corn syrup or corn starch, plus, of course, things like rice, noodles, potatoes, beans, and other ingredients we simply can't have.

So make some soup yourself. Most of these soups are quite simple to make, and many of them are filling, nutritious, one-dish meals. Making a big batch (or even a double batch) of soup over the weekend is one of the greatest things you can do to save cooking time all week long.

If you want to make a soup as an appetizer or snack, choose one of the soups with lowest carb counts. On the other hand, if you want a lunch or supper, keep an eye on the protein content, and figure that the vegetables in the soup will be all your carbs for that meal.

Note: You'll find that packaged broth generally comes in two sizes: 1-quart cans and 14 1/2-ounce cans. Why this should be, I have no idea. But in any of these recipes, if you substitute two 14 1/2-ounce cans for 1 quart of broth, no harm will come to your soup, you'll just get slightly less volume. You can make up the difference with water, if you really want to, but I don't see why you'd bother.

⌒ California Soup

A quick and elegant first course.

>   1 large or 2 small, very ripe avocados, pitted, peeled, and cut into chunks
>   1 quart chicken broth, heated

Put the avocados through the blender with the broth, puree until very smooth, and serve.

Yield: 6 servings (as a first course), each with 3 grams of carbohydrates and 1 gram of fiber, for a total of 2 grams of usable carbs and 4 grams of protein.

🍓 If you like curry, you've got to try this: Melt a tablespoon or so of butter and add 1/2 teaspoon or so of curry powder. Cook for just a minute, and add the mixture to the blender with the broth and avocados.

⌒ Corner-Filling Consommé

>   2 tablespoons butter
>   4 ounces sliced mushrooms
>   1 small onion, sliced paper-thin
>   1 quart beef broth
>   2 tablespoons dry sherry
>   1/4 teaspoon pepper

Melt the butter in a skillet, and sauté the mushrooms and onions in the butter until they're limp. Add the beef broth, sherry, and pepper. Let it simmer for 5 minutes or so, just to blend the flavors a bit, and serve.

Yield: 6 appetizer-size servings, each with 5 grams of carbohydrates and 1 gram of fiber, for a total of 4 grams of usable carbs and 8 grams of protein.

꩜ Crock-Pot Tomato Soup

Delicious tomato soup from *Splendid Low Carbing*, by Jennifer Eloff of sweety.com. So easy!

    2 1/2 cups V8 or other mixed vegetable juice

    2 1/2 cups boiling water

    8 ounces canned tomato sauce

    1 small onion, thinly sliced

    1 bay leaf

    3 tablespoons Splenda

    1 tablespoon beef bouillon granules or liquid beef-broth concentrate

    1/8 teaspoon pepper

    1/4 teaspoon dried basil

Combine all ingredients in a slow cooker and stir. Cover and cook on Low for 4 hours. Strain and serve.

Yield: 6 servings, each with 10 grams of carbohydrates and 2 grams of fiber, for a total or 8 grams of usable carbs and 2 grams of protein.

ᕫ Mulligatawny

This is a curried soup that came out of the British Colonial times in India. It's also wonderful made with broth made from a turkey carcass, or, for that matter, from the remains of a leg of lamb.

 2 quarts chicken broth

 2 cups or more diced cooked chicken or diced boneless, skinless chicken breast

 3 tablespoons butter

 1 clove garlic, crushed

 1 medium onion, chopped

 1 small carrot, shredded

 2 ribs celery, diced

 2 teaspoons to 1 $1/2$ heaping tablespoons curry powder
   (I like it with lots of curry!)

 1 bay leaf

 $1/2$ tart apple, chopped fine

 1 to 2 teaspoons salt or Vege-Sal

 $1/2$ teaspoon pepper

 $1/2$ teaspoon dried thyme

 Rind of 1 fresh lemon, grated, or $1/2$ to 1 teaspoon dried

 1 cup heavy cream

1. Put the broth and diced chicken in a large stockpot, and set the stockpot over low heat.

2. Melt the butter in a heavy skillet, and add the onion, garlic, carrot, celery, and curry powder. Sauté until the vegetables are limp, and add them to the stockpot.

3. Add the bay leaf, apple, salt, pepper, thyme, and lemon to the pot, and simmer for $1/2$ hour. Just before serving, stir in the cream.

Yield: 6 servings, each with 8 grams of carbohydrates and 2 grams of fiber, for a total of 6 grams of usable carbs and 18 grams of protein.

ᕫ Sopa Azteca

That's soup made by Aztecs, not soup made from Aztecs!

 3 quarts chicken broth

 2 cups diced cooked chicken or boneless, skinless chicken breast

1/4 cup olive oil

1 medium onion, chopped

4 or 5 cloves garlic, crushed

2 or 3 ribs celery, diced

1 green pepper, diced

1 small carrot, shredded

1 small zucchini, diced

2 cans (14 1/2 ounces each) diced tomatoes, including juice

1 package frozen chopped spinach

2 tablespoons dried oregano

2 tablespoons dried basil

2 teaspoons pepper

At least 8 ounces Mexican Queso Quesadilla or Monterey Jack cheese, shredded

Chipotle peppers in adobo sauce (these come canned)

5 ripe Haas avocados

1. Heat the broth and the chicken in a large pot over low heat.

2. Heat the olive oil in a skillet over medium heat, and sauté the onion, garlic, celery, pepper, carrot, and zucchini together until they're limp. Stir the oregano, basil and pepper into thevegetables and sautée for another minute and add them to the soup, along with the tomatoes and spinach. Let the whole thing simmer for 1/2 to 1 hour, to let the flavors blend.

3. When you're ready to serve the Sopa Azteca, put at least 1/4 to 1/2 cup of cheese (more won't hurt) in the bottom of each bowl, and anywhere from 1 to 3 chipotles, depending on how spicy you like your food. (If you don't like spicy food at all, leave the chipotles out entirely.) Ladle the hot soup over the cheese and peppers.

4. Use a spoon to scoop chunks of 1/2 ripe avocado onto the top of each bowl of soup.

Yield: 10 servings. Each serving of soup alone has 21 grams of carbohydrates and 6 grams of fiber, for a total of 15 grams of usable carbs and 25 grams of protein. 1/2 cup of shredded cheese adds only a gram or so of carbohydrates and 14 grams of protein. Each chipotle pepper adds no more than 1 gram or so of carbs, and 1/2 a Haas avocado has about 6 grams of carbohydrates and 2.5 grams of fiber, for a total of 3.5 grams of usable carbs per serving.

The totals on this soup may sound like a lot when you add them all up, but don't forget that this is a whole meal in a bowl: meat, vegetables, melted cheese, and lovely ripe avocado in each bite! You don't need to serve another thing with it, although if you could serve tortillas or quesadillas for the carb-eaters in the crowd.

Hot-and-Sour Soup

Really authentic Hot-and-Sour Soup uses Chinese mushrooms, but this is mighty good with any variety—especially when you have a cold!

> 2 quarts chicken broth
>
> 1 piece of fresh ginger about the size of a walnut, peeled and thinly sliced
>
> 1/2 pound lean pork (I use boneless loin.)
>
> 3 tablespoons soy sauce
>
> 1 to 1 1/2 teaspoons pepper
>
> 1/2 cup white vinegar
>
> 2 cans (6 1/2 ounces each) mushrooms
>
> 1 cake (about 10 ounces) firm tofu
>
> 1 can (8 ounces) bamboo shoots
>
> 5 eggs

1. Put the broth in a kettle and set it over medium heat. Add the ginger to the broth and let it simmer for a few minutes.

2. While the broth simmers, slice the pork into small cubes or strips. (I like strips.) Stir the soy sauce, pork, pepper, vinegar, and mushrooms (you don't need to drain them) into the broth. Let it simmer for 10 minutes or so, until the pork is done through.

3. Cut the tofu into small cubes. If you like, you can also cut the canned bamboo shoots into thinner strips. (I like them better that way, but sometimes I don't feel like doing the extra work.) Stir the tofu and bamboo shoots into the soup, and let it simmer another few minutes. Taste the soup; it won't be very hot—spicy-hot, that is, not temperature-hot—so if you like it hotter, add more pepper and some hot sauce. If you like, you can also add a little extra vinegar.

4. Beat the eggs in a bowl, and then pour them in a thin stream over the surface of the soup. Stir them in, and you'll get a billion little shreds of cooked egg in your soup. Who needs noodles?

   🍓 This is good served with a few finely sliced scallions on top (include some of the green part) and a few drops of toasted sesame oil. Since I like my soup hotter than my husband does, I use hot toasted sesame oil, rather than putting hot sauce in the whole batch.

Yield: 6 servings, each with 10 grams of carbohydrates and 2 grams of fiber, for a total of 8 grams of usable carbs and 25 grams of protein.

⌒ Peanut Soup

If you miss split pea or bean soup, try this. Try it even if you don't miss other soups—you may find you have a new favorite.

> 3 tablespoons butter
>
> 2 or 3 ribs celery, finely chopped
>
> 1 medium onion, finely chopped
>
> 2 quarts chicken broth
>
> 1/2 teaspoon salt or Vege-Sal
>
> 1 1/4 cups natural peanut butter (I use smooth.)
>
> 1 teaspoon guar gum (optional)
>
> 2 cups half-and-half or heavy cream
>
> Salted peanuts, chopped

1. Melt the butter in a skillet, and sauté the celery and onion in the butter. Add the broth, salt, and peanut butter, and stir. Cover and simmer on the lowest temperature for at least 1 hour, stirring now and then.

   🍓 If your slow cooker will hold this quantity of ingredients (mine will), it's ideal for cooking this soup. Set it on High, cover it, and let it go for 2 to 3 hours.

2. If you're using guar gum (it makes the soup thicker without adding carbs; most peanut soup is thickened with flour), scoop 1 cup of the soup out of the kettle about 15 minutes before you want to serve it. Add the guar gum to this cup, run the mixture through the blender for a few seconds, and whisk it back into the soup.

3. Stir in the half-and-half, and simmer for another 15 minutes. Garnish with the peanuts.

Yield: 5 servings, The carb count will depend on what brand of natural peanut butter you use (they have varying amounts of fiber) and whether you use half-and-half or heavy cream. Figure each serving has about 19 grams of carbohydrates and 3 grams of fiber, for a total of 16 grams of usable carbs and 29 grams of protein.

ꙮ Spring Chicken Soup

This soup is a great way to use up leftovers—just substitute 1 cup of leftover chicken for the chicken breast called listed with the ingredients.

     6 cups chicken broth

     1 can (6 1/2 ounces) mushrooms

     1 can (6 1/2 ounces) cut asparagus

     1 boneless, skinless chicken breast, diced into small cubes

     1/4 cup dry sherry

     1 tablespoon soy sauce

     Pepper

     Sliced scallions

Combine the broth, mushrooms, asparagus, chicken, sherry, and soy sauce in a pot, and heat. If you're using raw chicken, let it cook for 5 to 10 minutes (that's all it should take to cook small cubes of chicken through). Add pepper to taste, and serve with a scattering of scallions on top.

🍓 If you're feeling ambitious, there's no reason you couldn't make this with fresh mushrooms and fresh asparagus; you'll just have to simmer it a little longer. As it is, though, this soup is practically instantaneous!

Yield: 4 servings. Depending on the broth you use, this should have no more than about 17 grams of usable carbs in the whole pot, plus about 0.5 gram for the little bit of scallion you put on top of each bowl. Figure each serving has 6 grams of carbohydrates and 2 grams of fiber, for a total of 4 grams of usable carbs and 23 grams of protein.

ꙮ Judie's Chicken "Noodle" Soup

Judie Edwards created this when she was craving chicken noodle soup, and it's a cinch to make.

     2 cups chicken broth

     1 can Chinese vegetables, drained

Simply combine, heat, and serve.

Yield: 1 serving, with 7 grams of carbohydrates and 2.5 grams of fiber, for a total of 4.5 grams of usable carbs and 7 grams of protein.

↶ Easy Tomato-Beef Soup

1/4 to 1 1/2 pound ground beef

2 cans (14 1/2 ounces each) beef broth

1 can (14 1/2 ounces) diced tomatoes

In a skillet, brown the ground beef. Pour off the grease, and add the broth and tomatoes. Heat through, and serve.

Yield: 4 servings, each with 9 grams of carbohydrates, a trace of fiber, and 19 grams of protein.

↶ Italian Tuna Soup

Okay, it's not authentically Italian, but it's a lot like minestrone. It's easy, too.

1 quart chicken broth

1 can (14 1/2 ounces) diced tomatoes

1 can (14 1/2 ounces) Italian green beans or 1 package (10 ounces) frozen Italian green beans

1/2 cup frozen broccoli cuts

1/2 cup frozen cauliflower cuts

1 cup thinly sliced zucchini, frozen or fresh

3 tablespoons tomato paste

1 teaspoon Italian seasoning

2 cans (6 ounces each) tuna

Tabasco

Combine the broth, tomatoes, beans, broccoli, cauliflower, zucchini, tomato paste, seasoning, and tuna. Add a few drops of Tabasco (more if you like it hotter, less if you just want a little zip), and simmer until the vegetables are tender.

Yield: 5 servings, each with 14 grams of carbohydrates and 3 grams of fiber, for a total of 11 grams of usable carbs and 23 grams of protein.

🍓 Check the frozen foods section of your supermarket for mixed bags of broccoli and cauliflower, and substitute 1 cup of the mix for the separate cauliflower and broccoli. That way, you'll only have one partially eaten bag of veggies in the freezer to use up, rather than two.

ᕗ Zesty Seafood Soup

Marilee Wellersdick came up with this. Just make sure you use real crab, not the high-carb fake crab that's widely available these days, when you make this soup.

2 tablespoons olive oil

1 medium onion, chopped

2 cloves garlic, minced

1 cup chopped celery

2 tablespoons fresh or dried parsley, chopped

1 teaspoon dried basil

1/2 teaspoon dried rosemary

1/2 teaspoon dried thyme

Dash of cayenne

3 cans (8 ounces each) tomato sauce

8 ounces clam juice

1 can (14 1/2 ounces) chicken broth

1 pound firm fish (such as cod, halibut, or snapper), cut into 1-inch cubes

4 1/2 ounces small canned, fresh, or frozen shrimp

1 can (8 ounces) crabmeat, or 1 fresh crab

Salt

1. Heat the oil in a Dutch oven. Add the onion, garlic, and celery, and sauté until the onion is limp.

2. Stir in the parsley, basil, rosemary, thyme, cayenne, tomato sauce, clam juice and chicken broth. Cover and simmer for about 10 minutes.

3. Add the fish; cover and simmer until the fish flakes (about 7 minutes). Stir in the shrimp and crab. Cover and cook for a few minutes, until everything is thoroughly heated. Salt to taste.

Yield : About 8 servings, each with 12 grams of carbohydrates and 2 grams of fiber, for a total of 10 grams of usable carbs and 12 grams of protein.

↷ Cream of Cauliflower

You'll be surprised by how much this tastes like Cream of Potato!

> 3 tablespoons butter
> 3/4 cup diced onion
> 3/4 cup diced celery
> 1 quart chicken broth
> 1 package (10 ounces) frozen cauliflower
> 1/2 teaspoon guar or xanthan (optional)
> 1/2 cup heavy cream
> Salt and pepper

1. Melt the butter over low heat, and sauté the onion and celery in it until they're limp. Combine with the chicken broth and cauliflower in a large saucepan, and simmer until the cauliflower is tender.

2. Use a slotted spoon to transfer the vegetables into a blender, and then pour in as much of the broth as will fit. Add the guar or xanthan (if using), and puree the ingredients.

3. Pour the mixture back into the saucepan. Stir in the cream, and salt and pepper to taste.

Yield: 4 servings, each with 9 grams of carbohydrates and 3 grams of fiber, for a total of 6 grams of usable carbs and 7 grams of protein.

Skydancer's Zucchini Soup

Jo Pagliassotti, an artist who works under the name Skydancer, came up with this savory and versatile soup.

> 4 cups chopped zucchini, cut into chunks
>
> 2 cups chopped Spanish onion
>
> 4 cups chicken stock, homemade or canned (if homemade, salt to taste)
>
> 1 to 2 teaspoons dry summer savory
>   or 1/4 cup fresh summer savory leaves, chopped
>
> 1 tablespoon dry basil or 1/2 cup fresh leaves, lightly packed
>
> 8 ounces cream cheese, at room temperature

1. Place the zucchini, onion, stock, summer savory, and basil into a pan. Cook over low heat until the vegetables are soft (30 minutes minimum).

    🍓 It won't hurt this soup a bit if you turn the burner to low, cover the pan, and forget it for a couple of hours. You want it to be squashy (pun intended!).

2. Put the cream cheese and a small quantity of the cooked mixture into a blender, and blend until smooth. (Add more liquid if needed to get the cheese smooth.) Pour that into another pan. Add more of the cooked squash and onion mixture to the blender, and blend until smooth (or as smooth as you like it). Blend the rest of the cooked mixture, pouring each blended batch into the soup and cheese mixture as you go.

3. Once everything is pureed, stir it well to mix in the initial cheese and zucchini blend, and rewarm over low heat if necessary.

Yield: 9 servings, each with 6 grams of carbohydrates and 2 grams of fiber, for a total of 4 grams of usable carbs and 3 grams of protein.

Try making this with a mixture of yellow squash and zucchini, but note that yellow squash has more carbs than zucchini. You can also use green onion or leeks instead of the Spanish onion. Keep in mind that 2 cups of green onion will give you 9.6 grams of carbs instead of 22 and 2 cups of leeks will give you 61.6 grams of carbs (why are they so high?) instead of 22.

Want even more variety and some more protein along with it? Leftover flaked salmon and chunks of cold leftover chicken are both great in this. You can garnish the soup with some sliced green onions or shallots, and that's also wonderful. This soup lends itself to many variations—be creative. Oh, and it freezes well! The cream cheese seems to hold up to this just fine.

ᔕ Jodee's Zucchini Soup

Here's another take on zucchini soup, from reader Jodee Rushton. She says this is satisfying as a quick between-meals snack, not to mention versatile: "In the summer, pour it into a mug and drink it cold. In the winter, you might microwave it."

1/4 cup butter

1 medium onion, chopped

1 1/2 pounds zucchini, washed and sliced

28 ounces chicken broth

1/8 teaspoon salt

1/8 teaspoon pepper

1/2 teaspoon ground nutmeg

1/2 cup half-and-half

1. Melt the butter and sauté the onion in it until golden. Add the zucchini and sauté over medium-high heat until limp (10 to 15 minutes).

2. Add the chicken broth, salt, pepper, and nutmeg. Simmer for 15 minutes, add the half-and-half, and let the mixture cool.

3. Puree the broth mixture in a blender. (Do this in batches, if necessary.) Refrigerate for a minimum of 4 hours, to allow the flavors to blend. Serve hot or cold.

Yield: 8 servings, each with 5 grams of carbohydrates and 1 gram of fiber, for a total of 4 grams of usable carbs and 2 grams of protein.

ᕫ Jamaican Pepperpot Soup

Unbelievably hearty, almost like a stew, and very tasty!

1/2 pound bacon, diced

2 pounds boneless beef round or chuck, cut into 1-inch cubes

1 large onion, chopped

4 cups water

1 cup canned beef broth

2 packages (10 ounces each) frozen chopped spinach

1/2 teaspoon dried thyme

1 green pepper, diced

1 can (14 1/2 ounces) sliced tomatoes

1 bay leaf

2 teaspoons salt

1/2 teaspoon pepper

1 teaspoon hot sauce (or to taste)

1 package (10 ounces) frozen sliced okra, thawed

3 tablespoons butter

1/2 cup heavy cream

Paprika

1. Place the bacon, beef cubes, onion, water, and beef broth in a large, heavy soup pot. Bring to a boil, turn the burner to low, and let the mixture simmer for 1 hour.

2. Add the spinach, thyme, green pepper, tomatoes, bay leaf, salt, pepper, and hot sauce. Let it simmer for another 30 minutes.

3. Sauté the okra in the butter over the lowest heat for about 5 minutes, then add to the soup, and simmer just 10 minutes more.

4. Just before serving, stir in the cream and sprinkle just a touch of paprika on each serving.

Yield: 6 servings, each with 16 grams of carbohydrates and 5 grams of fiber, for a total of 11 grams of usable carbs and 49 grams of protein.

Eggdrop Soup

Quick and easy, but filling, and it can practically save your life when you've got a cold. You don't have to use the guar, but it gives the broth the same rich quality that the cornstarch-thickened Chinese broths have.

> 1 quart chicken broth
>
> 1/4 teaspoon guar (optional)
>
> 1 tablespoon soy sauce
>
> 1 tablespoon rice vinegar
>
> 1/2 teaspoon grated fresh ginger
>
> 1 scallion, sliced
>
> 2 eggs

1. Put a cup or so of the chicken broth in your blender, turn it on Low, and add the guar (if using). Let it blend for a second, then put it in a large saucepan with the rest of the broth. (If you're not using the guar, just put the broth directly in a saucepan.)

2. Add the soy sauce, rice vinegar, ginger, and scallion. Heat over medium-high heat, and let it simmer for 5 minutes or so to let the flavors blend.

3. Beat your eggs in a glass measuring cup or small pitcher—something with a pouring lip. Use a fork to stir the surface of the soup in a slow circle and pour in about 1/4 of the eggs, stirring as they cook and turn into shreds (which will happen almost instantaneously). Repeat three more times, using up all the egg, then serve!

Yield: 3 biggish servings, or 4 to 5 small ones (but this recipe is easy to double). In 4 servings, each will have 2 grams of carbohydrates, a trace of fiber, and 8 grams of protein.

↻ Stracciatella

This is the Italian take on eggdrop soup, and it's delightful.

> 1 quart chicken broth
> 2 eggs
> 1/2 cup grated Parmesan cheese
> 1/2 teaspoon lemon juice
> Pinch of nutmeg
> 1/2 teaspoon dried marjoram

1. Put 1/4 cup of the broth in a glass measuring cup or small pitcher. Pour the rest into a large saucepan over medium heat.

2. Add the eggs to the broth in the measuring cup, and beat with a fork. Then add the Parmesan, lemon juice, and nutmeg, and beat with a fork until well blended.

3. When the broth in the saucepan is simmering, stir it with a fork as you add small amounts of the egg and cheese mixture, until it's all stirred in.

    🍓 Don't expect this to form long shreds like Chinese eggdrop soup; because of the Parmesan, it makes small, fluffy particles, instead.

4. Add the marjoram, crushing it a bit between your fingers, and simmer the soup for another minute or so before serving.

Yield: 4 servings, each with 2 grams of carbohydrates, a trace of fiber, and 12 grams of protein.

ꙭ Manhattan Clam Chowder

4 slices bacon, diced

1 large onion, chopped

2 ribs celery, diced

1 green pepper, chopped

2 1/2 cups diced white turnip

1 grated carrot

1 can (14 1/2 ounces) diced tomatoes

3 cups water

1 teaspoon dried thyme

4 cans (6 1/2 ounces each) minced clams, including liquid

Tabasco

1 teaspoon salt or Vege-Sal

1 teaspoon pepper

1. In a large, heavy bottomed stock pot, start the bacon cooking. As the fat cooks out of it, add the onion, celery, and green pepper, and sauté them in the bacon fat for 4 to 5 minutes.

2. Add the turnip, carrot, tomatoes, water, and thyme, and let the whole thing simmer for 30 minutes to 1 hour.

3. Add the clams, including the liquid, a dash of Tabasco, the salt or Vege-Sal, and pepper. Simmer for another 15 minutes, and serve.

Yield: 10 servings, each with 11 grams of carbohydrates and 1 gram of fiber, for a total of 10 grams of usable carbs and 21 grams of protein.

↺ Lo-Carb Clam Chowder

New England Clam Chowder fans will want to try this recipe from reader Tricia Hudgins.

8 pieces bacon

1/2 cup finely chopped onion

1/2 cup finely chopped celery

2 cans clams (6 1/2 ounces each), drained and with the juice reserved

1 cup chicken broth

2 large turnips, peeled and chopped into small cubes

1/2 teaspoon pepper

1/2 teaspoon dried thyme

Salt

1 cup heavy cream

1. Fry the bacon and set it aside, reserving the bacon grease. Sauté the onion and celery in 3 tablespoons of the bacon grease until they're soft.

2. Remove the onion and celery from the heat, and add the clam juice, chicken broth, turnips, pepper, thyme, and salt. Cover and cook over medium heat, stirring occasionally, until the turnips are soft (about 15 minutes).

3. Remove from the heat and stir in the heavy cream and clams. Crumble the bacon and add it to the soup. Reheat over a low flame, and serve.

Yield: 4 servings, each with 13 grams of carbohydrates and 2 grams of fiber, for a total of 11 grams of usable carbs and 31 grams of protein.

🍓 The sharp or bitter part of the turnip is the outside layer near the skin. Peel your turnips with a paring knife, being careful to get all of the outer layer.

↻ Quick Green Chowder

>1 package (10 ounces) frozen chopped spinach, thawed
>2 cans (6 1/2 ounces each) minced clams, including the liquid
>1 cup half-and-half
>1 cup heavy cream
>1 cup water
>Salt and pepper

1. Put the spinach, clams, half-and-half, cream, and water in a blender or food processor, and puree.

2. Pour the mixture into a saucepan, and bring to a simmer (use very low heat, and don't boil!). Simmer for 5 minutes, and salt and pepper to taste.

🍓 If you prefer, you can puree everything but the clams, adding them later so they stay in chunks.

Yield: 4 servings, each with 12 grams of carbohydrates and 2 grams of fiber, for a total of 10 grams of usable carbs and 29 grams of protein.

Artichoke Soup

> 3 to 4 tablespoons butter
>
> 1 small onion, finely chopped
>
> 2 stalks celery, finely chopped
>
> 1 clove garlic, crushed
>
> 1 can (14 ounces) quartered artichoke hearts, drained
>
> 4 cups chicken stock
>
> 1/2 teaspoon guar or xanthan
>
> 1 cup half-and-half
>
> Juice of 1/2 lemon
>
> Salt or Vege-Sal
>
> Pepper

1. In a heavy skillet, melt the butter and sauté the onion, celery, and garlic over low to medium heat. Stir from time to time.

2. Drain the artichoke hearts, and trim off any tough bits of leaf that got left on. Put the artichoke hearts in a food processor with the S blade in position. Add 1/2 cup of the chicken stock and the guar gum, and process until the artichokes are a fine puree.

3. Scrape the artichoke mixture into a saucepan, add the remaining chicken stock, and set over medium-high heat to simmer.

4. When the onion and celery are soft, stir them into the artichoke mixture. When it comes to a simmer, whisk in the half-and-half. Bring it back to a simmer, squeeze in the lemon juice, and stir again. Salt and pepper to taste. You can serve this immediately, hot, or in summer you can serve it chilled.

Yield: 6 servings, each with 10 grams of carbohydrates and 3 grams of fiber, for a total of 7 grams of usable carbs and 4 grams of protein. (Note: Much of the carbohydrates in artichokes is inulin, which remains largely undigested, so this carb count is actually misleadingly high.)

⌒ Olive Soup

Olives are so good for you that you should be eating more of them!
This makes a fine first course.

> 4 cups chicken stock
>
> 1/2 teaspoon guar or xanthan
>
> 1 cup minced black olives (you can buy cans of minced black olives)
>
> 1 cup heavy cream
>
> 1/4 cup dry sherry
>
> Salt or Vege-Sal
>
> Pepper

1. Put 1/2 cup of the chicken stock in the blender with the guar gum, and blend for a few seconds. Pour into a saucepan, and add the rest of the stock and the olives.

2. Heat until simmering, then whisk in the cream. Bring back to a simmer, stir in the sherry, and salt and pepper to taste.

Yield: 6 servings, each with 3 grams of carbohydrates and 1 gram of fiber, for a total of 2 grams of usable carbs and 2 grams of protein.

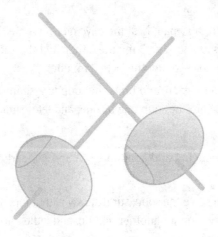

Turkey Meatball Soup

This makes a light, quick, and tasty supper all by itself.

> 1/2 pound ground turkey
>
> 1 1/2 tablespoons oat bran
>
> 2 tablespoons minced fresh parsley
>
> 1/2 teaspoon salt or Vege-Sal
>
> 1/2 teaspoon poultry seasoning
>
> 1/8 teaspoon pepper
>
> 1 tablespoon olive oil
>
> 1/2 cup grated carrot
>
> 2 cups diced zucchini
>
> 1 tablespoon minced onion
>
> 1 clove garlic, crushed
>
> 1 quart chicken broth
>
> 1 teaspoon dried oregano
>
> 2 eggs, beaten
>
> 1/4 cup grated Parmesan cheese

1. In a mixing bowl, combine the ground turkey with the oat bran, parsley, 1/2 teaspoon salt or Vege-Sal, poultry seasoning, and pepper. Mix well, and form into balls the size of marbles or so. Set aside.

2. In a large, heavy-bottomed saucepan, heat the olive oil over a medium-high burner. Add the carrot, and let it sauté for 2 to 3 minutes. Then add the zucchini, onion, and garlic, and sauté the vegetables for another 5 to 7 minutes.

3. Add the chicken broth and oregano, and bring the soup to a simmer for 15 minutes. Drop the turkey meatballs into the soup one by one, and let it simmer for another 10 to 15 minutes.

   🍓 Taste the soup at this point, and add more salt and pepper to taste, if desired.

4. Just before you're ready to serve the soup, stir it slowly with a fork as you pour the beaten eggs in quite slowly. Simmer another minute, and ladle into bowls. Top each serving with 1 tablespoon of Parmesan, and serve.

Yield: 4 servings, each with 7 grams of carbohydrates and 2 grams of fiber, for a total of 5 grams usable carbs and 21 grams of protein.

⌒ Kim's Week-After-Thanksgiving Soup

This is what my sister did with the carcass from her Thanksgiving turkey. Our mother always made turkey and rice soup, but we low-carbers needed a new tradition, and here it is.

> 1 turkey carcass
>
> 1 tablespoon salt
>
> 2 tablespoons vinegar
>
> 5 small turnips, cut into largish cubes
>
> 4 ribs celery, cut into 1/2-inch lengths
>
> 1/2 pound mushrooms, sliced
>
> 1 large onion, chopped
>
> 2 zucchini, each about 6 inches long, diced into small chunks
>
> 2 cups frozen, cut green beans
>
> 1 chicken bouillon cube or 1 teaspoon chicken bouillon crystals
>
> 2 tablespoons dried basil
>
> Salt and pepper

1. In a large pot, break up the turkey carcass, leaving bits of meat clinging to it. Cover it with water, add the salt and vinegar, and simmer on low until the water is reduced to about 4 quarts. Let cool.

2. Pour the whole thing through a strainer, and return the broth to the pot. Pick the meat off the turkey bones. Discard the bones, cut up the meat, and return it to the pot.

3. Add the turnips, celery, mushrooms, onion, zucchini, beans, bouillon, and basil, and simmer until the vegetables are soft. Salt and pepper to taste, and serve.

Yield: 12 servings, each with 12 grams of carbohydrates and 4 grams of fiber, for a total of 8 grams of usable carbs. Your protein count will depend on how much meat was left on your turkey carcass, but assuming 2 cups of diced turkey total, you'll get 15 grams of protein per serving.

⌒ Portuguese Soup

If this were really authentic, it would have potatoes in it. But this
decarbed version is delicious, and it's a full meal in a bowl. Read the
labels on the smoked sausage carefully—they range from 1 gram of carb
per serving up to 5.

> 1/3 cup olive oil
>
> 3/4 cup chopped onion
>
> 3 cloves garlic, crushed
>
> 2 cups diced turnip
>
> 2 cups diced cauliflower
>
> 1 pound kale
>
> 1 1/2 pounds smoked sausage
>
> 1 can (14 1/2 ounces) diced tomatoes
>
> 2 quarts chicken broth
>
> 1/4 teaspoon Tabasco
>
> Salt and pepper

1. Put 1/4 cup of the olive oil in a large soup pot, and sauté the onion, garlic, turnip,
   and cauliflower over medium heat.

2. While that's cooking, chop the kale into bite-size pieces, and add it to the pot, as
   well. (You may need to cram it in at first, but don't worry—it cooks down quite a
   bit.) Let the vegetables sauté for another 10 minutes or so, stirring to turn the whole
   thing over every once and a while.

3. Slice the smoked sausage lengthwise into quarters, then crosswise into 1/2-inch
   pieces. Heat the remaining 2 tablespoons of oil in a heavy skillet over medium heat,
   and brown the smoked sausage a little.

4. Add the browned sausage, tomatoes, and 7 1/2 cups of the chicken broth to the kettle, and use the last 1/2 cup of broth to rinse the tasty browned bits out of the frying
   pan, and add that, too. Bring to a simmer and cook until the vegetables are soft (30
   to 45 minutes). Stir in the Tabasco and salt and pepper to taste, and serve.

Yield: 10 servings, each with 13 grams of carbohydrates and 2 grams of fiber, for a
total of 11 grams of usable carbs and 23 grams of protein.

CHAPTER THIRTEEN

Condiments, Seasonings, and Sauces

Once you start reading labels, you'll be shocked at how many of your favorite seasonings, sauces, and especially condiments, are simply loaded with sugar, corn syrup, cornstarch, flour, and other things you'd rather keep to a minimum. Most brands of ketchup have 4 grams of carbohydrates per tablespoon, for heaven's sake, and barbecue sauce tends to run even higher! You can carve significant chunks of carbohydrates out of your diet by making your own sauces at home, instead.

☌ Cheese Sauce

Try this over broccoli or cauliflower. It's wonderful!

> 1/2 cup heavy cream
> 3/4 cup shredded Cheddar cheese
> 1/4 teaspoon dry mustard

1. In a heavy-bottomed saucepan over the lowest heat, warm the cream to just below a simmer.

2. Whisk in the cheese about 1 tablespoon at a time, only adding the next tablespoonful after the last one has melted. When all the cheese is melted in, whisk in the dry mustard, and serve.

Yield: Enough to sauce 1 pound of broccoli or cauliflower, or about 4 servings of sauce, each with 1 gram of carbohydrates, no fiber, and 6 grams of protein.

∩ Stir-Fry Sauce

If you like Chinese food, make this up and keep it on hand. Then you can just throw any sort of meat and vegetables in your wok or skillet and have a meal in minutes.

1/2 cup soy sauce

1/2 cup dry sherry

2 cloves garlic, crushed

2 tablespoons grated fresh ginger

2 teaspoons Splenda

Combine the ingredients in a container with a tight-fitting lid, and refrigerate until you're ready to use.

Yield: 1 cup. Each 2-tablespoon serving has 2 grams of carbohydrates, no fiber, and no protein.

∩ Not-Very-Authentic Peanut Sauce

This is inauthentic because I used substitutes for such traditional ingredients as lemon grass and fish sauce. I wanted a recipe that tasted good but could be made without a trip to specialty grocery store.

1 piece of fresh ginger about the size of a walnut, peeled and thinly sliced across the grain

1/2 cup natural peanut butter, creamy

1/2 cup chicken broth

1 1/2 teaspoons lemon juice

1 1/2 teaspoons soy sauce

1/4 teaspoon Tabasco sauce

1 large or 2 small cloves garlic, crushed

1 1/2 teaspoons Splenda

Put all the ingredients in a blender, and run it until everything is well combined and smooth. If you'd like it a little thinner, add another tablespoon of chicken broth.

Yield: About 2 cups, or 16 servings, each with 2 grams of carbohydrates, a trace of fiber, and 2 grams of protein.

∽ Hoisin Sauce

This Chinese sauce is usually made from fermented soybean paste, which has tons of sugar in it. Peanut butter is inauthentic, but it tastes quite good here.

> 4 tablespoons soy sauce
>
> 2 tablespoons creamy natural peanut butter
>
> 2 tablespoons Splenda
>
> 2 teaspoons white vinegar
>
> 1 clove garlic, crushed
>
> 2 teaspoons toasted sesame oil
>
> 1/8 teaspoon Chinese Five Spice powder

Put all the ingredients in a blender, and run it until everything is smooth and well combined. Store in a snap-top container.

Yield: Roughly 1/3 cup. Each 1-tablespoon serving contains 2 grams of carbohydrates, a trace of fiber, and 2 grams of protein.

🍓 Of course, this sauce is essential for Mu Shu Pork (or Mu Shu Anything, for that matter), but it's also good for dipping plain chicken wings in.

↷ Taco Seasoning

Many store-bought seasoning blends include sugar or cornstarch—my food counter book says that several popular brands have 5 grams of carbs in 2 teaspoons! This is low-carb, very easy to put together, tastes great, and is even cheaper than the premixed stuff.

2 tablespoons chili powder

1 1/2 tablespoons cumin

1 1/2 tablespoons paprika

1 tablespoon onion powder

1 tablespoon garlic powder

1/8 to 1/4 teaspoon cayenne pepper (less makes a more mild seasoning, more takes the spice up a notch)

Combine all the ingredients, blending well, and store in an airtight container. Use 2 tablespoons of this mixture to flavor 1 pound of ground beef, turkey, or chicken.

Yield: About 8 tablespoons, or 4 batches worth. 2 tablespoons will add just under 2 grams of carbohydrates to a 4-ounce serving of taco meat.

↷ Chicken Seasoning

This is wonderful sprinkled over chicken before roasting.

3 tablespoons salt

1 teaspoon paprika

1 teaspoon onion powder

1 teaspoon garlic powder

1 teaspoon curry powder

1/2 teaspoon black pepper

Combine all the ingredients well, and store in a salt shaker or the shaker from an old container of herbs. Sprinkle over chicken before roasting; I use it to season at the table, as well.

Yield: Just over 1/4 cup. There are 7 grams of carb in this whole recipe and 1 gram of fiber, for a total of 6 grams of usable carbs, so the amount in the teaspoon or so you sprinkle over a piece of chicken is negligible.

◌ Cajun Seasoning

This New Orleans–style seasoning is good sprinkled over chicken, steak, pork, fish, or just about anything else you care to try it on.

> 2 1/2 tablespoons paprika
>
> 2 tablespoons salt
>
> 2 tablespoons garlic powder
>
> 1 tablespoon black pepper
>
> 1 tablespoon onion powder
>
> 1 tablespoon cayenne pepper
>
> 1 tablespoon dried oregano
>
> 1 tablespoon dried thyme

Combine all ingredients thoroughly, and store in an airtight container.

Yield: 2/3 cup. In the entire batch there are 37 grams of carbohydrates and 9 grams of fiber, for a total of 28 grams of usable carbs. Considering how spicy this is, you're unlikely to use more than a teaspoon or two at a time, and 1 teaspoon has just 1 gram of carbohydrates and a trace of fiber.

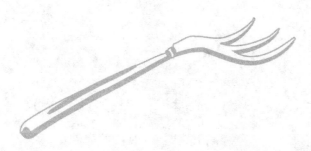

↻ Jerk Seasoning

Sprinkle this over chicken, pork chops, or fish before cooking for an instant hit of hot, sweet, and spicy flavor.

 1 tablespoon onion flakes

 2 teaspoons ground thyme

 1 teaspoon ground allspice

 1/4 teaspoon ground cinnamon

 1 teaspoon black pepper

 1 teaspoon cayenne pepper

 1 tablespoon onion powder

 2 teaspoons salt

 1/4 teaspoon ground nutmeg

 2 tablespoons Splenda

Combine all the ingredients, and store in an airtight container.

Yield: About 1/3 cup. Each teaspoon contains 1 gram of carbohydrates, a trace of fiber, and no protein.

⌒ Dana's No-Sugar Ketchup

Store-bought ketchup has more sugar in it per ounce than ice cream does! This great-tasting ketchup has all the flavor of your favorite brand, without the high carb count. The guar or xanthan isn't essential, but it makes your ketchup a little thicker and helps keep the water from separating out if you don't use it up quickly.

> 1 can (6 ounces) tomato paste
>
> 2/3 cup cider vinegar
>
> 1/3 cup water
>
> 1/3 cup Splenda
>
> 2 tablespoons finely minced onion
>
> 2 cloves garlic, crushed
>
> 1 teaspoon salt or Vege-Sal
>
> 1/8 teaspoon ground allspice
>
> 1/8 teaspoon ground cloves
>
> 1/8 teaspoon pepper
>
> 1/4 teaspoon guar or xanthan

Put all the ingredients in a blender, and run the blender until the bits of onion disappear. (You'll have to scrape down the sides as you go, because this mixture is thick.) Store in the refrigerator, in a container with a tight-fitting lid.

Yield: 1 1/2 cups of ketchup. 1 tablespoon has 2.25 grams of carbohydrates, a trace of fiber, and a trace of protein.

⌒ Low-Carb Steak Sauce

> 1/4 cup Dana's No-Sugar Ketchup (see above)
>
> 1 tablespoon Worcestershire sauce
>
> 1 teaspoon lemon juice

Combine well and store in an airtight container in the fridge.

Yield: 5 servings of 1 tablespoon, each with 2.25 grams of carbohydrates, a trace of fiber, and a trace of protein.

↻ Cocktail Sauce

Use this for dipping your cold, boiled shrimp in, of course. Commercial cocktail sauce, like so many other condiments, is full of sugar.

> 1/4 cup Dana's No-Sugar Ketchup (see page 407)
>
> 1 teaspoon prepared horseradish
>
> 2 or 3 drops Tabasco
>
> 1/2 teaspoon lemon juice

Just stir together, and dip!

Yield: 1/4 cup, with 10 grams of carbohydrate, a trace of fiber, and a trace of protein in the whole batch.

↻ Aioli

This is basically just very garlicky mayonnaise. It's good on all kinds of vegetables, and on fish, too.

> 4 cloves garlic, crushed very thoroughly
>
> 1 egg
>
> 1/4 teaspoon salt
>
> 2 tablespoons lemon juice
>
> 1/2 to 2/3 cup olive oil

Put the garlic, egg, salt, and lemon juice in a blender. Run the blender for a second, and then pour in the oil in a very thin stream, as you would when making mayonnaise. Turn off the blender when the sauce is thickened.

Yield: About 1 cup, or 8 servings of 2 tablespoons, each with 1 gram of carbohydrates, only a trace of fiber, and 1 gram of protein.

↷ Wonderful Memphis-Style Dry Rub BBQ

The Mystery Chef sends this recipe. Good on ribs, chops, or chicken, and far lower-carb than barbecue sauce.

    1 tablespoon paprika
    2 teaspoons chili powder
    3/4 teaspoon salt
    1/4 teaspoon dry mustard
    1/4 teaspoon garlic powder
    1/8 teaspoon pepper

Mix all the ingredients together, and store the mixture in a salt shaker. Sprinkle on both sides of whatever meat you're cooking, and grill.

Yield: Enough for 3 1/2 pounds of ribs, or about 3 servings. If, indeed, 3 of you eat this entire recipe, you'll each get 2 grams of carbohydrates and 1 gram of fiber, for a total of 1 gram of usable carbs and no protein.

Reduced-Carb Spicy Barbecue Sauce

1 clove garlic, crushed

1 small onion, finely minced

1/4 cup butter or oil

4 tablespoons Splenda

1 teaspoon salt or Vege-Sal

1 teaspoon dry mustard

1 teaspoon paprika

1 teaspoon chili powder

1/2 teaspoon black pepper

2 teaspoons blackstrap molasses

1 1/2 cups water

1/4 cup cider vinegar

1 tablespoon Worcestershire sauce

1 tablespoon prepared horseradish

1 can (6 ounces) tomato paste

1 tablespoon Liquid Smoke (made by Colgin and available in most large grocery stores)

1. In a saucepan, cook the garlic and onion in the butter for a few minutes.

2. Stir in the Splenda, salt, mustard, paprika, chili powder, and pepper. Add in the molasses, water, vinegar, Worcestershire sauce, and horseradish, and stir to combine. Let the mixture simmer for 15 to 20 minutes.

3. Whisk in the tomato paste and Liquid Smoke, and let the sauce simmer another 5 to 10 minutes.

4. Let the mixture cool, transfer it to a jar with a tight-fitting lid, and store in the refrigerator.

Yield: About 2 2/3 cups of sauce. Each 2-tablespoon serving has 3 grams of carbohydrates and 1 gram of fiber, for a total of 2 grams of usable carbs and no protein.

 If you're wondering whether it's worth it to make your own barbecue sauce from scratch, chew on this for a moment: Your average commercial barbecue sauce has between 10 and 15 grams of carbs per 2-tablespoon serving—and do you know anyone who ever stopped at 2 tablespoons of barbecue sauce?

ꙅ Tequila Lime Marinade

$1/3$ cup lime juice (bottled is fine)

$1/3$ cup water

3 tablespoons tequila

1 tablespoon Splenda

1 tablespoon soy sauce

2 cloves garlic, crushed.

Combine the ingredients, and store in the refrigerator until ready to use.

Yield: Roughly $3/4$ cup (enough for a dozen boneless, skinless chicken breasts or a couple of pounds of shrimp). In the whole batch there are 13 grams of carbohydrates and 1 gram of fiber, for a total of 12 grams of usable carbs and no protein, but since you drain most of the marinade off, you won't get more than a gram or two of carbs total.

ꙅ Teriyaki Sauce

Good on chicken, beef, fish—just about anything.

$1/2$ cup soy sauce

$1/4$ cup dry sherry

1 clove garlic, crushed

2 tablespoons Splenda

1 tablespoon grated fresh ginger

Combine all the ingredients, and refrigerate until ready to use.

Yield: Just over $3/4$ cup. Each 1-tablespoon serving will have about 3 grams of carbohydrates, a trace of fiber, and a trace of protein.

Jerk Marinade

Jerk is a Jamaican way of life. Make it with one pepper if you want it just nicely hot or with two peppers if you want it traditional—also known as take-the-top-of-your-head-off hot.

    1 or 2 Scotch Bonnet or habenero peppers, with or without seeds
        (the seeds are the hottest part)
    1/2 small onion
    3 tablespoons oil
    1 tablespoon ground allspice
    2 tablespoons grated fresh ginger
    1 tablespoon soy sauce
    1 teaspoon dried thyme
    1 bay leaf, crumbled
    1/4 teaspoon cinnamon
    1 tablespoon Splenda
    2 cloves garlic, crushed

Put all the ingredients in a food processor with the S blade in place, and process until it's fairly smooth. (You'll get a soft paste that looks like mud but smells like heaven!) Smear this over the meat of your choice, and let it sit for a day before cooking. Always wash your hands after handling hot peppers!

Yield: Enough for about 4 servings of meat, each serving serving of Jerk Marinade adding 4 grams of carbohydrates and 1 gram of fiber, for a total of 3 grams of usable carbs and no protein.

> If you just can't take the heat, you can chicken out and use a jalapeño or two instead of the habeneros or Scotch Bonnets, and your jerk marinade will be quite mild, as these things go. But remember: There is no such thing as a truly mild jerk sauce.

Looing Sauce

This is a Chinese sauce for "red cooking." You stew things in it, and it imparts a wonderful flavor to just about any sort of meat.

> 2 cups soy sauce
>
> 1 star anise
>
> 1/2 cup dry sherry (the cheap stuff is fine)
>
> 4 tablespoons Splenda
>
> 1 tablespoon grated fresh ginger
>
> 4 cups water

🍓 Star anise is available in Oriental markets, and my health food store carries it, too. It actually does look like a star, and it's essential to the recipe. Don't try to substitute regular anise.

Combine the ingredients well and use the mixture to stew things in. (Specifically, see Looed Chicken on page 245, and Looed Pork on page 348.) After using Looing Sauce, you can strain it and refrigerate or freeze it to use again, if you like.

Yield: 6 1/2 cups of looing sauce, or plenty to submerge your food in. In the whole batch there are about 50 grams of usable carbohydrates, but only a very small amount of that is transferred to the foods you stew in it.

Cranberry Sauce

Unbelievably easy, and good with roast chicken or turkey—as though you needed to be told!

> 1/2 teaspoon plain gelatin (optional)
>
> 1 cup water
>
> 1 bag (12 ounces) fresh cranberries
>
> 1 cup Splenda

Combine water, cranberries, and Splenda in a sauce pan over medium-high heat. (If you're using the gelatin, dissolve it in 1/2 cup of the water, then add it to the cranberries and Splenda in a saucepan over medium-high heat.) Bring the mixture to a boil, and boil it hard until the cranberries pop. Keep it in a tightly covered jar in the fridge.

Yield: Roughly 2 cups. Each 2-tablespoon serving will have 4 grams of carbohydrates and 1 gram of fiber, for a total of 3 grams of usable carbs.

🍓 Fresh cranberries are available only in fall, but they freeze beautifully. Just stick them in a plastic bag in the freezer, and pull them out when you need them.

↷ Cranberry Chutney

Think of this as cranberry sauce with a kick. It's good with any curried poultry, or even with plain old roast chicken.

> 1 bag (12 ounces) cranberries
>
> 1 cup water
>
> 1/2 cup Splenda
>
> 2 cloves garlic, crushed
>
> 1 tablespoon pumpkin pie spice
>
> 1/8 teaspoon salt

Combine all the ingredients in a saucepan over medium heat, bring it to a boil, and boil until the cranberries pop (7 to 8 minutes).

Yield: Roughly 2 cups. Each 2-tablespoon serving will have just over 3 grams of carbohydrates and 1 gram of fiber, for a total of 2 grams of usable carbs and only a trace of protein.

🍓 This recipe improves if you let the boiled mixture sit for a while before serving. Try it with a little cinnamon, too.

Hollandaise for Sissies

An easy, unintimidating sauce for asparagus, artichokes, broccoli, or whatever you like.

    4 egg yolks
    1 cup sour cream
    1 tablespoon lemon juice
    1/2 teaspoon salt or Vege-Sal
    Dash of Tabasco

You'll need either a double boiler or a heat diffuser for this; it needs very gentle heat. If you're using a double boiler, you want the water in the bottom hot, but not boiling. If you're using a heat diffuser, use the lowest possible heat under the diffuser.

Put all the ingredients in a heavy-bottomed saucepan or the top of a double boiler. Whisk everything together well, let it heat through, and serve it over vegetables.

Yield: 6 to 8 servings, each with about 2 grams of carbohydrates, a trace of fiber, and 3 grams of protein.

∽ No-Fail Hollandaise

This recipe is courtesy of *Lowcarbezine!* reader Linda Carroll-King.
Make sure you follow her directions to use room-temperature eggs—
that's what makes this recipe no-fail.

> 1/2 cup butter
>
> 4 eggs yolks at room temperature
>
> 1 tablespoon fresh lemon juice
>
> White pepper

1. Heat the butter to a bubble in a saucepan over low heat; don't let it burn.

2. While the butter is heating, put the egg yolks, lemon juice, and pepper to taste in a blender.

3. When the butter is bubbling, start the blender. Without giving the butter time to cool, slowly pour it into the blender. Whir for several seconds, and it's done.

> *Yield:* This is about 1/2 cup, or 4 servings, each with 1 gram of carbohydrates, a trace of fiber, and 3 grams of protein.

∽ Green Tomato Chutney

Most chutneys are full of sugar, so I invented my own—now I plant
extra tomatoes in the summer to have enough to make this. It's wonderful with anything curried.

> 4 quarts green tomatoes, cut into chunks
>
> 3 cups apple cider vinegar
>
> 1 whole ginger root, sliced into very thin rounds
>
> 5 or 6 cloves garlic, thinly sliced
>
> 1 tablespoon whole cloves
>
> 5 or 6 sticks whole cinnamon
>
> 1/2 cup Splenda
>
> 1 tablespoon blackstrap molasses
>
> 3 teaspoons stevia/FOS blend

> 🍓 There are two things you need to know when buying and cooking with gin-
> ger. The first is that a whole gingerroot is also called a "hand" of ginger. The
> second is that you should always cut ginger across the grain, not along it, or
> you'll end up with woody ginger.

Combine all the ingredients in a large stainless steel or enamel kettle—no iron, no aluminum. (This is an acidic mixture, and if you use iron or aluminum you'll end up with your chutney chock full of iron, which will turn it blackish, or aluminum, which simply isn't good for you.) Simmer on low for 3 to 4 hours. Store in tightly closed containers in the refrigerator.

Yield: Roughly 2 quarts. Each 2-tablespoon serving will have 5 grams of carbohydrates and 1 gram of fiber, for a total of 4 grams of usable carbs and no protein.

⌒ Duck Sauce

What are you going to eat duck sauce on, now that you're not eating egg rolls? Well, Crab and Bacon Bundles, for one thing. It's good with chicken, too. This does have the sugar that's in the peaches, of course, but not all the added sugar of commercial duck sauce. And it tastes better, too.

> 1 bag (1 pound) unsweetened frozen peaches or 2 1/2 to 3 cups sliced,
>   peeled fresh peaches
> 1/2 cup water
> 2 tablespoons cider vinegar
> 2 tablespoon Splenda
> 1/4 teaspoon blackstrap molasses
> 1/8 teaspoon salt
> 1 teaspoon soy sauce
> 1 clove garlic, crushed

1. Put all the ingredients in a heavy-bottomed saucepan, and bring them to a simmer. Cook, uncovered, until the peaches are soft (about 30 minutes).

2. Puree the duck sauce in a blender, if you like, or do what I do: simply mash the sauce with a potato masher or a fork. (I like the texture better this way.)

Yield: About 2 cups. Each 2-tablespoon serving has 3 grams of carbohydrates and 1 gram of fiber, for a total of 2 grams of usable carbs and no protein.

🍓 It's best to freeze this if you're not going to use it up right away.

Tootsie's Pesto

Tootsie is my friend Kay's mother, and this is her recipe. Store-bought pesto is okay for us, but it's awfully expensive and not nearly so fresh and good! This makes a highly concentrated product; feel free to thin it a bit with olive oil before you use it.

> 2 cups fresh basil leaves, washed and patted dry
> 4 good-size garlic cloves
> 1 cup shelled walnuts or pine nuts
> 1 cup extra-virgin olive oil
> 1 cup freshly grated Parmesan cheese
> 1/4 cup freshly grated Romano cheese
> Salt and pepper to taste

1. Combine the basil, garlic, and nuts, and chop in a food processor with the S blade. Leave the motor running, and add the olive oil in a slow steady stream.

2. Shut off the food processor, and add the Parmesan, Romano, a big pinch of salt, and a liberal grinding of pepper. Process briefly to blend.

Yield: 2 cups. Each 1-tablespoon serving will have 1 gram of carbohydrates, a trace of fiber, and 2 grams of protein.

🍓 Your can store your pesto by freezing it in an ice cube tray and then wrapping it in small pieces of plastic wrap, or you can keep it in a plastic container with a snap-on lid in the fridge. Kay says she particularly likes this thinned a bit with olive oil and served on cooked green beans—to quote her: "Yummy yum yum." Pesto is also good with chicken and seafood.

CHAPTER FOURTEEN

Cookies, Cakes, and Other Sweets

I am of two minds about this chapter (a chapter which, by the way, contains recipes for treats as delicious as any sugary desserts you've ever made). On the one hand, I think it's a bad idea to get in the habit of eating these sugarless sweets with the same frequency with which you used to eat the sugary stuff. I feel strongly that weaning yourself away from wanting sweets all the time, from not considering a meal complete until you've had a dessert, is a very good and important thing.

On the other hand, I understand—boy, do I understand!—the lure of sweets. Heck, as a kid I quite literally stole to get sugar. And I know that for some of you, these recipes will be the thing that lets you stick to your diet and break your sugar addiction altogether.

So this is what I suggest: If you're fighting severe sugar cravings or if you're subject to frequent temptation, keep one or two of these desserts on hand. They really do taste great and satisfy your taste buds. However, they will not cause the blood sugar rush—or crash—of the sugary stuff, and therefore, with the help of these desserts, you should be able to slowly back away from sweets until they're just an occasional treat. And that, my friend, is where I would love for you to be.

Butter Cookies

    1 cup butter

    8 ounces cream cheese

    1/4 cup plus 1 tablespoon Splenda

    1 egg

    2 cups sifted soy powder

    1/2 teaspoon baking powder

    1/2 teaspoon ground cinnamon

1. Use an electric mixer to cream the butter and cream cheese together until well blended and soft. Add 1/4 cup Splenda, and cream until completely combined. Beat in the egg.

2. Sift the soy powder, then sift again with the baking powder (to combine the baking powder with the soy powder and to break up any lumps in the baking powder). Sift the combined powders into the mixing bowl, and mix to make a soft dough.

3. Chill the dough for several hours in a covered container or wrapped in foil; this will make it easier to handle.

4. When the dough is chilled, preheat the oven to 375°F. Make small balls of the dough and place them on an ungreased cookie sheet.

5. Mix 1 tablespoon of Splenda with the cinnamon on a small plate or saucer. Take a flat-bottomed glass, measuring cup, or something similar (I use an old scoop from a jar of protein powder), and butter the bottom. Then dip the buttered cup in the cinnamon and Splenda, and use it to press the cookies flat.

   🍓 You'll need to dip your "pressing glass" in the cinnamon and Splenda for each cookie, but you won't have to rebutter the bottom each time. The butter just keeps the cup from sticking to the cookies and, of course, puts yummy cinnamon and Splenda on each one!

6. Bake for about 9 minutes, checking at 8 minutes, to make sure the bottoms aren't browning too fast. The cookies are done when the bottoms are just starting to brown.

Yield: About 6 dozen, each with 1 gram of carbohydrates, a trace of fiber, and 1 gram of protein.

🍓 Don't butter the cookie sheet or spray it with nonstick cooking spray. Why not? These cookies are so rich, they practically float on the butter that cooks out of them. I had no trouble with them sticking—I had trouble with them sliding around the cookie sheet while they were baking! I call them The Incredible Migrating Cookies. Hopefully your cookie sheets are flatter and your oven more level than mine.

Chocolate Walnut Balls

These are great to make around Christmastime, when high-carb temptations abound.

> 1/2 cup butter, at room temperature
>
> 2 ounces cream cheese
>
> 1/2 cup Splenda
>
> 2 tablespoons stevia/FOS blend
>
> 1 egg
>
> 1 teaspoon vanilla extract
>
> 1 1/2 cups sifted soy powder
>
> 1/4 teaspoon salt
>
> 1 1/2 teaspoons baking powder
>
> 2 ounces unsweetened baking chocolate
>
> 1/2 cup chopped walnuts

1. Preheat the oven to 375°F.

2. With an electric mixer, cream the butter and cream cheese until soft and well combined. Add the Splenda and stevia/FOS blend, and cream until well combined. Add the egg and the vanilla, and beat until well combined.

3. Sift the soy powder, then resift with the salt and baking powder. Add the powders to the butter mixture. (It's easier to beat it in if you add it one-half at a time.)

4. Melt the chocolate and beat that in, then add the nuts and beat them in well.

5. Butter or spray cookie sheets with nonstick cooking spray. Roll the dough into small balls and place them on the sheets. Bake for 8 to 10 minutes.

Yield: About 40 cookies, each with 2 grams of carbohydrates and 1 gram of fiber, for a total of 1 gram of usable carbs and 1 gram of protein.

↻ Peanut Butter Cookies

I can't tell these from my mom's peanut butter cookies!

1/2 cup butter, at room temperature

1/2 cup Splenda

2 tablespoons plus 1 teaspoon stevia/FOS blend

1 tablespoon blackstrap or dark molasses

1 egg

1 cup natural peanut butter (creamy is best)

1/2 teaspoon salt

1/2 teaspoon baking soda

1/2 teaspoon vanilla

1 cup soy powder

2 tablespoons oat bran

1. Preheat the oven to 375°F.

2. Use an electric mixer to beat the butter until creamy. Add the Splenda, stevia/FOS blend, and molasses, and beat again until well combined.

3. Beat in the egg, peanut butter, salt, baking soda, and vanilla. Beat in the soy powder and oat bran.

4. Butter or spray cookie sheets with nonstick cooking spray. Roll the dough into small balls, and place them on the sheets. Use the back of a fork to press the balls of dough flat, leaving those traditional peanut butter cookie crisscross marks. Bake for 10 to 12 minutes.

Yield: About 4 1/2 dozen cookies, each with 2.3 grams of carbohydrates and 1 gram of fiber, for a total of 1.3 grams of usable carbs and 2 grams of protein.

ͻ Hazelnut Shortbread

Love Walker's Shortbread cookies? Meet their new low-carb replace-ment.

> 2 cups hazelnuts
> 1 cup butter, at room temperature
> 1/2 cup Splenda
> 1 egg
> 1/2 teaspoon salt
> 1/4 teaspoon baking powder
> 1 cup vanilla-flavored whey protein powder
> 2 tablespoons water

1. Preheat the oven to 325°F.
2. Grind the hazelnuts to a fine meal with a food processor. Set aside.
3. Use an electric mixer to beat the butter until it's fluffy. Add the Splenda, and beat well again. Beat in the egg, again combining well.
4. Sprinkle the salt and baking powder over the top of the mixture, and add half of the ground hazelnuts. Beat them in, add the rest of the hazelnuts, and beat again.
5. Beat in the vanilla-flavored whey protein powder, and then the water to make a soft, sticky dough.
6. Line a shallow baking pan (a jelly roll pan is best, and mine is 11 1/2" x 15 1/2") with baking parchment, and turn the dough out onto the parchment. Cover it with another piece of parchment, and through the top sheet, press the dough out into an even layer covering the whole pan. (The pressed dough should be about 1/4" thick.)
7. Peel off the top sheet of parchment, and score the dough into squares using a pizza cutter or a knife with a straight, thin blade. Bake for 25 to 30 minutes, or until golden.

> 🍓 You'll need to rescore the lines before removing the shortbread from the pan. Use a straight up-and-down motion, and the shortbread will be less likely to break outside the score lines.

Yield: 4 dozen cookies, each with 1.5 grams of carbohydrates, a trace of fiber, and 1 gram of protein.

ꙮ Almond Cookies

Crumbly and delicate, but delicious!

> 1 cup butter, at room temperature
>
> 1 cup Splenda
>
> 1 egg
>
> 1 cup smooth almond butter
>
> 1/2 teaspoon salt
>
> 1/2 teaspoon baking soda
>
> 1 1/2 cups vanilla-flavored whey protein powder
>
> 2 tablespoons water
>
> 30 whole, shelled almonds

1. Preheat the oven to 375°F.

2. Use an electric mixer to beat the butter until smooth and fluffy. Add the Splenda and beat again, scraping down the sides, until very well combined.

3. Beat in the egg, then add the almond butter, salt, and baking soda.

4. Beat in the protein powder about 1/2 cup at a time.

5. Add the water, and beat until everything is well combined.

6. Use a measuring tablespoon to scoop heaping tablespoons of dough onto greased cookie sheets (each cookie should be made of about 2 tablespoons of dough). Press an almond into the center of each cookie. Bake for 10 to 12 minutes, or until the cookies just begin to brown around the edges.

Yield: 2 1/2 dozen nice big cookies, each with 3.5 grams of carbohydrates and 0.5 grams of fiber, for a total of 3 grams of usable carbs and 4 grams of protein.

Sesame Cookies

> 1/2 cup butter
>
> 1 cup Splenda
>
> 1 egg
>
> 1 cup tahini (roasted sesame butter)
>
> 1/2 teaspoon salt
>
> 1/2 teaspoon baking soda
>
> 1 1/2 cups vanilla-flavored whey protein powder
>
> 1/4 cup sesame seeds

1. Preheat the oven to 375°F.

2. Use an electric mixer to beat the butter and Splenda together until smooth and fluffy. Beat in the egg, mixing well, and then the tahini, again mixing well.

3. Add the salt and baking soda, then beat in the protein powder 1/2 cup at a time. Beat in the sesame seeds last.

4. Spray a cookie sheet with nonstick cooking spray and drop the dough onto it by spoonfuls. Bake for 10 to 12 minutes, or until golden.

Yield: About 4 1/2 dozen cookies, each with 2 grams of carbohydrates, a trace of fiber, and 6 grams of protein.

Mom's Chocolate Chip Cookies

With this recipe, I assume the title of Low-Carb Cookie God.

    1 cup butter, at room temperature

    1 1/2 cups Splenda

    1 1/2 teaspoons blackstrap molasses

    2 eggs

    1 cup ground almonds

    1 cup vanilla-flavored whey protein powder

    1/4 cup oat bran

    1 teaspoon baking soda

    1 teaspoon salt

    1 cup chopped walnuts or pecans

    12 ounces sugar-free chocolate chips

If you can't get sugar-free chocolate chips, you need to make some from sugar-free chocolate bars. Break 7 or 8 of the bars, which are 1.3 to 1.5 ounces each, into three or four pieces each, and place the pieces in a food processor with the S blade in place. Pulse the food processor until your chocolate bars are in pieces about the same size as commercial chocolate morsels, and set them aside until you're ready to use them.

Note: If you haven't ground your almonds yet, now would be a good time to do that, as well.

1. Preheat the oven to 375°F.

2. Use an electric mixer to beat the butter, Splenda, and molasses until creamy and well blended. Add the eggs, one at a time, and beat well after each addition.

3. In a separate bowl, stir together the ground almonds, protein powder, oat bran, baking soda, and salt. Add this mixture, about 1/2 cup at a time, to the Splenda mixture, beating well after each 1/2-cup addition, until it's all beaten in. Stir in the nuts and chocolate chips.

4. Spray a cookie sheet with nonstick cooking spray, and drop the dough by rounded tablespoons onto it. These cookies will not spread and flatten as much as standard chocolate chip cookies, so if you want them flat, flatten them a bit now.

5. Bake for 10 minutes, or until golden. Cool on baking sheets for a couple minutes, then remove to wire racks to cool completely.

Yield: About 4 1/2 dozen cookies, each with 3 grams of carbohydrates, a trace of fiber, and 5 grams of protein. (This carbohydrate count does not include the polyols used to sweeten the sugar-free chocolate, since it remains largely undigested and unabsorbed.)

℘ Coconut Shortbread

1/2 cup butter, at room temperature

1/2 cup coconut oil

3 tablespoons Splenda

1 1/2 cups vanilla-flavored whey protein powder

1 cup finely shredded, unsweetened coconut

2 tablespoons water

1. Preheat oven to 375°F.

2. Using an electric mixer, beat together the butter, coconut oil, and Splenda until light and creamy. Beat in the protein powder, coconut, and water, in that order, scraping down the sides of the bowl several times to make sure everything is well blended.

3. Line a jelly roll pan with baking parchment, and turn the dough out onto it. Place another sheet of baking parchment on top, and press the dough out into a thin, even sheet. Use a sharp knife, or better yet, a pizza cutter, to score the dough into small rectangles. Bake for 7-10 minutes, or until golden. Cool and break apart.

Yield: 4 dozen cookies, each with 1 gram of carbohydrates, a trace of fiber, and 6 grams of protein.

Pecan Sandies

Peggy Witherow sent me a recipe for Pecan Sandies that she wanted de-carbed, and this is the result.

> 1 cup butter, at room temperature
>
> 1 cup Splenda
>
> 1 egg
>
> 1 1/2 cups vanilla-flavored whey protein powder
>
> 1 1/2cups chopped pecans
>
> 1/2 teaspoon salt

1. Preheat the oven to 325°F.

2. Beat the butter and Splenda together until light and creamy. Beat in the egg, mixing well. Then beat in the protein powder, pecans, and salt.

3. Spray a cookie sheet with nonstick cooking spray. Form the dough into balls about the size of a marble, and flatten them slightly on the cookie sheet. Bake for 10 to 15 minutes, or until golden.

Yield: 4 1/2 dozen cookies, each with 2 grams of carbohydrates, a trace of fiber, and 5 grams of protein.

◯ Oatmeal Cookies

Oh. My. God.

> 1 cup coconut oil
>
> 1 cup butter, at room temperature
>
> 1 1/2 cups Splenda
>
> 1 teaspoon molasses
>
> 2 eggs
>
> 1 cup ground almonds
>
> 1 cup vanilla-flavored whey protein powder
>
> 1/2 teaspoon salt
>
> 1 teaspoon baking soda
>
> 1 teaspoon cinnamon
>
> 1 cup rolled oats
>
> 1 cup chopped pecans

1. Preheat the oven to 350°F.

2. With an electric mixer, beat together the coconut oil, butter, and Splenda until well combined, creamy, and fluffy.

3. Beat in the molasses and eggs, combining well, followed by the ground almonds, protein powder, salt, and baking soda, scraping down the sides of the bowl a few times and making sure the ingredients are well combined.

4. Beat in the cinnamon, rolled oats, and pecans.

5. Spray a cookie sheet with nonstick cooking spray, and drop dough onto it by the scant tablespoonful, leaving plenty of room for spreading. Bake for 10 minutes, or until golden. Transfer the cookies carefully to wire racks to cool.

Yield: About 5 dozen outrageously good cookies, each with 3 grams of carbohydrates, a trace of fiber, and 4 grams of protein.

♆ Cocoa-Peanut Logs

This very simple recipe is an adaptation of a recipe using Cocoa Krispies that was around back in the '60s.

> 4 sugar-free dark chocolate bars (about 1.5 ounces each)
> or 6 ounces sugar-free chocolate chips
>
> 1/2 cup natural peanut butter (salted is best)
>
> 4 cups crisp soy cereal (like Rice Krispies, only made from soy)

1. Over very low heat (preferably using a double boiler or a heat diffuser), melt the chocolate and the peanut butter. Blend well. Stir in the cereal until it's evenly coated.

2. Coat a 9 x 11-inch pan with nonstick cooking spray, or line it with foil. Press the cereal mixture into the pan, and chill for at least a few hours. Cut into squares and store in the refrigerator until ready to serve.

Yield: About 3 dozen logs, each with 1.5 grams of carbohydrates, a trace of fiber, and about 5 grams of protein. (This does not include the polyols in the chocolate. And remember, those polyols have to be eaten in moderation, or you'll be in gastric distress!)

◯ Peanut Butter Brownies

This was the first recipe I ever tried from Diana Lee's *Baking Low Carb*, and I've been recommending her book ever since. The peanut butter topping sinks to the bottom, and you get fudgy brownie on top and chewy peanut butter cookie on the bottom.

Brownie Layer

5 tablespoons butter

1/4 cup unsweetened baking cocoa

2 eggs

1/4 cup heavy cream

1/4 cup water

1 teaspoon vanilla extract

1/4 cup Splenda

1 teaspoon liquid saccharine

3/4 cup vanilla-flavored whey protein powder

2 tablespoons oat flour

1 tablespoon baking powder

Peanut Butter Topping

1/4 cup natural peanut butter

3 tablespoons butter

2 tablespoons Splenda

1 egg

2 tablespoons vanilla-flavored whey protein powder

1. Preheat the oven to 350°F.

2. Melt the butter and stir in the cocoa. Add the eggs, cream, water, vanilla, Splenda, and saccharine, and mix well.

3. Add the protein powder, oat flour, and baking powder, and mix just until well moistened.

4. Spray an 8 x 8-inch baking pan with nonstick cooking spray, and pour the batter into it.

5. Mix the peanut butter, butter, Splenda, egg, and protein powder together, and spoon the mixture on top of the brownie batter. Bake for 15 minutes—do not overbake.

Yield: 16 brownies, each with 5 grams of carbohydrates and 1 gram of fiber, for a total of 4 grams of usable carbs and 12 grams of protein.

↻ Fudge Toffee

Jen Eloff of sweety.com, says her husband Ian is mad for this candy. Another winner from *Splendid Low-Carbing*.

2 cups Splenda

1 cup whole milk powder (available in health food stores)

1 cup natural whey protein powder

1/2 cup unsalted butter, melted

1/4 cup whipping cream

2 tablespoons water

2 ounces unsweetened baking chocolate, melted

1. In a large bowl, combine the Splenda, milk powder, and protein powder.

2. In a small bowl, combine the butter, cream, and water. Stir this into the dry ingredients. Stir in the melted chocolate until well combined.

3. Press the mixture into a 9 x 9-inch baking dish. Freeze for approximately 30 minutes, then refrigerate. Cut into squares and serve.

Yield: Makes 36 squares, each with 3 grams of carbohydrates, a trace of fiber, and 3 grams of protein.

Sugar-Free Chocolate Mousse To Die For!

This is the very first low-carb dessert I came up with, and it still blows people away.

1 package (4-serving size) chocolate sugar-free instant pudding mix

1 package (about 10 ounces) soft tofu

1 heaping tablespoon unsweetened cocoa powder

1/4 to 1/2 teaspoon instant coffee crystals (more, if you like mocha flavoring)

1 to 1 1/2 cups heavy whipping cream, chilled

1. Use an electric mixer to beat the pudding mix, tofu, cocoa powder, and coffee crystals until very smooth.
2. In a separate bowl, whip the cream until just about stiff.
3. Turn the mixer to its lowest setting, blend in the pudding mixture, and turn off the mixer—quickly. (If you over-beat, you'll end up with chocolate butter.)

Yield: Made with 1 cup of heavy cream, you'll get 6 servings, each with 8 grams of carbohydrates and 1 gram of fiber, for a total of 7 grams of usable carbs and 5 grams of protein. Made with 1 1/2 cups of heavy cream, your yield increases to at least 7 servings, each with 7.5 grams of carbohydrates and just under 1 gram of fiber, for a total of about 6.5 grams of usable carbs and 4 grams of protein. (I like this made with the smaller amount of cream, for a sturdier texture, but I know folks who like it with the larger amount, for a fluffier texture. It's your choice.)

Sugar-Free Vanilla Mousse To Die For! Here's one for those non-chocoholics out there: Just use sugar-free vanilla instant pudding mix and a teaspoon of vanilla extract, and omit the cocoa powder and the coffee crystals.

Yield: Made with 1 cup of cream, you'll get 6 servings, each with 7 grams of carbohydrates, a trace of fiber, and 4 grams of protein. Made with 1 1/2 cups of cream, you'll get 7 servings, each with 6.5 grams of carbohydrates, a trace of fiber, and 4 grams of protein.

◯ Strawberry Cups

This is a good make-ahead company dessert, and it's a really beautiful color.

> 1 cup water
>
> 1 package (4-serving size) sugar-free lemon gelatin
>
> 10 ounces frozen unsweetened strawberries, partly thawed
>
> 1 cup heavy cream
>
> 1/2 teaspoon vanilla extract
>
> 1 teaspoon Splenda (if desired)

1. Bring the water to a boil. Put the gelatin and boiling water in a blender, and whirl for 10 to 15 seconds to dissolve the gelatin. Add the strawberries, and whirl again, just long enough to blend in the berries.

2. Put the blender container in the refrigerator for 10 minutes, or just until the mixture starts to thicken a bit.

3. Add 3/4 cup of the heavy cream, and run the blender just long enough to mix it all in (10 to 15 seconds). Pour into 5 or 6 pretty little dessert cups and chill. Whip the remaining 1/4 cup of cream with the vanilla and a teaspoon of Splenda (if using), to garnish.

Yield: About 5 servings, each with 6 grams of carbohydrates and 1 gram of fiber, for a total of 5 grams of usable carbs and 3 grams of protein.

⌒ Mixed Berry Cups

For you raspberry and blackberry lovers, here's a quick and tasty dessert.

> 1 package (4-serving size) sugar-free raspberry gelatin
>
> 1 cup boiling water
>
> 2 teaspoons lemon juice
>
> Grated rind of 1/2 orange
>
> 3/4 cup frozen blackberries, partly thawed
>
> 1 cup heavy cream
>
> 1/2 teaspoon vanilla extract
>
> 1 teaspoon Splenda (optional)

1. Put the gelatin, water, lemon juice, and orange rind in a blender, and whirl for 10 to 15 seconds to dissolve the gelatin. Add the blackberries and blend again, just long enough to mix in the berries.

2. Put the blender container in the refrigerator for 10 minutes, or just until the mixture starts to thicken a bit. Add 3/4 cup heavy cream, and run the blender just long enough to mix it all in (10 to 15 seconds). Pour into 5 or 6 pretty little dessert cups, and chill.

3. Whip the remaining 1/4 cup of cream with vanilla and a teaspoon of Splenda (if using), to garnish.

Yield: 5 servings, each with 5 grams of carbohydrates and 1 gram of fiber, for a total of 4 grams of usable carbs and 2 grams of protein.

Hazelnut Crust

This is a great substitute for a graham cracker crumb crust with any cheesecake. And I think it tastes even better than the original.

> 1 1/2 cups hazelnuts
>
> 1/3 cup vanilla-flavored whey protein powder
>
> 4 tablespoons butter, melted

1. Preheat the oven to 350°F.

2. Put the hazelnuts in a food processor with the S blade in place. Pulse the processor until the hazelnuts are ground to a medium-fine texture. Add the protein powder and butter, and pulse to combine.

3. Spray the pie plate or springform pan, depending on which your recipe specifies, with nonstick cooking spray, and press this mixture firmly and evenly into the pan. Don't try to build your crust too high up the sides, but if you're using a springform pan, be sure to cover the seam around the bottom and press the crust into place firmly over it.

4. Place your crust in a preheated oven on the bottom rack, and bake for 12 to 15 minutes, or until lightly browned and slightly pulling away from the sides of the pan. Remove the crust from the oven, and let it cool while you make the filling.

Yield: Assuming 12 slices of cheesecake, this crust will add to each slice 4 grams of carbohydrates and 1 gram of fiber, for a total of 3 grams of usable carbs and 10 grams of protein.

Almond Crust. Here's another great nut crust for you to try. Just substitute 1 1/2 cups almonds for the hazelnuts in the **Hazelnut Crust** (above) and decrease the vanilla-flavored whey protein powder to 1/4 cup. Follow the directions to make the crust, and bake for 10 to 12 minutes, or until lightly golden. Cool.

Yield: Assuming 12 slices of cheesecake, this crust will add to each slice 4 grams of carbohydrates and 2 grams of fiber, for a total of 2 grams of usable carbs and 7 grams of protein.

↺ Chocolate Cheesecake

You'll be surprised how good a cheesecake you can make from cottage cheese! It's high in protein, too.

 2 cups cottage cheese

 2 eggs

 1/2 cup sour cream

 2 ounces unsweetened baking chocolate, melted

 1/4 cup Splenda

 1 Hazelnut Crust or Almond Crust (see page 436),
 prebaked in a large, deep pie plate

1. Preheat the oven to 375°F.

2. Put the cottage cheese, eggs, and sour cream in your blender. Run the blender, scraping down the sides now and then, until this mixture is very smooth. Add the melted chocolate and Splenda, and blend again.

3. Pour into the prebaked crust. Place the cake on the top rack of the oven, and place a flat pan of water on the bottom rack. Bake for 40 to 45 minutes.

4. Cool, then chill well before serving. Serve with whipped cream.

Yield: 12 servings, each with 7 grams of carbohydrates and 2 grams of fiber, for a total of 5 grams of usable carbs and 16 grams of protein. (Analysis includes the crust.)

↷ Cheesecake to Go with Fruit

This lemon-vanilla cheesecake is wonderful with strawberries, blueberries, cherries—any fruit you care to use. It also makes a nice breakfast.

> 2 cups cottage cheese
>
> 2 eggs
>
> 1/2 cup sour cream
>
> 1/4 cup vanilla-flavored whey protein powder
>
> 1/4 cup Splenda
>
> Grated rind and juice of 1 fresh lemon
>
> 1 teaspoon vanilla extract
>
> 1 Hazelnut Crust or Almond Crust (see page 436), prebaked in a large, deep pie plate

1. Preheat the oven to 375°F.

2. Put the cottage cheese, eggs, sour cream, protein powder, Splenda, lemon rind and juice, and vanilla extract in a blender, and blend until very smooth.

3. Pour into the prebaked crust. Place the cake on the top rack of the oven, and place a flat pan of water on the bottom rack. Bake for 30 to 40 minutes. Cool, then chill well before serving.

Yield: 12 servings, each with 8 grams of carbohydrates and 2 grams of fiber, for a total of 6 grams of usable carbs and 21 grams of protein. (Analysis includes crust.)

🍓 Serve this cheesecake with the fruit of your choice. I like to serve it with thawed frozen, unsweetened strawberries, blueberries, or peaches, mashed coarsely with a fork and sweetened slightly with Splenda. If you use 1 1/2 cups of strawberries with 2 tablespoons Splenda for the whole cake, you'll add 2 grams of carbohydrates per slice, plus a trace of fiber and a trace of protein. Use 1 1/2 cups sour cherries—you can get these canned, with no added sugar—and sweeten them with 1/4 cup Splenda, and you'll add 3 grams per slice. I'm lucky enough to have a sour cherry tree, and cherry cheesecake is one of the joys of early summer around here!

Sunshine Cheesecake

This has a lovely, creamy texture and a bright, sunshiney orange flavor. Using the stevia/FOS blend keeps the carb count very low.

1 cup cottage cheese

1 package (8 ounces) cream cheese, softened

1 cup sour cream

4 eggs

Grated rind of 1 orange

1 tablespoon orange extract

1 tablespoon plus 1 teaspoon stevia/FOS blend

2 tablespoons lemon juice

Tiny pinch salt

1 Hazelnut Crust or Almond Crust (see page 436), prebaked in a springform pan

1. Put the cottage cheese, cream cheese, sour cream, eggs, orange rind, orange extract, stevia, lemon juice, and salt in a blender, and run the blender until everything is well-blended and a bit fluffy.

2. Pour into the prebaked crust. Place the cake on the top rack of the oven, and place a flat pan of water on the bottom rack. Bake for 50 minutes. The cheesecake will still jiggle slightly in the center when you take it out.

3. Cool, then chill well before serving.

Yield: 12 servings, each with 8 grams of carbohydrates and 2 grams of fiber, for a total of 6 grams of usable carbs and 17 grams of protein. (Analysis includes crust.)

This is wonderful with sugar-free chocolate syrup. Many grocery stores carry it; it's worth your while to take a look-see.

↻ Blackbottomed Mockahlua Cheesecake

You'll have to make yourself some Mockahlua before you can make this. What better incentive could you have?

Blackbottom Layer

3 sugar-free dark chocolate bars (about 1.5 ounces each)

1/4 cup heavy cream

1 Almond Crust (see page 436), prebaked in a springform pan

Mockahlua Filling

3 packages (8 ounces each) cream cheese, softened

3/4 cup Splenda

3/4 cup sour cream

1 tablespoon vanilla extract

4 eggs

1/3 cup Mockahlua (see page 463)

1. Preheat the oven to 325°F.

2. Over the lowest possible heat, melt the chocolate bars (preferably in a heat diffuser or a double boiler, to keep the chocolate from burning). When the chocolate is melted, stir in the cream, blending well. Pour over the crust, and spread evenly.

3. In large bowl, use an electric mixer to beat the cream cheese until smooth, scraping down the sides of the bowl often. Beat in the Splenda and sour cream, and mix well. Beat in the vanilla and eggs, one by one, beating until very smooth and creamy. Beat in the Mockahlua last, and mix well.

4. Pour into the chocolate-coated crust. Place the cake in the oven, and on the rack below it or on the floor of the oven place a pie pan of water. Bake for 1 hour.

5. Cool in the pan on a wire rack. Chill well before serving.

Yield: 12 servings, each with 10 grams of carbohydrates and 2 grams of fiber, for a total of 8 grams of usable carbs and 18 grams of protein. (Analysis includes crust, but omits the polyols in the sugar-free chocolate.)

Butter-Pecan Cheesecake

All you butterscotch fans are going to love this one.

Pecan Cookie Crust

1 stick butter, softened

1/2 cup Splenda

3/4 cups vanilla-flavored whey protein powder

3/4 cups chopped pecans

1/2 teaspoon salt

Butterscotch Filling

3 packages (8 ounces each) cream cheese, softened

3/4 cup Splenda

3/4 cup sour cream

2 teaspoons butter flavoring

1 tablespoon vanilla extract

1 tablespoon blackstrap molasses

4 eggs

1. Preheat the oven to 325°F.

2. Beat the butter and Splenda together until light and creamy. Then beat in the protein powder, pecans, and salt. Spray a springform pan with nonstick cooking spray, and press the crust evenly and firmly into the bottom of the pan, plus just far enough up the sides to cover the seam at the bottom.

3. Bake for 12 to 15 minutes, until lightly golden. Set aside to cool while you make the filling.

4. In a large bowl, use an electric mixer to beat the cream cheese until smooth, scraping down the sides of the bowl often. Next beat in the Splenda and the sour cream, and mix well. Beat in the butter flavoring, vanilla, and molasses; add the eggs one by one, beating until very smooth and creamy.

5. Pour the mixture into the crust. Place the cake in the oven, and on the oven rack below it or on the floor of the oven place a pie pan of water. Bake for 1 hour.

6. Cool in the pan on a wire rack. Chill well before serving.

For a nice touch, decorate this with some pretty pecan halves.

Yield: 12 servings, each with 9 grams of carbohydrates and 1 gram of fiber, for a total of 8 grams of usable carbs and 18 grams of protein. (Analysis includes crust.)

↻ Pumpkin Cheesecake

Vicki Cash gives us this elegant alternative to pumpkin pie for Thanksgiving dessert. It's from her *Low Carb Success Calendar*, and it's not to be missed.

Butter

1/2 cup pecans, coarsely chopped

2 packages (8 ounces each) cream cheese, softened

1/2 to 3/4 cup Splenda sweetener

2 teaspoons vanilla extract

1 1/2 cups pure canned pumpkin

1/2 cup sour cream

4 eggs

1 1/2 teaspoons cinnamon

1 teaspoon ginger

1/2 teaspoon nutmeg

1/4 teaspoon ground cloves

1/4 teaspoon salt

1. Preheat the oven to 300°F.
2. Butter the bottom and sides of a 9 1/2 -inch springform cheesecake pan. Sprinkle the bottom of the pan with chopped pecans, distributing evenly.
3. In a large mixing bowl, use an electric mixer to beat the cream cheese, Splenda, and vanilla until fluffy, stopping occasionally to scrape the sides of the bowl and beaters.
4. Add the pumpkin and sour cream, mixing thoroughly on medium speed. Add the eggs one at a time, mixing thoroughly between each one. Mix in the cinnamon, ginger, nutmeg, cloves, and salt.
5. Pour the batter over the nuts in the pan. Bake for 60 to 70 minutes, or until a knife placed in center comes out clean. Cool for 20 minutes before removing from the pan, and chill for at least 2 hours before serving.

Yield: 12 servings, each with 7 grams of carbohydrates and 1 gram of fiber, for a total of 6 grams of usable carbs and 6 grams of protein.

◯ Grasshopper Cheesecake

If you're a mint-chocolate chip ice cream fan, this is your cheesecake! Chocolate extract can be a little hard to find, but it's worth it for this. If you can only find "flavoring," not extract (you'll know because flavorings are in teeny little bottles), keep in mind that these are far more concentrated, so taste as you go.

Chocolate Layer

3 sugar-free dark chocolate bars (about 1.5 ounces each)

1/4 cup heavy cream

1 Almond Crust or Hazelnut Crust (see page 436), prebaked in a springform pan

Grasshopper Filling

3 packages (8 ounces each) cream cheese, softened

3/4 cup Splenda

3/4 cup sour cream

3/4 teaspoon peppermint extract

1 1/2 tablespoons chocolate extract

1 or 2 drops green food coloring (optional, but pretty)

4 eggs

1. Preheat oven to 325°F. In the top of a double boiler over hot water (or in a heavy-bottomed saucepan over the lowest possible heat), melt the chocolate and whisk in the cream until smooth. Spread this mixture evenly over the crust, and set aside.

2. In a large bowl, use an electric mixer to beat the cream cheese until smooth, scraping down the sides of the bowl often. Beat in the Splenda and the sour cream, and mix well. Beat in the peppermint and chocolate extracts, food coloring (if using), and eggs, one by one, beating until very smooth and creamy.

3. Pour the mixture into the chocolate-coated crust. Place the cake in the oven, and on the oven rack below it or on the floor of the oven place a pie pan of water. Bake for 1 hour.

4. Cool in the pan on a wire rack. Chill well before serving.

Yield: 12 servings, each with 9 grams of carbohydrates and 2 grams of fiber, for a total of 7 grams of usable carbs and 18 grams of protein. (Analysis includes crust, but omits the polyols in the sugar-free chocolate.)

ꙅ Kathy's Peanut Butter Protein Bars

From reader Kathy Miller. These would make a filling snack, or even breakfast or lunch.

1/4 cup butter

1/2 cup natural peanut butter (preferably chunky), at room temperature

4 ounces cream cheese, softened

1 3/4 cups vanilla-flavored whey protein powder

1 tablespoon vanilla

2 tablespoons Splenda

1/2 cup chopped peanuts

1. Melt the butter (a microwave works well for this), and add the peanut butter and softened cream cheese to it. Mix together with a spoon (no need to drag out a blender or mixer), and then add the protein powder, vanilla, Splenda, and peanuts; stir well. (It will be very crumbly.)

2. Taste and see if it is sweet enough. If not, add a little more Splenda.

3. Press the mixture firmly into an 8 x 8-inch pan. Slice into 12 pieces and put the whole pan in the freezer. Remove when the bars are firm.

Yield: 12 bars, each with 9 grams of carbohydrates and 1 gram of fiber, for a total of 8 grams of usable carbs and 31 grams of protein.

🍓 For storage, it's a good idea to package these in individual zipper-lock bags in the freezer.

◯ Great Balls of Protein!

You may recognize this updated version of an old health food standby.

> 1 jar (16 ounces) natural peanut butter, oil and all
> 2 cups vanilla-flavored whey protein powder
> Splenda, saccharine, stevia, or whatever sweetener you prefer (optional)
> Sesame seeds (optional)
> Unsweetened shredded coconut (optional)
> Sugar-free chocolate bars (optional)
> Unsweetened cocoa powder (optional)
> Splenda (optional)

🍓 This is easiest to make if you have a powerful stand mixer or a heavy-duty food processor. If you don't, don't try to use a smaller appliance—you'll only burn it out and destroy it! Rather than dooming your old mixer, just roll up your sleeves, scrub your hands, and dive in.

1. Thoroughly combine the peanut butter with the protein powder. (I find that working in about 1/3 cup of the protein powder at a time is about right.) This should make a stiff, somewhat crumbly dough.

2. Work the sweetener of your choice (if using) into the dough. My whey protein powder is sweetened with stevia, and I find that that's enough sweetener for me. But if you want your Great Balls of Protein to be sweeter, simply add sweetener.

   🍓 If you're using stevia, dissolve it in a couple of tablespoons of water and sprinkle it evenly over the mixture before working it in, or it's not likely to spread throughout the mixture very well. Actually, it's best to sprinkle any sweetener evenly before combining it with a mixture this thick.

3. Roll into balls about 1 inch in diameter.

4. It's nice to coat these with something. If you like sesame seeds, you can toast them by shaking them in a dry, heavy skillet over medium heat until they start popping and jumping around the pan, and then roll the balls in them while they're still warm. You could roll them in coconut, if you prefer; most health food stores carry it unsweetened and shredded. Again, you can toast it lightly in a dry frying pan, and add a little Splenda. Or you could melt sugar-free chocolate bars, and dip your Balls of Protein in chocolate—although it would probably be simpler to chop them up and mix them in. Another option is to roll them in unsweetened cocoa mixed with a little Splenda.

Yield: About 50 balls, each with 3 grams of carbohydrates, a trace of fiber, and 10 grams of protein. (Analysis does not include coatings for balls.)

⌒ Whipped Topping

The pudding adds a very nice texture to this topping, and it helps the whipped cream "stand up," as well as adding a slightly sweet vanilla flavor to the cream, of course.

> 1 cup heavy cream, well chilled
>
> 1 tablespoon vanilla sugar-free instant pudding powder

Whip the cream and pudding mix together until the cream is stiff.

Yield: About 2 cups, or 16 servings of 2 tablespoons, each with only a trace of carbohydrates, no fiber, and a trace of protein.

🍓 This is incredible with berries, as a simple but elegant dessert. I like to serve strawberries and whipped cream in my nice chip-and-dip; it looks so pretty, and it makes the whole thing engagingly informal. This whipped topping is also great on any dessert, and terrific on Irish Coffee!

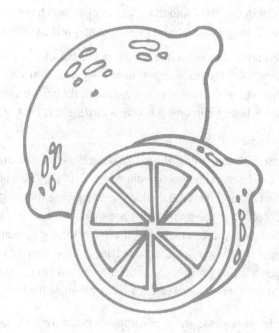

↻ Lemon Sherbet

Low-carb, low-fat, low-calorie—and delicious!

> 1 package (4-serving size) sugar-free lemon gelatin
>
> 2 cups boiling water
>
> 2 cups plain yogurt
>
> 2 teaspoons lemon extract
>
> 3 tablespoons Splenda
>
> 1/4 cup vanilla-flavored whey protein powder

1. Put the gelatin powder in the blender, and add the water. Blend for 20 seconds, or just long enough to dissolve the gelatin.

2. Add the other ingredients, and blend well. Put the blender container in the refrigerator and let it chill for 10 to 15 minutes. Take it out and blend it again for about 10 seconds, then chill it for another 10 to 15 minutes, and then give it another quick blend it when it's done chilling.

3. Pour the sherbet mixture into a home ice cream freezer, and freeze according to the directions for your freezer.

Yield: 8 servings of 1/2 cup—but just try to eat only 1/2 cup! Just try! Each serving has 2.5 grams of carbohydrates (if you use the GO-Diet figure of 4 grams of carbs in a cup of plain yogurt); even if you go with the count on the label, this only has 4 grams of carbohydrates per serving, no fiber, and 9 grams of protein.

Creamy Strawberry Popsicles

From sweety.com's Jennifer Eloff and her terrific cookbook *Splendid Low-Carbing*, these popsicles are bound to liven up your summer.

   1 1/2 cups plain yogurt

   1 cup heavy cream

   2/3 cup Splenda

   1/2 cup frozen, unsweetened strawberries

   1/4 teaspoon strawberry Kool-Aid powder

In a blender, blend the yogurt, cream, Splenda, strawberries, and Kool-Aid powder until smooth. Pour into popsicle molds, and freeze.

Yield: 13 popsicles, each with 3 grams of carbohydrates, a trace of fiber, and 1 gram of protein.

Orange Popsicles. Make just like Creamy Strawberry Popsicles, only substitute 2 tablespoons of frozen orange juice concentrate for the strawberries, and instead of the Kool-Aid powder, add 2 teaspoons lemon juice and 1/4 teaspoon orange extract.

Yield: 13 popsicles, each with 4 grams of carbohydrates, a trace of fiber, and 1 gram of protein.

Coconut Banana Cream Popsicles. In a blender, blend the following until smooth: 1 can (14 ounces) unsweetened coconut milk, 1 cup plain yogurt, 1 cup Splenda, 2/3 cup heavy cream, 1 medium banana (sliced), and 1/2 teaspoon banana or vanilla extract. Pour into popsicle molds and freeze.

Yield: 16 popsicles, each with 5 grams of carbohydrates and 1 gram of fiber, for a total of 4 grams of usable carbs and 1 gram of protein.

↻ Flavored Whip

Reader David Drake Hunter sends this easy dessert recipe.

        1 pint heavy cream, chilled
        1 to 2 teaspoons sugar-free fruit-flavored drink mix powder
          (your choice of flavor)

Pour the cream into a bowl, add the drink mix crystals to taste, and beat into whipped cream.

Yield: About 8 servings, each with only a trace of carbohydrates, fiber, and protein.

Maria's Flan

My childhood friend Maria found me on the Internet a couple of years ago, and we got together. Her mom is Colombian, so Maria had grown up eating flan, a traditional Latin American dessert. Here's the version we came up with together.

Syrup

2 tablespoons Splenda

1 teaspoon blackstrap molasses

2 tablespoons water

Custard

1 cup heavy cream

1 cup half-and-half

6 eggs

1 teaspoon vanilla extract

Pinch of nutmeg

Pinch of salt

2/3 cup Splenda

1. Preheat the oven to 350°F.

2. Combine the Splenda, molasses, and water, stirring until the lumps are gone.

3. Spray a glass pie plate with nonstick cooking spray, and pour the mixture into it, spreading it over the bottom. Microwave for 2 minutes on Medium power.

   🍓 You could substitute the sugar-free syrup of your choice for this syrup; just use 2 to 3 tablespoons.

4. Whisk together well the heavy cream, half-and-half, eggs, vanilla, nutmeg, salt, and Splenda, and pour the mixture over the syrup in the pie plate.

5. Place the pie plate carefully in a large, flat baking dish, and pour water around it, not quite up to the brim of the pie plate. Put the baking pan with the pie plate in its water bath in the oven. Bake for 45 minutes, or until a knife inserted in the center comes out clean.

6. Cool, and cut the flan into wedges. Traditionally, each piece is served inverted on a plate, with the syrup on top.

Yield: 8 generous servings, each with 5 grams of carbohydrates, no fiber, and 6 grams of protein.

↷ Mocha Custard

  1 cup boiling water

  1 ounce unsweetened baking chocolate

  1 rounded teaspoon instant coffee crystals

  1 cup heavy cream

  3 eggs

  1/3 cup Splenda

  A pinch of salt

1. Preheat the oven to 300°F.

2. Put the boiling water in your blender container, and drop in the chocolate. Let it sit for 5 minutes or so.

3. Add the coffee crystals, heavy cream, eggs, Splenda, and salt, and blend for a minute or so.

4. Spray a 1-quart casserole with nonstick cooking spray, and pour the mixture into it. (If you prefer, pour into individual custard cups.)

5. Place the casserole or custard cups in a larger pan filled with hot water, and place the entire thing in the oven. Bake for 1 hour and 20 minutes.

6. Cool, then chill well before serving. (The chilling makes a big difference in the texture.)

Yield: 4 generous servings, each with 6 grams of carbohydrates and 1 gram of fiber, for a total of 5 grams of usable carbs and 6 grams of protein.

↻ Lemon-Vanilla Custard

Don't save this just for dessert—it makes a lovely breakfast, too.

 1 cup heavy cream
 1 cup half-and-half
 3 eggs
 1/3 cup Splenda
 1 teaspoon lemon extract
 1/2 teaspoon vanilla extract
 2 tablespoons vanilla-flavored whey protein powder
 Pinch of salt
 Grated rind of 1/2 lemon

1. Preheat the oven to 300°F.

2. Put all the ingredients in a blender, and blend well.

3. Spray a 1-quart casserole with nonstick cooking spray, and pour the mixture into it. (If you prefer, use individual custard cups.) Place the casserole or custard cups in a larger pan filled with hot water, and place the entire thing in the oven. Bake for 2 hours. Cool, and chill well.

Yield: 4 generous servings, each with 8 grams of carbohydrates, a trace of fiber, and 13 grams of protein.

↻ Peanut Butter Silk Pie

Incredible, decadent, outrageous, utterly scrumptious. A real special-occasion dessert, and a surefire crowd pleaser.

Crust
 1 1/4 cup shelled raw hazelnuts
 1/2 stick butter, melted
 1/2 cup vanilla-flavored whey protein powder

Chocolate Layer
 4 sugar-free dark chocolate bars (about 1.5 ounces each)
 5 tablespoons heavy cream
 1/4 teaspoon instant coffee crystals

Peanut Butter Slik Layer

1 package (8 ounces) cream cheese, softened

1 cup Splenda

1 cup creamy natural peanut butter

1 tablespoon butter, melted

1 teaspoon vanilla extract

1 cup heavy cream

1. Preheat the oven to 325°F.

2. Use the S blade in a food processor to grind the hazelnuts to a meal. Add the butter and protein powder, and pulse until well combined.

3. Spray a large pie plate with nonstick cooking spray, and press the hazelnut mixture firmly into bottom of the pie plate (it won't build up the side very far).

4. Bake for 10 to 12 minutes, or until lightly browned. Remove from the oven to cool.

5. Melt the chocolate over the lowest possible heat, as chocolate burns very easily. (If you have a double boiler or a heat diffuser, this would be a good time to use it!) Whisk in the cream and coffee crystals, and continue stirring until the crystals disappear. Spread this mixture evenly over the bottom of the hazelnut crust.

6. Use an electric mixer to beat the cream cheese, Splenda, peanut butter, butter, and vanilla together until creamy.

7. In a separate bowl, whip the heavy cream until stiff. Turn the mixer to the lowest setting, and beat the whipped cream into the peanut butter mixture one-third at a time.

8. Spread the peanut butter filling gently over the chocolate layer, and chill. (This is best made a day in advance, to allow plenty of time for chilling.)

Yield: 10 generous servings, each with 12 grams of carbohydrates and 2 grams of fiber, for a total of 10 grams of usable carbs and 20 grams of protein.

ᔕ Pumpkin Pie with Pecan Praline Crust

I'm very proud of this recipe. Serve it at Thanksgiving Dinner, and no one will guess it's made without sugar.

Crust

2 cups shelled raw pecans

1/4 teaspoon salt

2 1/2 tablespoons Splenda

1 1/2 teaspoons blackstrap molasses

4 tablespoons butter, melted

2 tablespoons water

Pumpkin Pie Filling

1 can (15 ounces) pumpkin

1 1/2 cups heavy cream

3 eggs

3/4 cup Splenda

1/2 teaspoon salt

2 teaspoons blackstrap molasses

1 tablespoon pumpkin pie spice

1. Preheat the oven to 350°F.

2. Put the pecans and salt in a food processor with the S blade in place. Pulse until the pecans are chopped to a medium consistency.

3. Add the Splenda, molasses, and butter, and pulse again until well blended. Add the water and pulse again, until well combined. At this point, you'll have a soft, sticky mass.

4. Spray a 10-inch pie plate with nonstick cooking spray, or butter it well. Turn the pecan mixture into it, and press firmly in place, all over the bottom, and up the sides by 1 1/2 inches or so. Try to get it an even thickness, with no holes, and if you wish, run a finger or a knife around the top edge, to get an even, nice-looking line.

5. Bake for about 18 minutes. Cool.

6. Increase the oven temperature to 425°F.

7. Combine the pumpkin, heavy cream, eggs, Splenda, salt, molasses, and spice in a bowl, and whisk together well. Pour into the prebaked and cooled pie shell. Bake for 15 minutes, lower the oven temperature to 350°F, and bake for an additional 45 minutes. Cool, and serve with whipped cream.

Yield: 8 servings, each with 14 grams of carbohydrates and 4 grams of fiber, for a total of 10 grams of usable carbs and 6 grams of protein.

🍓 Wondering how many carbs you're really saving by making your pumpkin pie from scratch? A lot—especially when you consider that a slice of Mrs. Smith's frozen pumpkin pie has 37 grams of usable carbs, or well over three times as much!

☽ Helen's Chocolate Bread Pudding

Helen was my dad's mom, and this was our family's traditional Christmas dessert the whole time I was growing up. People have threatened to marry into the family to get the secret recipe, but since this is the decarbed version, it's not secret! It is still high-carb enough that you'll want to save it for a special occasion, though.

> 2 cups half-and-half
>
> 1 cup heavy cream
>
> 1 cup water
>
> 6 slices "lite" white bread (5 grams of usable carbs per slice or less —the squishiest you can find)
>
> 3 ounces unsweetened baking chocolate
>
> 2/3 cup Splenda
>
> 2 eggs, beaten
>
> 1 teaspoon vanilla extract
>
> Pinch salt

1. Preheat the oven to 375°F.

2. Combine the half-and-half, cream, and water, and scald; bring it just up to a simmer.

3. While it's heating, spray a large casserole with nonstick cooking spray, tear the bread into small bits, and put them in the dish. Pour the hot half-and-half mixture over the bread, and let it sit for 10 minutes.

4. Melt the chocolate, and add it to the bread mixture; it's good to use a little of the hot cream to rinse out the pan you melted the chocolate in, so you get all of it. Stir well. Now stir in the Splenda, eggs, vanilla, and salt, mixing very well. Bake for 1 hour, or until firm. Serve with Not-So-Hard Sauce (see page 456).

Yield: 8 servings, each with 12 grams of carbohydrates and just over 1 gram of fiber, for a total of 11 grams of usable carbs and 7 grams of protein.

∩ Not-So-Hard Sauce

Traditional hard sauce is made with sugar, butter, and egg, plus vanilla, rum, or brandy, and when it's refrigerated it gets quite hard—hence the name. However, with Splenda instead of sugar, my hard sauce just didn't work—it fell apart in little globs. I added cream cheese, and it all came together, but it doesn't get quite so hard when refrigerated, which is why this is Not-So-Hard Sauce. It still tastes great, though!

> 1 cup Splenda
>
> 5 tablespoons butter, softened
>
> 1/8 teaspoon salt
>
> 1 teaspoon vanilla extract
>
> 1 egg
>
> 1 ounce cream cheese, softened
>
> Nutmeg

1. Use an electric mixer to beat the Splenda and butter together until well blended. Beat in the salt, vanilla extract, and egg. At this point, you'll be sure you've made a dreadful mistake.

2. Beat in the cream cheese, and watch the sauce smooth out! Mix very well, until light and fluffy. Pile your Not-So-Hard Sauce into a pretty serving dish, sprinkle it lightly with nutmeg, and refrigerate until well-chilled.

Yield: About 1 cup, or a 2-tablespoons serving of sauce for each serving of Helen's Chocolate Bread Pudding (see page 455). Each serving will have 3 grams of carbohydrates, no fiber, and 1 gram of protein.

꧂ Couer a la Crème

This is a classic French dessert, traditionally made in a heart-shaped mold. Couer a la Crème molds are hard to come by, but you can buy a regular 2-cup heart-shaped mold and stick three or four holes in it with a nail, which is what I did. Serve with fresh strawberries or Strawberry Sauce (see page 458) for a truly beautiful Valentine's Day dessert.

> 2 packages (8 ounces each) cream cheese, softened
>
> 2 tablespoons Splenda
>
> 3 tablespoons heavy cream
>
> 2 tablespoons sour cream
>
> 1/4 teaspoon salt

🍓 Warning: This is not a quick dessert to whip up before your sweetheart comes over. You need to start making this dessert at least 24 hours in advance, to give it plenty of time to chill.

1. Use an electric mixer to beat the cream cheese until it's very creamy. Beat in the Splenda, heavy cream, sour cream, and salt, mixing very well.

2. Line your mold with a double layer of dampened cheesecloth, and pack the cheese mixture into it, pressing it in well. Place the mold on a plate to catch any moisture that drains out, and chill for at least 24 hours.

Yield: 8 servings, each with 2 grams of carbohydrates, no fiber, and 5 grams of protein.

Strawberry Sauce

Traditionally, Couer a la Crème is served with fresh strawberries, but I make this for Valentine's Day, and I'm generally not impressed with the quality of the fresh strawberries I can get in February. I'd rather use frozen.

> 1 bag (1 pound) frozen, unsweetened strawberries, thawed
> 1 tablespoon lemon juice
> 2 or 3 tablespoons Splenda

Simply pour your strawberries and any liquid in the package into a bowl, and stir in the lemon juice and Splenda. Mash your strawberries a little with a fork, if you'd like; I like mine fairly chunky.

Yield: 8 servings, each with 6 grams of carbohydrates and 1 gram of fiber, for a total of 5 grams of usable carbs and only a trace of protein.

Zucchini-Carrot Cake

About 1 1/4 cups hazelnuts

2 eggs

1/2 cup oil

2/3 cup Splenda

1/2 cup yogurt

1/2 cup vanilla-flavored whey protein powder

1 teaspoon baking soda

1/2 teaspoon salt

1 1/2 teaspoons cinnamon

1/4 teaspoon nutmeg

3/4 cup shredded zucchini

1/4 cup shredded carrot

1. Preheat the oven to 350°F.

2. In a food processor with the S blade in place, use the pulse control to grind the hazelnuts to a mealy consistency. (You want 1 1/2 cups of ground hazelnuts when you're done, and for some inexplicable reason they seem to actually grow a little rather than shrink a little when you grind them.) Set the ground hazelnuts aside.

3. In a large mixing bowl, whisk the eggs until well blended. Add the oil, yogurt, ground hazelnuts, protein powder, baking soda, Splenda, salt, cinnamon, and nutmeg, mixing well after each addition. (It's especially important that the baking soda be well distributed through the mixture.) Add the zucchini and carrots last, mixing well.

4. Thoroughly coat a ring mold or bundt pan with nonstick cooking spray, and turn the batter into it.

   🍓 If you sprayed your pan ahead of time, give it another shot just before adding the batter. And don't expect the batter to fill the pan to the rim; it fills my bundt pan about halfway.

5. Bake for 45 minutes and turn out gently onto a wire rack to cool.

Yield: 8 generous servings, each with 8 grams of carbohydrates and 2 grams of fiber, for a total of 6 grams of usable carbs and 16 grams of protein.

🍓 This doesn't need a darned thing—it's simply delicious exactly the way it is. If you wish to gild the lily, however, you could top it with whipped topping, pumpkin cream, or cream cheese frosting. This cake, by the way, makes a fabulous breakfast, and since it's loaded with protein and good fats, it should keep you going all morning.

Adam's Chocolate Birthday Cake

I made a low-carb feast for my friend Adam's birthday, and this was the cake. It's not a layer cake, it's a snack-type cake: dense, moist, and fudgy—a lot like brownies. It's easy, too, because it needs no frosting, tasting great just as it is.

1 cup finely ground hazelnuts

1/2 cup vanilla-flavored whey protein powder

3 tablespoons unsweetened cocoa powder

1 teaspoon baking soda

1 cup Splenda

1/2 teaspoon salt

5 tablespoons oil (peanut, sunflower, canola, or whatever)

1 tablespoon cider vinegar

1 cup cold water

1. Preheat the oven to 350°F.

2. In a bowl, combine the hazelnuts, protein powder, cocoa, baking soda, Splenda, and salt, and stir them together quite well. (Make sure there are no lumps of baking soda!)

3. Spray a 9 x 9-inch baking dish with nonstick cooking spray, and place the combined ingredients in it. Make two holes in this mixture. Pour the oil into one, the vinegar into the other, and the water over the whole thing. Mix with a spoon or fork until everything's well combined. Bake for 30 minutes.

Yield: 9 servings, each with 7 grams of carbohydrates and 1 gram of fiber, for a total of 6 grams of usable carbs and 12 grams of protein.

↻ Gingerbread

I've always loved gingerbread, and this is as good as any high-carb gingerbread I've ever had! Don't worry about that zucchini; it completely disappears, leaving only moistness behind.

1 cup ground almonds (or 2/3 cup raw almonds finely ground in a food processor)

1/2 cup vanilla-flavored whey protein powder

1 teaspoon baking soda

1/2 teaspoon salt

2 1/2 teaspoons ground ginger

1/2 teaspoon ground cinnamon

1/2 cup Splenda

1/2 cup plain yogurt

1/4 cup oil

1 teaspoon blackstrap molasses

1 egg

2 tablespoons water

1/2 cup shredded zucchini

1. Preheat the oven to 350°F.

2. In a mixing bowl, combine the almonds, protein powder, baking soda, salt, ginger, cinnamon, and Splenda, and mix them well.

3. In a separate bowl or measuring cup, whisk together the yogurt, oil, molasses, egg, and water. Pour into the dry ingredients, and whisk until everything is well combined and there are no dry spots. Add the zucchini, and whisk briefly to distribute evenly.

4. Spray an 8 x 8-inch baking pan with nonstick cooking spray, and turn the batter into it. Bake for 30 minutes, or until a toothpick inserted in the middle comes out clean.

Yield: 9 servings, each with 9 grams of carbohydrates, a trace of fiber, and 17 grams of protein.

🍓 Try serving this with Whipped Topping (see page 446).

◌ Cream Cheese Frosting

This is my sister's recipe. It's good on the Zucchini-Carrot Cake (see page 459) or the Gingerbread (see page 461).

3/4 cup heavy cream, chilled

1 package (8 ounces) cream cheese, softened

1/2 cup Splenda

1 teaspoon vanilla

1. Whip the heavy cream until it's stiff.

2. In a separate bowl, beat the cream cheese until very smooth, then beat in the Splenda and vanilla. Turn the mixer to its lowest speed, and blend in the whipped cream, then turn off the mixer, quick!

Yield: 9 servings, each with 3 grams of carbohydrates, no fiber, and 2 grams of protein.

◌ Gingered Melon

Light and elegant—and people following a low-fat diet can eat it, too.

1/2 ripe cantaloupe

1/2 ripe honeydew

1/3 cup lime juice

2 tablespoons Splenda

1 teaspoon grated fresh ginger

1. Peel the cantaloupe and honeydew, and cut it into bite-size chunks or, if you have a melon baller, cut balls from it. Place in a serving dish.

2. Combine the lime juice, Splenda, and ginger. Pour over the melon, toss, and serve.

Yield: 8 servings, each with 12 grams of carbohydrates and 1 gram of fiber, for a total of 11 grams of usable carbs and 1 gram of protein.

Strawberries in Wine

Simple, and simply delicious.

> 8 ounces fresh strawberries
>
> 1/2 cup burgundy wine
>
> 1 tablespoon Splenda
>
> Cinnamon stick

1. Hull the strawberries, and slice or cut them into quarters.

2. Mix the wine and the Splenda, and pour the mixture over the berries. Add the cinnamon stick and refrigerate, stirring from time to time, for at least 12 hours (but 2 days wouldn't hurt!).

Yield: 4 servings, each with 8 grams of carbohydrates and 3 grams of fiber, for a total of 5 grams of usable carbs and 1 gram of protein.

Mockahlua

My sister, a longtime Kahlua fan, says this is addictive. And my husband demanded to know, "How did you do that?" You can make this with decaf if caffeine bothers you.

> 2 1/2 cups water
>
> 3 cups Splenda
>
> 3 tablespoons instant coffee crystals
>
> 1 teaspoon vanilla
>
> 1 bottle (750 milliliters) 100-proof vodka (use the cheap stuff)

1. In a large pitcher or measuring cup, combine the water, Splenda, coffee crystals, and vanilla. Stir until the coffee and Splenda are completely dissolved.

2. Pour the mixture through a funnel into a 1.5- or 2-liter bottle. (A clean 1.5-liter wine bottle works fine, so long as you've saved the cork.) Pour in the vodka. Cork, and shake well.

Yield: 32 servings of 1 1/2 ounces—a standard "shot." Each will have 2 grams of carbohydrates, no fiber, and the merest trace of protein.

Mochahlua. Try this one if you like a little chocolate with your coffee. Just cut the water back to 1 1/2 cups and substitute a 12-ounce bottle of sugar-free chocolate coffee flavoring syrup for the Splenda and vanilla. This has only a trace of carbohydrates per shot, because the liquid Splenda used to sweeten the chocolate coffee flavoring syrup doesn't have the maltodextrin used to bulk the granular Splenda.

Mockahlua and Cream. This makes a nice "little something" to serve at the end of a dinner party, in lieu of a heavier dessert. For each serving you'll need a shot of Mockahlua (or Mochalua) and 2 shots of heavy cream. Simply mix and sip!

Yield: Each Serving has 4 grams of carbohydrates, no fiber, and 2 grams of protein.

⌒ Kay's Hot Rum Toddy

A delicious winter libation—for adults only! The rum is carb-free, but it will slow down your metabolism, so go easy.

> 2 1/4 cups Splenda
> 2 teaspoons blackstrap molasses
> 1 teaspoon ground nutmeg
> 1 teaspoon ground cinnamon
> 1 teaspoon ground cloves
> 1 teaspoon ground cardamom
> 1 bottle (750 milliliters) top-quality dark rum

1. Put the Splenda, molasses, nutmeg, cinnamon, cloves, and cardamom in a food processor with the S blade in place. Process until it's smooth and creamy, scraping down the sides of the processor once or twice to make sure everything combines evenly.

2. Scoop this "batter" mixture into a snap-top container, and keep it in the fridge. (The batter will keep well, and that means you make only a serving or two at a time, if you like.)

3. To serve the toddy, warm a coffee mug by filling it with boiling water and pouring it out. Then fill it again, halfway, with more boiling water. Add 1 to 2 tablespoons of the batter, and stir until it dissolves into the water (a small whisk works well for this). Add two shots of dark rum, stir, and sip.

Yield: About 12 servings. Each 2-tablespoons serving of batter will have 5 grams of carbohydrates, a trace of fiber, and a trace of protein.

🍓 Kay says that one theory of hot-toddy making is that it is impossible to use too much batter and you should keep stirring more in until you are bored with stirring. Another theory of hot toddy making is that it is impossible to use too much rum, and that you should keep stirring in more until your friends panic. Use your best judgment.

☌ Irish Coffee

If you're having this after dinner, you may want to use decaf instead of regular coffee.

    2 ounces Irish whisky
    6 ounces hot coffee
    1 to 2 teaspoons Splenda
    1 tablespoon Whipped Topping (see page 446)

Put the whisky into a stemmed Irish coffee glass or a mug. Fill with coffee. Stir in 1 to 2 teaspoons of Splenda, and top with whipped cream.

Yield: 1 serving, with 2 grams of carbohydrates, no fiber, and only a trace of protein.

☌ Cocoa

The lowest carbohydrate hot chocolate mix on the market is Swiss Miss Diet, but this is much better.

    1 cup heavy cream
    1 cup water
    2 tablespoons unsweetened cocoa powder
    1 1/2 or 2 tablespoons Splenda
    2 tablespoons vanilla-flavored whey protein powder
    Tiny pinch salt

Over the lowest possible heat (it doesn't hurt to use a heat diffuser or a double-boiler) combine the cream and water. When they're starting to get warm, add the cocoa, Splenda, protein powder, and salt; whisk until well combined. Bring just barely to a simmer, and pour into cups.

Yield: 2 servings, each with 10 grams of carbohydrates and 2 grams of fiber, for a total of 8 grams of usable carbs and 15 grams of protein.

🍓 The amount of protein in this cocoa means that a cup of this doesn't make a bad breakfast. And for grownups, this is very nice with a shot of Mockahlua or Mochalua (see page 464) in it—but not in the morning!

Creamy Vanilla Coffee

Reader Honey Ashton sends this sweet little treat, and says it's also good iced.

>   1 hot cup decaffeinated coffee
>
>   2 tablespoons low-carb vanilla shake meal-replacement powder
>
>   1 to 2 teaspoons sugar-free vanilla coffee-flavoring syrup
>
>   Cinnamon (optional)

Combine the coffee, vanilla shake powder, and coffee-flavoring syrup. Garnish with cinnamon (if using).

Yield: 1 serving, with no more than 2 grams of carbohydrates, no fiber, and no protein.

Chai

My darling friend Nicole is a devotee of this spiced Indian tea. She suggested I come up with a low-carb version for this book, and here it is. Make up a batch, and your whole house will smell wonderful.

> 1 tablespoon fennel seed or anise seed
>
> 6 green cardamom pods
>
> 12 whole cloves
>
> 1 cinnamon stick
>
> 1/4 inch of fresh ginger root, thinly sliced
>
> 1/4 teaspoon whole black peppercorns
>
> 2 bay leaves
>
> 7 cups water
>
> 2 tablespoons loose Darjeeling tea
>
> 1/3 cup Splenda
>
> 1/8 tablespoon blackstrap molasses
>
> 1/2 cup heavy cream mixed with 1/2 cup water, or 1 cup half-and-half

1. Combine the fennel, cardamom, cloves, cinnamon, ginger, peppercorns, bay leaf, and water. Bring to a simmer, and let simmer for 5 minutes.

2. Add the tea, turn off the burner, cover, and let the mixture steep for 10 minutes.

3. Strain, and stir in the Splenda, molasses, and cream.

🍓 You can refrigerate this for a day or two, and reheat it in the microwave whenever you want a cup.

Yield: 8 servings of 1 cup each. Made with heavy cream, each serving will have about 7 grams of carbohydrates, no fiber (you've strained it out), and 2 grams of protein. Made with half-and-half, it'll have 8 grams of carbs, no fiber, and 2 grams of protein.

↶ Eggiweggnog

This is for those of you who are unafraid of raw eggs. My husband would gladly have this for breakfast every day!

    3 eggs
    1/2 cup heavy cream
    1/2 cup half-and-half
    2 tablespoons Splenda
    1 teaspoon vanilla extract
    Pinch of salt
    Pinch of nutmeg

Put the eggs, heavy cream, half-and-half, Splenda, vanilla, and salt in a blender, and run it for 30 seconds or so. Pour into glasses, sprinkle a little nutmeg on top, and drink up.

Yield: 2 servings, each with 9 grams of carbohydrates, no fiber, and 11 grams of protein.

↻ Cooked Eggnog

This is for you safe-living folks who would never consider eating a raw egg—and it's mighty tasty, too. It just takes more work.

> 2 cups half-and-half
>
> 1 cup heavy cream
>
> 1/4 cup Splenda
>
> 1 teaspoon vanilla extract
>
> 1/4 teaspoon salt
>
> 6 eggs
>
> 1 cup water
>
> Nutmeg

1. In a big glass measuring cup, combine the half-and-half and cream. Microwave it at 70 percent power for 3 to 4 minutes, or until it's very warm through, but not boiling. (This is simply a time-saver, and is not essential; if you prefer, you can simply heat the half-and-half and cream over a low flame in the saucepan you'll use to finish the recipe.)

2. After microwaving, pour the half-and-half mixture into a heavy-bottomed saucepan, and whisk in the Splenda, vanilla, salt, and eggs. Turn the burner to lowest heat (if you have a heat diffuser or a double boiler, this would be a good time to use it), and stand there and stir your eggnog constantly until it's thick enough to coat a metal spoon with a thin film. This will, I'm sorry to say, take at least 5 minutes, and maybe as many as 20.

3. Stir in the water, and chill. Sprinkle a little nutmeg on each serving, and feel free to spike this, if you like!

Yield: About 6 servings of 1 cup, each with 5 grams of carbohydrates, a trace of fiber, and 9 grams of protein.

A Refresher on Measurements

Just in case these details have slipped your mind since junior high school home ec class:

3 teaspoons = 1 tablespoon	2 cups = 1 pint
2 tablespoons = 1 fluid ounce	4 cups = 1 quart
2 ounces = 1/4 cup	2 pints = 1 quart
4 ounces = 1/2 cup	4 quarts = 1 gallon
8 ounces = 1 cup	

Help! I Use the Metric System!

The problem with being an American cookbook author is that your recipes end up being confusing to the vast majority of the world—namely, the millions of folks out there who don't use quarts, cups, teaspoons, and tablespoons, and whose ovens are calibrated for Celsius rather than Fahrenheit. That most of the world measures dry ingredients by weight rather than volume just adds to the confusion.

Here, for all you nice folks who live in that great big world outside the United States, are some useful measurement conversions. I'm afraid I can't convert measurements of volume to measurements of weight, but I can give you the volumes in liters and the oven temperatures in Celsius. It's good to know that a liter and a quart are so close as to make almost no difference and that for our purposes, we're going to assume they're the same. Be aware that there are two different sorts of ounces in the measurement system used in America—an ounce of weight, and a "fluid ounce," which is measure of volume equal to

2 tablespoons. If a liquid is being measured in ounces, this will always refer to a fluid ounce, rather than an ounce of weight.

Measurements of Volume

1 quart = 1 liter

1 cup = 250 milliliters

3/4 cup = 200 milliliters

1/2 cup = 125 milliliters

1/3 cup = 105 milliliters

1/4 cup = 75 milliliters

1 fluid ounce = 30 milliliters

1 tablespoon = 15 milliliters

1 teaspoon = 5 milliliters

Measurements of Weight

1 ounce = 28.4 grams, but in most cases you can round to 25 or 30

1 pound = 454 grams, or about half a kilo

In America, we measure butter both by the pound and by volumetric measurements:

1 pound butter = 2 cups

1 stick butter = 1/4 pound = 1/2 cup = 8 tablespoons = 113 grams

1 cup butter = 226 grams

1 tablespoon butter = 14 grams

Oven Temperatures

225°F = 110°C

250°F = 130°C

275°F = 140°C

300°F = 150°C

325°F = 170°C

350°F = 180°C

375°F = 190°C

400°F = 200°C

425°F = 220°C

450°F = 230°C

475°F = 240°C

Acknowledgments

There were a great number of people whose collective efforts have made this cookbook possible in what seemed like an impossibly short time:

First, I'd like to thank my husband, Eric Schmitz, who has been my unfailing right hand all through this project, grocery shopping, recipe testing, eating my failures without complaint, and accepting the strain on the food budget. He also helped me run the nutritional calculations for these recipes, which is about the only reason this book was done by its deadline. I quite literally couldn't have done it without him.

Three cookbook authors have kindly allowed me to reprint recipes from their cookbooks. They're great books and great recipes, and you should buy them all. Those cookbooks and their authors are:

Baking Low Carb and *Bread and Breakfast: Baking Low Carb II*, both by my pal Diana Lee. The best place to get Di's books is through Amazon.com, but you can most likely order them through your local bookstore. These are the only books I know that are solely devoted to low-carb baking. Recipes reprinted with permission from *Baking Low Carb*, 1999, Diana Lee. Recipes reprinted with permission from *Bread and Breakfast: Baking Low Carb II*, 2001, Diana Lee.

Splendid Low-Carbing, by Jennifer Eloff. Jen is the Splenda Queen, and since she lives in Canada, where Splenda's been available far longer than in the United States, Jen's had far more experience with it than I. Jennifer sells her book herself through her Web site, sweety.com, and she has other books on cooking with Splenda, as well. Recipes reprinted with permission from *Splendid Low-Carbing*, 2001, Jennifer Eloff.

Lo-Carb Cooking, by Debra Rowland, is the source, among other things, for recipes for "cornbread" and cheese popovers—and there are many more great-sounding recipes in her book that I didn't have room for. Deb sells *Lo-Carb Cooking* herself; you can reach her at d_rowland3@hotmail.com. Recipes reprinted with permission from *Lo-Carb Cooking*, 2001, Debra Rowland.

Also contributing greatly to this book is Vicki Cash, who allowed me to use the recipes from her *2002 Low Carb Success Calendar*. If Vicki puts out a calendar again, I strongly suggest you snap it up! Recipes reprinted with permission from The *2002 Low Carb Success Calendar*, 2001, Just Ducky Productions.

My *Lowcarbezine!* readers responded to my requests with piles of great low-carb recipes for this book. The ones whose recipes have been used are named with their recipes. I thank them, but I also thank those folks who sent recipes I didn't use. Quite often it was because we already had a similar recipe or because the carb count was judged to be just a bit too high; it was very rarely because we just didn't like a recipe. So whether your recipe is here or not, thank you, thank you, from the bottom of my heart. And who knows? We may use your recipe in another book! I also thank all of you who have come up with ideas for recipes you wanted me to develop. My *Lowcarbezine!* readers are one of the genuine joys of my life.

I was far too busy coming up with recipes of my own to test all of the recipes coming in from readers, so I recruited a crack troop of recipe testers. Again, I couldn't have done it without them. My recipe testers were Kim Carpender, Deborah Crites, Jane Duquette, Julie McIntosh, Ray Todd Stevens, Carol Vandiver, Maria Vander Vloedt, and Kay Winefordner—not to mention their families and friends. Thank you, one and all.

Finally, I'd like to thank my mom, Jane Carpender, for letting me help her cook from the time I was tiny. Because of her, I knew how to measure accurately, separate an egg, bake cookies, make gravy, knead bread, rice potatoes, and perform dozens of other cooking tasks by the time I was 7 or 8 years old. If I know my way around a kitchen, it's because of my mother. Thanks, Mom! All you parents out there, cook with your kids. Not only is it terrific quality time together and a great defense against junk food, but it also teaches kids skills that will serve them well for the rest of their lives.

Index